ENGLISH THOUGHT
IN THE EIGHTEENTH CENTURY

VOLUME II

History of English Thought in the Eighteenth Century

Sir Leslie Stephen

IN TWO VOLUMES

VOLUME II

with a new preface by Crane Brinton

A Harbinger Book

HARCOURT, BRACE & WORLD, INC.

NEW YORK & BURLINGAME

First Harbinger Books edition 1962
First published in 1876, third edition 1902

Preface by Crane Brinton © 1962 by Harcourt, Brace & World, Inc.

Library of Congress Catalog Card No.: 62–20104

Printed in the United States of America

PREFACE TO THE HARBINGER EDITION

by *Crane Brinton*

The modern reader will almost certainly find more of direct interest in the subject matter of this second volume of Leslie Stephen's *History of English Thought in the Eighteenth Century* than in the first. The deist controversy, the whole problem of natural versus revealed religion, and much else in the first volume, though basically still important to us today, seems far away and a bit dreary; but in this volume Stephen deals with morals, with political thought, with economics, and in a final chapter, under the modest title of "Characteristics," with general literature, Methodism, and nascent romanticism. He is in fact here trying to analyze what less unassuming writers would call the "spirit of the age" or the "climate of opinion." Stephen had in his first volume treated such figures as Toland, Tindal, Warburton, Paley, and Butler of the *Analogy*; here he brings his gifts of analysis to much greater men—Locke and Hume (more lightly touched on in Volume I), Burke, Adam Smith, Pope, Samuel Johnson, Wesley, and many others. On Wesley and the Methodist movement Stephen is much more succinct than his contemporary Lecky in his *History of England in the Eighteenth Century;* but the wise reader will go to Lecky also, especially for the social and political effects of Methodism. Stephen himself in 1903 gave a series of lectures published under the title *English Literature and Society in the Eighteenth Century* which by no means repeats his briefer treatment here, and is fuller in its handling of literature.

Leslie Stephen wrote a great deal. For his "field" we have in English no good single term; the French *politique et moraliste*, neither term meaning quite what its apparent English equivalent does, is perhaps as close as we can come. He was indeed an essayist, an editor, a biographer, a historian; he was concerned at bottom with the range of the behavior of man as—this time we must turn to Aristotle's Greek—a *political animal*. A sample of his range: biographies of Samuel Johnson, Henry Fawcett, George Eliot, his brother Sir James Fitzjames Stephen, and a four-volume collection of shorter biographical sketches, *Studies of a Biographer*; three series of essays, mostly on literary subjects, entitled

Hours in a Library; Essays on Free-Thinking and Plain-Speaking and *An Agnostic's Apology and Other Essays*; critical editions of works of Thackeray, Fielding, and Richardson; several collections of essays on Alpine climbing; and finally, in a sense a continuation of the *English Thought in the Eighteenth Century,* a three-volume study, *The English Utilitarians.*

Once more, as in the first volume of the *English Thought in the Eighteenth Century,* Stephen is in this second volume in many ways astonishingly modern in his approach to the history of ideas. He was, of course, as all the thumbnail biographical and bibliographical comments now point out, a Victorian fully aware of the difference between right and wrong, as well as between the lofty and the vulgar. Of Mandeville of the scandalous *Fable of the Bees,* for example, he writes, "His brutality and his love of paradox revolt us as a display of cynical levity," and he adds, "the fairest flowers, as Tucker says, may be rooted in dunghills, and the genuine observer must examine the dunghill as well as the flower." The phrasing is no doubt Victorian, but we should find it hard to disagree with the precept, and with the way Stephen carries it out. Stephen's temperament and training combined to impel him to "examine" whatever he found; he also judged what he found, but to judge is surely not in the good judge a form of suppression. Again, Stephen was too much of an English Victorian gentleman to like revolutions—but not too much one to understand them. On Godwin and Paine he is as illuminating as on Burke. He does not write about ideas in a vacuum; men and their societies always figure in his work.

Stephen the scholar and writer is by no means wholly of a piece with the gentleman, the father of a family, the sickly little boy grown up into a pioneer mountain climber. Yet Stephen the man, the Stephen who appears in his daughter Virginia's *To the Lighthouse* as "Mr. Ramsay," a by no means controlled and judicious character, is worth our attention for himself. He is worth such attention also from the point of view of the historian of ideas or the sociologist of knowledge, for he and his family circle make up a curious link between two such remarkably English groups as the Clapham Sect of the early nineteenth century and the Bloomsbury Group of the early twentieth.

Stephen, after his loss of faith and his drastic decision of 1862 to resign his safe fellowship at Cambridge and risk the life of what we now call the free-lance writer, moved to London, where he soon established himself as a successful and adequately paid writer for serious magazines. In 1867 he married a daughter of the novelist Thackeray and went to Switzerland on a honeymoon. Even in Zermatt, however, he nobly and perhaps not unnaturally, as he wrote Oliver Wendell Holmes, Sr., "stayed at the bottom instead of bounding from peak to peak across the fathomless abysses of the glacier." Mrs. Stephen died suddenly in 1875 after eight years of a happy marriage, leaving one son. Three years later Stephen married again, and again most happily. The bride was a widow, Mrs. Herbert Duckworth, born Jackson, a friend of the Thackerays, and a member of the same close-knit class of English intellectuals, lawyers, and civil servants as her husband. There were three children, one boy and two girls.

The girls helped set up the Bloomsbury Group. Vanessa married Clive Bell, art critic and indeed philosopher of art. Virginia in 1912 married Leonard Woolf, who had spent seven years in the Civil Service in Ceylon, and had returned to England to write and preach what an outsider may call a variety of Fabian Socialism. After her father's death in 1904 Virginia had settled with her brothers in Bloomsbury, a section of London around the British Museum developed in the eighteenth century largely by the Russell family, Dukes of Bedford. Like most such groups at least in British literary life, those who met in Bloomsbury *salons* were likely to deny that they formed a "school" of closely knit artists and writers with a common aim. And Lytton Strachey, T. S. Eliot, Roger Fry, Clive Bell, Stephen Spender, Elizabeth Bowen, Virginia Woolf, and the rest had differing personalities, differing political and ethical philosophies, even different ideas about the beautiful. T. S. Eliot in the May, 1941, issue of *Horizons* after the death of Mrs. Woolf wrote:

> Any group will appear more uniform, and probably more intolerant and exclusive from the outside, than it really is; and here, certainly, no sub-scription of orthodoxy was imposed. Had it, indeed, been a matter of limited membership and exclusive doctrine, it would not have attracted the exasperated attention of those who objected to it on these supposed grounds . . . I only mention the matter in order to make the point that Virginia Woolf was the centre, not merely of an esoteric group, but of the literary life of London. Her position was due to a concurrence of qualities and circumstances which never happened before, and which I do not think will ever happen again. It maintained the dignified and admirable tradition of Victorian upper middle-class culture—a situation in which the artist was neither the servant of the exalted patron, the parasite of the plutocrat, nor the entertainer of the mob—a situation in which the producer and the consumer of art were on an equal footing, and that neither the highest nor the lowest.

There does indeed seem a great gap between the evangelical Clapham

Sect of Virginia Woolf's great-grandfather and the Bloomsbury Group of devoted, and in the eyes of their critics snobbish, seekers after all the refinements and subtleties of modern art and letters. Leslie Stephen himself, with his moral fervor and his agnostic's righteousness, seems at first sight nearer to his ancestors than to his children. Yet there are many like-minded people in this century-long chain, and Bloomsbury is after all not very far from Clapham. For what unites them is something very important in modern English culture, something for the most part lacking in both those imperfectly egalitarian societies so influenced by the eighteenth-century Enlightenment, the United States and France. This common link is membership in an intellectual privileged class sure of its position, little troubled by what we now call problems of status, of pecking order, relatively free from economic worries, with no drive toward conspicuous consumption, much addicted to understatement and ambivalent—perhaps for all concerned profitably ambivalent —in their feelings about the behavior and potential behavior of the "lower classes."

All the Stephens, from the two Jameses through Leslie to Virginia, disliked the vulgar—or better, perhaps, disliked vulgarity. For the great-grandfather the evil was no doubt more fully the kind of evil the puritan has always disliked, carnal self-indulgence, loss of self-control, worldly pride; for the great-granddaughter the evil was bad taste, bad manners, cruelty, the "pooled self-esteem" of common nationalism. It is easy to call the first idealism, the second snobbery, but the two often meet in specific behavior. The Bloomsbury Group wanted a better world, were indeed reformers, evangelicals of a sort. Leslie Stephen himself displays an interesting reaction in which the moral and the aesthetic mingle. He hated those very nineteenth-century evidences of the fact that the increasingly prosperous many were not pursuing the beautiful and the good. He hated *villes de plaisir*. He writes on his first visit to the United States in 1863:

> Leaving Boston, I went, I don't exactly know why, to a place called Newport in Rhode Island, which is one of the most popular watering-places round about. Why it should be popular is more than I can say, as it is hatefully flat and apparently devoid even of good bathing. However, I could not stay in it long, for I felt that disgust arising which always comes to me at Interlaken or any of those vile haunts of all that is most contemptible in humanity, called watering-places.

One shudders to think of the effect contemporary Las Vegas would have on him.

Yet there is another side to this distrust of the masses, distrust in fact of democracy. Evangelicals, nineteenth-century British liberals, Fabians, were very far indeed from the kind of aristocrat's contempt for—better, perhaps, aloofness from—the commoner associated, not always fairly, with the feudal aristocracy of birth, with the Prussian *Junkers* and the old French *noblesse*. Nor were these British groups, not even the Bloomsbury one, dwellers in an ivory tower. They were crusaders, men and women trying very hard to push and pull the many up to the standards of the few. The wisest and most moderate of them—a Leslie Stephen, a Walter Bagehot, a Graham Wallas—had reconciled themselves to the slowness of the process of making the many as good as the few, to its incompleteness and complexities. They were not in a hurry, not in despair. Their twentieth-century successors were less serene, understandably enough in the face of events. In our own day those who are left of them have had to face the angry young men who were not born to assured status, and they have had to see their world in many ways rather farther from the beautiful and good than it was in their youth. Perhaps the race of the Stephens is dying out. But something of them, something of the Enlightenment Leslie Stephen writes about with such fairness and balance in this book, is still our heritage on both sides of the Atlantic.

June 1962

CHAPTER XI

POLITICAL ECONOMY

CHARACTERISTICS

CHAPTER IX

MORAL PHILOSOPHY

I. Introductory.

1. The different religions of the world tell us, each in its own fashion, what is the plan and meaning of this universe. Thence true believers may infer what is the best method of employing our brief existence within it. We ought to be good, say all moralists, and the questions remain, what is meant by 'ought' and by 'goodness,' and what are the motives which induce us to be good? Theology, so long as it was a vital belief in the world, and preserved a sufficient infusion of the anthropomorphic element, afforded a complete and satisfactory answer to these questions. Morality was of necessity its handmaid. Believe in an active ruler of the universe, who reveals his will to men, who distributes rewards and punishments to the good and the evil, and we have a plain answer to most of the problems of morality. God's will, so far as known to us, must determine what is good. We are obliged to be good, because, whether from love or from fear, man must obey his Creator and preserver. Nor does the enquiry into the nature of our moral sentiments naturally suggest itself. Men who live under a visible monarch do not speculate as to the origin of the sentiment which makes them obey his laws. Their loyalty and the fear of his power are sufficient reasons; and it would never strike them that any special faculty was needed to produce dread of his vengeance or an enthusiastic reverence for his goodness. So long, therefore, as the older theological conception of the universe is unhesitatingly accepted, the only moral enquiry which is likely to flourish is casuistry, or the discussion as to the details of that legal code whose origin and sanction are abundantly clear.

2. But wider speculations as to morality inevitably occur as soon as the vision of God becomes faint; when the Almighty retires behind second causes, instead of being felt as an immediate presence, and his existence becomes the subject of logical proof, or belief is refined into sentiment. If the old system of government disappears, what is to take its place? The prohibition of murder is no longer uttered by a visible Deity from Mount Sinai. Why, then, should we not commit murder?

and how do we know that it is wrong? Hell no longer yawns before us; what punishment has the murderer to dread? This sentiment of disapproval survives the clearly divine character of the prohibition. What, then, is its meaning and origin? In England attention had been recently called to these important questions by Hobbes, the keenest and most audacious of all contemporary speculators. Throughout the seventeenth and the first years of the eighteenth century he represented the evil principle to moralists as well as to theologians. The two classes were indeed one. The whole theology of the eighteenth century has a specially moral turn. Religion was regarded far less as providing expression for our deepest emotions, or as a body of old tradition invested with the most touching poetical associations, than as a practical rule of life. This preoccupation with the direct moral bearing of theology gives a prosaic turn to the writing of the day; but, in fact, this aspect of the great problem was of vital importance. How could order be preserved when the old sanctions were decaying? Can a society of atheists be maintained? was a question put by Bayle, and taken up by Shaftesbury. It was nothing more than an epigrammatic form of a question, to which it was of the deepest importance to find an answer, and which was rightly discussed with an eagerness tending rather to cast into the shade the more poetical aspects of religion. How, to put the question less bluntly, should morality survive theology? Various answers were given in England by various schools of thought—by Clarke, Wollaston, and Price, by Shaftesbury, Butler, and Hutcheson, by Hartley and Adam Smith, by Locke, Hume, Tucker, Paley, and Bentham. What was the nature of the solutions suggested? and what relation do the various theories bear to each other?

II. The Intellectual School.

3. That which comes first in the order of thought is represented by the writers generally known as the intellectual school of moralists. Its leading representatives are Clarke, Wollaston, and Price. The first two names have already encountered us in the deist controversy. Price belonged to a later generation. He was born in 1723, the year preceding Wollaston's death, and six years before the death of Clarke. He was more conspicuous in political than moral or theological controversies, and is remembered chiefly as the inventor of the younger Pitt's sinking fund, and as affording the occasion of one of Burke's most brilliant invectives against revolutionary principles. His 'Review of the principal Questions and Difficulties in Morals' was first published in 1758, before

he had taken part in political discussions and become the friend of Priestley and Shelburne. His writings are of interest as illustrating the connection, so often noticed by Burke, between revolutionary theories in politics and the *a priori* doctrines of metaphysicians. The advocate of the most mathematical view of morality naturally became the advocate of the indefeasible rights of man in politics. The absolute spirit is the same in both cases. His philosophical speculations are curious, though they hardly possess high intrinsic merit. His book on morality is the fullest exposition of the theory which it advocates; but the theory was already antiquated; and Price, though he makes a great parade of logical systematisation, is a very indistinct writer. It is often difficult to discover his precise drift, and the discovery does not always reward the labour which it exacts. Clarke's theory is contained in his 'Sermons on Natural and Revealed Religion,' and Wollaston's in his 'Religion of Nature Delineated.' Both of these books have a reference to the deist controversy, with which the first is principally occupied. The theory which they expound was accepted by the whole school of which Clarke was the most conspicuous leader. We have already been led to notice it in the history of the deist controversy, and it is simply the application to ethical speculations of the metaphysical system which dates from Descartes. A brief examination will sufficiently indicate the main cause of the rapid decay of a doctrine which had so little influence upon the main problems of human life.

4. The starting-point is the identification of God with nature. The Almighty is not with these philosophers the ruler of a universe, in some sort independent of him, or external to him, but the first cause of all things. He moves the stars and directs the course of a bubble. The moral as well as the material universe is absolutely dependent on his laws. Men like Hobbes and Spinoza, who dared to push their logic to its legitimate consequences, saw that the most trifling and transitory phenomenon must be ascribed as distinctly as those which, in our language, are most important and lasting, to the action of an omnipotent and omniscient Creator. It matters not how many links intervene between the earthly end of the chain perceptible to our senses and the heavenly end which is in the immediate grasp of the Creator. He who, with absolutely infallible knowledge, has present to his mind the remotest ramifications of the infinite series of causes and effects, guides the raindrop, or moves the hand of the murderer as distinctly as if he directly intervened at the moment. If, then, 'law' means the same thing when we speak of moral and natural laws, it would seem that morality is annihilated by this conception. 'Fish,' says Spinoza, 'are determined

by nature to swim; and big fish to eat little fish, and therefore it is by the highest natural right that fish possess the water, and that big fish eat little fish.'[1] Whatever is, it would seem, on this showing, is in the strictest sense of the word right. A murderer obeys a natural 'law' as much as a saint; a 'Borgia and a Catiline' are as much the products of nature as a shark or a St. Paul. If, in short, the moral law expresses simply the will of the legislator, and the legislator is nature, everything which happens is, by the very definition, in conformity with the law. To break the law is not wrong, but impossible.

5. Spinoza's method of escaping the difficulty need not be considered, for though his name is often quoted by the English writers of the time, neither opponents nor followers appreciated his position. Hobbes's writings, on the contrary, were, as I have said, the most potent stimulant to English thought in the last half of the seventeenth, and even during the first half of the eighteenth, century in England. He had, indeed, fewer disciples than antagonists; but the writer who provokes a reaction does as much in generating ideas as the writer who propagates his own ideas. Hobbes, as his opponents understood him, identified the moral with the positive law. That is wrong, he said, which the sovereign forbids; that is right which he allows. Hobbes indeed declared that the 'laws of nature' are immutable and eternal: but they do not become binding until the commonwealth has been instituted; and the sovereign has the power of defining their application.[2] It follows that the moral standard varies according to time and place; for that which is wrong in Turkey may be right in England. His precise meaning need not here be discussed. The doctrine in its extreme form is that which later English moralists sought to impugn, and of which they considered Hobbes to be the chief representative.

6. The particular form of the theory which commended itself to Clarke—for the skill of metaphysicians has woven doctrines substantially identical into various forms at different periods of speculation—follows from the fundamental assumptions of the metaphysical school, from which he was an offshoot. The mathematical universe in which he believed consisted of two elements; on one side was matter with its primary qualities, or, in other words, the objects of sense stripped of all qualities except those of which the mathematician takes cognisance; and, on the other, the hierarchy of spirits from the divine to the human. All other qualities were merely the modifications raised in the spirit in

---

[1] Spinoza, 'Tract. Theologico-Politicus,' p. 252.
[2] See 'Leviathan,' pt. i. chs. 14, 15.

consequence of the mysterious action and reaction between itself and matter. The reason was the faculty by which the invariable relations between these ultimate facts were perceived; whilst the senses presented us with a shifting phantasmagoria of unrealities. To prove, then, that morality was not arbitrary and variable seemed to him to be the same thing as proving that it belonged to those eternal and immutable relations, and not to the sphere of observation, where the accidental and the essential were indistinguishably blended. The foundation of his argument for revealed religion was a proof that there was an unalterable natural law, to which revelation provided a necessary supplement. Clarke attacks Hobbes as asserting that 'there is no such real difference originally, necessarily, and absolutely in the nature of things; but that all obligation to God arises merely from his absolutely irresistible power; and all duty towards men merely from positive compact.'[3] In opposition to this view, some of the consequences of which he exposes with great clearness, he sets up his system of mathematical morality. He that wilfully refuses to honour and obey God is 'really guilty of an equal absurdity and inconsistency in practice as he that in speculation denies the effect to owe anything to its cause, or the whole to be bigger than its part. He that refuses to deal with all men equitably' makes the same mistake as 'he that in another case should affirm one number or quantity to be equal to another, and yet that other, at the same time, not to be equal to the first.'[4] The three great primary duties, to God, to each other, and to ourselves, may be deduced in the same way as the propositions of Euclid. 'There is no congruity or proportion in the uniform disposition and correspondent order of any bodies or magnitudes, no fitness and agreement in the application of similar and equal geometrical figures one to another,'[5] so plain as the fitness of God's receiving honour from his creatures. To deny that I should do for another man what he in the like case should do for me, and to deny it,[6] 'either in word or action' (a phrase which suggests the singular crotchet soon afterwards expounded by Wollaston), 'is as if a man should contend that, though two and three are equal to five, yet five are not equal to two and three.' It is characteristic that Clarke does not perceive that this interpretation of the common precept reduces it to a truism. The essence of the rule would be, according to him, that if the circumstances are the same, the same law will give the same results; and it would be as compatible, for example, with a law of mutual hatred as of mutual love. In fact, he argues that the identity of reason is implied in a more special assertion;

[3]Clarke's Works, ii. 609.   [4]Ib. p. 613.   [5]Ib. p. 618.   [6]Ib. p. 619.

and then assumes that the universal postulate is the vital principle of the assertion. Finally, our duty to ourselves is deduced from our duty to God, and, therefore, rests upon the same intuitions.

7. An obvious difficulty underlies all reasoning of this class, even in its most refined shape. The doctrine might, on the general assumptions of Clarke's philosophy, be applicable to the 'Laws of Nature,' but is scarcely to be made applicable to the moral law. Every science is potentially deducible from a small number of primary truths; to which Clarke would have added that those truths were intuitively apprehended, and that their denial involved a contradiction in terms. Thus, for example, a being of sufficient knowledge might construct a complete theory of human nature, of which every proposition would be either self-evident or rigorously deducible from self-evident axioms. Such propositions would take the form of laws in the scientific, not in the moral, sense; the copula would be 'is,' not 'ought;' the general formula would be 'all men do so and so,' not 'thou shalt do so and so.' Clarke would have denied the possibility of such a science, because he disjointed the system which would otherwise have conducted him to Spinozism by the unphilosophical hypothesis of free-will. The language, however, which he uses about the moral law is, in reality, applicable to the scientific law alone. It might be said with plausibility (we need not ask whether it could be said with accuracy) that the proposition 'all men are mortal' is capable of being deductively proved by inference from some self-evident axioms. A denial of it would, therefore, involve a contradiction. But the proposition 'thou shalt not kill' is a command addressed to the will, not a statement of a truth addressed to the intellect; and Clarke's attempt to bring it under the same category involves a confusion fatal to his whole theory. It is, in fact, a confusion between the art and the science of human conduct.

8. If, to evade this difficulty, we throw the statement into a different form, we obtain, indeed, a body of doctrines to which Clarke's arguments may be applicable; but then we introduce precisely the considerations which he endeavoured to exclude. It may, for example, be a demonstrable proposition that all murderers will be damned, or that they will all be hateful, or that their conduct diminishes the sum of general happiness. Such propositions are the groundwork of ethical science, if not the science itself. But, if Clarke's doctrine were stretched so as to include them, it would be merged in a system of theological, or intuitional, or utilitarian morality. Any such formula includes of necessity some references to the feelings with which we regard actions, or to their consequences to mankind. It forms part of the science of

human nature, and it was Clarke's ambition, as it has substantially been the ambition of other metaphysicians, to expound a theory of human conduct which should be entirely independent of any observation of human nature. Morality must not be 'subjective.' That means, it must be independent of the idiosyncrasies of individuals. Clarke translates this into the statement: Morality must be independent of the character of the race. He wished to elevate morality into the sphere of pure mathematics, or, what he held to be equivalent, of absolute truth, where the promptings of passion and the lessons of experience should be entirely excluded. He tried to argue from our *a priori* knowledge of the essence of the divine and human natures, and not from the *a posteriori* experience of their relations. Once more, he was transporting a method, applicable in the theological stage of thought, into a metaphysical region where it collapsed from want of the necessary supports. Theologians who—it matters not how—were capable of defining the character of God, could deduce a set of rules independent of, or even contradictory to, experience. Given a just or vindictive and omnipotent ruler, it was easy to infer what should be the conduct of his creatures. But when for Jehovah or the Christian Trinity was substituted the colourless conception of a supreme nature, the *a priori* method could give no results except certain neutral rules applicable to every fact, and, therefore, condemnatory or approbatory of none. From this fatal circle Clarke vainly endeavours to free himself, when he has once taken the suicidal course of refusing to interrogate nature, in order to discover what is pleasing to the God of nature. He is forced, in order to give any plausibility to his arguments, to supplement them by heterogeneous reasonings drawn from other systems of morality. When his wings fail to support him in the heavenly spaces beyond the atmosphere, he has recourse to purely utilitarian arguments drawn from the influence of morality upon human happiness.

9. The nugatory character of his system appears in the curious development given to it by Wollaston. Wollaston's doctrine is the expansion of the hint just quoted from Clarke. The system which results is sufficiently ingenious to supply an excellent thesis for attack and defence in the schools; whilst his contemporaries were so impressed as to receive it with the 'highest applause.'[7] So, at least, Conybeare assures us, who himself speaks of the theory as though it were a discovery in morals, fit to be placed beside the Newtonian discoveries in astronomy. He who acts upon the hypothesis that things are so and so, says

[7]Conybeare's 'Defence' &c. p. 239.

Wollaston, proclaims by his acts that they are so and so; and no act that interferes with a true proposition (as if any act could 'interfere' with a true proposition!) can be right. Hence, I ought not to kill a man because, by so doing, I deny him to be a man. To which it was obvious to reply that my action proclaims the very reverse, and that, in any case, it is a mere verbal juggle to call an action a lie. The doctrine, whether in Clarke's or Wollaston's hands, is, in fact, a kind of offshoot from the common theory of metaphysicians which identifies crime with error, and which had lately been presented in more imposing forms by many more famous metaphysicians. Many schools of moralists may admit that all immorality involves an element of intellectual error. To one who had adequate conceptions of the universe, and to whose intellect, therefore, all the consequences of his actions were immediately present, the wisdom of virtue would be so evident that crime would be impossible. God's omniscience implies his moral perfection. Our passions lead us into error by distorting our judgments; and perfectly sound judgment would disperse the mists excited by the passions. This doctrine, whatever its value, took a peculiar form in the school of Clarke. One would have thought it plain that, whether the intellectual error or the passionate impulse were the essential element in wrongdoing, either of them was produced by nature. We obey the law of nature when we blunder as much as when we judge soundly; for to break that law is not a crime, but an impossibility. The confusion, however characteristic of metaphysicians generally, between the objective and subjective, generated an indistinct impression that a confusion in our conceptions was, in some sense, a confusion in the order of nature itself. If every error involved a contradiction, it seemed that a wrong belief was the ultimate element in every wrong action, and the mistake was identified with the impossible crime of disobedience to nature. Wollaston capped this confusion by calling the blunder a lie.

10. He inevitably fails to extract any intelligible results from this fanciful form of an illusory theory. He is either confined to a series of those barren statements for which metaphysicians have found high-sounding names, such as the doctrine that 'whatever is, is;' or that 'A is not not-A;' or has to interpret his doctrine as including any statement reconcilable with those propositions. Thus Wollaston slides into utilitarianism. He proclaims that 'happiness must not be denied to be what it is; and' thus 'it is by the practice of truth that we arrive at that happiness which is true,'[8] 'true' being characteristically used as identical

---

[8]'Religion of Nature,' p. 52.

with 'real.' Hence he makes room for a utilitarian or even a purely selfish system of morality. For if the obligation to truth is interpreted as including the obligation to pursue happiness, we find that all or any of the ordinary sanctions are admissible under this scheme.

11. The nugatory character of the doctrine is still clearer in the application which was most important in the eyes of its supporters. Clarke's doctrine had its root in the laudable desire to prove that morality was not a mere fashion; and with him and his followers the phrase 'eternal and immutable' becomes a kind of catchword. Yet, after all, it was obvious to remark that a proposition is either true or not true; and that to add 'eternal and immutable' makes no real difference. Those words properly refer to the matter of the proposition, not to its formal truth. Every true proposition is, in a sense, 'eternally and immutably' true. If it is true that in the year 1700 a particular bubble burst, it will always be true to the end of time, and it always was true from the beginning of time to say that the bubble burst or would burst in 1700. The real question is not whether the statement that men should not commit murder in the eighteenth century was eternally and immutably true, granting it to be true at the time; for that would be allowed by Hobbes as freely as by Clarke; but whether the wickedness of murder in the eighteenth century proved the wickedness of murder in all times and places. Yet Clarke interprets his phrases in such a way as to make them equivalent to the truism, and to leave the other proposition untouched. 'The nature and relations, the proportions and disproportions, the fitnesses and unfitnesses of things,' he says, 'are eternal, and in themselves absolutely unalterable; but this is only upon supposition that the things themselves exist, and exist in such a manner as they actually do.'[9] So that the thing which is really 'immutable and eternal' is that mysterious entity—a bare proposition which may be applicable to nothing that exists, or ever did exist. Nobody surely need trouble himself much as to the truth or falsehood of an abstract proposition which is entirely independent of any concrete embodiment. The point is stated more explicitly by one of Clarke's disciples, Balguy. After asserting that the moral relations are manifestly 'independent and immutable in whatever state or relation rational creatures may be supposed to be placed,' he adds that we may 'conceive human nature so framed that the relations of princes and subjects, parents and children, masters and servants, &c., should have no place in our duty, or lie dormant, as it were, in respect of mankind; nevertheless these relations, and all truths connected with them, will be in themselves, that is, in the divine under-

[9]Clarke, p. 640.

standing, precisely what they are now.'[10] He goes on to qualify this admission by adding that some duties, such as love to God and justice to men, will be binding on all rational creatures under any circumstances. The admission, however, is obviously wide enough for all purposes. In spite of the eternal and immutable nature of the abstract laws, the concrete law may vary as widely as even Mandeville could have desired.

12. The tenet of free-will adopted by the whole school encouraged the delusion that to make morals a science of observation was equivalent to making it arbitrary. They would have been under a similar delusion if they had argued that the art of healing was dependent upon fashion because its principles have to be deduced from facts and not from *a priori* and quasi-mathematical axioms. Price, the last teacher of the school, dwells at greatest length upon this part of the subject. Shaftesbury and Hutcheson had popularised the theory of a 'moral sense.' Price understood them to mean that our moral judgments were merely the dictates of a blind instinct, in which the intellect had no share. Their theory, as expounded by him, would have been that murder was wrong simply because we disliked it; or the dislike would have been alleged as its own justification. He argues, in opposition to this theory, which would certainly have been disowned by its supposed sponsors, that the intellect has not only a share in laying down moral laws and enforcing our obedience, but that it operates, or ought to operate, without the assistance of the emotions. His language upon those points is rendered obscure by his systematically confusing the questions of the criterion and the motive. It is comparatively plausible to say that the intellect is the sole agent in framing the criterion. His language upon this subject may occasionally remind us of Kant's 'Categorical Imperative;' and he seems to have been confusedly aiming at the same truths or errors from which the great German elaborated a moral theory more ingenious, though (as I should say) involving the same fundamental fallacy. He finds fault with the language of some of his own school who had said that virtue consisted in 'conformity to the relations of truths and things'—on the ground that virtue cannot be defined. It is an ultimate form of thought. 'If we will consider why it is right to conform ourselves to the relations in which persons and objects stand to us, we shall find ourselves obliged to terminate our views in a simple immediate perception, or in something ultimately approved; and for which no justifying reason can be assigned.'[11]

[10]Balguy, 'Second Letter to a Deist,' Tracts, p. 304.
[11]Price's 'Review' &c. p. 210.

This intuition constitutes the obligation to act rightly. He asserts 'that the perception of right and wrong does excite to action, and is alone a sufficient principle of action.'[12] 'It seems extremely evident that excitement belongs to the very ideas of moral right and wrong, and is essentially inseparable from the apprehension of them. When we are conscious that an action is fit to be done, or that it ought to be done, it is not conceivable that we can remain uninfluenced or want a motive to action.'[13] . . . 'Instincts, therefore, as before observed in other instances, are not necessary to the choice of ends. The intellectual nature is its own law. It has within itself a spring and guide of action which it cannot suppress or reject.'[14]

13. Hence we come to the conclusion that our actions do not, as philosophers have maintained, spring exclusively from a desire of pleasure or a dread of pain, but from the mere perception of a truth. Though Price cannot altogether dissociate our emotions from our actions, he endeavours to represent the passions as properly subsidiary to the intellect, and as superfluities of which we might rid ourselves entirely in a higher state of existence. He admits that 'some degree of pleasure is inseparable from the observation of virtuous actions;'[15] but he seems to hold that this is a merely subsidiary, and so to speak illusory, phenomenon. It would be as unreasonable to infer that 'the discernment of virtue is nothing distinct from the reception of this pleasure' as to infer that the so-called primary qualities are only modes of sensation. According to his philosophy, that is, virtue depends upon those real relations of things themselves which are apprehended only by the intellect. The pleasure given to the emotions, like the sensations produced by external phenomena on our ears or noses, have no independent reality. We should be better if we could do without them altogether. 'The occasion for them' (our passions and appetites) 'arises entirely from our deficiencies and weaknesses: Reason alone, did we possess it in a higher degree, would answer all the ends of them. Thus there would be no need of the parental affection were all parents sufficiently acquainted with the reasons for taking upon them the guidance and support of those whom nature has placed under their care, and were they virtuous enough to be always determined by those reasons.'[16] How there could be any reasons, when the passions and appetites had been eliminated, or how such reasons could determine anybody's conduct, does not appear. Price's argument on this point resembles the assertion that, because the process of intellectual development might enable us at some future day to draw our supplies of heat

[12]Price, p. 308.   [13]Ib. 310.   [14]Ib. p. 311.   [15]Ib. p. 99.   [16]Ib. p. 124.

from some central reservoir instead of maintaining a fire on every hearth, we should therefore be able, if we were clever enough, to do without heat altogether.

14. Not only are the affections superfluous, but any given action is deprived of its merit in so far as they are present. The intellectual determination is, he says, the '*only* spring of action in a reasonable being, so far as he can be deemed morally good and worthy,' and the 'only principle from which all actions flow which engage our esteem of the agents.'[17] It follows that 'instinctive benevolence is no principle of virtue, nor are any actions flowing merely from it virtuous. As far as this influences, so far something else than reason and goodness influence, and so much I think is to be subtracted from the moral worth of any action or character.'[18] He argues, for example, that the tenderness of a mother is less valuable morally, as it flows more from instincts and is less attended with reflection on their reasonableness and fitness; and in the same way as virtue is only virtue when it is the product of an intellectual perception, so vice is only vicious so far as the agent knows his actions to be vicious.[19] The fallacy here is not peculiar to Price or his school; but it is useless to attempt to unravel any further doctrine which has been more adequately set forth by philosophers of higher pretensions both in ancient and modern times. Englishmen of the eighteenth century were little inclined to regard the ideal man as a mere calculating machine without passions or affections, employed in meditating on the eternal relations of things in a universe purified of all emotion, or likely to accept a theory according to which infallibility and not impeccability constitutes the ultimate perfection, and the perfect man would be lost, not in the love of God or of his race, but in the profoundest mathematical speculations. Price, oddly enough, represents himself as a disciple of Butler, of whom he speaks with the highest reverence, and does not perceive that Butler is in closer agreement with his adversary Shaftesbury than with himself.

III. Shaftesbury and Mandeville.

15. It soon appeared that the moral Euclid which was the ideal of these philosophers would never get beyond the primary axioms which are equally true and trifling. Their metaphysical system decayed, leaving as its sole relic a magniloquent trick of language about the eternal and immutable nature of things. The phrase was familiar to the schools

[17]Price, p. 313.   [18]Ib. p. 318.   [19]Ib. p. 326.

of Clarke and Tindal, but it gradually became too empty for use even in theological controversy. The serious discussion of ethical problems was continued by two schools, which correspond to the speculative tendencies embodied in Reid's Common Sense and Hume's scepticism. Both of them recognised tacitly or explicitly the impossibility of constructing a moral code from the ontological bases.

16. The common-sense school was alarmed by the apparent consequences of this admission. The same logic justified the belief in God and the belief in virtue. If that logic were admitted to be insecure, might not God and virtue disappear from the universe? The common-sense philosophers held, as we have seen, that the vital principles might be preserved, though their truth could not be exhibited as a necessary conclusion of the pure reason. A principle which cannot be demonstrated, and which is yet held to possess independent authority, must be recognised by a kind of intellectual instinct. In ethical discussions, the faculty in which this mysterious power resided was generally described as the moral sense or the conscience. To the ontologist such a theory appeared to be mere empiricism, for it abandoned the claim of tracing back moral dogmas to an ultimate truth. The empiricist, on the other hand, was offended by the recognition of certain dogmas as possessing an authority requiring no confirmation from experience. The radical weakness, indeed, of a philosophy which tries to save the superstructure whilst abandoning the foundation, which multiplies first principles at will because it cannot prove them, was sufficiently exhibited by the barrenness of Reid's philosophy. In ethical questions the same weakness appears in another form. The intellectual cowardice which refuses to ask fundamental questions is naturally connected with the moral cowardice which refuses to look facts in the face. In the moralists whom we are about to consider there is generally a provoking tendency to an easy optimism. They inherit the pantheistic sentiment that 'whatever is, is right,' though they do not adopt the pantheistic logic; and as nature is still their God, they overlook the dark side of nature. The instinct which believes in God and virtue is very apt to disbelieve in the existence of natural evil and moral wickedness. There was, as we shall see, one great exception in Butler, who owes much of his power to his peculiar position in this respect. His conscience gives an account of the world very unlike that of his complacent brother philosophers. The want of thoroughness common to most of the school, the desire to obtain a comfortable and symmetrical theory at the expense of facts, did not prevent them from discharging a most important function. When the world is without a genuine philosophy, it becomes extremely de-

sirable to assert the existence and value of those impulses which (whatever their nature) we call conscience. The sceptical school was sapping the very foundations of the system with which, rightly or wrongly, the whole moral doctrine had been connected. In such a case, a blind and inexplicable instinct was at least better than none. The common-sense school might be wrong in asserting that the conscience was essentially a primitive and inexplicable faculty. They might, nevertheless, be right in saying that it existed, and that neither they nor their opponents could disprove its reality nor explain its origin. In the sphere of practice they maintained an ideal of virtuous action which was seriously threatened; in the sphere of speculation they at least kept before the world an important problem—what, namely, is the origin of the virtuous impulses?

17. Round this point raged the most active controversies of the period which we have to consider. Is conscience a reality or a sham? an ultimate or a derivative faculty? The sceptics and the intuitionalists discussed the question from various points of view. The typical representatives of the two schools of thought in the early part of the century were Shaftesbury and Mandeville, both of them writers of remarkable ability and of great influence upon their contemporaries and successors. I will begin by considering their attitude and relation.

18. The school of Shaftesbury retained the general doctrine of a divine guidance, but generally denied or relegated to the background the doctrine of supernatural sanctions. Anxious to retain a theological conception of the universe, they made a God out of Nature—a God immanent in the world, not acting upon it from without. Good impulses were at once divine and natural. The old God dwelt in a supersensual heaven, and our corrupt world could only reflect scattered lights from its benign Creator. Nature was revealed in the visible universe, and, therefore, the universe was everywhere pervaded by profound harmonies fitted to excite our enthusiastic veneration. It was the new temple, sanctified everywhere by the omnipresent Deity. Our aspirations were gratified within the visible order, instead of seeking for gratification elsewhere. Heaven and hell were no longer required to balance the corrupt desires of man, for man's loftiest impulses were natural. It was unnecessary as in orthodox divinity to call a new world into existence to redress the balance of the old.

19. The school, of which I have called Mandeville the representative, generally retained, by an equally natural process, the doctrine of supernatural sanctions, but rejected the doctrine of the divine guidance.

They cared comparatively little for a comprehensive theory of the universe, and fixed their eyes upon the facts immediately around them. A strong grasp of realities distinguished them, as a love of wider generalisation distinguished their adversaries. They recognised the important truth involved in the theological doctrine of human corruption. Man was, in fact, an animal moved by base and ferocious passions. As a matter of observation, religion was the best restraint upon his impulses, and the most tangible part of religion was the belief in future rewards and punishments. They had no desire, therefore, to abolish damnation, unless, with Mandeville, they accepted the doctrine that all virtue was an empty sham. But they refused to see any signs of supernatural agency in the world around them. Inspecting every theory, to use an illustration of Tucker's, with the microscope of science, they thought that human passions, bad as they might generally be, quite accounted for all the phenomena around them. Theology might still be true as regarded the dim distance beyond their ken, but theology was not applicable to ordinary life. Just as in the deist controversy, it was assumed that God might have revealed himself to the ancient Jews, but never appeared to modern Englishmen, so in ethical controversy, it was thought that God was not a present guide, but it might very well be proved that he would reward or punish us elsewhere. Thus, with thinkers of this class, the divine glory retired from the present and the tangible world, to concentrate itself in a distant past and future; whilst, with their opponents, that glory grew dim and indefinite indeed, but still continued to irradiate the present world. These two currents of speculation run side by side throughout the century; the utilitarian gradually becoming the most conspicuous, as being most in harmony with the tendencies of the age and of English thought. I shall trace them separately, after describing Shaftesbury and Mandeville as their typical representatives.

20. The third Lord Shaftesbury is one of the writers whose reputation is scarcely commensurate with the influence which he once exerted. His teaching is to be traced through much of our literature, though often curiously modified by the medium through which it has passed. He speaks to us in Pope's poetry, and in Butler's theology. All the ethical writers are related to him, more or less directly, by sympathy or opposition. During his life, he and his friend Lord Molesworth were the chief protectors of Toland; and Tindal and Bolingbroke took many hints from his pages. The power is perhaps due less to his literary faculty—for, in spite of high merits, he is a wearisome and perplexed

writer—than to the peculiar position which he occupied in speculation, and which at once separates him from his contemporaries, and enabled him to be a valuable critic and stimulator of thought.

21. A grandson of Dryden's Achitophel, and brought up under the influence of Locke, he had imbibed from his cradle the political principles of the great Whig families. He professed, indeed, to adhere to the genuine party creed, with an independence not shown by its official representatives. Above all, he shared the Whig hatred to high-church principles; and contempt for the slavish political doctrines of nonjurors and highflyers was naturally allied in his mind, and as in the minds of many other members of his party, with an equally hearty contempt for their theology. The Church, according to his view, was useful in so far as it tied the hands of priests and fanatics, and acted as a gag instead of a trumpet; it would be pernicious if it could be made an engine of priestly power. He contemptuously professes his 'steady orthodoxy, resignation and entire submission to the truly Christian and catholic doctrines of our Holy Church, as by law established'[1]—a profession in which the stress is, of course, to be laid upon the last three words. His Utopia implied an era of general indifference, in which the ignorant might be provided with dogmas for their amusement; and wise men smile at them in secret. The Church, in short, was excellent as a national refrigerating machine; but no cultivated person could believe in its doctrines.

22. Shaftesbury, however, by native intellectual power, and by force of cultivation, was raised far above the ordinary politicians of his day. On the rude stock of commonplace Whiggism were grafted accomplishments strange to most of his countrymen. Driven from a public school by the unpopularity of his grandfather, he had acquired the rare power of enjoying classical literature, without being drilled by grammatical pedants. He had travelled abroad, and there learnt to value, even to excess, the advantages of cosmopolitan culture in art and philosophy. In Italy he had become a connoisseur, and could frame high-sounding æsthetic canons of taste. In Holland, he had made the acquaintance of Bayle and Le Clerc, the leaders of European criticism. He is never tired of preaching the advantages obtainable by the refining process of which he was thus a brilliant example. He complains of the narrow prejudices of his countrymen. Those only will relish his writings 'who delight in the open and free commerce of the world, and are rejoiced to gather views and receive light from every quarter.'[2] A highly cultivated taste is the sole guide both in art and philosophy. 'To philosophise in a just

[1]Misc. v. ch. iii.   [2]Ib. iii. ch. i.

signification is but to carry good breeding a step higher.'[2] 'The test of beauty and the relish of what is decent, just, and amiable, perfects the character of the gentleman and the philosopher.'[3] The person who is thus thoroughly trained is called, in his old-fashioned dialect, the 'virtuoso;' and if Shaftesbury has a full measure of the pedantry and conceit belonging to the character, he has still more of the intellectual sensibility which the virtuoso arrogates as his peculiar merit.

23. Shaftesbury's writings appeared between 1708 and 1711.[4] His first two treatises explain his view of contemporary theologians. I have not discussed them in speaking of the deist controversy, although their influence was considerable. Shaftesbury, however, confines himself chiefly to indicating his general attitude of mind, and deals but little in those specific attacks upon the letter of the Bible which formed the staple of contemporary controversy. He looks upon the whole struggle with the supercilious contempt of an indifferent spectator. His 'Letter on Enthusiasm,' provoked by the strange performances of the French prophets, and its sequel, called 'Sensus Communis,' or an 'Essay on the Freedom of Wit and Humour,' explains his theory. His strongest antipathies are excited by that ugly phenomenon which our ancestors condemned under the name of enthusiasm—a word, the change in whose signification is characteristic of many other changes. 'Inspiration,' he says, 'is a real feeling of the Divine presence, and enthusiasm a false one;'[5] to which he adds, significantly, that the passions aroused in the two cases are much alike. This false belief in a supernatural influence is at the bottom of the disgusting manifestations of popular superstition, in which men mistake mental diseases for divine inspirations; and equally at the bottom of the superstitions which the Church of Rome has succeeded, with marvellous skill, in fettering and turning to account for the support of its majestic hierarchy. To provide for the enthusiasm of the loftier kind, the rulers of that Church allowed 'their mystics to write and preach in the most rapturous and seraphic strains.'[6] To the vulgar they appealed by temples, statues, paintings, vestments, and all the gorgeous pomp of ritual. No wonder, he exclaims, if Rome, the seat of a monarchy resting on foundations laid so deep in human nature, still appeals to the imagination of all spectators, though some are charmed into a desire for reunion, whilst others conceive a deadly hatred for all priestly rule.

[2]Misc. iii. ch. i.   [3]Ib. iii. ch. i.

[4]The essay on 'Virtue' had been published in an imperfect state by Toland in 1698. The 'Characteristics,' containing his collected treatises, first appeared in 1711, the year of his death.   [5]'Enthusiasm,' sec. 7.   [6]Misc. ii. ch. ii.

24. Shaftesbury, of course, belongs to the latter category, and for both evils he prescribes the same remedy. Ridicule is the proper antidote to every development of enthusiasm. Instead of breaking the bones of the French charlatans, we had the good sense to make them the subject of 'a puppet-show at Bartle'my fair;'[7] and if a similar prescription had been applied by the Jews seventeen centuries before, he thinks that they would have done far more harm to our religion. For enthusiasm in priestly robes, and armed with the implements of persecution, there is the same remedy as for the enthusiasm serving the passions of a mob by counterfeit miracles. He maintained as a general principle that ridicule was the test of truth; a theory which produced a very pretty quarrel between Warburton and Akenside. Truth, he argues, 'may bear all lights,'[8] and one of the principal lights is cast by ridicule. This is an anticipatory justification of the practice of the deists and their pupil Voltaire. Ridicule is the natural retort to tyranny. "Tis the persecuting spirit that has raised the bantering one.'[9] The doctrine, questionable enough in this dogmatic form, may perhaps be admitted with some limitation. Ridicule, out of place, when men are still in earnest enough to fight for their creeds, may be fairly employed in destroying the phantoms of dead creeds. When the prestige has survived the power, when heterodoxy in unfashionable, but not criminal, when priests bluster but cannot burn, satire may fairly come into play. Dogmas whose foundations have been sapped by reason may be toppled over by the lighter bolts of ridicule. The method is hardly possible till some freedom of discussion is allowed, nor becoming when free discussion has brought all disputants to equal terms. Ridicule clears the air from the vapours of preconceived prejudice. Shaftesbury, though insisting even to tediousness upon its importance, is awkward in its application. Nor, indeed, is he to be reckoned amongst the unscrupulous employers of the weapon. It is 'good humour,' not a scoffing humour, which he professes to desire. 'Good humour,' he tells us, 'is not only the best security against enthusiasm, but the best foundation of piety and true religion.'[10] Good humour, in fact, is the disposition natural to the philosopher when enthusiasm has been finally exorcised from religion. All turbulent passions and vehement excitements are alien to his nature. The sour fanatic and the bigoted priest are at opposite poles of disturbance, whilst he dwells in the temperate latitudes of serene contemplation. With the more rational forms of religion he would be the last man to quarrel. He sets himself at one place to prove that 'wit and humour are corrob-

[7]'Enthusiasm," sec. 3.   [9]Ib. sec. 4.
[8]'Wit and Humour,' part i. sec. 1.   [10]'Enthusiasm,' sec. 3.

orative of religion and promotive of true faith;' that they have been used by 'the holy founders of religion;' and that ours is 'in the main a witty and good-humored religion.'[11] He passes with suspicious lightness over the proof of the last head; and the phrase 'in the main' is obviously intended to exclude a large, but undefined, element of base alloy. So long, however, as religion makes no unpleasant demands upon him he will not quarrel with its general claims. He 'speaks with contempt of the mockery of modern miracles and inspiration;' he is inclined to regard all pretences to such powers as 'mere imposture or delusion;' but on the miracles of past ages he resigns his judgment to his superiors, and on all occasions 'submits most willingly, and with full confidence and trust, to the opinions *by law established*.'[12] A miracle which happened seventeen centuries before could hurt nobody; but the miracles of the French prophets, or at the tomb of the Abbé Paris, were noxious enough to require a drastic remedy in the shape of satire. One exception, indeed, must be admitted. Shaftesbury's philosophic calm is slightly disturbed by any mention of the Jews. The idol of the Puritans was naturally the bugbear of the deists. The Jew was the type of all that was fanatical, superstitious, narrow-minded, and offensive, and Shaftesbury hated him with the hatred of Voltaire. When writing as a literary critic, his examples of subjects upon which no poet could confer any interest are taken from Jewish history. Nothing, as the friend of Bayle naturally thinks, could be made of David. 'Such are some human hearts that they can hardly find the least sympathy with that only one which had the character of being after the pattern of the Almighty.'[13] When writing as a moralist the same fertile source supplies him with abundant instances of the fearful consequences of superstition. Deism may be evil when it implies belief in a bad God. If religion gives a divine warrant for cruelty, persecution, barbarity to the conquered, human sacrifices, self-mutilation, treachery, or partiality to a chosen race, the practices which it sanctions are still 'horrid depravity.'[14] The reference to the Jews is more explicitly pointed in his later writings, where, for example, he explains the allusion to human sacrifice by the story of Abraham and Isaac,[15] and discovers the origin of enthusiasm in priest-ridden Egypt, whence it was derived by the servile imitation of the Jews.[16] Shaftesbury was a theist; but he was certainly not a worshipper of Jehovah.

25. The destructive element of Shaftesbury's writings is, however,

---

[11]'Misc. ii. ch. iii.   [14]'Virtue,' book i. part ii. sec. 3, and pt. iv. sec. 2.
[12]Ib. ii. ch. ii.   [15]Misc. ii. ch. iii.
[13]'Soliloquy,' part iii. sec. 3.   [16]Ib. ii. ch. i.

strictly subordinate to his main purpose. He differs from Hobbes, the typical representative of the destructive impulses, as profoundly, though he does not hate him so heartily, as the soundest contemporary divines. Suppose, he says, that we had 'lived in Asia at the time when the Magi, by an egregious imposture, had got possession of the empire,'[17] but had endeavoured to obviate the hatred justly due to their cheats by recommending the best possible moral maxims, what would be our right course? Should we attack both the Magi and their doctrines; repudiate every moral and religious principle, and make men as much as possible wolves to each other? That, he says, was the course pursued by Hobbes, who, both in religion and politics, went on the principle of 'Magophony,' or indiscriminate slaughter of his opponents. Shaftesbury, on the contrary, aims at slaying, or rather fettering, the Magi, whilst retaining the precious treasures of which they had become the depositories. He had been profoundly influenced by Hobbes's great opponents, the Cambridge Platonists, and had even written a preface to a volume of sermons published by Whichcote—one of their number. His sceptical tendencies, indeed, prevented him from being a thorough disciple of the school, though their spirit permeates his pages. Metaphysical speculation, again, was not congenial to his temper, and his cosmopolitan training had impressed him with the belief that the day of the great systemmongers was past. The vast tower of Babel, by which the school of Descartes and Leibnitz had hoped to scale the heavens, was crumbling into ruin, leaving for its only legacy a jargon detestable to all intelligent men. Of metaphysics he always speaks with a bitter contempt. It was a pseudo-science, leading to barren formulæ fit only for scholastic pedants. Philosophers are 'a sort of moonblind wits who, though very acute and able in their kind, may be said to renounce daylight and extinguish, in a manner, the bright visible outside world, by allowing us to know nothing besides what we can prove by strict and formal demonstration.'[18] He ridicules the philosophical speculations about 'formation of ideas; their compositions, comparisons, agreement and disagreement.'[19] Philosophy, in his sense, is nothing but the study of happiness,[20] and all these discussions as to substances, entities, and the eternal and immutable relations of things, and pre-established harmonies and occasional causes, and primary and secondary qualities, are so much empty sound. 'The most ingenious way of becoming foolish,' as he very truly says, 'is by a system,'[21] and, in truth, the systems then existing

---

[17]'Wit and Humour,' part ii. sec. 1.   [20]'Moralists,' iii. sec. 3.
[18]Misc. iv. ch. ii.   [21]'Soliloquy,' part iii. sec. 1.
[19]'Soliloquy,' part iii. sec. 1.

were rapidly decaying. Should Shaftesbury, then, join the sceptical assault of his tutor, Locke, and endeavour to anticipate Berkeley and Hume? His dislike to purely sceptical speculation, and his want of metaphysical acuteness, precluded such a direction of his studies. The first is illustrated by his unequivocal condemnation of Locke; the second by the fact that, whilst repudiating the metaphysical theories, he really borrows from them the central support of his own doctrine.

26. His theory is given in its most systematic shape in the 'Inquiry concerning Virtue,' but various corollaries and corroborative doctrines are scattered through his discursive disquisitions upon things in general. Shaftesbury is pre-eminently a moralist; for the main purpose of his writings is to show how, amidst the general wreck of metaphysical and theological systems, a sufficient base may still be discovered on which to construct a rational scheme of life. Moreover, his morality is still theological and metaphysical. A belief in God, though hardly in the Christian, any more than in the Jewish God, is an essential part of his system. The belief in justice must, as he urges, precede a belief in a just God.[22] A sound theism follows from morality, not morality from theism. And thus 'religion' (by which he means a belief in God) 'is capable of doing great good or great harm, and Atheism nothing positive in either way.'[22] The worship of a bad deity will produce bad worshippers, as the worship of a good deity produces good worshippers. Atheism, indeed, implies an unhealthy frame of mind, for it means the belief that we are 'living in a distracted universe,' calculated to produce no emotions of love or reverence, and thus it tends to sour the temper and impair the 'very principle of virtue, viz.: natural and kind affection.'[23] A belief in God means, on the other hand, a perception of harmonious order, and a mind in unison with the system of which it forms a part. Atheism is the discordant, and theism the harmonious, utterance drawn from our nature, according as it is, or is not, in tune with the general order of things. Though at times Shaftesbury uses language which would fit into an orthodox sermon about a 'personal God,'[24] his teaching seems to adapt itself more naturally to the pantheism of Spinoza.

27. Intimately connected with this theology is the metaphysical doctrine which lies at the base of his system. With Leibnitz he is a thoroughgoing optimist. He holds with Pope, who perhaps learnt the doctrine from him, that 'whatever is, is right;' or, in the phrase of Pangloss, 'everything is for the best in this best of all possible worlds.' The 'Enquiry into Virtue' opens with a demonstration that there can be no real

[22]'Virtue,' book i. part iii. sec. 2.
[23]Ib. part iii. sec. 3.   [24]See *e.g.* 'Moralists,' part ii. sec. 3.

ill in the universe. Apparent evil is merely the effect of our ignorance. The weakness of infants is the cause of parental affection; and all philanthropical impulses are founded on the wants of man. 'What,' he asks, 'can be happier, than such a deficiency as is the occasion of so much good?' If there be a supremely good and all-ruling mind, so runs his argument, there can be nothing intrinsically bad. Or, rather, the absence of evil proves the existence of the all-wise and all-good ruler. Theism is another name for universal optimism. The universe is a veil which but half disguises the presence of an all-pervading essence of absolutely pure benevolence. And, therefore, Shaftesbury exhausts all the resources of eloquence, pedantic and stilted enough, yet at times touched by some genuine emotion, in exalting the wondrous harmonies of nature. Much of his writings is simply an exposition of Dryden's verses:—

> From harmony, from heavenly harmony,
>   This universal frame began.
> From harmony to harmony
>   Through all the compass of the notes it ran,
> The diapason closing full in man.

Harmony is Shaftesbury's catchword. On that text he is never tired of dilating. What discords may exist in the general current of harmony are to be resolved into a fuller harmony as our intelligence widens. If we complain of anything useless in nature, we are like men on board a ship in a calm complaining of the masts and sails as useless encumbrances.[25] He dwells, however, less upon metaphors of this kind, which suggest Paley's Almighty watchmaker, than upon the universal harmony which speaks of, or which, we might almost say, is God. Theocles, the expounder of his views in the 'Moralists,' bursts into a prose hymn to nature, conceived in this spirit—'O mighty nature!' he exclaims; 'arise, substitute of Providence, empowered creatress! O, Thou empowering Deity, supreme Creator! Thee I evoke, and Thee alone adore! To Thee this solitude, this place, and these rural meditations are sacred; whilst thus inspired with harmony of thought, though uninspired by words and in loose numbers, I sing of nature's order in created beings, and celebrate the beauties which resolve in Thee, the source and principle of all beauty and perfection.'[26] There is beauty, as he goes on to show, in this queer compromise between blank verse and prose, which naturally embodies a strange mixture of bombast and eloquence, in the laws of matter, in sense and thought, in the whole universe, in earth, air, water, light, in the animal creation, and in natural scenery. Stilted, frigid, and

---

[25] 'Moralists,' part ii. sec. 4.   [26] Ib. part iii, sec. 1.

most awkward when he attempts to enliven his style by playful humour and sarcastic insinuation, there is yet a true vigour and originality in Shaftesbury, which entitles him to high respect.

28. Shaftesbury's theology is thus an attempt to reconcile the old and new by banishing the supernatural, whilst retaining the divine, element of religion. God is to be no longer a ruler, external to the world, but an immanent and all-pervading force. He wishes to retain so much of the old conceptions as may enable him to regard the universe as a coherent whole, and to look upon it with reverence and affection; but he would reject under the name of enthusiasm all the degrading beliefs which imply the occasional interference, under whatever forms, of a supernatural agent. The evil which he wishes to extirpate is the obstinate anthropomorphism of divines. The advantage which he desires to retain is the power of regarding nature with the sentiments expressed in the higher forms of theology, and not to allow it to fall to pieces in a blind chaos of mutilated fragments. The light is to be diffused throughout the universe, not concentrated into a single external focus.

29. Hence arises his fundamental quarrel with the divines. He charges them with blaspheming God, the universe, and man. They blaspheme God when they represent him as angry with his creatures, as punishing the innocent for the guilty, and pacified by the sufferings of the virtuous. They blaspheme the universe, because in their zeal to 'miraculise everything,' they rest the proof of theology on the interruptions to order rather than upon order itself.[27] They paint the world in the darkest colours in order to throw the future world into brighter relief, and thus, as Bolingbroke afterwards put it, the divines are in tacit alliance with the atheists. Make the universe a scene of wrong and suffering, and is not the inference that there is no God more legitimate than the inference that a God exists, to provide compensation elsewhere? We cannot, indeed, understand the whole. The spider is meant for the fly, and the fly for the spider; the web and the wing are related to each other; to understand the leaf we must go to the root.[28] Every naturalist must understand the organisation in order to explain the organs.[29] 'All are but parts of one stupendous whole,' as Pope puts it, whose 'Essay on Man' frequently coincides with Shaftesbury. His incessant reference to the 'mighty union,' to a 'uniform consistent fabric,' and to 'a universal mind,'[29] by which the whole is animated, is the keynote of Shaftesbury's writings. The theory is in part identical with Butler's, but with this vital difference—that whereas, with Butler, na-

[27]'Moralists,' part ii. sec. 5.

[28]'Virtue,' book i. part ii. sec. 1.   [29]'Moralists,' part ii. sec. 4.

ture testifies to an external Creator, nature is with Shaftesbury itself divine. The supernatural element is thus excluded; for if nature be God or the veil of God, how should God interfere with his work?

30. But Shaftesbury's conception of man is that which places him in most radical opposition to the divines, for they had blasphemed man even more than they blasphemed God and the universe. Man, as the chief work of nature, must show the plainest marks of the divine power. The theological dogma of corruption, and Hobbes's doctrine of the state of nature as a perpetual warfare, are equally alien to him. The state of nature—to quote Pope once more—

The state of Nature was the reign of God;

as how should it be otherwise if God be nature? And therefore, Shaftesbury repudiates with special indignation the doctrine of supernatural rewards and punishments. They have no proper place in a system which restores the divinity of man and represents the universe as self-balanced without the aid of external considerations. He believes, indeed, in an immaterial soul, and he does not deny that a belief in hell has its advantages for the vulgar. But his whole energy is bent to show that hopes and fears of a future state are so far from being the proper reward of virtue that they are rather destructive of its essence. The man who obeys the law under threats is no better than the man who breaks it when at liberty. 'There is no more of rectitude, piety, or sanctity in a creature thus reformed than there is of weakness or gentleness in a tiger strongly chained, or innocence and sobriety in a monkey under the discipline of the whip.'[30] The greater the obedience, the greater the servility. The habit of acting from such motives strengthens self-love and discourages the disinterested love of God for his own sake. In short, 'the excellence of the object, not the reward or punishment, should be our motive,' though where the higher motive is inadequate the lower may be judiciously brought in aid.[31] 'A devil and a hell,' as he elsewhere puts it, 'may prevail where a gaol and a gallows are thought insufficient;' but such motives, he is careful to add, are suited to the vulgar, not to the 'liberal, polished, and refined part of mankind,' who are apt to show that they hold such 'pious narrations to be no better than children's tales for the amusement of the more vulgar.'[32] Hell, in short, is a mere outpost on the frontiers of virtue, erected by judicious persons to restrain the vulgar and keep us from actual desertion; but not to provide an animating and essential part of the internal discipline.

[30]'Virtue,' book i. part iii. sec. 3.
[31]'Moralists,' part ii. sec. 3.   [32]Misc. iii. ch. ii.

31. Meanwhile, the removal of this external barrier naturally associates itself with a vigorous assertion of the efficacy of the internal guidance. The doctrine, however, is radically transformed. To believe in a supernatural interference with our conduct would be to fall into the errors of enthusiasm. Human nature is itself divine, and the external guide becomes a natural organ. The term 'moral sense,' which Shaftesbury invented to express his doctrine, became a technical phrase with his successors. With him, it indicates that natural tendency to virtue which was implicitly denied in the dogma of human corruption. The moral sense, as a divine or natural instinct (for the two phrases are equivalent), directs us by its own authority, and thus in practice supersedes the necessity of an appeal to our selfish instincts. Should anyone ask me, he says, why I would avoid being nasty when nobody was present, I should think him a very nasty gentleman to ask the question. If he insisted, I should reply, Because I have a nose. If he asked further, What if you could not smell, I should reply that I would not see myself nasty. But if it was in the dark? 'Why even then, though I had neither nose nor eyes, my *sense* of the matter would still be the same; my nature would rise at the thoughts of being sordid; or, if it did not, I should have a wretched nature indeed, and hate myself for a beast.'[33] Our hatred to vice, then, is a primitive instinct; and Shaftesbury is rather inclined to cut summarily the knot, which arises from the possible conflict between interest and virtue. He declares roundly that it does not exist. 'To be wicked and vicious,' as he argues elaborately and with much vigour, 'is to be miserable and unhappy;' and 'every vicious action must be self-injurious and ill.'[34] Why, then, one is disposed to ask, it is so hard to be virtuous? But to be a consistent optimist, one must learn the art of shutting one's eyes.

32. The moral sense thus supplies—to the 'virtuoso' at least—the necessary sanctions and motives; and it is in this vindication of human nature from the charges made against it by cynics and by theologians that Shaftesbury's merits are most conspicuous. The further question remains, what is the criterion of morality thus established? What are the actions which the moral sense approves? To such questions, Shaftesbury replies—so far as he makes any explicit reply—by dwelling upon his favourite doctrine of the universal harmony. The moral sense is merely a particular application of the faculty by which we apprehend that harmony. The harmony, as revealed to our imagination, produces the sense of the beautiful; as partially understood by reason, it generates philosophy; as shown in the workings of human nature, it gives rise

[33]'Wit and Humour,' part iii. sec. 4.   [34]'Virtue,' conclusion.

to the moral sense. The æsthetic and the moral perceptions are in fact the same, the only difference lying in the objects to which they are applied. 'Beauty and good with you, Theocles,' he says, 'I perceive, are still one and the same.'[35] Or, as he elsewhere puts it, 'what is beautiful is harmonious and proportionable; what is harmonious and proportionable is true; and what is at once both beautiful and true is of consequence agreeable and good.'[36] And thus Shaftesbury's last word is cultivate your taste. The virtuoso is the best judge of manners as of art. Criticism is of surpassing importance with him, because criticism gives the theory of judging in religion, in art, or in morality. Human passions are divided into the natural affections, which lead to the public good; the 'self-affections' (the 'self-regarding affections,' as later utilitarians would say), 'which lead only to the good of the private,' and those which, as simply injurious, may be called the 'unnatural affections.'[37] To eliminate the last, and to establish a just harmony between the others, is the problem of the moralist; and he will judge of the harmonious development of a man as a critic would judge of the harmony of a pictorial or a musical composition. Man, again, can be fully understood only as part of the human race. He is a member of a vast choir, and must beat out his part in the general music. Hence, Shaftesbury dwells chiefly on the development of the social affections, though admitting that they may be developed in excess. The love of humanity must be the ruling passion. To the objection that one may love the individual but not the species, which is 'too metaphysical an object,'[38] he replies by maintaining that to be a 'friend to anyone in particular, it is necessary to be first a friend to mankind.'[39] He has been in love, he says, with the people of Rome in many ways, but specially under the symbol 'of a beautiful youth called the genius of the people.'[39] But the full answer to the difficulty is given in the Hymn to Nature, of which I have already quoted a fragment.

33. But what, after all, it might be asked, was this 'harmony' of which Shaftesbury speaks so fluently? Does not his moral system crumble in one's hands when one endeavours to grasp it firmly? Admit that a 'virtuoso' is the ideal man, and who is to decide between the virtuosos? Is the standard of morality to be as fluctuating and uncertain as the standard of æsthetic taste? One 'virtuoso' swears by Gothic and one by Greek architecture—which is right? The answer might conceivably be, it does not much matter. Let each man go his own way. But

[35]'Moralists,' part iii. sec. 2.   [38]'Moralists,' part ii. sec. 1.
[36]Misc. iii. ch. ii.   [39]Ib. part ii. sec. 2.
[37]'Virtue,' book ii. part i. sec. 3.

that answer is scarcely open to the moralist whose object is to discover some inflexible moral standard, and who is put off with this elastic virtuoso jargon. Lord Shaftesbury is doubtless a polished gentleman, but when he gives us his canons of criticism in place of a moral rule, we feel that he is a rather poor substitute for St. Paul or Marcus Aurelius. Shaftesbury anticipated and endeavoured to answer this objection. He declared that political maxims, drawn from considering the balance of power, were as 'evident as those in mathematics;'[40] and inferred that moral maxims, founded on a theory as to the proper balance of the passions, would be equally capable of rigid demonstration. The harmony of which he spoke had an objective reality. The moral sense required cultivation to catch the divine concords which run through creation; but the judgment of all cultivated observers would ultimately be the same. If a writer on music were to say that the rule of harmony was caprice, he would be talking nonsense. 'For harmony is harmony by nature, let men judge ever so ridiculously of music.' Symmetry and proportion are equally founded in nature, 'let men's fancy prove ever so barbarous, or their fashions ever so Gothic in their architecture, sculpture, or whatever other designing art. 'Tis the same case where life and manners are concerned. Virtue has the same fixed standard. The same numbers, harmony, and proportion will have place in morals; and are discoverable in the characters and affections of mankind, in which are laid the just foundations of an art and science, superior to every other of human practice and comprehension.'[41] Shaftesbury thus vindicates his claim to be a 'realist' in his theism and his morality. Virtue is a reality, and can be discovered by all who will go through the same process of self-culture. And yet one would like to have a rule rather more easy of application than this vague analogy of music. With thy harmony, one might say, thou beginnest to be a bore to us.

34. This pedantic fine gentleman, whose delicacy placidly ignores the very existence of vice and misery, who finds in the cultivated taste of a virtuoso sufficient guidance and consolation through all the weary perplexities of the world, had very real power in him in spite of his pedantry; but he was ill qualified to impress shrewd men of the world, or the philosophical school, which refuses to sink hard facts in obedience to fine-spun theories. In Germany, where sentimentalism is more congenial to the national temperament, he found a warmer reception than amongst his own countrymen.[42] In England, the contempt for flimsy speculation, which often leads to the rejection of much that is

---

[40]'Wit and Humour,' part iii. sec. 1.   [41]'Soliloquy,' part iii. sec. 3.
[42]See some remarks on this in Spicker's 'Shaftesbury.'

valuable because it is not palpable and definite, brought Shaftesbury
into unmerited neglect. The first critic who laid a coarse hand on his
pretentious philosophy was Mandeville.

35. Bernard de Mandeville published the 'Fable of the Bees' in
1714.[43] It consists of a doggrel poem, setting forth how a hive of bees
were thriving and vicious, and how, on their sudden reformation, their
prosperity departed with their vice. A comment follows, expounding
his theory in detail. In later editions there were added an 'Essay on
Charity and Charity Schools,' a 'Search into the Nature of Society,' and
a series of dialogues upon the Fable. The 'Fable of the Bees' was presented as a nuisance by the Grand Jury of Middlesex in 1723. Mandeville became a byword with all the respectable authors of the day; and
his book was attacked as a kind of pot-house edition of the arch-enemy
Hobbes. Berkeley, Law, Hutcheson, Warburton, and Brown may be
named amongst his most eminent opponents. To say the truth, the
indignation thus excited was not unnatural. Mandeville is said to have
been in the habit of frequenting coffee-houses, and amusing his patrons
by ribald conversation. The tone of his writings harmonises with this
account of his personal habits. He is a cyincal and prurient writer, who
seems to shrink from no jest, however scurrilous, and from no paradox,
however grotesque, which is calculated to serve the purpose, which he
avows in his preface to be his sole purpose, of diverting his readers—
readers, it may be added, not very scrupulous in their tastes. Yet a vein
of shrewd sense runs through his book, and redeems it from anything
like contempt. Nay, there are occasional remarks which show great
philosophical acuteness. A hearty contempt for the various humbugs of
this world is not in itself a bad thing. When a man includes amongst
the humbugs everything that passes with others for virtue and purity,
it is repulsive; though even in such a case we may half forgive a writer
like Swift, whose bitterness shows that he has not parted with his illusions without a cruel pang. Mandeville shares Swift's contempt for the
human race; but his contempt, instead of urging him to the borders of
madness, merely finds vent in a horse-laugh. He despises himself as
well as his neighbours, and is content to be despicable. He is a scoffer,
not a misantrope. You are all Yahoos, he seems to say, and I am a
Yahoo; and so—let us eat, drink, and be merry.

36. His view of this world is, therefore, the obverse of Shaftesbury's,
of whom he speaks with bitter ridicule. 'Two systems,' he says, 'cannot

---

[43]The poem itself was first published in 1705. It did not excite much attention until republished with comments in 1723.

be more opposite than his lordship's and mine.'[44] 'The hunting after this *pulchrum et honestum*'—Shaftesbury's favourite expression—'is not much better than a wild-goose chase;'[45] and, if we come to facts, 'there is not a quarter of the wisdom, solid knowledge, or intrinsic worth in the world that men talk of and compliment one another with; and of virtue and religion there is not an hundredth part in reality of what there is in appearance.'[46] This is his constant tone. Mandeville speaks in the favourite character of the man of the world, whose experience has shown him that statesmen are fools, and churchmen hypocrites, and that all the beautiful varnish of flimsy philosophy with which we deceive each other is unable to hide from him the vileness of the materials over which it forms a superficial film. He will not be beguiled from looking at the seamy side of things. Man is corrupt from his head to his foot, as theologians truly tell us; but the heaven which they throw in as a consolation is a mere delusion—a cheat invented to reconcile us to our-selves. Tell your fine stories to devotees or schoolgirls, he seems to say, but don't try to pass them off upon me, who have seen men and cities, and not taken my notions from books.

37. The particular paradox which gave the book its chief notoriety is summed up in the alternative title, 'Private Vices, Public Benefits.' The fallacy which lies at the bottom of his argument is sufficiently trans-parent, though it puzzled many able men at the time, and frequently reappears at the present day in slightly altered forms. The doctrine that consumption instead of saving is beneficial to labourers has a permanent popularity. Mandeville puts it in the most extravagant shape. 'It is,' he declares, 'the sensual courtier that sets no limit to his luxury; the fickle strumpet that invents new fashions every week; the haughty duchess, that in equipage, entertainment, and all her behaviour, would imitate a princess; the profuse rake and lavish heir, that scatter about their money without wit or judgment, buy everything they see, and either destroy or give it away the next day; the covetous and perjured villain that squeezed an immense treasure from the tears of widows and orphans, and left the prodigals the money to spend' . . . it is of these that we are in need to set all varieties of labour to work, and 'to procure an honest livelihood to the vast numbers of working poor that are required to make a large society.'[47] He pronounces the Reformation to have been scarcely more efficacious in promoting prosperity 'than the silly and capricious invention of hoop'd petticoats.'[47] 'Religion,' he adds, is one thing and trade is another. He that gives most trouble to thousands of

---

[44]Mandeville's 'Fable of the Bees,' p. 205.   [45]Ib. p. 210.   [46]Ib. p. 508.
[47]Ib. pp. 227, 228.

his neighbours, and invents the most operose manufactures, is, right or wrong, the greatest friend to society.'[47] Going still further, he thinks that even the destruction of capital may be useful. 'The fire of London was a great calamity, but if the carpenters, bricklayers, smiths,' and others set at work 'were to vote against those who lost by the fire, the rejoicings would equal, if not exceed, the complaints.'[48] Foolish paradoxes, it may be said, and useful at most as an extravagant statement of a foolish theory, may help to bring about its collapse. And yet the writer who propounded such glaring absurdities was capable of attacking a commercial fallacy with great keenness, and of anticipating the views of later authorities.[49]

38. Mandeville, in fact, has overlaid a very sound and sober thesis with a number of showy paradoxes which, perhaps, he only half believed. When formally defending himself, he can represent his audacities as purely ironical. He confesses that he has used the words: 'What we call evil in this world, moral as well as natural. is the grand principle that makes us social creatures, the solid basis, the light and support of all trades without exception.'[50] The phrase, he admits, has an awkward sound; but had he been writing for people who could not read between the lines, he would have explained in good set terms that he only mean to argue that 'every want was an evil; that on the multiplicity of those wants depended all those mutual services which the individual members of a society pay to each other; and that, consequently, the greater variety there was of want, the greater the number of individuals who might find their private interest in labouring for the good of others; and, united together, compose one body.'[51] The streets of London, to use his own illustration,[52] will grow dirtier as long as trade increases; and, to make his pages more attractive, he had expressed this doctrine as though he took the dirt to be the cause, instead of the necessary consequence. The fallacy, indeed, is imbedded too deeply in his argument to be discarded in this summary fashion. The doctrine that the heir who scatters, and not the man who accumulates, wealth, really sets labour at work, was so much in harmony with the ideas of the age, that even Berkeley's acuteness only suggests the answer that an honest man generally consumes as much as a knave. There is, however, a core of truth in the sophistry. Large expenditure is a bad commercial symptom, so far as it indicates that consumption is outrunning accumulation; it is good so far as it indicates that large accumulations render

---

[47]Mandeville, pp. 227, 228.   [48]Ib. p. 230.
[49]See *e.g.* his remarks, at p. 58, upon the balance of trade; and at p. 465, on the division of labour.   [50]Mandeville, p. 246.   [51]Ib. p. 251.   [52]Preface, p. viii.

large consumption possible. Mandeville, confusing the two cases, attacks the frugal Dutchman, who saves to supply his future wants, and the frugal savage, who, consuming little, yet consumes all that he produces, and produces little because he has no tastes and feels no want. As against the savage his remarks are perfectly just. The growth of new desires is undoubtedly an essential condition towards the improvement of society, and every new desire brings new evils in its train.

39. The importance of the doctrine appears in its moral aspect; and it was here that Mandeville gave most scandal, whilst here, too, he indulged in the most daring paradoxes. He is, in fact, radically opposed to the ascetic doctrine of theologians. Accept in all sincerity the doctrine of contempt for the world and its wealth, and the further doctrine that all natural passions are bad, and we should be a set of naked savages. He anticipates the teaching of later economists, that accumulation of wealth affords the essential material base of all the virtues of civilisation. And it is perfectly true that the industrial view of morality is, on this point, vitally opposed to the old theological view. Mandeville gives an appearance of paradox to his doctrine by admitting, with the divine, that the pursuit of wealth is intrinsically vicious, and by arguing, with the economist, that it is essential to civilisation. Luxury, he says emphatically, should include everything that is not necessary to the existence of a naked savage.[53] Virtue consists in renouncing luxury. Hence the highest conceivable type of virtue is to be found in religious houses, where the inmates bind themselves by rigid vows of poverty and chastity to trample the flesh under foot; or, rather it would be found there, if all monks and nuns did not cover the vilest sensuality under a mask of hypocrisy.'[54] The ideal of a Trappist monk is plainly incompatible with the development of an industrious community. Pushing the theory to an extreme, which is, however, sanctioned by some less paradoxical authorities, he denies the name of virtuous to any doctrine which is prompted by natural instinct. The 'vilest women,' he tells us, have exerted themselves in behalf of their children 'as violently as the best.'[55] And this, which might seem to prove that there is virtue even in the vilest, is converted to a proof that there is no virtue even in the most excellent. For, says Mandeville, we are prompted to such actions 'by a natural drift or inclination, without any consideration of the injury or benefit the society receives from it,' and 'there is no merit in pleasing ourselves.'[55] A murderer or a highwayman would be thrilled with horror if, without being able to interfere, he should see a pretty child torn in pieces by 'a nasty overgrown sow,'[56] and, therefore, there

[53]Mandeville, p. 56.   [54]Ib. p. 87.   [55]Ib. p. 35.   [56]Ib. p. 156.

is no virtue in compassion. In the same spirit, he argues with offensive coarseness, that modesty is no virtue, because it does not imply an extinction, but only a concealment, of the natural passions.

40. The military as well as the industrial virtues are condemned by theologians, and are yet necessary to society. Duelling, for example, is forbidden by divines, and yet is an essential part of the code of honour, without which there would be no living in a large nation.[57] The contrast between honour and religion is vigorously summed up, and the conclusion is simple. 'Religion is built on humility, honour on pride. How to reconcile them must be left to wiser heads than mine.'[58] After describing a perfect gentleman, who might have stood for the portrait of Sir Charles Grandison, he argues that all his virtues might proceed from nothing but a thirst for praise;[59] and proves it by asserting that such a man would fight a duel in spite of his religious principles, and thus obey man rather than God.[60] In fact, Richardson found this dilemma a very awkward one. This and much more might pass for an attack on the ascetic virtues, to which the writer has wilfully given the form of an attack upon virtue itself. It is, however, mixed up with a more unequivocal depreciation of human nature. Mandeville puts in its most offensive form the dogma that what we call virtue is but selfishness masquerading. His theory is summed up in the assertion that 'the moral virtues are the political offspring which flattery begot upon pride.'[61] Lawgivers, moralists, and philosophers, it appears, entered into a strange conspiracy for their own vile purposes to persuade men into submission. For this purpose they 'thoroughly examined all the strength and frailties of our nature,'[62] and discovered that flattery was the most powerful instrument for moving human beings. 'Having by this artful way of flattery insinuated themselves into the hearts of men, they began to instruct them in the notions of honour and shame,'[62] and by various cunning devices of the same kind gradually persuaded the multitude to submit quietly to the yoke imposed upon them by the ambitious. This preposterous theory is precisely analogous to the ordinary deist doctrine that the sacred writings were mere forgeries. Virtue, like religion, was assumed to be a mere figment when it was no longer believed to come straight from heaven. Human cunning is the substitute for final causes.

41. Mandeville is, in this respect at least, as much opposed to Shaftesbury as to the theologians. He agrees with the orthodox in regarding Shaftesbury's scheme as too flimsy to influence human beings; though

[57]Mandeville, p. 131.   [59]Ib. p. 317, &c.   [61]Ib. p. 18.
[58]Ib.   [60]Ib. p. 319.   [62]Ib. p. 14.

he differs from them in denying that any more powerful scheme can be set up in its place. With Shaftesbury virtue corresponds to a certain harmony pervading all the works of nature, and recognisable by the human intellect. With Mandeville it is a mere fashion, changing as rapidly as taste in dress or in architecture.[63] Mandeville, like Shaftesbury, can talk of nature when it suits his purpose; but the difference of their conceptions is characteristic. With Shaftesbury nature is an impersonal deity, of whose character and purpose we can form a conception, inadequate and yet sufficient for our world, by tracing out the design manifested in the marvellous order of the visible universe. With Mandeville nature is a power altogether inscrutable to our feeble intelligence. In a certain sense, indeed, we can see that she has formed animals for inhabiting this world; but, in fact, 'every part of her works, ourselves not excepted, are an impenetrable secret to us, that eludes all enquirers.'[64] Nature makes animals to feed upon each other; waste of life, cruelty, voracity, and lust are parts of her mysterious plan; 'all actions in nature, abstractedly considered, are equally indifferent;'[65] and cruelty and malice are words applicable only to our own feelings. Nature, in short, is a dark power, whose action can only be inferred from facts, not from any *a priori* theory of design, harmony, and order.[66] We know, because we see, that the passions of men, pride, lust, and cruelty, have been and still are the great moving forces which have shaped society as we see it, and brought out the complex structure of a civilised nation; and, what is more, they are still the great moving powers, though we hide them under decorous disguises. Revolting as is the picture of human nature which results, Mandeville is very superior to Shaftesbury from a purely scientific point of view. He owes his superiority to a resolution to look facts in the face, instead of being put off by flimsy rhetoric. Whilst Shaftesbury contemptuously rejects the theory of the savage origin of man as inconsistent with the conception of a designing providence,[67] Mandeville anticipates, in many respects, the views of modern philosophers. He gives a kind of conjectural history describing the struggle for existence by which man gradually elevated himself above the wild beasts, and formed societies for mutual protection. He shows how the development of the military passions would gradually strengthen the rising order.[68] He discovers the origin of religion in the natural fetichism which induces young children to fancy

[63]Mandeville, p. 209 *et seq.*   [64]Ib. p. 422.   [65]Ib. p. 441.

[66]In the 'Free Thoughts on Religion' (1720) Mandeville expressly says that the Manichæan theory is the most consonant to reason (p. 105).

[67]'Moralists,' part ii. sec. 4.   [68]Mandeville, p. 442, &c.

that everything thinks and feels as they do themselves.[69] He describes the slow growth of language;[70] and he makes the general remark, which is really instructive and significant, that many things which are ordinarily attributed to one man's genius are really the result of long time and many generations slowly and unconsciously co-operating to build up arts without any great variety in natural sagacity.[71]

42. These and other observations, much in advance of the general speculation of the time, exhibit Mandeville's acuteness. His brutality and his love of paradox revolt us as a display of cynical levity. He ruthlessly destroys the fine coating of varnish which Shaftesbury has bestowed upon human nature, and shows us with a grin the hideous elements that are fermenting beneath. The grin is simply detestable; but we cannot quite deny the facts. Mandeville was giving up to the coffee-houses a penetration meant for loftier purposes. The man of science has this much in common with the cynic, that he must not shrink from tracing the origin of the most beautiful forms in repulsive substances. The fairest flowers, as Tucker says, may be rooted in dunghills, and the genuine observer must examine the dunghill as well as the flower. No object must be excluded from his laboratory because it is of ill savour and repulsive aspect. To say that all virtue can be analysed into brutal passion is, doubtless, a gross libel upon human nature; and yet too many of our virtues are, in fact, barbarous passions decorously disguised, and we must not shrink from acknowledging that fact more than any other fact. There is, indeed, a common fallacy which Mandeville perversely encourages to give a higher flavour to his pages. People of the present day refuse to believe in our descent from apes, because they illogically infer that the admission would prove that we are apes still. Mandeville assumes that because our virtues took their rise in selfish or brutal forms, they are still brutality and selfishness in masquerade. The assumption is erroneous; but, from a scientific point of view, it has the merit of calling attention to the necessity of investigating primitive conditions of society, in order to account for our existing sentiments. And hence we may appreciate the unintentional co-operation of Shaftesbury and Mandeville. Shaftesbury as setting forth the 'dignified,' and Mandeville as exclusively dwelling upon the baser, aspect of our nature, are equally unsatisfactory. Neither optimism nor pessimism is a tenable form of belief; but the two opinions are rather complementary than antagonistic. When Shaftesbury finds an instinct which he cannot explain, he declares it to be inexplicable. When Mandeville finds it, he

[69]Mandeville, p. 409.   [70]Ib. p. 466.   [71]Ib. p. 361.

declares that it does not really exist. Shaftesbury and his followers kept before their countrymen the belief in a higher doctrine of morality than the popular theory of gross selfishness. Mandeville, by attempting to resolve all virtue into selfishness, stimulated the efforts towards a scientific explanation of the phenomena. With Shaftesbury we may admit the existence of a moral sense; with Mandeville we may admit that it is not an ultimate and irresoluble instinct. The theory that virtue is divine recognises the transcendent importance and the independent force of the virtuous instincts. The theory that virtue is an invention is a crude form of the doctrine that, valuable as those instincts are, they are derivative, and that their origin may be the legitimate subject of scientific enquiry. The action and reaction of the opposing schools continued throughout the century, for each school ignored the element of truth contained in its opponent.

43. Although the names of Shaftesbury and Mandeville appear in most contemporary writings, neither of them became the centre of any formal controversy, apart from the main current of discussion. They were, however, attacked by three writers of marked ability. In 1724 appeared Law's 'Remarks on the Fable of the Bees.'[72] In 1732 Berkeley published the 'Minute Philosopher,' the second dialogue of which refers to Mandeville, and the third to Shaftesbury. Many years later (in 1751) Brown published a formal Essay on the 'Characteristics,' in which Mandeville, too, comes in for a brief notice.

44. Law's pamphlet is, perhaps, the ablest of these attacks. With the controversial ability in which he had scarcely a superior in that time, he assaults some of Mandeville's singular paradoxes. He points out, for example, with admirable clearness, that an action is not the less virtuous because we are prompted to it by natural instincts or by acquired habits. It is virtuous 'because it is in obedience to reason and the laws of God, and does not cease to be so because the body is either formed by use or created by disposition, easy and ready for the performance of it. . . . Nay, all habits of virtue would, upon this foot, be blamable, because such habits must be supposed to have rendered both body and mind more ready and exact in goodness.'[73] The fallacy thus attacked is rather an outlying part of Mandeville's system, though he makes great use of it by giving a libellous tone to his remarks on human nature. Oddly enough, the cynic Mandeville asserts the reality of benevolent impulses in order to throw doubt upon human virtue. The more serious question

[72]Law's pamphlet was republished in 1844, with a preface by Mr. Maurice.
[73]Law's Works, ii. 41.

remains, whether virtue is to be called real. Mandeville and Law follow the intellectual school in the assumption that, if virtue included an element of taste and observation, it was in some sense 'unreal.' Mandeville argues that the taste for philanthropy, humility, and chastity may vary like the taste for big or little buttons. The true answer would be that a taste for buttons is just as much the product of fixed laws as a taste for philanthropy; though as incomparably less permanent instincts are concerned, the taste is correspondingly variable. Assuming, however, that virtue would become purely arbitrary if admitted to depend on the changing elements of human nature, Law asserts, with great vigour, that 'moral virtue is founded on the immutable relations of things, in the perfections and attributes of God, and not in the pride of man or the craft of cunning politicians.'[74] The singular hypothesis indicated in the last phrase is attacked with admirable force. 'Do but suppose *all* first principles to be invented,' he says, 'and then it will follow that nothing could be invented in any science.' If the primary reasons of mathematicians are mere arbitrary assumptions, the science disappears. 'Were we not all mathematicians and logicians, there would be no such sciences; for science is only an improvement of those first principles which nature has given us.'[75] He ingeniously compares Mandeville's theory of the invention of virtue to an imaginary invention of an erect posture. 'The first legislators,' says his supposed theorist, 'having examined the strength and weakness of man's body, discovered that he was not so top-heavy but that he might stand upright on his feet; but the difficulty was how to raise him up. Some philosophers, more sanguine than the rest, found out that, though man crept on the ground, yet he was made up of pride, and that, if flattery took hold of that, he might easily be set on his legs. Making use of this bewitching engine, they extolled the excellence of his shape above other animals, and told him what a grovelling thing it was to creep on all fours like the meanest animals. Thus did these philosophers shame poor man out of his natural state of creeping, and wheedled him into the dignity and honour of standing upright to serve their own ambitious ends, and that they might have his hands to be employed in their drudgery.'[76] The parallel is only too perfect. Law does not perceive that, beside the theory which represents man as wheedled into walking, and that which represents him as walking by an inherent and immutable necessity of his nature, there is the theory that the walking may have been evolved from the creeping animal by the operation of natural laws.

[74]Law's Works, ii. 29.   [75]Ib. p. 22.   [76]Ib. p. 20.

45. Berkeley's 'Minute Philosopher' is the least admirable performance of that admirable writer. The most characteristic part is the attempt to erect a proof of theology upon his own peculiar metaphysical theory. The remainder consists for the most part of the familiar commonplaces, expressed in a style of exquisite grace and lucidity, but not implying any great originality. The general tendency of his remarks, both upon Mandeville and Shaftesbury, may be described as utilitarian. Although, as already noticed, he seems to be incapable of detecting the economical fallacy involved in Mandeville's eulogy upon extravagance, he, of course, sees, and has no difficulty in proving, that vice is prejudicial to a community. He establishes with rather superfluous care that immorality of all kinds is ruinous to the constitution of individuals, and destructive to a state. Virtue is not a mere fashion, but implies obedience to the laws upon which men's physical and spiritual health depends. Shaftesbury is condemned on the same grounds. Admitting Shaftesbury's leading principle of the beauty of virtue, Berkeley argues that our sense of beauty consists essentially in our perception of the right adaptation of means to ends. The beauty of the universe consists, therefore, in the existence of an intelligent principle, governing all things, punishing the wicked, protecting the virtuous. 'In such a system, vice is madness, cunning is folly, wisdom and virtue all the same thing;'[77] and whatever seems amiss, will, in the last act, be ultimately wound up according to the strictest rules of wisdom and justice. Shaftesbury's ruling mind must, therefore, be either the Christian Deity, or another name for blind Fate. In the latter case, a man must be a 'Stoic or a Knight-errant'[77] to be virtuous; the 'minute philosopher' is the devotee of 'an inexplicable enthusiastic notion of moral beauty,'[78] or, as Lysicles, the representative of Mandeville, puts it, his doctrine 'hath all the solid inconveniences, without the amusing hopes and prospects, of the Christian.'[79]

46. John Brown, better known as the author of the 'Estimate,' was a writer of genuine ability.[80] His style is clear, and he is free from the coarse abuse and the cavilling at petty details, which are the prevailing faults of controversialists of the time. His essays, directed against a writer who had been nearly forty years dead, may be regarded as some testimony to the enduring influence of Shaftesbury; but they are, perhaps, rather an indication that poor Brown, who had a hard struggle

[77]Dial. iii. sec. 10.   [78]Ib. sec. 12.   [79]Ib. sec. 7.

[80]Mr. Mill, in his essay on Bentham, refers with very high praise to this performance of Brown.

to win fame and some solid rewards, was rather looking out for a good text for the display of his talents than anxious to encounter a vital error. The immediate suggestion came from Warburton, who had been told by Pope that the 'Characteristics' had to his knowledge done more harm to revealed religion in England than all other infidel books. The essays are three in number. In the first, directed against Shaftesbury's theory of ridicule as the test of truth, which had been attacked by Warburton and supported by Akenside, he establishes without much trouble the obvious truism that raillery is not argument. In the last, he puts the ordinary arguments against Shaftesbury's sneers at revelation. The second considers the moral theory of Shaftesbury, and more briefly that of Mandeville. The argument depends on the utilitarian principle, which he had probably learnt from Hume, though he only refers to him as 'a late writer of subtlety and refinement,'[81] in order to controvert his view of the existence of purely benevolent affections. Brown, in substance, anticipates Paley, and insists in the same spirit upon the necessity of some effective sanction to the moral law. 'Where selfish or malevolent affections happen to prevail, there can be no internal motive for virtue,'[82] and, therefore, we cannot do without a hell. He separates very clearly the question of the criterion from that of the sanction; and he points to the fundamental weakness which is common to the intellectual and to the moral-sense school, whose opposition he accordingly regards as a mere logomachy, of setting up no really intelligible standard of virtue. That standard he discovers in the tendency of all good actions to promote happiness. Virtue is the 'voluntary production of the greatest possible happiness.'[83] Thus he tries to supplant Shaftesbury's vague declamation and Clarke's nugatory metaphysics by a fixed and intelligible standard. In fact, the criticism strikes at Shaftesbury's fundamental weakness. He had no more escaped than the intellectual school from the dilemma produced by identifying God with nature, or rather his escape was palpably a mere evasion. He makes nature divine by denying the most patent facts; and is obliged to introduce a kind of tacit Manichæism, by calling the evil passions, when he condescends to speak of them, 'unnatural.' But if there are unnatural things in nature, what becomes of his optimism? Brown's utilitarianism provides a practical rule, though, of course, it does not attempt to answer the problem of the existence of evil. The clearness of his exposition is remarkable, but I may postpone the consideration of the development of his theory in other hands till I have followed the series of writers who may be considered as embodying Shaftesbury's impulse.

[81]Dial. ii. 163.   [82]Ib. p. 184.   [83]Ib. p. 158.

IV. The Common-Sense School.

47. The greatest of these, and, with the exception of Hume, the acutest moralist of the century, is Butler, and the characteristic doctrine of Butler is another mode of solving the difficulty just noticed. No two men can present a greater contrast than exists in some respects between Butler and Shaftesbury; the contemplative nature shrinking from the rude contact of the world, and the polished 'virtuoso;' the man to whom life is a weary burden, lightened only by hopes of a future happiness, and yet rendered heavier by the dread of future misery, and the man who is so resolute an optimist as almost to deny the existence of evil— are at opposite poles of feeling; and yet their intellectual relation is close and unmistakable, as, indeed, explicitly admitted by Butler.

48. Butler's sermons, published in 1726, repose fundamentally upon a conception identical with that which was afterwards expounded in the 'Analogy.' The whole theory may be regarded as a modification from a theological point of view of Shaftesbury's doctrines. The fifteenth sermon, for example, on 'the ignorance of man,' contains the germ of the 'Analogy;' and the germ of the fifteenth sermon is to be found in Shaftesbury's conception of the universe as embodying a partially understood 'frame of things.'[1] Shaftesbury's optimism is, indeed, radically opposed to Butler's melancholy temper. The world, regarded as the ante-room to heaven and hell, is no longer that harmonious whole which excited Shaftesbury's facile artistic enthusiasm. Butler—and it is the great secret of his power—is always depressed by the heavy burden of human misery and corruption. The horror of sin and death weighs upon his spirits. Our wisest course in life is to 'endeavour chiefly to escape misery.'[2] Mitigation of sorrow, rather than actual happiness, is all that can be hoped by his sorely tried soul. Hence nature, the deity of Shaftesbury, is invested by him with the terrible attributes of a judging and avenging God. To prove that the existence of such a God may be inferred from the facts of the universe, is the purpose of the 'Analogy.' To prove the same doctrine from the facts of human nature is the purpose of the Sermons. Nature, as interpreted by Shaftesbury or by Clarke, is too impartial a deity to satisfy his conceptions. It is the cause of evil as well as of good. A beast, drawn to his destruction by a bait, acts 'naturally,' because he gratifies his ruling appetite; a man, drawn to destruction by his ruling appetite, might seem to be in the same case. But 'since such an action is utterly disproportionate to the

---

[1] See, for example, 'Moralists,' part iii. sec. 1.
[2] Butler's Works, ii. 82, sermon vi.

nature of man, it is, in the strictest and most proper sense, unnatural; this word expressing that disproportion.'[3] Whence this difference in our judgments? Why condemn a Catiline and not condemn a tiger? Shaftesbury's vague declamation gave, it seemed, no sufficient reply. The *a priori* mode of reasoning, though Butler, with characteristic caution, admits its validity,[4] was not so applicable to the men whom he desired to meet. His special method consists in inferring from nature a Creator distinguished, so to speak, by personal idiosyncrasies. He has to show that the God who made alike the good and the bad instincts, takes part with the good and not with the bad; and, moreover, he has to show this from the inspection of the instincts themselves. Nature is to testify to a special design, not to an impartial and abstract reflection of itself. This is the problem ever present to Butler's mind, and his answer to it is the essence of his writings.

49. We have seen how this was done in the 'Analogy.' In the Sermons, the starting-point is identical. The independent system of morality supplied the external point of view from which Butler discovered the character of this life as a probationary state. In the Sermons, the instincts which enable us to recognise this moral law enable him to solve the problem of human nature. Shaftesbury's moral sense becomes with him the conscience—the conscience being no longer an æsthetic perception of the harmony of the universe, but rather the sense of shame which makes our moral nature 'tremble like a guilty thing surprised' in the presence of its Creator. The weakness which he indicates in Shaftesbury's teaching is the absence of a due recognition of the authoritative character of conscience.[5] For conscience is God's viceroy; our nature means 'the voice of God within us.'[6] To stifle its commands is mere usurpation.[7] He compares human nature to a civil constitution, in which conscience plays the part of sovereign.[8] And thus we discover the true meaning of the ancient phrase of acting in conformity to nature. That formula might be taken to mean acting from any natural impulse, in which case, the same action would at once obey and contradict nature; or it might mean obeying our strongest passions; which, as Butler says with characteristic pessimism, 'being vicious ones, mankind is in this sense naturally vicious.'[9] As these two meanings fail to reveal a moral law, we must take refuge in a third; namely, that to act according to nature is to obey that power which has a natural supremacy. The con-

[3]Butler's Works, p. 28, sermon ii.   [7]Ib. ii. 33, sermon ii.
[4]Ib. preface, p. vii.   [8]Ib. ii. 34, sermon iii.
[5]Ib. ii. preface, p. xiv.   [9]Ib. ii. 25, sermon ii.
[6]Ib. ii. 80, sermon vi.

science, enthroned within our souls, passes an authoritative judgment upon our actions; declares which are right and which wrong; approves the one, condemns the other, and anticipates 'a higher and more effectual sentence.' It is by this 'faculty natural to man that he is a moral agent, that he is a law to himself; by this faculty, I say, not to be considered merely as a principle in his heart, which is to have some influence as well as others; but considered as a faculty in kind and in nature supreme over all others, and which bears its own authority of being so.'[10] 'Had it strength, as it has right,' he says of the conscience; 'had it power, as it has manifest authority, it would absolutely govern the world.'[11] This is Butler's most characteristic doctrine. The constitution of man, like the constitution of his dwelling-place, points unmistakably to his Creator. In both cases we recognise the final causes of the phenomena. 'A man,' he says, 'can as little doubt that his eyes were given him to see with as he can doubt of the truth of the science of optics, deduced from ocular experiments;' he can as little doubt that shame 'was given to him to prevent his doing shameful actions as he can doubt whether his eyes were given him to guide his steps.'[12] The exact correspondence between the natural and moral world, or between the 'inward frame of man' and his external circumstances, is a particular instance of that general law of mutual adaptation which runs through the universe. Thus 'The several passions and affections in the heart of man' afford 'as certain instances of final causes as any whatever, which are more commonly alleged for such.' The correspondence between the organism and the medium, which, from the scientific point of view, is a condition of existence, is with Butler, in morality as in all other questions, a proof of a special purpose of the Creator. What is peculiar to him is the character of those purposes and of the Creator whom they reveal.

50. Butler anticipates and gives a rather singular answer to one difficulty. Why should I obey my conscience? asks the objector. 'Your obligation to obey the law,' he replies, 'is its being the law of your nature;'[13] for conscience is 'the guide assigned to us by the author of our nature.' But why should I obey the law? persists the objector; meaning, what private interest have I in obeying it? In answer to this, Butler labours like Shaftesbury to prove that virtue and private interest generally coincide in their directions.'[14] This anxiety to establish the proposition that it is, on the whole, profitable to be virtuous, fits in rather awkwardly with his system, and is an unfortunate concession to

[10]Butler's Works, ii. 27, sermon ii.   [13]Ib. ii. 37, sermon iii.
[11]Ib. ii. 31, sermon ii.   [14]Ib. ii. 4, sermon i.
[12]Ib. ii. 21, sermon ii.

the general spirit of the age.[15] He expressly promises in the beginning of the eleventh sermon that 'all possible concessions' shall be 'made to the favourite passion' of his age—namely, self-love.[16] Feeling that the coincidence between the dictates of virtue and a rational self-love is not absolutely perfect, he introduces apologetically, and by way of supplement, what he might more fitly have proclaimed as a leading principle of his system; and, even then, promises that the discord shall not be definitive. Although exceptions to the general principle are, he says, 'much fewer than are commonly thought,' they exist here, but 'all shall be set right at the final distribution of things.'[17] Thus the selfish will find at last that the man who has sacrificed present advantages to virtue 'has infinitely better provided for himself and secured his own interest and happiness.'[18]

51. That strain we heard was of a lower mood. Even Butler is bowing his knee in the house of Rimmon; and, in spite of the depth of his moral sentiments, is consenting to make virtue a question of profit and loss. The whole significance of his theory lies in the mysterious attributes with which conscience is surrounded; and yet in his anxiety to 'make all possible concessions,' he is endangering the very core of his teaching. This view, however, might be excised with benefit to the general argument. But, meanwhile, a difficulty more vital from a logical point of view passes unnoticed. The supremacy of conscience, says Butler, is a supremacy *de jure* and not *de facto*. We can disobey its dictates; but, if we disobey them, we act wrongly. What, then, is meant by acting wrongly? Disobeying conscience? Then his assertion comes to be that those who disobey conscience—disobey conscience. We disapprove immoral actions, and immoral actions are those which we disapprove. What then is this special supremacy of conscience? Why is it exceptional? Every instinct, good or bad, avenges itself by inflicting pain when we resist its dictates. What is the specific peculiarity of the pangs inflicted by conscience? Conscience, says Butler, brings with it its own credentials; the supremacy is 'a constituent part of the idea, that is, of the faculty itself;'[19] it is implied in the very meaning of the word duty. The conception of a self-evidencing power seems to involve a vicious circle. Exclude the idea of right from the supremacy, and the statement becomes inaccurate; admit it, and the definition includes the

[15]See, too, the remarkable passage in sermon xi. (ii. 170), where he seems to admit that we cannot justify ourselves in pursuing virtue, or anything else, 'till we are convinced that it will be for our happiness, or, at least, not contrary to it.'   [16]Butler's Works, ii. 152, sermon xi.

[17]Ib. ii. 41, sermon iii.   [18]Ib. ii. 42, ib.   [19]Ib. ii. 31, sermon ii.

very thing to be defined. Conscience must, in some way, derive its credentials from some other authority than itself. If, for example, conscience be an infallible guide to those actions which increase the happiness of mankind, its right to govern follows from the beneficial effects of its rule. Butler, however, expressly and indignantly repudiates the doctrine which measures the goodness of actions by their consequences. The inward 'judge of right and wrong,' he tells us, approves or disapproves many actions 'abstracted from the consideration of their tendency' to the happiness or misery of this world.[20] Butler's escape from the vicious circle really consists in his assumption that the conscience represents the will of God. He is blind to the difficulty, because he conceives the final cause of conscience to be evident. This mysterious power, claiming an absolute supremacy, can derive its origin from nothing else than the divine source of all mystery. A blind instinct, ordering us to do this and that, for arbitrary or inscrutable reasons, is entitled to no special respect so long as we confine ourselves to nature. But when behind nature we are conscious of nature's God, we reverence our instincts as implanted by a divine hand, and enquire no further into their origin and purpose. No suspicion occurred to him that the marks of a divine origin which he supposed himself to be discovering by impartial examination, might be merely the result of his having stated the problem in terms of theology. As in the 'Analogy' his argument depends on assuming suffering to be supernatural punishment, so here it depends on assuming the promptings of conscience to be supernatural commands.

52. Around the conscience, in Butler's conception of human nature, are grouped a number of instincts, inferior in authority, but each ruling over the province assigned to it—impelling forces, regulated and controlled by the higher power. The two nearest the throne are benevolence and self-love; beneath them come such passions as, for example, resentment, which also are 'implanted in our nature by God,' and destined to excite us against 'injury and wickedness.'[21] Even the lower appetites and passions are 'placed within as a guard and further security,' without which our private interests would be neglected.[22] Were it not for hunger, thirst, and weariness, our reason would tell us in vain that food and sleep were necessary for our preservation. The testimony which these arrangements give to a divine design is heightened by a peculiar refinement. The passions, he says, urge us towards *external things*

[20]Butler's Works, ii. 191, note, sermon xii., and 'Dissertation on Virtue,' i. 382. See above, ch. v. sec. 13.   [21]Ib. ii. 114, sermon viii.

[22]Ib. ii. 69, sermon v.

themselves distinct from the *pleasure arising from them*.'[23] We eat, that is, for the sake of eating, not because eating is pleasant. The purpose of this doctrine appears more plainly as it was afterwards worked out by Lord Kames, a disciple of Shaftesbury and Butler. Kames tries to evade the doctrine that our will is always determined by pain or pleasure by substituting the words attraction and aversion, and by maintaining, for example, that many unpleasant things have an attraction for us.[24] Self-love thus plays a peculiar part in the hierarchy of passions. According to other psychologists, self-love is the aggregate of all our passions; the sum of all the desires which seek for gratification. According to Butler, it is only 'one part of human nature,'[25] co-ordinate with a vast variety of other passions. It differs from them, however, in this —that its only office is to prompt us to gratify its colleagues. If, he says, there were no passion but self-love, there could be no such thing as happiness.[26] Thus hunger makes us eat without regarding the pleasure which is to be derived from eating; and then self-love supplies the singular defect by ordering us to gratify our hunger in order to gain the pleasure. It would be simpler to portion out the self-love amongst the various passions instead of distributing the provinces in this curiously arbitrary manner. The psychology is manifestly defective, and its complexity was one reason why Butler failed to impress his contemporaries more decidedly. A cumbrous system, expressed in very loose phraseology, is likely to deter all but the most resolute students. And yet it was only by help of this complex hypothesis, or series of hypotheses, that Butler could manage to put into shape his expression of what was doubtless a most important truth.

53. Butler was protesting, like Shaftesbury, against the popular doctrine of the time, which resolved all human actions into selfishness. There is an ambiguity in the statement which has perplexed the speculations of many moralists. Philosophers wished to explain everything, and to explain everything by deduction from a few axiomatic principles. Such a principle seemed to be the selfishness of all actions. The most general statement that can be made about a voluntary action is that it is voluntary; or, in words which seem to be identical, that it is done because the actor pleases, or because the will is determined by the balance of pleasure over pain. All actions, then, may be called selfish in the sense that they are the product of motives acting on a man's self. The proposition is so wide as to be harmless, or, as some writers main-

[23]Butler's Works, ii. 153, sermon xi.
[24]'Essays on Principles of Morality,' &c. See pp. 8, 124.
[25]Butler's Works, ii. 156, sermon xi.   [26]Ib. ii. 156, sermon xi.

tain, useless.[27] 'If,' says Butler, 'because every particular affection is a man's own ... such particular affection must be called self-love; according to this way of speaking, no creature whatever can possibly act but from self-love.'[28] The doctrine thus understood is compatible with belief in the most disinterested motives. But, unluckily, selfish had been changed into a sense much narrower, more fruitful of consequences, and essentially debasing. It became, for example, in Mandeville's hands, equivalent to the opinion that men always act upon a calculation of their own private interests. The calculations might be wrong, but the motive was in all cases the same; and actions of self-sacrificing heroism, such, for example, as that of Regulus, became unintelligible paradoxes. Such an axiom was highly convenient as affording an easy foundation for a calculus of human motive. The reaction against the false simplification which it introduced shows itself in Butler's view of the strangely complex constitution of human nature, a peculiarity which is still more conspicuous in some later writers of the school, whilst it urged him to deny that even the particular passions had immediate pleasure for their object.[29] They are divinely implanted impulses, and have no relation to any grovelling motives.

54. Butler's denial that benevolence could by any possibility be resolved into selfishness might dispense with this questionable psychology. He asserts that self-love may be developed in excess, even with a view to our private happiness. 'Disengagement,' he says, 'is absolutely necessary to enjoyment,' and a person may attend so rigidly to his own interests as to lose many opportunities of gratification.[30] Overfondness for ourselves, like overfondness for children, may defeat its own object. Taking Butler's psychology, the assertion is doubtful; for the injury to our happiness would seem to result not from the excessive strength of the passion, but from an intellectual error, which perplexes our view of our own interests; or from a want of due impartiality, which leads it to prefer one passion to another. But the assertion, less rigidly construed, is undeniable. A man in whose eyes self assumes a disproportionate

[27]See the obvious argument in Shaftesbury, 'Moralists,' p. 2, sec. 1. 'When will and pleasure are synonymous; when everything which pleases us is called pleasure, and we never choose or prefer but as we please, 'tis trifling to say "pleasure is our good." For this has as little meaning as to say, we choose what we think eligible, and we are pleased with what delights and pleases us.'

[28]Butler's Work, ii. 154, sermon xi.

[29]Shaftesbury puts this very clearly ('Wit and Humour,' part iii. sec. 3), where he objects to those who would reduce all the balances and weights of the human heart to simple selfishness.   [30]Butler's Works, ii. 157, sermon xi.

magnitude is less likely to be happy than one who is absorbed by desire for the happiness of others. Butler shows conclusively the inadequacy of the analysis of all heroism and philanthropy into a love of our own trumpery individuality. He is puzzled and perplexed in his utterance; he mixes his theories with many irrelevant and inconclusive doctrines; he painfully builds up an elaborate system which will not bear serious inspection; he makes needless concessions to the demoralising doctrine which he is denouncing, even at the moment of denouncing it; and yet the protest was as honourable as it was needed at a time when most theologians agreed that nothing but threats of hell could make men virtuous, whilst the belief in hell was yet daily weakening. The theological conception of human vileness remained, whilst the only check applicable to vile creatures was disappearing. Butler would enthrone the conscience in place of self-love. In exalting conscience, it is true, he exemplifies the facile dogmatism of the Common-Sense school, and his attempted expulsion of self-love makes the mechanism of human nature singularly cumbrous. But, with all his faults, Butler remains, in a practical sense, the deepest moralist of the century. He alone refuses to shut his eyes with the optimistic theists to the dark side of the world, and yet does not, with their opponents, implicitly deny the existence of virtue. Seeing God through conscience, the same faculty which reveals to him the prevalence of vice, reveals also the antagonistic force opposed to it. The description of the sense of duty as the voice of God must be pronounced an error, if by those words we mean that it implies a supernatural guidance, that it is enforced by supernatural sanctions, and inculcates a course of conduct directed to fit men, not for this world, but for the next. But Butler's language, regarded as the utterance of a deep conviction of the unspeakable importance of our moral instincts, conveyed a profound rebuke to his age. Talk about nature and harmony, he says to the easy-going optimists of the Shaftesbury type, may be very charming to æsthetic philosophers, but it will not sway the brutal passions of mankind. Your denial that virtue exists, he says to Mandeville, or your assertion that virtue is merely a name for clever calculation of your own private interests, he says to the utilitarians of his time, is in various degrees debasing and unsatisfactory. You have not yet found a successor to the old God. Theology, in him, seems to utter an expiring protest against the meanness and the flimsiness of the rival theories by which men attempted to replace it. His theory of the universe is distorted, gloomy, and radically unscientific. But it takes into account the dark side from which shallow metaphysicians averted their faces; it rejects the debasing conceptions which followed when the divine element was exiled from the existing world with nothing offered in its place; and it emphatically asserted that conscience was a mystery which had not yet received a sufficient explanation. His error lay in the assumption that because the instinct, which moved him so deeply, was unexplained, it was therefore supernatural. He endeavours to honour conscience by taking it altogether out of the sphere of scientific observation, and forcing it to bear testimony not to the goodness which counteracts the many vices and weaknesses of humanity, but to the interference of an extramundane power; and thus clinging to the dogma of corruption whilst asserting the existence of virtuous instincts in man.

55. Butler has thus endeavoured to evade the great dilemma by absorbing nature in God as revealed to conscience, instead of absorbing God in nature. Each man is a little kingdom in himself, with a constitution of divine origin; and our duty consists in observing its laws, though we know not the purpose for which they were ordained. The position occupied by Hutcheson may be roughly described by saying that, whilst holding a very similar theory, the constitution, with him, no longer rests upon divine right, but is justified as conducive to the welfare of the subject. He therefore forms a connecting link between the utilitarians and the intuitional school; and his writings bring out very distinctly the relations between the two systems.

56. Francis Hutcheson[31] was the son of a dissenting minister, in the North of Ireland, and the descendant of a Scotch family. He represents that variety of theology in which the old Calvinism was replaced by eighteenth-century rationalism, whilst the old hatred to priestcraft survived. Like Butler, he had an early correspondence with Clarke, and is said to have retained a profound conviction of the futility of the *a priori* method of that philosopher. Perhaps his dislike to orthodox systems went a little further. At any rate, he accepted the offer of a 'private academy' in Dublin, instead of becoming a minister according to his first intention. Whilst in Dublin he published his 'Enquiry into the Ideas of Beauty and Virtue,' and soon afterwards a 'Treatise on the Passions.' In 1729 he accepted the chair of moral philosophy in the University of Glasgow, and remained there till his death in the fifty-third year of his age (1747). The only blemish which his enthusiastic biographer can discover in his character is a certain quickness of temper. He gave offence, it seems, by 'honest freedom;' but otherwise lived as became a professor of moral philosophy. The tone of his writings is amiable, though in him, as in most of his contemporaries, we are apt to be annoyed at the exceeding placidity and complacency with which

[31] See Life by Leechman, prefixed to 'System of Moral Philosophy.'

this questionable world is contemplated. The awful shadow of sin and misery never clouds his spirits. In striking contrast to Butler, he is smooth, voluble, and discursive; and the even flow of his eloquence is apt to become soporific. The 'System of Moral Philosophy' appeared in 1755, eight years after his death, and gives the fullest account of his system; but the essence is contained in his earlier treatises.

57. Hutcheson is a far more servile disciple of Shaftesbury than Butler, and his easy-going optimism resembles that of his master. 'Happiness,' he tells us, 'is far superior to misery, even in this present world,' and he lays little stress upon the other.[32] God is everywhere revealed in nature. The 'stupendous orbs' (a cant phrase which at once stamps the argument), the convenient arrangements of the earth and the solar system, and the structure of animals, testify unmistakably to the beneficient Creator. Our sufferings are 'the kind admonitions and exhortations of the Universal Parent;'[33] and we may enable ourselves to meet cheerfully all apparent evils by 'a firm persuasion of an omnipotent, omniscient, and most benign Universal Parent, disposing of all things in this system for the very best . . . and permitting no further evil than what the most proper constitution requires or necessarily brings along with it.'[34] His theology differs from Shaftesbury's, by attributing a slightly more distinct personality to the Creator; the Universal Parent is not so closely identified with nature; and, instead of an all-pervading harmony, Hutcheson prefers to use the more technical and definite phraseology of final causes. The chief difference between the master and the disciple is, that Hutcheson forces into the framework of a system the doctrines which are in a state of solution in Shaftesbury's rather turbid eloquence. This is especially the case with the 'moral sense'—a term which had been used by Shaftesbury, though with no special emphasis, whilst in Hutcheson it becomes the keystone of an elaborate system. By explaining its nature and functions, we shall give the essential principle of Hutcheson's philosophy.

58. 'The mind,' says Shaftesbury, ' . . . cannot be without its eye and ear, so as to discern proportion, distinguish sound, and scan each sentiment and thought which comes before it.' It detects the harmonious and the dissonant in affections as the bodily eye detects them in outward things.[35] Hutcheson takes up this hint, and presents the resulting theory in a compact form in the opening of the 'Enquiry concerning Beauty and Virtue.' We have, as he puts it, internal as well as external senses; the external perceiving sounds and colours as the internal perceive

[32]'System of Moral Philosophy,' i. 190.   [33]Ib. i. 185.
[34]Ib. i. 215.   [35]Shaftesbury, 'Virtue,' book i. part ii. sec. 3.

moral excellence or turpitude.[36] This theory is worked up into an elaborate psychological analysis in the opening chapters of the 'System of Moral Philosophy.' He there endeavours to anatomise the complex internal organisation by which our actions are determined; for, as he remarks, 'human happiness which is the end of this art' (the art, that is, of morality) 'cannot be distinctly known without the knowledge of the constitution of this species.'[37] Beyond and above the senses which reveal the external world and provide us with all our 'materials of knowledge,'[38] we have a number of 'finer perceptions,'[39] which he proceeds to enumerate. There are the senses of beauty and harmony, or of the imagination; the sympathetic sense, the sense which causes us to take pleasure in action, the moral sense, the sense of honour, the sense of decency and dignity, a parental, and social, and religious sense. Each of these senses produces, or is identical with, a certain 'determination of the will.' There is a determination of the will towards our own happiness, and another, not resoluble into the first, and entitled to override it in cases of conflict, towards the 'universal happiness of others.'[40] The system, already sufficiently complex, is further perplexed by cross-divisions of the various passions which appear to be identical with the senses, into selfish and benevolent, extensive and limited, calm and turbulent; and we are ready, after reading the list, to agree fully with Hutcheson's observation that human nature must 'appear a very complex and confused fabric, unless we can discover some order and subordination among these powers.'[41] The complexity is reached by the simple device, common to many metaphysicians, of assuming that to every name that can be given corresponds a distinct entity. He makes, however, very little use of these elaborate divisions and cross-divisions in working out his theory; and we need only remember that human nature is, in his opinion, a machine of innumerable parts, skilfully put together for benign purposes by the Divine artisan; and that each sense has a final cause which reveals itself to the reverent observer.

59. It is enough to speak of the moral sense. The proof that it is an independent faculty is, that none of the methods hitherto applied have resolved it into simpler elements. It cannot be analysed into sympathy, for we approve the virtues of our enemies; nor into the pleasure derivable from virtuous action, for it is the root and not the fruit of that pleasure; nor into a perception of utility to the agent or the approver, for bad actions may be useful as well as good; nor can it be derived

[36]Hutcheson's 'Inquiry' &c. i. sec. 10.   [39]Ib. p. 7.
[37]'Moral Philosophy,' i. 1.   [40]Ib. p. 9.
[38]Ib. p. 6.   [41]Ib. p. 38.

from approval of conformity to the divine will, for the moral attributes of God must be previously known; nor from conformity to the truth or fitness of things, for that is a nugatory definition.[42] It remains, then, so Hutcheson assumes, that the moral sense must be a primitive faculty.

60. What, in the next place, are its functions? Is it an internal teacher, making known to us, by declarations from which there is no appeal, that such an action is right, and such another action wrong? In that case, our duty would be revealed to us by a series of direct intuitions. Hutcheson, however, follows Locke in denying that we have innate ideas. The moral sense perceives virtue and vice as the eye perceives light and darkness; but it no more frames general propositions than the external sense provides us with mathematical theorems.[42] The object of the sense is merely the internal feeling; and our judgments of actions may vary indefinitely as we infer that they proceed from one or other motive. He anticipates and retorts the ordinary objection that, to make the moral sentiments dependent upon feeling, is to make them variable. The variety in our judgments is 'not owing to any irregularity in the moral sense, but to a wrong judgment or opinion.'[43] If putting the aged to death 'really tends to the public good,'[44] it is a good action; and circumstances are conceivable in which this would actually be the case; as, for example, in an overloaded boat in a storm. Different courses of action may be approved as they may flow from the same affections. And thus the moral sense is simply a natural tendency to approve certain affections which tend to the public good. It approves the benevolent affections directly, and indirectly it leads us to approve such actions, and such actions alone, as flow from goodwill, or, at lowest, from dispositions 'which exclude the highest selfishness.'[45] Benevolence, for example, meets with the highest, fortitude and veracity[46] meet with lower degrees of approval. To the self-regarding virtues he assigns, like Shaftesbury, an inferior place, and, indeed, falls into the assumption that a tendency to promote the public happiness is not only the measure of goodness in actions, but should be the sole motive to performing them.

61. The complication which follows from Hutcheson's theory that 'to each of our powers we seem to have a corresponding taste or sense commending the proper use of it to the agent, and making him relish or value the like exercise of it by another,'[47] is characteristic; and were it removed, the moral sense would become identical with the benevolent

---

[42]'Moral Philosophy,' book i. ch. iv.   [45]'System,' i. 63.

[43]'Inquiry,' sec. iv.   [46]Ib. i. 66.

[44]'Inquiry,' sec. i. § 8, and 'System,' i. 97. [47]Ib. i. 59.

instincts. The result of this false analysis is to produce a curious and more important confusion. The moral sense, as we discover, and as is apparent from remarks just quoted, approves the benevolent affections because, and in so far as, they conduce to the public good. From considering the moral sense, he tells us, we might 'proceed to consider more particularly the several offices of life, and to discover what partial affections and actions consequent upon them are to be entirely approved, as beneficial to some part of the system, and perfectly consistent with the general good; and what appetites and affections, even of a beneficial kind, though they may be useful to a part, are pernicious to the general system, and thus deduce the special laws of nature from this moral faculty and generous determination of soul.'[48] We find, in short, that Hutcheson uses two standards—the public good, and the approval of the moral sense—and uses them indifferently, because he is convinced of their absolute identity. In his discussion of particular problems, the moral sense passes out of sight altogether, and he becomes a pure utilitarian.

62. Hutcheson, indeed, appears to have been the first person to proclaim the celebrated formula, 'the greatest happiness of the greatest number.'[49] This principle is thoroughly interwoven into his system. 'The moral faculty,' he tells us, 'most approves and recommends such dispositions as tend most to the general good, and, at the same time, such as may give the noblest enjoyment to the agent upon consideration;'[50] for, like Shaftesbury, he takes great pains to prove that virtue is happiness even to the individual. Still more expressly, he declares that 'the ultimate notion of right is that which tends to the universal good.'[51] He attacks Butler for asserting that there can be any other justification of punishment than 'the tendency of sufferings to the public

---

[48]'System,' i. 98.

[49]Hutcheson's use of this phrase occurs in the 'Inquiry concerning Moral Good and Evil,' sec. iii. § 8. 'In the same manner,' he says, 'the moral evil or vice' (of a given action) 'is as the degree of misery and number of sufferers; so that that action is best which procures *the greatest happiness of the greatest numbers.*' In Bentham's Works, x. 79, 80, it is said that Bentham first thought of the principle on reading Priestley's 'Treatise on Government.' At p. 142 the alternative is suggested that the phrase may have been borrowed from Beccaria; who, in the preface to his essay on crimes and punishments, condemns laws which have not been made from the point of view of *la massima felicità divisa nel maggior numero.* Hutcheson has clearly the right of priority, whatever the value of the thing claimed.

[50]'System,' i. 139.   [51]Ib. p. 266.

good,'[52] and points out very clearly the confusion produced in this instance by Butler's habitual confusion between punishment and suffering. Finally, he maintains that a precept of the Law of Nature is 'no more than a conclusion from observation of what sort of conduct is ordinarily useful to society.'[53] Hutcheson, in short, though he occasionally refers to the metaphysical doctrine of compacts underlying certain social arrangements, refers habitually and distinctly to utility as the sole and sufficient measure of virtue.

63. Hutcheson, then, substantially propounds a problem. His 'moral sense' is nothing but the approval of such affections, and consequently of such courses of action, as are most conducive to the public welfare. How, then, does it happen that such affections and actions are approved? Hutcheson assumes that because none of the ordinary explanations are sufficient, no explanation can be given except the divine ordinance. God enters his system, not as the supreme judge and awarder of rewards and penalties, but as the skilful contriver of an harmonious system. Man is a machine of vast complexity, so put together that the resultant of its various forces always points in that direction which is most beneficial to society. The origin of our moral sentiments remains, as with Butler, a mystery; but the end to which they point is no longer mysterious. The moral sense is a kind of Ithuriel's spear, which, when brought into contact with our affections, reveals their true quality, showing the angelic nature of those which are conducive to the public good and the diabolical character of those which are opposed to it. Or it resembles the fabulous cups which detected the poison lurking in any drink poured into them; and enables us to reject the anti-social, and accept the social emotions. When utility was thus recognised as the criterion of virtue, it required but one step to admit that it was also the cause of moral approbation. That step was taken by Hume, who had some personal relations with Hutcheson; but Hutcheson explicitly declined to accept an explanation which appeared to be equivalent to resolving virtue into selfishness.

64. The ethical speculations of Reid, the most eminent writer of the Common-Sense school, are contained in his 'Essays on the Active Powers,' but would scarcely justify a prolonged analysis. They may be described briefly as a combination of the views of Clarke and Shaftesbury, though most resembling those of Butler. Recognising the nugatory character of Clarke's theory,[54] he also thinks that to adopt Shaftesbury's theory would be to make morality arbitrary, as dependent upon a

---

[52]'System,' p. 256.   [53]Ib. p. 273.   [54]Reid's Works, p. 676.

'natural or acquired taste.'[55] The conscience, therefore, which guides our moral judgments, is at once, in his language, an intellectual and an active power, and its supremacy is, as with Butler, an ultimate and self-evident fact.[56] This power, which is simply common sense applied to moral questions, is, of course, capable of laying down as many first principles as may be required.[57] Here, as elsewhere, the difficulty of finding an ultimate justification for axioms is evaded by simply declaring that no justification is needed; but there is nothing in Reid's ethical doctrine which had not been more articulately worked out by his predecessors, except that his facility in multiplying first principles is, perhaps, more marked and his ethical philosophy proportionally weaker.

V. Hartley and Adam Smith.

65. Two remarkable attempts were made at explaining the mechanism of the mysterious power postulated by the Common-Sense school. Hutcheson had spoken slightingly of sympathy, and of the association of ideas as means of explaining our moral judgments. Sympathy was, in his eyes, merely a variety of selfishness. We dislike seeing pain in others because it produces a sympathetic pain in ourselves. And such a feeling would not account for a moral sentiment in cases where his sympathetic action could not be set up. A brave man dying is interested in the fate of his family, though he would know that their suffering after his death could inflict no pain upon him.[1] Association again is briefly noticed as useful in many ways, but also as exciting a disturbing influence. It leads us, for example, to dislike or admire certain actions, without asking whether our feelings are justified by reason, or produced only by an accidental collocation of circumstances. Hartley endeavoured to make association the fundamental law of our intellectual and emotional nature; and Adam Smith tried to resolve all our moral sentiments into sympathy.

66. David Hartley published his 'Observations on Man' in 1749. He had been a Fellow of Jesus College, Cambridge, but being deterred by some scruples from taking orders, became a physician. To the writings of Sir Isaac Newton and Locke he owed, as his son tells us,[2] the first stimulant to his intellect, but the hint which immediately suggested his peculiar theory came from a Mr. Gay, who afterwards published his sentiments in a dissertation prefixed to Law's translation of King's

[55]Reid's Works, p. 534.
[56]Ib. pp. 597, 598.   [1]'System,' i. 48.
[57]Ib. p. 637, &c.   [2]See Life prefixed to vol. iii. of Works.

'Origin of Evil.' The candour which prompted this avowal is in harmony with the admirable simplicity, truthfulness, and elevation which animated his book and his life. Anyone who should read the last pages of his treatise, in which he prophesies, with singular insight, the approach of a terrible revolution,[3] might probably declare that Hartley's peculiar characteristic was his opposition to the materialising tendencies of his age. And yet Hartley was philosophically a materialist. He was preaching substantially the same doctrines which were advocated by his contemporary Condillac. Man, according to him, is nothing but a bundle of 'vibratiuncles'—a kind of barrel-organ set in motion by the external forces of the world. Yet turn over a few pages and Hartley appears in the character of a Christian advocate, refuting the infidel by the same arguments, though not with the same brutality, as his friend Warburton. Go a little further, and it might appear that Hartley is a disciple of Spinoza, to whom the highest good is self-annihilation and absorption in the Deity. Certainly, a strange combination; and yet it must be added that Hartley is a consecutive reasoner, whose theory sins rather by excessive simplicity than by undue complication. The explanation of the paradox is partly to be sought in the ease with which the phraseology of any system may be pressed into the service of any other; partly in a real inconsistency due to his desire to satisfy his moral instinct even at the price of his logic; but partly, also, in the fact that the inconsistency is not so great as appears at first sight.

67. The doctrine which lies at the bottom of Hartley's scheme is the belief in necessity. He realises almost as clearly as Spinoza the truth that all events in the universe, including the phenomena of human action, are links in an eternal chain of causes and effects. 'The cause of the cause,' he says, is also 'the cause of the thing caused'[4]—a truism which many people allow to lie in their minds without really affecting their conceptions. Now 'God is the cause of all things'—matter is a 'mere passive thing,' and therefore every motion comes ultimately from a divinely communicated impulse.[5] God is eternal, omnipresent, immutable, and has all possible perfections; he is free, though freedom can only be predicated of him in the sense of his not being subject to any external compulsion.[6] Neither is man any exception to the universal action of the Deity. Hartley denied that he was a materialist, in the sense of believing the materiality of the soul. When arguing for a future state, he leaves it doubtful whether the soul is an immaterial

---

[3]See the very remarkable passage, Hartley 'On Man,' ii. 440 *et seq.*

[4]Ib. ii. 423; part ii. prop. 94.   [5]Ib. ii. 31; part ii. prop. 6.

[6]Hartley, ii. 35; part ii. prop. ix.

substance or an 'elementary infinitesimal body,' a germ or atom which receives the sensation, and whose existence survives that of the organism within which it is placed.[7] His system, however, clearly renders a soul a superfluity, if not an anomaly. The will, the thoughts, and the emotions, not only result from, but, as it would seem, are 'vibratiuncles,' that is, miniature vibrations set up in our bodies. Like all other material motions, they are therefore due—it matters not whether directly or indirectly—to the Divine Impulse. God is the one efficient cause, and all the phenomena of human life are but the waves stirred by him in the infinite ocean of existence. Hartley is, so far, a materialist Spinoza; nor, it would seem, does it make very great difference whether we call that substance which is the medium transmitting the divine impulses matter or spirit. In either case we are equally ignorant of its ultimate essence. There are, indeed, with Hartley, two substances; but matter is merely the senseless mass tossed hither and thither by the omnipresent and omnipotent force which we call God.

68. Further, it necessarily follows from this conception that Hartley is a consistent optimist. The universe being but the raw material provided for the display of the divine energy, corresponds to the perfection of its Creator. It is the cast moulded in its minutest details upon infinite beneficence. The infinite happiness and perfection of God is a 'pledge of the ultimate happiness and perfection of all his creatures.'[8] Assuming the Calvinist doctrine of the supreme will of God, he rejects the Calvinist conclusion that some men can have been made for eternal happiness and others for eternal misery.[9] Nay, he even ventures to maintain, though some of his terms require a special interpretation, a doctrine 'which at first sight seemed not only contrary to obvious experience, but even impossible—viz. that all individuals are actually and always infinitely happy.'[10] The theory sounds like optimism run mad. It is curious that Hartley should have persuaded himself that such opinions were consistent with the Christian dogmas, elastic as those dogmas had become in the hands of the rationalist school. The explanation is partly that a philosophy resting exclusively upon experience can adapt itself easily to a religion resting upon evidence. Hartley, for example, is ready to accept miracles which Spinoza declared upon *a priori* grounds to be irrational. The difference between Hartley and the older metaphysicians may be described by saying that with them the type of all reasoning is to be found in pure mathematics, whilst with him it is to

[7]Hartley, ii. 383, &c.; part ii. prop. 86, and see his comparison of his own system with those of Leibnitz and Malebranche (i. 111; part i. prop. 21, cor. 3).
[8]Ib. ii. 421; part ii. prop. 94.   [9]Ib. ii. 421.   [10]Ib. ii. 29; part ii. prop. 4.

be found in applied mathematics. He seeks to do for human nature what Newton did for the solar system. Association is for man what gravitation is for the planets; and as Newton imagined that God's will must be the efficient cause of gravitation, so Hartley imagined the same will to be the cause of those movements in the human organism which are the immediate cause of all mental phenomena.[11] He is about the last writer who affects the mathematical form common to the metaphysicians of the previous generation, but in his mind the analogy is not with the pure mathematics which, dealing with ideas of space and time, seem to have an *a priori* validity, but with those laws of motion which he would have asserted (as indeed he would have asserted of all axiomatic truths) to be derived from experience.

69. Dropping the peculiar theory of vibratiuncles which Priestley afterwards excised from his system with small injury to its coherency,[12] the theory, so far as morality is concerned, may be pretty simply stated. He holds, in opposition to Locke, that all ideas are derived from sensation, the remaining ideas of reflection being simply the residuum which Locke was incapable of sufficiently analysing.[13] The ideas which thus enter the mind are gradually transformed by force of association into more complex products. The pleasures and pains which are compounded of the primary sensations may be divided into seven classes: (1) sensation; (2) imagination; (3) ambition; (4) self-interest; (5) sympathy; (6) theopathy; and (7) the moral sense. The pleasures and pains of sensation are the ultimate irresoluble facts. From them are generated the pleasures and pains of the imagination. From these two, again, in various combinations, arise the pleasures and pains of ambition. From the three thus obtained, the pleasures and pains of self-interest, and so on. But, again, each class of pleasures and pains reacts upon the previous classes; and thus we have wholes too complex to admit of complete analysis.[14] In mathematical language it may be said that six equations arise from stating each of the latter six classes in terms of all the others; and thus it is possible to determine every one of the other classes as functions of the primitive sensations. The problem is ingeniously worked

---

[11]See Hartley, i. 351, where he says that all enquiries may ultimately be put into mathematical forms, and all categories be reduced to quantity alone. His classification of the sciences, part i. prop. 88, evidently implies this conception. All 'natural philosophy' is with him reducible to laws such as those of gravitation. Hume also compares association to gravitation (see Works, i. 321).   [12]See 'The Theory of the Human Mind,' by Priestley, 1775.

[13]Hartley, i. 360; part i. prop. 88.   [14]Ib. i. 369; part i. prop. 89.

out in each case; but the process is too complicated and too unsatisfactory to be worth following.

70. Upon this foundation Hartley erects his theory of the rule of life. The innumerable pains and pleasures, as they strike upon our sense, cause vibrations which tend to coalesce. Association thus converts a state in which both pleasure and pain are felt by turns into a state in which pure pleasure and pure pain are alone perceived. But as pleasures are more numerous than pains, the resulting state will be generally one of pleasure alone; and thus, ultimately, association has 'a tendency to reduce the state of those who have eaten of the tree of the knowledge of good and evil back again to a paradisaical one.'[15] The painful element is gradually absorbed in the pleasurable, until at last it is altogether eliminated. By a similar process we may trace the proper course to be pursued by each individual. Mankind is endued with a desire of obtaining happiness;[16] but this desire, when properly regulated, leads not to selfishness, but to an utter annihilation of self. Analysing each of the classes of the pleasure, Hartley discovers that in each case the purest enjoyment is derived from those pleasures which border upon the higher class. The sensual and the purely selfish pleasures should be sought only in strict subordination to the love of man and the love of God. By a process of successive approximations (the mathematical analogy is always present to his mind) the lower desires will thus be gradually merged in the higher, till we arrive at 'perfect self-annihilation and the pure love of God.'[17] The moral sense in Hartley's classification lies above theopathy; but the moral sense is the 'sum total'[18] of all the others, and not a distinct faculty. It represents the state of mind which results when the whole nature is brought into its final harmony. We begin as animals, with nothing but sensations; we should end as angels rapt in the beatific vision of the all-perfect Creator. Hartley expresses his conclusion in that queer mathematical mysticism which is characteristic of the strange contrasts of his system. Let W., he says, represent the love of the world; F, the fear, and L, the love of God. Then we may say that $W : F :: F : L$ or $W = \frac{F^2}{L}$. In our initial state we fear God infinitely more than we love him; and love the world infinitely more than we fear God. In our final state, the ratios should be reversed, and the love of the world be swallowed up in the fear, and that again in the love of God. W, that is, should approach indefinitely

---

[15]Hartley, i. 83; part i. prop. 14, cor. 9.   [17]Ib. ii. 282; part ii. prop. 67.
[16]Ib. ii. 197; part ii. prop. 46.   [18]Ib. i. 497; part i. prop. 99.

to zero; and L must, therefore, be indefinitely greater than F.[19] The good Hartley smiles complacently at the 'new and compendious light' which he has thus thrown upon the most important of all problems. He has compressed religion into a pocket formula.

71. The kernel of his system of course lies in that theory of association which provides the machinery for this curious transformation, by which vibratiuncles set up in the medullary substance of the brain are ultimately converted into the pure love of God. The general doctrine is familiar enough. The miser loves money as an end, because he has associated it with the pleasures produced by money. As we thus learn to value the cause from first valuing the thing caused, we are led by the necessity of our natures to rest at last 'upon him who is the inexhaustible fountain of all power, knowledge, goodness, majesty, glory, property, &c.'[20] By the same process children learn to love the parents, attendants, or playfellows, who are the cause of most of their pleasures. The amusements which we share with others have the same tendency; the honour procured by benevolence, and the pleasures of religion and the moral sense, tend to strengthen the early associations, and thus, without any direct expectation of reward, or even of subsidiary pleasure, benevolence becomes an ultimate object for its own sake. 'And this,' says Hartley, 'I take to be a proof from the doctrine of association, that there is, and must be, such a thing as pure disinterested benevolence; also a just account of the origin and nature of it.'[21]

72. This is Hartley's contribution to a moral theory. Its value and its limitations are tolerably clear. The great problem of contemporary moralists was to solve an apparent contradiction. The purely selfish solution—the doctrine, that is, that the man neither does nor can act except from a regard to his own interest—has a terrible plausibility, especially when all philosophy is obliged to start from the consideration of the individual mind, instead of contemplating the social organism. The very existence of 'altruistic' sentiments appears to be contradictory, from this point of view. Some writers denied, with Mandeville, that they existed, or, with Butler and Hutcheson, regarded the faculty which sanctions them as in some sense supernatural. Hartley still retains the conception of final causes, but endeavours to lay bare the machinery by which they work. The process by which a regard for self is gradually refined into pure love of God or our neighbours is still the work of a divine hand, but it may be studied, analysed, and shown to conform to

---

[19]Hartley, ii. 329; part ii. prop. 72 (Scholium).   [20]Ib. i. 463; part i. prop. 96.
[21]Ib. i. 474; part i. prop. 97.

certain general laws.'[22] No one had explained the power of association in regard to the emotions with so much ingenuity, and, as association is doubtless a true cause, Hartley had the merit of really improving our conception of the mode in which the moral sentiments are generated in the individual. So few men have really added to our limited stock of moral theories, that the merit must be regarded as a very high one. On the other hand, the value of Hartley's speculation is confined to this branch of ethical speculation. It is a general weakness of his system, resulting from its mode of ignoring ultimate philosophical problems, that he never seems to allow for general truths. Why does not each of those bundles of vibratiuncles which we call brains, differing in nature, and exposed to infinitely various conditions, grind out a different set of truths? How can there be a universal system of morality? Hartley seems to prove that each individual must tend, as times goes on, to become more exclusively animated by the love of God —a result which is at least opposed to the ordinary views of human experience. The formation of a moral standard is not definitely explained; though some theory might be accommodated to his system. But, without going into metaphysical questions, it is plain that this weakness is significant of the individualist method of Hartley, and that, on his own showing, the doctrine requires to be supplemented by a study of the reciprocal action upon each other of different members of the race. In other words, Hartley's doctrine is defective from the absence of any sociology, or even of the perception that some sociological theory is necessary to frame a moral doctrine based upon experience. He might then have anticipated the teaching of some cognate schools in later times.

73. Adam Smith's 'Theory of Moral Sentiments' appeared in 1759,[23] and won a rapid popularity, though producing little conviction. The qualities of thought and style which afterwards caused the success of the 'Enquiry into the Wealth of Nations' are equally visible in its predecessor. Smith's ingenious and discursive intellect pours itself out in streams of diffuse eloquence, often brilliant with felicitous illustrations, and quick flashes of historical insight, and yet wide rather than deep, rather dexterous in new combinations than penetrating the essence of the subject, and therefore apt to disappoint us by a certain superficiality. Smith's ingenuity in tracing the working of the mecha-

---

[22]Hartley's doctrine coincides curiously on some points with Comte's teaching as to the cultivation of the altruistic sentiments.

[23]A tenth edition in 1804.

nism of human nature is so marked and so delightful to himself that he almost forgets to enquire into the primary forces which set it in action. He describes the mutual action and reaction of the passions with more fidelity than the passions themselves. Smith, in fact, is a thorough representative of that optimistic Deism which we have seen illustrated by Shaftesbury and Hutcheson. Hutcheson, Smith's predecessor in the chair of Moral Philosophy in Glasgow,[24] was in this respect nearer to Smith than was Smith's friend and teacher, Hume. The characteristic difference appears in this, that Smith follows Hutcheson and departs from Hume in making the doctrine of final causes an essential part of his system. Although we have no longer that extraordinary complex machinery of primitive instincts which, according to Butler and Hutcheson, had been mysteriously implanted in our bosom as divinely appointed monitors, yet Smith constantly regards human nature as a mechanism skilfully contrived to carry out the divine purposes. He simplifies the construction with a view to a rational explanation; but the action of the artificer is still discernible. Superfluous wheels and pulleys have been removed, but the general conception remains.

74. His theology rests essentially upon the 'whatever is, is right' dogma. He believes in a 'great, benevolent, and all-wise Being,' who is determined by his own perfections to maintain in the universe at all times 'the greatest possible quantity of happiness.'[25] A belief in a future life is necessary to make us happy in this, and to "illumine the dreary prospect of its continually approaching mortality.'[26] The doctrine is so cheering that every virtuous man must earnestly wish to believe it; and disbelief has only been produced by its perversion to ascetic purposes.[27] He quotes with indignation a passage in which Massillon, in preaching to a military audience, eloquently compares the hardships endured by a soldier to the penances endured by a monk; and proclaims that one day of a soldier's devotion might, if applied in a different direction, have won eternal happiness. When the rewards and penalties of futurity are perverted to secure the salvation of gloomy ascetics, and to ensure the damnation of heroes, statesmen, and philosophers, the doctrine is unnaturally opposed to all our moral sentiments.[28] A cheerful discharge of daily duties proceeding from an equable and social temper is, in his opinion, the truest wisdom. 'Happiness,' he says,

[24]Hutcheson died in 1747. Craigie, his successor, was succeeded by Smith, in 1752.

[25]Smith's 'Moral Sentiments,' ii. 98; part vi. sec. 2, ch. iii.

[26]Ib. i. 267; part iii. ch. ii.   [27]Ib. i. 268, part iii. ch. ii.   [28]Ib. i. 271, ib.

'consists in tranquillity and enjoyment.'[29] and enjoyment follows almost of necessity from tranquillity. With this moderate estimate of human wants it is easy to believe, and to rejoice in the belief, that there are twenty people happy for one in misery.[30] 'What,' he characteristically asks, 'can be added to the happiness of a man who is in health, who is out of debt, and has a clear conscience?'[31] and this, he adds, is the actual condition of the greatest part of mankind. The sight of the universe and of the human race excites in him neither lofty raptures nor melancholy misgivings, but a kind of placid complacency, which he describes as belief in God.

75. The benevolence of the Creator shows itself in the skilful adaptation of human passions to produce this result. Nature (which is the polite term for God) has made us worshippers of rank and fortune, because she 'wisely judged' that order would be more secure when resting on visible distinctions than on the obscure qualities of virtue and wisdom. Hume explains the snobbishness of mankind by the obvious consideration that we naturally admire what is useful to us. In Adam Smith's view it becomes a mysterious arrangement of Providence, designed for the good of society.[32] The theory of the method is given with great clearness by Smith himself. After adducing the ordinary illustration of the watch, he remarks that we frequently mistake the end promoted by the existence of a given sentiment for the efficient cause of the sentiment; and thus 'imagine that to be the wisdom of man which in reality is the Wisdom of God.'[33] Thus, as he goes on to say in tacit reference to Hume, the utility of just laws being obvious, it has been supposed that the utility was the cause of our approval of the enforcement of such laws. In opposition to this Smith argues that, although the utility has a certain influence, the sentiment of justice is excited in all men, and especially in the unthinking, by a spontaneous movement which does not take utility into account. Sympathy with the injured man excites our anger against a thief, and not any concern for the general interests of society. Smith's argument would be conclusive against a reasoner who should assert that the utility of an action was

[29]Adam Smith, i. 302; part iii. ch. ii.

[30]Ib. i. 282, ib.

[31]Ib. i. 87; part i. sec. 3, ch. i. The phrase perhaps comes from Pope ('Essay on Man,' iv. 80), who says that all happiness consists in 'health, peace, and competence;' and Pope here follows Bolingbroke almost verbally (Bolingbroke's Works, v. 298).

[32]Adam Smith, ii. 78; part vii. sec. 2, ch. i.

[33]Ib. i. 178; part ii. sec. 2, ch. iii.

not merely the criterion of its morality, but also the immediate ground of our approval or disapproval. That would, of course, be a very crude statement of the utilitarian view. Smith's criticism, however, is significant of his position, and gives the starting-point of his special theory.

76. He holds that the moral sentiments contribute blindly to promote the happiness of mankind. Our anger against evildoers falls in by an undesigned coincidence—undesigned, that is, so far as we are concerned—with the general disposition of Providence to promote the greatest possible amount of happiness. But if not designed by us, it must have been designed by the Creator. The theory is, therefore, directed against a palpable weakness of the doctrine as generally expounded. It is easy to perceive that a dim perception of the utility of certain actions may have gradually generated moral sentiments which have no longer a conscious reference to the necessity which produced them. But until this distinction had been plainly drawn, it was a natural objection to the utilitarian theory that moral approval frequently did not involve any distinct recognition of the utility of actions. The instincts which had grown up by a complex process seemed, to observers still unable to place themselves at the historical point of view, to have something mysterious about them. Philosophers talked not of concrete men, but of abstract human nature, assumed, or rather loudly asserted, to be the same in all times and places. They did not think of our instincts as slowly developed under the influence of a thousand modifying causes through long generations, but as suddenly springing into existence ready made. And to such observers it was natural that the conformity between our wants and our sentiment should appear to be the result of special contrivance, rather than of slow evolution. Smith, however, regards the moral sense described by Hutcheson as a superfluity, and as not properly explaining the phenomena. Our judgments of different vices and virtues vary too widely to be explained as the dictates of one sense; and it would be strange if an instinct so important and so peculiar should have been discovered for the first time within a few years, and not even have received a name.[34] For this and other reasons, he rejects the theory of a specific moral faculty, and substitutes a theory of his own, which, however, seems to have gained few adherents.

77. In the place of Butler's conscience and Hutcheson's moral sense, Smith erects an internal monitor, who is the object of much eloquence, and who is generally described as the 'man,' or 'the demigod within the

---

[34]Adam Smith, ii. 299 *et seq.;* part vii. sec. 4, ch. ii.

breast—the great judge and arbiter of conduct.'[35] What, then, is this demigod? Whence his authority, and what his origin? Smith's general reply is that he is formed by sympathy. God has given us the gift, though not in such perfection as might be desired, to see ourselves as others see us. We invent, as it were, an impartial spectator, and approve or disapprove of our conduct as we feel that another man would or would not sympathise with our actions.[36] Or, to use an appropriate metaphor, we form a mirror from the opinions of other men, by supposing ourselves the spectators of our own behaviour. 'This is the only looking-glass by which we can in some measure, with the eyes of other people, scrutinise the propriety of our own conduct.'[37] The theory becomes complex as it is worked out. We have to take into account not merely the primary but the secondary reflections; and, indeed, we must imagine two opposite mirrors, reflecting images in indefinite succession. We must consider A's sympathy for B, and then B's sympathy with A's sympathy, and then A's own sympathy with B's sympathy with A's sympathy for B, and we are finally rather puzzled to discover the ultimate basis of the sympathy. From some points the doctrine seems to resolve itself into a regard for public opinion as embodied in the hypothetical 'impartial spectators.' But which sympathies are right and which wrong? Where is the ultimate criterion? Impartiality is, doubtless, an essential condition for a sound moral judgment, but can it be the only condition? The standard of morality seems to be too fluctuating to serve any intelligible purpose. We can understand the process by which, according to Smith, the 'amiable virtues' are generated by the spectator's sympathy with the sufferer, and the 'respectable virtues' by the sufferer's sympathy with the spectator's sympathy, and consequent desire to restrain his emotions within moderate bounds.[38] But how are these inconsistent demands to be regulated? How far should the spectator sympathise, and within what bounds should the sufferer restrain his demands for sympathy? The 'man within the breast' is not an incorruptible judge. He may be persuaded to make reports very different from what circumstances would authorise.[39] Who, then, is to correct his judgments? Man, says Smith, has been constituted a judge of his brethren, and is thus the 'vicegerent upon earth' of his Creator. But he is only judge in the first instance. An appeal lies from him to the higher tribunal of conscience, or, what is identical, to that of the supposed

---

[35]Adam Smith, ii. 127; part vi. sec. 3.
[36]Ib. i. 226; part iii. ch. i.   [38]Ib. i. 35; part i. sec. 1, ch. v.
[37]Ib. i. 230, ib.   [39]Ib. i. 320; part iii. ch. iv.

well-informed and impartial spectator, to that of the 'man within the breast, the great judge and arbiter of their' (that is, mankind's) 'conduct.'[40] The jurisdiction of the 'man without' is founded in the desire of simple praise; that of the 'man within' in the desire of praiseworthiness. Does, then, the impartial spectator give a final judgment? No; for it seems that this demigod is partly of mortal, though partly of immortal extraction.[41] His judgment is perverted by the clamour of the 'man without.' There lies, therefore, another appeal to a still higher tribunal—that of the 'all-seeing Judge of the world,'[42] from whom perfect justice may be anticipated in another life, if not in this.

78. But how is the appeal to be made? Smith avoids all reference to supernatural revelation, and we must assume that the decisions of this final and absolute tribunal are to be sought in nature. But on what principal they are to be discovered is nowhere apparent. Smith asserts that, beyond the standard of conduct which is formed from the ordinary opinions of the world, there is a higher standard, slowly framed by the 'demigod,' and approximating indefinitely to the 'archetype of perfection' framed by the Divine artist[43]—but we seek in vain for any definite account of its nature. The appeal is ultimately made to an inaccessible tribunal, or, in other words, the standard of absolute morality seems to be hopelessly uncertain. It is in heaven, not on earth, and heaven is shrouded in impenetrable mystery. Here, as elsewhere, Smith's copious and rather unctuous eloquence enables him to glide over the real difficulty, quite unconscious of its existence. His ultimate analysis of the sources of approbation is given in his concluding account of 'Systems of Moral Philosophy.' First, he says, we sympathise with the motives of the agent; secondly, with the gratitude of those he has benefited; 'thirdly, we observe that his conduct has been agreeable to the general rules by which those two sympathies generally act; and, last of all, when we consider such actions as making a part of a system of behaviour which tends to promote the happiness either of the individual or of the society, they appear to derive a beauty from this utility, not unlike that which we ascribe to any well-contrived machine.'[44] And this he asserts to be a complete analysis of the sentiment.

79. The general laws of morality, then, are merely formulæ expressive of the mode in which sympathy habitually acts, and are convenient

---

[40]Adam Smith, i. 264; part iii. ch. ii. The 'great judge and arbiter of conduct' is a kind of cant phrase with Smith. He appears again, for example, i. 276, and ii. 127.   [41]Ib. i. 266, ib.   [42]Ib. i. 267, ib.

[43]Ib. ii. 128; part vi. sec. 3.   [44]Ib. ii. 304; part vii. sec. 4, ch. iii.

standards of reference, but not the ultimate foundation of morality.[45] Utility, again, occupies a strictly subordinate position. Smith rejects Hume's explanation of our sentiments as founded upon it, because we praise a man for other reasons than those which lead us to praise 'a chest of drawers;' and because the usefulness of any disposition is not the 'first ground of our approbation.'[46] Utility acts chiefly as facilitating sympathy. We readily fall in with the sentiments which dictate an action plainly useful to mankind, and in this indirect fashion, the utility stimulates, though it does not cause, approbation. 'Many an honest Englishman,' he says, would have been more grieved by the loss of a guinea than by the loss of Minorca; and yet, had it been in his power, would have sacrificed his life a thousand times to defend the fortress.[47] It is because he naturally sympathises with the nation to whom Minorca was of importance, though the utility to him personally may be infinitesimal. Smith, as before, is arguing against the hypothesis that each man acts from calculations of private interest, and does not consider that loyalty and patriotism may have been generated by their obvious utility, though, when developed, their origin passes out of sight.

80. The name of Adam Smith must always be mentioned with high respect; but it cannot be said that as a writer upon ethics he equals his own achievement as a writer upon economics. It may be fully admitted that he shows great ingenuity, and great fertility of illustration, and that he calls attention to a fact which must be taken into account by the moralist. But it is impossible to resist the impression, whilst we read his fluent rhetoric, and observe his easy acceptance of theological principles already exposed by his master Hume, that we are not listening to a thinker really grappling with a difficult problem, so much as to an ambitious professor who has found an excellent opportunity for displaying his command of language, and making brilliant lectures. The whole tone savours of that complacent optimism of the time which retained theological phrases to round a paragraph, and to save the trouble of genuine thought. Smith's main proposition was hardly original, though he has worked it out in detail, and it is rather calculated to lead us dexterously round difficult questions than to supply us with a genuine answer.

81. The moralists, whom I have thus considered, may be regarded as successively developing or modifying the theory originally expounded by Shaftesbury. There is, it is maintained by them all, a certain mysterious

---

[45]See vol. i. p. 327; part iii. ch. iv.

[46]Adam Smith, i. 395; part iv. ch. ii.   [47]Ib. i. 403; part iv. ch. iii.

harmony or order in the universe which reveals itself to the divine faculty of conscience. With Shaftesbury the faculty is almost identified with the æsthetic perceptions, and is rather a sentiment than a power of intellectual intuition. By his followers the doctrine takes a more formal shape. The sense of harmony is made more definite as a perception of final causes. If we may use the old analogy of the watch, Butler holds that the hand of conscience always points to duty, and that its dictates justify themselves. Hutcheson says that, by a prearranged harmony, the hand of the moral sense points to the course productive of the greatest happiness. Hartley and Adam Smith endeavour to take the watch to pieces and describe the mechanism by which this result is attained. Yet they still hold that the perfection of the contrivance implies a divine artificer. The morality most naturally connects itself with that philosophical Deism which, though it had never much vital power, survived the deist controversy. Except Butler, these writers are all optimists, in regard both to human nature and the universe; they all lay stress upon final causes, and are forced to have recourse to a complex scheme of psychology to account for the assumed intuitions. These doctrines are a logical result from their fundamental conception. God is to them the informing and sustaining Spirit, manifested through the universe and recognised by the human soul. If the universe be thus the external veil of a divine power, everything, including the human mind which recognises it, must be naturally good. Evil is an illusion produced by our imperfect knowledge, or a result of the perverse exercise of that free-will which must be postulated to avoid a lapse into Pantheism. To maintain such a belief, it is necessary to avert one's eyes from the dark side of the world, from evil passions, from hopeless suffering, and to wrap oneself in a cloak of gentle complacency. It is dangerous to ask ultimate questions, or to pry too closely into human motives, in search of their more earthly elements. The origin of our instincts is best left shrouded in mystery, or they must be regarded as a mechanism which testifies to the design of an all-wise beneficence. If the conscience is the vicegerent of God, the impulse which theologians had placed in the external order is really within us. Yet the impulse still retains the divine attributes of inscrutability and supreme authority.

82. Butler alone retains the belief in human corruption, and with him the voice of nature testifies rather to a stern judge than a benevolent father. The universe is, therefore, ruled by a being who excites our dread more unequivocally than our affection. This view indicates the fundamental weakness of the intuitional system. No one who dares to look facts in the face can be a consistent optimist. Crime and misery

are no superficial phenomena to be dismissed as illusory or accidental; they are woven into the very tissue of the world. Men, therefore, who had the strong grasp of palpable facts, characteristic of the scientific temperament, preferred to put aside the beautiful but unsubstantial vision of the complacent school. Man is a strange mixture of good and bad, in whom we cannot trace the living image of a perfect Creator. The doctrine of corruption contains an undeniable truth. No plausible theory of final causes will clear up the strange maze of vice and virtue, folly and wisdom, misery and happiness. One thing alone is plain. Man wishes to be happy and dreads to be unhappy. There is the one solid fact, which may guide us through the perplexed labyrinth of good and evil, though it cannot explain why good and evil are so strangely blended. Virtue and vice must be resolved into these primitive desires. All *a priori* theories may be rejected as illusory, because all end by declaring facts to be an illusion. The tendency of these moralists was to deny the existence of instincts which they could not explain, as the tendency of their antagonists was to pronounce them inexplicable. Such theories as those of Hartley and Adam Smith opened a kind of *via media,* as suggesting that instincts which appear to be primitive, and which have come to be independent, may be ultimately derived from the simpler elements. But, in the earlier stages, the general tendency of the empirical school was to dispute the existence of an independent conscience rather than to explain the process by which it was generated.

83. Thus we have an apparently internecine conflict, which yet admits of a number of intermediate combinations of opinion. Those who retain some independent basis of intuitive knowledge are opposed to those who appeal exclusively to experience; the optimists are opposed to the pessimists; the believers in a general harmony to the believers in a universal corruption; the believers in a system of final causes to those who regard the existing order as a product of a blind struggle of opposing forces; the believers in an inspired conscience to those who resolve all conscience into self-love or prudence; and those who love symmetrical theories more than a definite statement of observed fact to those who prefer fact to theory. Shaftesbury and Mandeville represent the opposite tendencies in their purest shape. Other writers generally put together theories from more or less inconsistent fragments. If we admit that on each side there was a certain element of truth, we may infer that a theory is not necessarily the worse because it did not represent either tendency in its purest shape. The ultimate problem is to discover a moral system independent of the old theology. The natural inclination of the sceptical side was to reject every part of the old morality which

seemed to be inseparably connected with theology; but as that theology undoubtedly embodied essential truths, there is much to be said for those who would preserve fragments of the old doctrine, even when they could not accommodate them to a new philosophical basis.

VI. The Utilitarians.

84. We must now, however, turn our attention to the moralists who, in later phraseology, have been called utilitarians. Here as elsewhere we may trace the primary impulse to Locke. His attack upon the doctrine of innate ideas brought him into conflict with the intuitional school of morality. The third chapter of the first book of the Essay is directed against the ethical application of innate ideas. The argument there stated has served several generations of a utilitarian school; and its cogency within certain limits is irresistible. The theory which he is concerned to overthrow maintains the existence of certain self-evident moral axioms, the truth of which is recognised by all human beings as soon as they are propounded. The metaphysician regards them as ultimate facts, of which no account can be given, unless he chooses to say that they are divinely implanted in the mind. Nature—the metaphysical God—has directly revealed them to all her creatures. It would seem to follow—though there is room for some dispute upon this point—that these moral axioms, whatever they may be, should be recognised throughout the world, and that the moral code of all nations, though not identical to its furthest ramifications, should at any rate comprise a central core of unvarying truth.

85. Locke may be mistaken in imputing these doctrines to his opponents, but his answer is interesting inasmuch as it involves the germinal principles of the various utilitarian schools. The first doctrine which he avows is common to them all. He declares that he can find no 'innate practical principles,' except 'a desire of happiness and an aversion to misery;'[1] and these are appetites, not intellectual intuitions. 'Good or evil,' as he says in a later chapter, 'are nothing but pleasure and pain, or that which occasions pleasure or pain to us.'[2] The one universal motive being a desire for happiness, the moral impulses must be in some way resoluble into it. An ultimate appeal, as we may say, lies to this principle from every other. There is no moral rule, urges Locke, of which we may not ask the reason, and therefore none can be innate. The rule, for example, of doing as we would be done by is susceptible of

---

[1] Locke's Essay, book i. ch. iii. sec. 3.　　[2] Ib. book ii. ch. xxviii. sec. 5.

proof, and a man to whom it was proposed for the first time might fairly ask that its reasonableness should be made plain to him.[3] Virtue is approved because visibly conducive to happiness, and conscience is merely our opinion of the conformity of actions to certain moral rules, the utility of which has been proved by experience. It is no mysterious judge laying down absolute decisions for inscrutable reasons.

86. This, the fundamental doctrine of Locke and of all his disciples, is in fact a first form of the primary axiom, upon which depends the possibility of reducing morality within the sphere of scientific observation. It asserts that our moral sentiments have no inscrutable or exceptional character. Its essence consists in banishing mystery from the origin of our moral instincts. If it too easily degenerated into an assertion of the absolute selfishness of human nature, the assertion that the moral sense is derivative was a necessary preliminary to all fruitful investigation of the phenomena.

87. The doctrine, scientific in spirit if crude in form, is supported by the scientific method of an appeal to experience. Locke insists upon the variability of the moral standard in different races and ages. The 'Tououpinambos,' for example, thought that they would merit paradise by revenge, and by eating their enemies. 'They have not so much as a name for God, and have no religion and no worship,'[4] and these peculiarities of the Tououpinambos may be paralleled by equally strange aberrations of the moral instinct in other races. Now, though a special breach of the law may be no proof that it is unknown, a general permission to break it is a proof that it is not innate. The very recognition of any duty implies the presence in the mind of ideas of God, law, obligation, punishment, and a future life; and these ideas, so far from being universal, are not always clear and distinct, even in 'thinking and studious men.'[5] The vast diversity of opinion which exists would be impossible if threats of Almighty vengeance were stamped in indelible characters upon the minds of all men; nor can anyone, in fact, tell us what are these 'innate practical principles' which are yet asserted to be so palpably evident. Lord Herbert's five principles, for example, are illusory. To say that repentance for sin is a duty is idle, unless you are agreed as to the particular actions which are sinful. And the attempt to evade the appeal to experience by arguing that the innate principles are dulled by education and custom is really a mode of begging the question. The argument comes simply to this; 'the principles which all men allow for true are innate; those that men of right reason admit are the principles

[3]Locke's Essay, book i. ch. ii. sec. 4.   [4]Ib. book i. ch. iii. sec. 9.   [5]Ib. sec. 12.

allowed by all mankind; we, and those of our mind, are men of reason; wherefore, we agreeing, our principles are innate—which is a very pretty way of arguing and a short cut to infallibility.'[6] The real fact is, that men, having taken up many principles on trust, and having entirely forgotten whence they came, assume them to be divinely implanted axioms; and thus 'doctrines that have been derived from no better original than the superstition of a nurse and the authority of an old woman may, by length of time and consent of neighbours, grow up to the dignity of principles in morality and religion.'[7]

88. Locke brings down his logical sledgehammer on the principles of his antagonist with masculine vigour. If his objections were crudely stated, the dogmas which he smashes were at least equally crude. But it must be granted that he has left little behind him but ruins. We ask, in some alarm, what then is morality? The conscience as a mysterious and independent guide is annihilated; the only motive left is self-interest; and it almost seems as if the Tououpinambos had about as much to say for themselves as the English or the Jews. Mandeville, indeed, in his denial of the real existence of virtue has simply carried Locke's method one step further. Assume that the standard of virtue is so variable that no particular duty can be singled out as universally binding and recognised, and it is easy to infer that virtue is a mere sham.

89. No conclusion, of course, could be more repulsive to Locke himself, and it is curious that he did not perceive the application which might be made of his doctrines. Bending his whole energy to destroy the belief in the autocratic and irresponsible character of conscience, he never thinks of supplying its place. Apparently the need of reconstruction scarcely occurred to him. He speaks of the 'eternal and unalterable nature of right and wrong,'[8] and he asserts emphatically that 'morality is capable of demonstration as well as mathematics.'[9] If ethics are mathematically demonstrable, it must be possible to form a code applicable alike to Tououpinambos and Englishmen, or, at least, to assign some fixed principles from which the varying codes might be constructed. Locke would partly answer by referring to the will of God. The discussion is given in the twenty-eighth chapter of his second book, under the head of 'Moral Relations.' He there defines moral good and evil to be the conformity to 'some law,' whereby good and evil are drawn upon us

[6]Locke, sec. 20.   [7]Ib. book i. ch. iii. sec. 22.
[8]Ib. book ii. ch. xxviii., note to sec. 11.
[9]Ib. book iii. ch. xi. sec. 16; book iv. ch. iv. sec. 7; book iv. ch. xii. sec. 8; and see 'Reasonableness of Christianity,' Works, vi. 146.

by the will and power of the lawmaker.[10] We are subject to three kinds of laws, the law of God, the civil law, and the 'law of opinion or reputation.'[11] The law of God is enforced by the pains and penalties of the next world. Nobody can take us out of his hands. His will 'is the only true touchstone of moral rectitude; and by comparing them to his law it is that men judge of the most considerable moral good or evil of their actions; that is, whether as duties or sins they are likely to procure them happiness or misery from the hands of the Almighty.'[12] The civil law determines men's criminality or innocence, and the 'philosophical law,' or law of opinion, varying widely in different countries, determines their virtue or vice. This, though wanting in precision, is the law by which men most frequently govern themselves; for its sanctions, vaguer than those of other laws, are more continually present to the imagination than those of the divine law, and less easily evaded than those of the civil law. These various laws may, of course, conflict as in the case of duelling, which is a sin tried by the law of God, a virtuous action by the 'law of fashion'—another synonym for the law of opinion—and a capital crime according to the civil law of some countries.[13]

90. The law of God, then, is the only permanent and invariable standard; for the other laws vary—and, so far as Locke expounds his theory, vary indefinitely according to time, place, and circumstance. The law of God, too, must override the other laws in case of conflict; or, in his own language, be 'the only true touchstone of moral rectitude.' How, then, is the all-important question, can this law be discovered? If God's will be concealed in impenetrable mystery, virtue would apparently become a mere arbitrary fashion. That is Mandeville's solution. If the divine will be discoverable only by revelation, Locke's theory coincides with that of the theological utilitarians. The motive is with him, as with Paley, the dread of hell and the hope of heaven. He tells us himself that the Gospel gives an absolutely pure code of morality, and for that reason he excuses himself to Molyneux for not undertaking to write a treatise on the subject.[14] Locke, however, would not have admitted that our knowledge of morality was dependent on revelation. In fact, the whole argument of the treatise on the 'Reasonableness of Christianity' implies that the heathen philosophers could discover a system approximating very closely to that directly promulgated from heaven. How, then, could they arrive at a knowledge of the divine law? What was the criterion by which they were to distinguish between moral good and evil?

[10]Locke, book ii. ch. xxviii. sec. 5.   [12]Ib. sec. 8.
[11]Ib. sec. 7.   [13]Ib. sec. 15.
[14]See letter to Molyneux of March 30, 1696.

91. The curious vacillation which runs through Locke's reasoning upon morality, and which thus makes moral truth alternately quite uncertain and mathematically demonstrable, is but one instance of the general inconsistency in his theory of reality. According to Locke, as I have elsewhere observed, our knowledge of the external world cannot be 'scientifical.' We can only know phenomena, and know that they do not correspond (except in the case of the 'primary' qualities) to the objective facts beneath them. Certainty is attained only by comparison of ideas. We may know them adequately, for they exist entirely in our minds. Hence we may obtain certainty in mathematics; we have only to compare our ideas in order to discover geometrical relations, and we know (it matters not how) that those ideas are the counterparts of external realities. The same, according to Locke, may be said of moral relations. Though he expresses himself very indistinctly, his notion seems to be that in moral questions we are reasoning about certain things of which we know 'the precise real essence,' because they are entirely 'ideas in the mind.'[15] Thus, for example, we might compare our idea of justice with our idea of stealing, and observe that they did not correspond; whence the truth that stealing is unjust may be proved with the same certainty as the truth that three angles of a triangle are equal to two right angles. The obvious difficulty is, that this doctrine seems to make morality certain in the sense in which a verbal proposition is certain, and in that sense alone. We are merely unfolding our definition, or explaining that what we call just does not include what we call stealing. This remark was made by Berkeley. 'To demonstrate morality,' he says, in his commonplace book, 'it seems one need only make a discovery of words and see which included which. . . . Locke's instances of demonstration in morality are, according to his own rule, trifling propositions.'[16] Locke, it is clear, never distinctly realised his own position, and whatever escape he might have attempted, it is plain that no such process as he contemplates could be reconciled with his general utilitarianism. The certainty which he would attain is not a certainty as to the tendency of actions to produce happiness. Any such theory must involve an objective element, and, on Locke's general theory, cannot be part of scientifical knowledge. Here, as in the whole philosophy of which it forms a part, Locke's teaching is papably inconsistent, and the attempt to deduce a coherent doctrine would be waste of labour.

92. Berkeley's moral theory is not sufficiently prominent to require

[15]Locke's Essay, book iii. ch. xi. secs. 16 and 17.
[16]Berkeley, Works, iv. 449.

investigation. The next great theorist of Locke's school was Hume, and Hume preferred his moral treatise to all his other writings. The reason for this preference, so far as one ever can discover an author's motives for self-judgment, will be tolerably plain. Here, we may say, Hume has, at least, some excuse for saying that he has obtained a definite constructive result. When Hume gave a second version of his metaphysics and psychology in the Essays, he mangled the earlier 'Treatise of Human Nature' with singular want of parental affection. Part is rewritten, and much is altogether omitted. The later version of his ethics contained in the 'Enquiry' bears a different relation to the ethics of the treatise. All the essential principles reappear, though some points are more lightly touched; but they reappear in a substantially new exposition. The literary texture of the 'Enquiry' shows everywhere the magic touch of Hume's lucid intellect. Morality, perplexed or mysterious with most of his predecessors, becomes admirably simple. All the doctrines fall into their place spontaneously. One obvious principle solves all doubts. The very lucidity may appear suspicious to many thinkers; but all must admit that the essential doctrines of utilitarianism are stated by Hume with a clearness and consistency not to be found in any other writer of the century. From Hume to J. S. Mill, the doctrine received no substantial alteration. It was Hume's aim to state the principles of morality in such a way as to bring it entirely within the domain of science. Granting the truth of his theories, he succeeded admirably. 'The only object of reasoning,' he says (that is, of ethical reasoning), 'is to discover the circumstances on both sides which are common to these' (the estimable or blamable) 'qualities, to observe that particular in which the estimable qualities agree on the one hand, and the blamable on the other; and thence to reach the foundation of ethics, and find those universal principles from which all censure or approbation is ultimately derived. As this is a question of fact, not of abstract science, we can only expect success by following the experimental method, and deducing general maxims from a comparison of particular instances.'[17] The science of morality, then, is to be based on experience. Hume succeeded so far as he definitely and systematically admitted this appeal. He failed in so far as, from his standing-point, it was impossible to form an adequate conception of the method by which the appeal should be made.

93. This method of approaching the problem implies the dismissal of all ontological and teleological speculation. Clarke's method of deducing morality from the intuitions of pure reason must be abandoned along

---

[17] Hume's Works, iv. 174.

with Butler's method of discovering morality by divining the purposes of the Creator. Hume's objections to the first method are radical.[18] Reason by itself cannot prompt us to act. It can make us aware that an object which excites our passions does or does not exist, or it can show that the means by which we would gratify our passions are or are not adequate. But it is not by itself a motive. ' 'Tis not contrary to reason,' he says, 'to prefer the destruction of the whole world to the scratching of my finger. 'Tis not contrary to reason for me to choose my total ruin to prevent the least uneasiness of an Indian or person totally unknown to me.'[19] Strictly speaking, there is no such thing as a combat between reason and passion. 'Reason is and ought only to be the slave of the passions, and can never pretend to any other office than to serve and obey them.'[20] The phraseology is wantonly paradoxical in sound, because in his early treatise Hume aimed at being paradoxical. But it expresses the view which would be taken in sober seriousness by all scientific reasoners. The reason is the faculty which enables us to frame a mental picture of the world corresponding to the external reality. It would show that the total suffering caused by the destruction of the world was greater than the suffering caused by scratching my finger. But unless I were benevolent enough to feel for others, the bare fact would not impel me to scratch my finger to save the world, any more than the knowledge that a guinea was worth one-and-twenty shillings would make me prefer a guinea to a shilling if I had no love of money. If I were malevolent instead of benevolent, it might have the contrary effect. Hence all the reasonings of Clarke's school about the eternal and inherent essences of things are thrown away. If sound, they might reveal to us certain truths, but the mode in which those truths affected us would still be a question of experience. These moralists fill the gap in their system, as Hume points out,[21] by suddenly substituting for the copula 'is' or 'is not' the copula 'ought' or 'ought not.' The reason may regulate and guide the passions by enabling us to compare their objects. It cannot supply the place of the passions.

94. The distinction thus drawn between the reason and the passions raises the most difficult of psychological problems. The connection between the emotions and the intellect is indefinitely intricate. Every mental process has its emotional and its intellectual element.[22] It is impossi-

---

[18]'Treatise of Human Nature,' book ii. part iii. sec. 3; book iii. part iii. sec. 1; appendix i. to 'Enquiry.'   [19]Works, ii. 195.

[20]Ib. ii. 195.   [21]Ib. 245.

[22]Hume partly recognises the truth in the section 'Malice and Envy' of the Treatise, ii. 159.

ble, therefore, to describe the fully developed structure of the mind without taking into account a whole series of complex actions and reactions between the two factors. And, for this reason, Hume's psychology set forth in the second book of the Treatise, is the least satisfactory part of his work, as it was that which was most ruthlessly cut down in the Essays. Only a mangled remnant reappears as the brief 'Treatise on the Passions,' and ends abruptly with a half apology. Hume's attempt, indeed, was hopeless. The older philosophy had resolved feelings into beliefs. The passion, pride, for example, was identified with the conviction 'I am better than my neighbours.' Hume at once accepts a classification founded on this conception, and tries to get rid of the intellectual element implied. The attempt is contradictory. Pride, if pride be an elementary passion, must imply, at least, the intellectual processes necessary to frame some consciousness of myself and neighbours. Hume's effort to evade this conclusion is, at best, a display of wasted ingenuity. Human nature is compounded of too many elements, too intricately blended, for any offhand guesses of the cleverest philosopher to be of much value.

95. But the fact that Hume was not, and could not be, a scientific psychologist, does not destroy the value of his critical assault upon the ontologists. To confute the school of Clarke, little more was required than to show that ethics was not a branch of pure mathematics; for the truth and reality which they ascribed to morality were, on their showing, to be found in the mathematical world alone. Hume's criticism has a wider application. Morality, he says, in substance, cannot be deduced from absolute *a priori* truths, for it includes an empirical element. This follows from the fact that, if two men (or two races) shared the same intellectual convictions, the actions which resulted would vary according to their emotional compositions. The same truths which to the angelical nature would supply a motive for doing good, would supply to the diabolical nature a motive for doing evil. Hume, for this reason, compares the moral aspects of an action to the 'secondary' qualities.[23] An action is seen as coloured by our emotions as the external world is known, and can only be known, as it affects our senses. From the point of view of the earlier philosophy, this was to admit the unreality of vice and virtue, or, in a different phraseology, it would prove vice and virtue to be 'subjective.'

96. Hume's view of the passions as entirely independent of the intellect, and associated with certain objects by a tie in some sense arbi-

[23]Hume's Works, ii. 245.

trary, as indeed every causal tie is with Hume arbitrary, might seem to sanction this conclusion. If our likes and dislikes might be indefinitely altered or inverted, there could be no science of human conduct. In fact, however, Hume's aim is precisely to discover such a science, but to prove simultaneously that it must be a science of observation. The passions, he says, form a 'regular mechanism,' which is as susceptible of scientific investigation as any branch of natural philosophy.[24] Thus his argument virtually comes to the statement that a scientific morality would imply a psychology, and that psychology must be based upon experience alone. The relation is the same as that between sanitary and physiological science. The laws of moral as of physical health depend upon the structure of the organism, and the nature of that structure is only discoverable through the ordinary methods of scientific investigation. In this sense morality must include an empirical element, unless it be maintained that an *a priori* deduction of psychology is possible. The assumption of the possibility, to say nothing of the actual performance of such a deduction, depends upon the resolution of the passions into intellectual perceptions. If the passions are in some sense reason, there is some plausibility in attempting to frame an *a priori* scheme of psychological truths parallel to the so-called *a priori* scheme of mathematical truths. In that case, again, and in that case alone, morality would be in a sense capable of *a priori* deduction. We could not, indeed, even in that case, justify the identification of virtue and vice with truth and falsehood, or reason and error, implied in Clarke's substitution of 'ought' for 'is,' for that would be to show that bad actions were impossible as well as unusual, or to identify moral with scientific laws. But we might show that certain actions had always certain qualities or tendencies, which justified the moral distinction. That is to say, we might find an *a priori* justification for the utilitarian or 'moral sense' theories.

97. Meanwhile Hume is justified in declaring that morality must be based on experience if psychology be based on experience. We should amend his statement by adding that a complete science of morality would imply a science of sociology as well as of psychology, and requires a wider and more systematic interrogation of experience than he had fully contemplated. There must be not only an empirical, but a variable, element in morality; and this is enough to condemn the hypothesis of Clarke. A scheme of morality deduced from self-evident and necessary truths must produce a code as rigid as its fundamental axioms, and, therefore, incapable of varying with the development of the race.

[24]Last sentence of 'Treatise on the Passions.'

Morality, on the other hand, includes in its primary data an element which varies, though, of course, varies according to definite laws. It must, therefore, give rules varying as the subject-matter varies; just as sanitary science gives one set of rules for men and another for beasts, and prescribes different conduct to a negro and a European. Hume did not fully appreciate this view, because, accepting from the ontologists the doctrine that human nature is always the same, he contemplated only a variation of external circumstances. As he, like all his contemporaries, failed to make allowance for the slow evolution of new social and intellectual conditions, the observed inconsistencies of the ethical code seemed to imply an almost indefinite variability of the moral sense.

98. If this be the true view of the relation between ethics on the one hand, and the sciences of psychology and sociology on the other, and if again, as is perfectly clear, no scientific psychology or sociology existed (even if they now exist) till long after the foundation of morality, one of two results must follow. Either the moral law is revealed by an instinct or inspired faculty, which can act independently of reason, or morality must be an empirical science; that is to say, it must have been discovered like other truths—by a series of experiments. As sanitary rules preceded physiology, ethical rules have preceded psychology. Was the moral law known by revelation, or by a special faculty, or was it explicable by some admitted and normal faculties of human nature? Hume's object is to answer this question by showing the possibility of the last alternative. The ground was already prepared. Hutcheson, with whom Hume corresponded, had accepted the utilitarian criterion of morality, and he has been in great measure anticipated by Cumberland, who expounded this view, as against Hobbes, in 1672. The one necessary step was to get rid of the teleological view, and to represent this tendency to produce happiness, not as a case of preordained harmony, but as a simple case of cause and effect. Those actions are good, said Hume, which are useful, and are good because and in so far as they are useful, not useful because they are good. The inversion was very simple, but so fruitful as to justify the complacency with which Hume concludes the enquiry. His doctrine seems to him so obvious, that it must have been long ago accepted, were there not some hidden objection to it. It explains the various puzzles which had led some to reject morality, and others to regard it as a mystery. Locke and Mandeville, for example, had insisted upon the variability of the moral standard in different ages and countries. Locke cuts the knot by introducing the divine law; Mandeville accepts the conclusion that the taste for chastity

is as arbitrary as the taste for big buttons. Hume considers the same problem in the Dialogue which follows the 'Enquiry.' After pointing out with ingenious exaggeration the difference between the standard accepted in ancient Greece, in France, and in England, he asks how any fixed standard is discoverable? The answer is simple. 'By tracing matters a little higher, and examining the first principles which each nation establishes of blame and censure. The Rhine flows north, the Rhône south, yet both spring from the *same* mountain, and are also actuated in their opposite directions by the *same* principle of gravity.'[25] Utility is the moral force of gravitation. Qualities are admired as useful or agreeable. The many qualities admired by Greeks and Frenchmen were admired because useful both in Athens and Paris: the qualities approved by one nation and condemned by the other were differently judged, because the different circumstances of distant regions and periods made qualities valuable in one country which were prejudicial in the other. The military virtues are more admired because more essential in times of disorder than in times of peace; and customs, such as those which determine the relations between the sexes, will lead to corresponding varieties of moral sentiment.

99. The 'Enquiry' is devoted to an analysis of the moral qualities, with the object of showing that, in every case, approbation follows the useful or the agreeable qualities—the meaning of 'useful' and 'agreeable,' it must be noticed, being assumed instead of defined. Happiness ceases to be the reward of virtue, except in the sense in which the end is the reward of the means. The mysterious element vanishes. With Adam Smith our respect for wealth is a divinely implanted instinct; with Hume it is the natural effect of association and sympathy.[26] So, with Butler, resentment is a 'weapon put into our hands by nature against injury, injustice, and cruelty,' and justified because human nature, 'considered as the divine workmanship, should be considered sacred; for in the image of God made he man.'[27] With Hume, resentment would be simply a form of self-love, justified so far as conducive to happiness. Butler tells us that nature has caused us to disapprove falsehood, injustice, and cruelty more distinctly than folly and imprudence, because the punishment follows the fault more obviously in the latter case, and therefore additional punishment would be superfluous.[28] Hume would transfer the reason from 'nature' to man. Superfluous suffering being an evil, superfluous punishment is necessarily

[25]Hume's Works, iv. 297.   [27]Sermon viii.
[26]Ib. iv. 228.   [28]'Dissertation on Nature of Virtue.'

immoral. This change in the point of view is equivalent to that which takes place in science when the fins of a fish are regarded as developed by the conditions of life, instead of proofs of intelligent design. Their utility is equally obvious to all observers. The interpretation may be teleological or scientific.

100. The explanation given by Hume may be admitted in the case of the qualities immediately profitable to the individual; but how does it come to pass that we admire qualities, such as justice, which are profitable to our neighbours? It seems natural that we should be grateful to the benefactor who has supplied our wants; but why do we respect the judge who may punish our faults? The difference corresponds to a distinction which occupies a prominent place in the third book of the Treatise between the 'natural' and the 'artificial' virtues. Hume argues, in sufficient correspondence with modern methods of enquiry, that the artificial virtues, of which justice is the great type, take their origin in the gradual development of society, which is not, as earlier writers had supposed, based upon a contract, but which gradually generates a common understanding which may be compared to a contract. Men feel the necessity of living in society, common rules are essential to the social life, and their real or supposed utility is in all cases the cause of their adoption. The necessity of having some rule induces lawyers to catch at the most superficial analogies in order to justify particular modes of distributing property,[29] and these analogies are then represented as implying some metaphysical reason; but in all cases the ultimate ground of justice is simply the convenience of the society. The reasonings, again, by which we may prove the utility of certain arrangements, may appear to be too complex to have actually operated upon mankind; but they are worked out by the experience of the race. 'Speculative reasonings,' he says, in speaking of the theories of chastity, 'which cost so much pains to philosophers, are often formed by the world naturally and without reflection,'[30] and he proceeds to show how in this case a public opinion has been formed by the sense of immediate utility in persons directly interested. Though his doctrine, in short, is imperfect, Hume has a general conception of the method by which general rules may be blindly worked out through the conflict of opposing passions and the co-operation of common interests. Men, forced to live together, under fixed conditions, with limited means, have framed certain conventions under the mingled influences of sympathy and selfishness.[31]

101. The distinction of virtues into 'natural' and 'artificial' was cal-

[29]Works, ii. 279.   [30]See Treatise, part ii. sec. 2; ii. 258, &c.   [31]Ib. p. 332.

culated to give offence, as perhaps it was meant to excite attention, by the apparent implication that 'artificial' virtues were in some sense unreal. Hume, however, is careful to state distinctly that 'artificial' does not mean 'arbitrary.'[32] The laws of justice may even be called 'laws of nature,' meaning that they result from the qualities belonging to the species. 'Natural,' as he says in the 'Enquiry,' is taken in so many meanings that its application to justice may or may not be proper. 'If self-love, if benevolence, be natural to man; if reason and forethought be also natural, then may the same epithet be applied to justice, order, fidelity, property, society.'[33] His meaning is, in short, that these virtues are derivative, not primary; that they result from the operation of certain primary instincts working under given conditions; and are therefore as natural a product as any other qualities, though not due to the immediate teaching of a supernatural instinct or derivable from *a priori* reasoning.

102. The doctrine thus stated contains the germs of all later moral speculation which acknowledges the derivative character of morality. It expresses as accurately as the state of enquiry would admit the mode in which we must suppose the moral standard to have been actually formed. Moreover, it contains statements which, when their bearing is fully considered, may serve to correct some characteristic failings of the earlier utilitarians. If the process of building up a moral sense be such as Hume has indicated, it is obvious that instincts, for which it is difficult to assign any tangible reason, may yet deserve the highest respect. Men in past times felt the advantage of certain rules before they could prove their utility. That body of traditional prejudice or instinctive sentiment which is still the sole guide for most men should be treated with respect by philosophers as being, possibly at least, reason in the making. It represents a mass of inherited experience, which may, it is true, correspond to extinct needs, but which may also represent permanent and valuable truths. Utilitarians who were anxious to obtain a definite and tangible test generally treated such sentiment with simple contempt, especially if allied with the old theology. Hume, as we have seen, admits the value of rules which are designed for the protection of chastity, and explains how the experience of the race has felt out truths which a speculative philosopher could hardly have discovered by meditation. And yet Hume, like most of his contemporaries, speaks rather slightingly of the virtue, partly from undervaluing the importance of this very process, and partly because theologians had connected the doc-

[32]Treatise, ii. 258.   [33]See Ib. iv. 275.

trine of chastity with a narrow asceticism. A more curious, though less important, case is considered in the remarkable posthumous Essay on Suicide. Hume shows, with his usual acuteness, the futility of the reasoning by which it is generally condemned, and having exploded the theological objections, shows easily that suicide may frequently produce a balance of happiness. Why, then, should life be preserved when life means hopeless agony? This is one of the points upon which it is probable that some revision of existing morality is desirable. But a competent enquirer at the present day would see a class of difficulties which Hume ignores. He would have to trace out the true philosophy of the modern aversion to suicide, and to discover whether it is rooted in some exploded theological doctrine, or whether it may not be closely connected with sentiments of the sanctity of life with which it is dangerous to tamper. For the direct application of the test of utility he would have to substitute a more refined method of enquiry, recognising the principle of the complex correlations between the growth of particular sentiments, the social order, and the intellectual conceptions of the race. In other words, utilitarian calculations of the good and evil produced to the individual or to his neighbours would have to be supplemented by a careful consideration of the laws of growth of the social organism.

103. The full meaning of this criticism will appear more fully in considering a further characteristic of Hume's moral system. It is often said, as against utilitarians, that the happiness of which they speak is too vague a term to supply a sufficient criterion of morality. To this it may be replied that the moralists who argue—and what moralists do not argue?—that virtue produces happiness must understand the term distinctly enough to allow some meaning to the definition that actions which produce happiness are virtuous. It may be replied, again, that, whatever latitude is allowed to the word, the great moral rules may all be established by this mode of reasoning. Nobody can doubt that justice, benevolence, and temperance do in fact make the race happier in any admissible sense of happiness. The utilitarian, indeed, is forced to start from the postulate that there is a certain agreement as to what constitutes happiness in any society which has a common moral code. If so fundamental a difference existed that the pleasures of half the race were the pains of the other, there would be a moral anarchy, and one half would be sooner or later converted or extirpated. But the criticism points to a real difficulty. According to the ordinary assumption of the utilitarian, conduct can only be compared in respect of the happiness which it produces. Equal 'lots' of pleasure (in Bentham's phrase) are equally

desirable from whatever source they spring. Intellectual and sensual pleasures, the pleasures of love or of hatred, are to be counted as equal if equally intense. We are to measure the quantity, not the quality, of pleasure in forming our criterion. This doctrine is implicitly accepted by Hume, and colours his moral doctrine. The conscience, supreme with Butler, is with him no distinct faculty at all. The moral sense of which he speaks appears in the 'Enquiry' to be identified by humanity or sympathy.[34] In an appendix, 'On some Verbal Disputes,' he treats the distinction between the virtues and the talents as trifling or illusory. Why, he asks, should we discriminate between the social virtues and such endowments as 'sense and courage, temperance and industry, wisdom and knowledge'?[35] The corresponding sentiment may be 'somewhat different,' but not different enough to justify a different classification. He approves 'the definition of the elegant and judicious poet'—[36]

> Virtue (for mere goodnature is a fool)
> Is sense and spirit with humanity—

and he significantly ascribes the origin of the distinction to the connection between ethics and theology, which has warped reason and even language from its natural course, and by seizing the false analogy between civil and moral laws, has made the whole system turn on the unphilosophical and irrelevant distinction between voluntary and involuntary.[37]

104. The absence of that deep feeling which Butler associates with the word conscience; the want of sympathy with the emotions of remorse, and of that peculiar horror of sin which expresses itself in Christian morality, renders Hume's teaching greatly inferior to Butler's in practical force, far superior as it is in philosophical coherence. This superficiality of sentiment is to be traced partly to Hume's personal temperament, inclined to a quiet philosophical scepticism, and apt to look with indifference upon the more passionate emotions of imaginative minds, and illustrated in another direction by his preference of Racine to Shakespeare; and partly to the general temper of the age, and especially of the freethinkers of the age. The revolt from theology had blinded men to the deeper meanings veiled in theological teaching; and led to a contemptuous estimate of the great moving forces which had uttered themselves in theological language as mere fanaticism, 'enthusiasm,' and

---

[34]Hume's Works, iv. 219.   [36]Armstrong, 'The Art of Preserving Health.'
[35]Ib. 282.   [37]Hume, iv. 287.

superstition. But the tendency is also logically connected with Hume's philosophical position.

105. How, in fact, are we to frame our moral calculus? How are we to estimate the tendency of any action on happiness or unhappiness? Since we have no divine faculty to pronounce one kind of happiness to be better than another, let us assume all to be equal. In the same way, let us assume that, as Bentham says, each man is to count for one, and no man for two. Unless our units are assumed to be equal, we obviously cannot count to any purpose. But, however convenient the assumption, we may ask how it can be justified on empirical principles, and whether it does not lead us to practical difficulties? Why should the happiness of a Goethe or a Shakespeare be considered as of equal value with the happiness of a pickpocket? If all men's happiness is to be of equal value, does it not follow that we must accept the standard of the lowest, because the most numerous, class, and endeavour to promote those pleasures which they most appreciate? One man prefers art to gin; a thousand prefer gin to art. Why is the intellectual to be preferred to the sensual gratification? Because, it has been said, those who can appreciate both generally or always prefer the intellectual. But may that not imply merely that the power of gratifying the palate is lost as the power of gratifying the mental faculties increases? Can we obtain a sufficiently secure standing-point for asserting the value of the purest and what are generally called the highest pleasures? So long as we start simply from observation of the individual mind, and allow each testimony to be of equal value, there seems to be no sufficient escape from these difficulties. What is called morality becomes simply the judgment of the average mind as to the relative value of its pleasures. There must always be a tendency in thinkers of this class to regard the heroic few as fools, and men of lofty moral aspirations as mere dreamers.

106. The difficulty, indeed, is not so fatal as has been sometimes asserted. Human nature is so far uniform, and therefore, estimates of happiness so far alike, that we can deduce the ordinary rules of morality without much practical difficulty. The great moral commonplaces hold good upon any assumption; and in morality we have not got far beyond commonplace. It must be admitted, however, that this uncertainty as to the meaning of the fundamental conception leaves an apparently arbitrary assumption at the very base of the proposed science; and, moreover, tends to lower the resulting type of morality. In the proposed calculation, the most tangible pleasures are likely to be rated above their value, and the standard of happiness prevalent amongst the majority

of the race will be taken as determining the standard of morality. Morality becomes the art by which men obtain the greatest amount of gratification without attending to its quality.

107. How, then, are we to escape this uncertainty without attempting the impracticable task of an *a priori* deduction of morality? To give a satisfactory reply would be to indicate the true weakness, not only of Hume, but of his most distinguished disciples. A scientific morality, as I have said, would imply not only a psychology, but a sociology. To understand the conditions of human welfare, we must understand the laws of growth and equilibrium, both of the individual and the race. We must acquire a conception of society as a complex organism, not a mere aggregate of individuals in arbitrary or indefinitely variable combination; and, therefore, regulated and developed by processes not discoverable by simple inspection of the constituent atoms. If the laws which express those processes could be accurately stated, we should have, if not an actual moral code, the necessary basis for a moral code. Morality, according to the analogy already suggested, is to sociology what a sanitary code is to physiology; and the analogy may help us a step further. It must be defined as the art of attaining social health, not as the art of attaining the maximum of happiness, although we may admit that the two ends are ultimately identical. But is it not as necessary to have a definition of health in this case as of happiness in the other? The answer is suggested by the analogy. A physician does not start from defining health, but he aims at discovering the laws in virtue of which an organism preserves its equilibrium, and develops the greatest amount of strength, activity, and sensibility. He assumes that such an organism will enjoy greater happiness than one which does not conform to the rules laid down. If, instead of pursuing this method, he had made the attainment of pleasure at once the ultimate and immediate end, he would have arrived at different conclusions. The man, he would have said, is the happiest who gets the greatest amount of pleasures from his palate, his senses of hearing, touching, and so forth. But how from such a test could he deduce the right rule of life? How could he determine whether the ear was a worthier organ than the eye, or what amount of energy should be devoted to each mode of gratification? Some obvious rules of temperance or the like might be discovered; but he would be obviously in want of some method for bringing the conflicting series of observations into unity, and, so to speak, gathering the various indications to a focus. That want is supplied by the laws of organic unity. The ultimate criterion is the tendency of a given rule of life to maintain the organism in the highest degree of vigour. The

various modes of enjoyment are correlated by the tendency to preserve or destroy the equilibrium of the body; and a precisely analogous place is filled in ethical speculation by the study of the social organism.

108. A scientific sociology would bring the various estimates of happiness to a single focus. An individual may prefer sensual to intellectual gratification, but if it were proved that a rule which encouraged sensuality at the expense of the intellect tended to the decay of the social body, that it lowered its vitality, destroyed its equilibrium, and ultimately diminished even its powers of sensual gratification, he must either admit that the rule was a bad one, or declare that he preferred his own taste to the welfare of society. The existence of a certain social passion is undoubtedly necessary for the existence of society or of morality; but if its existence be once assumed, the moral question might be brought by sociology to a single test. Such and such rules tend, it would be shown, to the permanent vitality of society; everybody, then, must approve them who wishes well to society. This is the ultimate postulate of derivative morality, and one with which it is impossible to dispense. But if sociology were once constituted, it would supply a single and decisive test instead of the vague and complex calculus suggested by the cruder forms of utilitarianism, or what is called the greatest happiness principle.

109. Now, as we have already seen in speaking of Hume's philosophy, and as we shall hereafter see in treating of his political speculations, this conception of a social organism was just what was wanting to him. His scepticism reduced society to a mass of atoms, capable of being cast into any mould, and producing any set of results. A crude empiricism replaced a true experiential philosophy. Any cause might be joined to any effect; and, therefore, the tendency of actions to produce happiness, or, as he vaguely says, the fact that they are 'useful' or 'agreeable'— words never defined nor distinguished—could not be scientifically estimated. We must know how the organs are combined into a whole, as well as observe what amount of pleasure they produce; and the combination seemed to Hume to be more or less arbitrary. The expression of his theories in terms of social philosophy is individualism, and no scientific views can be reached when all methods of observation start from the individual, instead of taking into account the whole of which he forms a constituent part. One of the most important, for example, of moral questions is that which concerns the relations of the sexes; and a marked peculiarity of the school descended from Hume is its tendency to tamper with the moral code by which those relations are regulated. The case is significant in many ways. The only method by which the utilitarian can approach the subject is by endeavouring to reckon the

good and evil produced in individual cases. Here the indelibility of the
marriage law inflicts a hardship; there it prevents a cruelty. We must
strike an average as best we may of the good and ill effects, and condemn or approve the law accordingly. The old theological sanction implies a superstitious view, and may, therefore, be set aside altogether.
Every law inflicts some evil, because it forbids some gratification, and
therefore the presumption is always against law.[38] The scientific sociologist would have to take into account a series of observations to which
the utilitarian is apt to be altogether blind. He would observe, perhaps,
that the family is the primary germ of all society; that, in proportion as
its sanctity has been maintained, society has been in a healthy and
vigorous condition; that men in all ages have felt the necessity of
regulating the strongest instinct of our nature, so as to bring it upon
the side of the social, instead of the anti-social, tendencies; that the
theological sanction, however superstitious in form, is the expression of
the experience of many ages, blindly feeling its way to promote the
welfare of the race, and preserving those races in which it has been
allowed to operate with sufficient strength; that, therefore, the presumption is in favour of the social regulations in which it is embodied, however its form may be obsolete; and thus, that if any remedy is required
for existing grievances, it should be applied tentatively and cautiously.
A full understanding, in short, of the functions discharged by the family
in the social organisation would probably reveal many ulterior and
vitally important consequences of any change in its constitution to
which the rough calculations of the utilitarian are necessarily insensible. We are not at present, if we ever shall be, scientific sociologists, but
the bare recognition of the possibility of such a science, the knowledge
that there are laws, if only we could discover them, implies the application of a method of enquiry totally different from that which suggests
itself to a crude utilitarian.

110. Finally, we may remark that the same imperfection explains
Hume's inadequate appreciation of the true value of the great moral
forces. The conscience had always been associated with a belief in supernatural penalties. Those penalties had become incredible. Therefore, the
instincts called conscience had no real significance. A real historical
sense, which is but another side of a true conception of sociology, would
have suggested to him a more adequate measure of feelings, which have
played so vast a part in the development of the human race, even if he

---

[38]I shall remark hereafter how these principles were marked out by Godwin
—a distinguished disciple of Hume's philosophy.

had not personally sympathised with them. But Hume, like other philosophers of his time, was content to class the Puritan creed as 'enthusiastic,' and the Catholic as 'superstitious;' and, seeing the weakness of these beliefs, to infer, very illogically, the nullity of their positions. This inadequate view of history, or, in other words, of the unity and continuity of the race, is thus the main source of Hume's defects as a moralist, as well as of other shortcomings.

111. One side of Hume's theory remains to be considered, and it is of vital importance to the later history of moral speculation. How is morality to be preserved? What are the motives upon which we must ultimately rely to secure observance of the moral law, whatever its criterion or the faculty which discovers it? A moral law, supernaturally revealed and enforced by supernatural sanctions, may be enforced upon beings corrupt by nature. But if the law be derived from man as well as imposed upon man, it must reflect the qualities of the legislator. To anyone, then, who, like Hume, declines to look outside the visible universe for the explanation of any phenomena, it follows that the ultimate source of the virtuous affections must be discovered in the human heart. The theological dogmas, regarded by divines as imposed from without, can only be the modes by which the human intellect in its earlier stages interpreted its own aspirations to itself. Hume, therefore, agrees to some extent with Shaftesbury, in restoring the nobler element which theologians had banished from our nature. Man, according to Hume, has made God after his own image, and whatever appears in the divine ideal must be a reflection from the intellect which framed it.

112. It is, therefore, an essential part of Hume's theory to demonstrate the reality of the altruistic sentiments. A scientific method must admit the existence of feelings recognised by consciousness. We admire, so his argument runs, conduct which is useful. 'But *useful?* For what? For somebody's interest, surely. Whose interest, then? Not our own only; for our approbation frequently extends further. It must, therefore, be the interest of those who are served by the character or action approved of; and these, we may conclude, however remote, are not totally indifferent to us.'[39] Powerful as is the passion of self-love, it is easy to discover instances which are not resolvable into it; for moral approbation survives where our private interests are separable from, or even opposed to, the public interests. Sympathy, in short, is natural. Nobody would tread with equal indifference upon the pavement and upon the gouty toes of a man with whom he had no quarrel.[40] And,

[39]Hume's Works, iv. 206.   [40]Ib. p. 212.

however weak the sympathy is supposed, it is enough to prove the case. Once grant that a man is not purely selfish, and experience alone can prove how strong may be the unselfish element of our nature. The fact that it exists sufficiently upsets the antecedent metaphysical objections. These objections are considered in an appendix specially devoted to the subject. Hume argues that, even if true in a sense, they are irrelevant. Should a 'philosophical chemistry' be capable of resolving all passions into modifications of self-love, the distinction between self-love in its primitive state as regard to our own interests and its modified state as regard for the interests of others, is still of vital importance. The colour of a countenance would not be less beautiful though we should discover it to be produced by minute variations in the thickness of the skin.[41] The analysis, however, cannot be easily admitted. The explanation which admits the elementary character of benevolence is the simplest and probably the truest. Though we often conceal from ourselves the true nature of our motives, it is not because our motives are abstruse; nor is it easy to resolve the affections of animals into 'refined deductions of self-interest,'[42] and to suppose the maternal tenderness traceable through all orders of sensible beings to be self-love in disguise. Finally, in an argument borrowed from Butler, Hume tries to show that every appetite must exist antecedently to its gratification, and that self-love thus implies the existence of other passions, amongst which we may recognise benevolence, as naturally as thirst or hunger.

113. Whatever the force of this reasoning, it must be admitted that there is a great appearance of logic in a different conclusion. The doctrine that each man can only care for his own happiness is terribly plausible, and fits in admirably with individualism. If men have been moulded by their social relations, they should have impulses explicable only by reference to social conditions. If men are fully intelligible as isolated individuals, and this assumption seems to be in accordance with the general tenor of Hume's philosophy, such impulses must appear to be unaccountable. If society, in other words, is a mere aggregate of independent units, and not an organic compound of related units, altruistic emotions are superfluous. Hume, indeed, escapes by appealing to experience; and experience—we may fully agree—amply justifies him. But then it seems necessary to admit the truth of his theory that anything may cause anything, and therefore to accept as an infallible fact what could hardly be anticipated from his general principles; or, perhaps, we may admit that Hume had an indistinct view of results which

[41]Hume's Works, iv. 268.　　[42]Ib. iv. 270.

he could not explicitly formulate. Meanwhile, it was easier for most thinkers of his school to accept the explanation which he rejected, and to assume that altruism was merely self-love disguised. This indeed may be regarded as an early form of the explanation which we may probably regard as the soundest—namely, that the altruistic feelings are developed out of self-regarding feelings, though they have come to be something radically different. So long, however, as the development is supposed to take place in each individual, and an hereditary predisposition is tacitly denied, the doctrine tends to lapse into a more or less undisguised selfishness. In Mandeville it had appeared in the coarsest shape, as he denied that virtue is anything but a pretence. In later writers of the Benthamite school, the difficulty is more or less skilfully surmounted; but they generally show a reluctance, as did Bentham himself, to admit the possibility of a perfectly disinterested motive.

114. This tendency comes out in a different shape in another school of writers, which may probably be regarded as the dominant school of the century. Theological doctrine may be interpreted as purely selfish, though writers of more or less mystic tendency try to free it from the imputation. When the animating principle of the moral law is regarded as the will of a supernatural being, and that being is fashioned after the likeness of man, the penalties of disobeying the law become exaggerated to infinite proportions. Hell must be made more terrible the further it is removed from sensible perception; and the penalties and rewards become so tremendous, that, if they could be fully realised, selfishness would be inevitable. The fate of his own soul becomes of such importance to each man that he would be mad to care for anything else. What can it profit him if he confers any benefit upon others and loses himself? If man is corrupt by nature, the ultimate sanction which keeps him in order must be sheer terror of Almighty vengeance. As theology decayed, the tendency of the largest class was, as we have seen at length, to remove the miraculous from the present, and to leave it in the past. The sense of facts was too strong to admit of any belief in supernatural agency in the eighteenth century; but, if the desire for logical unity was weak, it would still be allowed to find a refuge in the first century. In moral speculation the same tendency exhibited itself in the admission that men's conduct must be regulated by ordinary prudence, but with a retention of the fear of hell as a sufficient motive to clench moral doubts. There was nothing, it was plain, supernatural about our immediate motives, but a supernatural object in the extreme distance might be allowed to have an occasional influence. In ninety-nine of a hundred actions men might be guided by common sense,

exerted upon obvious considerations; but, if in the hundredth a man was tempted to step beyond the line, or if he insisted upon raising some remote question as to ultimate grounds of action, it was convenient to have a hell in the background. How the existence of hell could be proved consistently with the ordinary philosophy was one of those awkward questions which concerned only philosophers, and in regard to which the ordinary philosopher was apt to reply by sending a man back to common sense. This kind of theological utilitarianism was specially prevalent during the last half of the century, and we must notice one or two of the principal writers.

115. Less philosophical, it was a more convenient compromise between the old and the new. The orthodox teachers protested against all attempts to found theism or morality upon unassisted reasoning. Human ignorance, according to them, made it necessary that God should be made known to man by supernatural intervention, and human corruption that his law should be enforced upon them by supernatural sanctions. As the evidences became more prominent in theological, so hell became of more importance in their ethical, speculations. And hence arose a coarse form of morality which, however, suited the temper of the age. Waterland, whose views upon the evidences of Christianity have already been noticed, may stand equally for a representative specimen of the Christian system of morality as Christianity was then understood. In a pamphlet which gave rise to a bitter controversy, he attacked Clarke's 'Exposition of the Catechism.' His wrath was aroused partly by certain symptoms of incipient Arianism in his adversary, but still more by a distinction drawn by Clarke between moral and positive duties. The distinction had been put into an epigrammatic form in Tillotson's assertion that a man had better never take the sacrament in his life than kill people for not taking it. In opposition to this doctrine, Waterland points out, with considerable logical vigour, that the distinction between moral and positive has been confounded by his adversaries with the distinction between external and internal. It is needless to follow him into the intricacies of the argument. Shortly stated, it is his view that all duties, whether moral or positive, are binding because they are imposed by God. Duty means simply obedience to a divine law, and it is not for us to enquire into the reasons for the commands given by the supreme authority. Obedience to a positive command may sometimes acquire greater value than obedience to a moral law; as is proved by his favourite case of Abraham's sacrifice of Isaac—a deed which, as he

assumes, has rendered its doer 'more famous both in heaven and on earth than all his moral virtues put together.'[43]

116. Waterland is a utilitarian so far as regards the criterion of morality, and he lays it down as a principle that we are to test the relative importance of divine commands, not by asking which is moral and which is positive, but by asking what depends upon our conscientious obedience to them; or, in other words, which is most conducive to the general good.[44] He is thus conducted to a definition of virtue substantially identical with the well-known dogma of Paley. 'Moral goodness,' he says, 'is choosing and performing those beneficial actions upon a principle of obedience and out of love to God.'[45] It is thus essential to a virtuous action that it should be performed not only from love of God, but from the love of the God revealed in the Bible. Accepting fully the orthodox dogma of the intrinsic vileness of all human actions, he speaks with the utmost contempt of all the pagan virtues. The good deeds of the heathen, like the good deeds of the brutes, are 'materially,' not 'formally,' virtuous. The absence of the right motive vitiates them. Socrates was hopelessly inferior to Abraham or St. Paul, because his acts, though externally of the same character, were not grounded on the same faith and hope. In fact, Socrates was not virtuous because he did not do right with a view to posthumous repayment. Rather, it seems, he should be called a fool or a madman. Suppose there was no God, he says, it might be fit for a man to discharge the moral duties 'so far as is consistent or coincident with his temporal happiness. That would be no virtue nor duty, but self-interest only, and love of the world. But if he proceeds further to sacrifice his own temporal happiness to the public, that, indeed, would be virtue and duty, on the supposition that God requires it; but without it, it is folly and madness. There is neither prudence nor good sense in preferring the happiness of others absolutely to our own, that is to say, without prospect of a future equivalent. But if God commands us to postpone our present interest, honour, or pleasure, to public considerations, it is then fitting and reasonable so to do; for God, by engaging us to it, becomes our security that we shall not finally or in the last result be losers by it. What would otherwise be folly now commences duty and virtue, and puts on obligation.'[46]

117. The theory thus expounded has an additional element of repulsiveness in Waterland's assumption, not only that virtue consists in giv-

---

[43]Waterland's Works, iv. 46.   [45]Ib. p. 78.
[44]Ib. p. 69.   [46]Ib. iv. 111.

ing credit to God for repayment of our sufferings, but that we should be mere fools to trust any God but his own. The doctrine is purified of that hideous corollary by later writers, and of the same school; but substantially the same theory was maintained by the most accepted teachers of the century. Its recommendation to men of strong common sense is obvious. It enabled them to threaten evildoers with hell-fire, instead of appealing to vague fitnesses of things, or to a moral sense only perceptible to philosophers. At the same time it kept God at a convenient distance. It exiled mystery from the affairs of daily life, but left a dark background of terror sufficient to keep criminals in awe. It may be considered, indeed, as a crude mode of expressing some important truths; on the one hand, it admitted that the rule of life was to be discovered from experience, and not from *a priori* theories, which had too little consistency to be a safe guide; on the other, it asserted— in a crude and brutal fashion enough—the necessity of some religious sentiment to restrain the selfish passions of mankind. And thus it was essentially a compromise which could not satisfy a truly philosophical mind, but which did well enough as a stopgap, borrowing its term from the old theology, and drawing upon experience for practical guidance.

118. The theory of Bishop Law, or of the Rev. Mr. Gay—for Gay, it seems, chiefly compiled the essay which was adopted by Law—is given in an introduction to Law's translation of Archbishop King's 'Origin of Evil.' This introduction is remarkable because, as already noticed, it helped to suggest Hartley's theory of association. Two or three propositions extracted from its pages will sufficiently indicate its general character.

'Virtue is conformity to a rule of life, directing the actions of all rational creatures with respect to each other's happiness; to which conformity everyone is in all cases obliged, and everyone that does so conform is, or ought to be, approved, esteemed, and loved for so doing.' 'Obligation is the necessity of doing or omitting any action in order to be happy.' God alone can make a perfect obligation, for he alone can, 'in all cases, make a man happy or miserable.' As God wishes men to be happy, the happiness of mankind 'may be said to be a criterion of virtue but once removed.' Happiness is the general end of all our actions, and 'moral goodness or moral virtue in man is not merely choosing or producing pleasure or natural good, but choosing it without a view to present rewards, and in prospect of a future recompense only.'

119. The ablest and most original exponent of this theory was Abraham Tucker, author of the 'Light of Nature Pursued.' Few men have

led more blameless or happier lives than this neglected philosopher. He was a rich country gentleman, spending his summers on his estate and his winters in London. But, unlike his neighbours, he delighted neither in fox-hunting nor in place-hunting. Philosophical theories were the game which he loved to follow through all the intricacies of some speculative labyrinth, and his ambition was to be received as a worthy colleague of Locke instead of Chatham. His devotion to abstract enquiries was free from the slightest tinge of moroseness or indifference to practical affairs. He was an example of that rarest of all intellectual compounds, the metaphysical humourist. He might have stood for a likeness of Mr. Shandy; and Montaigne is perhaps the writer to whom, though at a long distance, he bears the closest resemblance. The mixture of shrewdness and kindliness which made him active and amiable in all the relations of life shows itself in every page of his book. Listening to abstract disquisitions upon theology, ethics, and metaphysics, we strangely learn to love the author, whose eye is always twinkling with suppressed humour even in the gravest passages of his discourse. There is something so simple and childlike in his outbreaks of playfulness, that his incongruities never shock us. Indeed, his illustrations, quaint as they may be, have frequently the merit of an almost incomparable felicity. We can see the old gentleman writing in his study, and when perplexed to explain his theories, raising his eyes and smiling complacently, as he presses into his service the first object that meets his gaze. The childish game of cat's-cradle, the handiwork of the village carpenter, the groom saddling a horse, a girl going to a ball, or something that reminds him of his own courtship; these and a hundred other familiar objects enable him to expound his views on fate, free-will, a future life, the mechanism of the human mind, and the purposes of the Almighty. To be candid is part of his nature; a difficulty, instead of heating his temper, receives a genuine welcome, for does it not give one more problem over which he may brood for hours, and which may serve as a point of attachment for new webs of theory? No one ever more fully appreciated the maxim, that the search after truth—'Search' is the significant pseudonym which he adopts—is more delightful than the fruition. He would have regarded a fallacy which was too easily exposed just as a sportsman would regard a fox which did not give him a good run. An antagonist is therefore a friend in disguise, to be met with a quaint joke, instead of a bitter sarcasm. No man's pen was ever freer from gall. And, of course, it follows that Tucker is not seldom wearisome and immeasurably prolix. The last twenty years of his life were devoted to the composition of his book; and he has no intention to spare his readers one inch of the devious track which he has followed throughout that time. He never hurries; he cares nothing for concentration; the twentieth statement of any proposition is as prolix as the first; and he utterly ignores the principle that the secret of being tedious is to say everything.

120. This fault has been fatal to anything like a wide popularity of the 'Light of Nature.' Nine readers out of ten are probably repelled after a time by the boundless garrulity of his philosophical gossip. Vivacious, amiable, and cheerful as he may be, one longs to say, Do, for heaven's sake, take something for granted! But the old gentleman benignantly follows out his plan in its minutest details, and cares not for the diminution of his audience. Yet those who have the courage to follow him will be repaid, if by nothing else, at least by a curious exhibition of character, and by some curious illustrations of contemporary modes of thought.

121. To compress such a book into a few paragraphs is necessarily to do it injustice, for the irrelevant passages must be omitted, and the irrelevant passages are often just the most charming. It would be difficult, for example, to cite a more amusingly characteristic passage in any book than the chapter called the 'Vision,' which occupies over seventy closely printed octavo pages in the last edition of his works. But how give an idea within any shorter limits of the singular experience of the disembodied or partially disembodied Tucker; or the strange flashes of playful humour, and pathetic sentiment, and reverent emotion, which are blended into a unique whole, equally calculated to provoke smiles and sympathy? The dreaming soul is separated from his body, but still enveloped in a kind of minute bag, which, it appears, is the semi-corporeal abode of spirits in the 'vehicular state.' The bag has a strange power of shooting forth a head and limbs at the will of its occupant; and his first introduction in the new world is to a similar bag, looking like a bladder filled with air, from which protrudes the 'meagre lank-jawed face' of his master Locke.[47] By the instruction of his friend he learns to skate upon rays of light, and to talk after a new fashion, and, thus accomplished, performs strange journeys and hears strange converse in the world of spirits. He is put through a bit of dialectics by Socrates, and listens to an oration from Pythagoras, and talks sentiment with his long-lost Eurydice, and makes fun of Stahl, till the German philosopher shuts himself up in his bag; and is grievously bullied by Borgia in the likeness of a spider; and all the while, he and Locke carry on a queer running comment, changing strangely from grave to gay, but everywhere pervaded by a quaint tinge of humour. This bag bursts

[47] Tucker's 'Light of Nature,' i. 423.

for a time, and he is absorbed in the mundane soul, and hears unspeakable things and witnesses solemn visions; but he speedily returns
to his vehicle, and finally descending to a huge mountain, 'with a
monstrous gaping chasm on one side, from whence issue black streams
of fuliginous vapour,' discovers it to be his head, and entering with
difficulty through one of the pores, sticky and miry with insensible
perspiration, again takes his place in the seat of life.[48]

122. I must refrain, however, from following these strange flights of
fancy, in order to attempt a brief summary of the system which is
gradually shadowed forth in this strangely discursive performance.
Tucker, as already noticed, is a disciple of Locke, of whom he always
speaks with the warmest reverence. Indeed, he clings to those opinions
of his master which had been exploded by Berkeley and Hume. He
never, I believe, mentions Hume; but he frequently attacks Berkeley,
and by falling into the usual fallacies on the subject, exhibits his want
of metaphysical acuteness; for, indeed, it is exclusively as a psychologist
and as a moralist that Tucker has great speculative merit. From Hartley
he has borrowed much, whilst at the same time he regards the leader of
the association philosophy with a feeling as nearly approaching to dislike as can find room in his kindly bosom. Starting from such principles, Tucker's theological system presents no particular novelty, except
where his quaint fancy has engrafted some odd hypothesis upon the
older doctrines. He is a rationalist after the pattern of Locke; and
through many chapters of wearisome length he labours to accommodate
the mysterious dogmas of Christianity to a rational interpretation. By
the ordinary devices, he explains away the doctrines of the Trinity, the
Atonement, the Fall of Man, and the Sacraments, until they may be
accepted, even by a pure deist, without much effort—though in tread-
ing those perilous paths, it is probable that Tucker has unconsciously
stepped into some very heretical propositions. The fundamental method
of his reconciliation is significant.

123. God, according to him, is to the universe what the watchmaker
is to the watch[49]—an illustration which Paley may have borrowed,
along with much else, from his favourite author. Further, we may, if
we please, hold that the material universe is one stupendous engine,
which has been made from everlasting, and is never in want of wind-
ing up, or interference from the Creator.[50] Tucker, however, inclines to

[48]Tucker, 'Light of Nature,' i. 493.
[49]Ib. 'Things Providential,' sec. 11, ii. 83; and 'Providence,' sec. 9, i. 525.
[50]Ib. 'Things Providential,' ii. 85.

the opinion that the Almighty artificer does occasionally interfere, though only on rare and important occasions.[51] 'God is not profuse of his own omnipotence. He employs it rarely, upon those occasions only wherein he had rendered it necessary by leaving deficiencies in his plan of nature, purposely to admit these interpositions of his own hand, which he had predetermined from everlasting. Nor yet does he perform his extraordinary works wholly by his own power, but with the concurrence of second causes, turning and keeping them in the course wherein they will naturally bring forth the predestined event.'[52] Tucker, in short, is jealous of the Divine interference. It is equally important that we should believe in a God, and that we should make as little use of him as possible. The higher our reverence for the watchmaker, the less the need for his interfering with the instrument. This theory, however much it might satisfy Tucker the philosopher, was felt as unsatisfactory by Tucker the moralist and the religious thinker. A large part of his discursive performance is devoted to various attempts to reconcile the abstract doctrine with a doctrine more adapted for practical use; or, in other words, to show that the God thus revealed to us by reason is still the God whom we worship in church and obey in ordinary life. He applies his ingenuity in the spheres both of natural and revealed religion. Thus a chapter in the later part of his book is devoted to the distinction between 'esoterics and exoterics.' A man, he says, 'has one cast of mind for the closet, another to serve him when he enters into the busy world.'[53] The philosopher is the wholesale trader, who 'deals only in tons and hogsheads;' there is need also of the retailer who may 'pick or sort and parcel out his wares, and mingle them in such compositions as you shall scarce know the ingredients, yet shall find them fit for your immediate consumption.'[54] The first is the function of the reason, and the second of the imagination, which is the practical guide in ordinary affairs. 'Philosophy,' as he forcibly remarks, 'may be styled the art of marshalling the ideas in the understanding, and religion that of disciplining the imagination.' And thus it is possible, or rather necessary, to make assumptions in our daily life, which, though not inaccurate, cut short the long trains of reasoning which are required in speculation. Thus, for example, everything is providential to the philosopher, for everything comes by a longer or shorter chain of cause and effects from the action of the first great cause. But it would be considering too curiously—as Tucker cannot refrain from illustrating by some

[51]Tucker, 'Providence,' sec. 11, i. 527.   [52]Ib. 'Christian Scheme,' sec. 35, ii. 400.   [53]Ib. 'Esoterics and Exoterics,' sec. 5, ii. 20.   [54]Ib. sec. 7, ii. 22.

singular instances[55]—if we insisted on seeing in every trifling or disgusting object the immediate working of the Divine hand. It is wise
therefore to stop short, as a rule, at second causes. We should call only
those things providential which bear evident marks of wisdom and
goodness. 'When things are propounded as providential, let a man
examine impartially and courageously whether he feels them operate as
such upon his imagination; if he does not, they are not providential to
him.'[56] Or, to take a rather different instance, we may rightly pray for
external things; for, though prayer has no influence in obtaining them,
it obtains that 'ease and pleasure' which are the reasons for which we
desire them.[57] Yet, as a rule, it is best to keep the thought of Divine
interference at a distance. In Tucker's own language, he recommends
every man 'to remove the finger of God from him, as far as he can
without letting it go beyond the reach of his comprehension; if he believes the grace in his heart owing to a supernatural interposition of the
Spirit, still he may place a line of second causes between the act of God
and the effect he feels.'[58] Every movement of the watch is ultimately
attributable to the watchmaker; but, as a rule, we had better limit our
investigation to the works.

124. The system is illustrated still more curiously in his pure theology. God, he tells us, may be considered in two characters, as Creator
and as Governor of the universe.[59] As Creator, he dwells in inaccessible
light, where the eye of man is dazzled into blindness. As Governor, he
is more discernible, and is 'clothed with milder rays of glory, the subject of our hope and confidence as well as our admiration.'[60] It is here
that we can trace his power, wisdom, omnipotence, and goodness. In
order to give additional distinctness, he revives, after his own fashion,
the ancient hypothesis of the mundane soul. The atoms of which the
material world is composed are bathed, as it were, in a vast ocean of
spiritual substance. The infinite multitude of spirits in the 'vehicular
state' compose this ocean, lying in close contiguity to each other, and
every perception of one is immediately propagated through all the
intermediate spirits to every other. Had the modern discoveries in elec-
tricity been then familiar, Tucker would doubtless have pressed them
into his service for a more vivid illustration of his theories. These spirits

[55]See *e.g.* 'Divine Purity,' sec. 6, ii. 28.
[56]Tucker, 'Things Providential,' sec. 3, ii. 73; and see ib. sec. 9, ii. 80.
[57]Ib. 'Divine Services,' sec. 9, ii. 433.
[58]Ib. 'Grace,' sec. 5, ii. 179.
[59]Ib. 'Two Characters in God.' Theology, ch. xviii.   [60]Ib. sec. 5, i. 367.

form collectively a universal soul, which is unspeakably happy, and feels no more at the trivial evils which may happen to any of the comparatively small number of embodied spirits than a man who had just had a great piece of good fortune would feel at the breaking of a china saucer.[61] When God gave the order, this mundane soul formed the world in accordance with the Divine plan. 'The six days' formation being ended, though God rested from commanding, his agent did not rest from acting; for his reason could now direct him how to proceed in sustaining the work he had been taught to make. He still continued to turn the grand wheel of repulsion, that first mover in the wondrous machine of visible nature, all whose movements follow one another uninterruptedly for ages according to stated laws and in regular courses, without failure or disorder in any single wheel.'[62] When the fulness of time is come, God will give the signal for the reduction of everything to chaos—to be followed by the promulgation of a new plan and the employment of the mundane soul in its execution.

125. The purpose of this curious hypothesis—Tucker is superfluously careful to tell us that it is only an hypothesis—is to relieve the difficulty of our imaginations, and to present us with a secondary God not so mysterious as the Almighty himself. Tucker revels so much in discussing the complexities of his theory, and arguing for its possibility, that he seems half to lose sight of its hypothetical character, and still more completely of its utility. For, after all, it is plain enough that we are no nearer to any solution of the difficulty than we were before. God the Creator is still the true God, and the mundane soul is merely a wheel the more in the vast machinery of the universe. For Tucker realises fully, though he sometimes loses sight of the truth in his voluminous torrent of words, that neither chance, nor free-will, nor nature are in reality 'original springs of events.'[63] The Creator is really also the Disposer of events. The watchmaker has predetermined every movement of the watch. The mundane soul is merely a viceroy, to whom we may refer in imagination, but who is really the agent for carrying out the designs of the supreme sovereign.

126. His ethical theory, in fact, is constructed exclusively on the watchmaking plan. God, according to Tucker's conception, has framed the machine, and then allowed it to act by itself. From the beauty of the various contrivances we may infer his wisdom and power; from their tendency to promote our happiness we may infer his benevolence and

[61]Tucker, 'Mundane Soul,' sec. 23, i. 415.
[62]Ib. sec. 20, i. 414.
[63]Ib. 'Things Providential,' sec. 2, ii. 71.

justice. But he does not remain with us as a guide, nor leave any supernatural monitor within our breasts to warn us of what is pleasing to
him. Our own natural instincts are sufficient to lead us, as the force of
gravity is sufficient to keep the stars in their courses without further
interference. And thus morality, like everything else, is merely the
product of natural forces. Following his master Locke, Tucker has banished all innate ideas and everything that savours of the mysterious in
human nature. The one simple force which drives the machinery is our
desire for happiness. That is the ultimate end of all men. No one can
assert more emphatically that the measure of morality is the tendency of
actions to promote happiness, and that the aim of every particular individual is to secure his own happiness. In his chapter on 'Doing all for
the Glory of God' he says that a man's first step 'must be by a thorough
conviction of his judgment that acting for the divine Glory is acting
most for his own benefit.' 'I have observed all along,' he adds, 'that self
lies at the bottom of everything we do; in all our actions we constantly
pursue the satisfaction grounded on something apprehended beneficial
in our judgment or soothing in our fancy; the purest affections grow
from one or other of these roots, and the sublimest of our virtues must
be engrafted upon the former; therefore the love of God, to be sincere
and vigorous, must spring from the settled opinion of his goodness and
beneficence, and that every act of conformity to his will is beneficial to
the performer.'[64] The farsighted selfishness which teaches us to imitate
God supplies also the motives for obeying his commands. Tucker gives
us in one place a philosophical version of the Ten Commandments. He
imagines an angel sent from heaven to deliver a divine message in
these words: 'Know that if thou shalt worship chance or necessity, an
uncreated nature, or any God beside me; if thou shalt,' in short, break
any other of the commandment, 'know that in so doing thou actest
foolishly, for by all these things thou wilt lose far greater enjoyment
than thou canst gain for the present, and bring down intolerable mis-
chiefs upon thy head.'[65] God has spoken from this utilitarian Sinai, and
declares to all his creatures that vice is a bad speculation.

127. The harshness of this selfish doctrine is partly softened by the
theory which Tucker had learnt from Hartley. The principle of association, or, as Tucker chooses to call it, translation, is that which trans-
mutes the base metal of selfishness into the gold of benevolence. 'Though
flowers,' he says, 'grow out of the dirt,' they retain nothing of the
foulness of their original source; and so 'charity, though shooting most

---

[64]Tucker, 'Doing all for the Glory of God,' sec. 4, ii. 508.
[65]Ib. 'Divine Justice,' sec. 4, i. 626. -

vigorously from rational self-love, yet, when perfectly formed, has no tincture remaining of the parent root.'[66] Thus we forget the ultimate end in the means, and from doing good because it is our interest, learn to do it without conscious reference to any ulterior purpose. The benevolent impulses, however, though thus transformed, retain far more of their original character than in the scheme of Hartley. The ultimate end is not taken into account in every action, but it always remains in the background to be referred to, if necessary, in justification of our conduct. We resemble travellers carrying a general map of the country, which exhibits the right path as leading, though often by a circuitous route, to our ultimate destination. For practical purposes, we are often content with more limited plans, which represent the path as apparently deviating from the true direction; but we are content because we know that the larger map will show that the deviation is only in appearance.

128. Thus Tucker discusses at intervals the critical case of Regulus, which was a kind of standing puzzle for the moralists of the time. If Regulus did right, he says, it must have been because 'he acted more for his own happiness in the sequel than he could have done by any breach of faith.'[67] He admits it to be possible, theoretically, that the satisfaction which Regulus felt in acting rightly might have 'overbalanced the pain of the tenters.'[68] And yet it seems, on further consideration, that a man ought to know when to make exceptions to general rules, and should have known in such a case that the suffering could not be compensated by the pleasure. 'Upon the whole,' he says, 'we are forced to acknowledge that hitherto we have found no reason to imagine a wise man would ever die for his country or suffer martyrdom in the cause of virtue, how strong propensity soever he might feel in himself to maintain her interests.'[69] After 'searching every corner of the human breast'[70] we have found our own satisfaction to be the sole spring of all our actions and the ultimate end of all our contrivances.[70] How, then, are we to escape from the dilemma? for Tucker begs his readers not to imagine, even for a time, that this atrocious condemnation of all self-sacrifice is really his last word. To discover a satisfactory solution of the enigma, Tucker has to lead us through all the labyrinths of his theological system. Ultimately he emerges with a discovery which is made known to us in a chapter on the 'Re-enlargement of Virtue.' After

---

[66]Tucker, 'Charity,' sec. 3, ii. 281.　[67]Ib. 'Rectitude,' sec. 7, i. 214.
[68]Ib. 'Virtue,' sec. 10, i. 222.
[69]Ib. 'Temptation of Virtue,' sec. 8, i. 272.　[70]Ib. i. 273.

explaining its nature, we may now, he says, 'do ample justice to Regulus, whom we left under a sentence of folly for throwing away life with all its enjoyments for a phantom of honour. For he may allege that he had not a fair trial before, his principal evidence being out of the way, which, having since collected in the course of his second book, he moves for a rehearing.' In fact, Regulus now pleads that he was doing great good by his example. 'He was persuaded, likewise, that all the good a man does stands placed to his account, to be repaid him in full value when it will be most useful to him; so that whoever works for another works for himself, and by working for numbers earns more than he possibly could by working for himself alone. Therefore he acted like a thrifty merchant, who scruples not to advance considerable sums, and even to exhaust his coffers, for gaining a large advantage to the common stock in partnership.'[71] Regulus, therefore, is acquitted with flying colours. The mode in which Regulus is repaid appears very plainly by the comparison of heaven to a 'universal bank, where accounts are regularly kept and every man debited or credited for the least farthing he takes out or brings in.'[72] The bank of heaven has many advantages, indeed, over the Bank of England; not only is the security perfect, but the rate of interest is enormous; whenever and wherever I may be in want, 'the runner angel' will 'privately slip the proper sum into my hand at a time when I least expect it;'[72] and, finally, we can have no reason to be jealous of the larger balances of other customers, for we are all dealing in partnership and we shall all profit equally.

129. This last phrase suggests one curious whim of the worthy Tucker, with which I may conclude my account of his system. He persuades himself that, since God gives everything, he must give an equal share to everybody; or that, as he puts it, 'the value of each person's existence, computed throughout the whole extent of his being,' must be 'precisely the same.'[73] This singular inference would appear to cut at the very roots of Tucker's theory; for it would prove that, as in the long run all actions are indifferent, rational self-love could not prompt one course of conduct more than another. Tucker succeeds in reconciling himself to the conclusion by various ingenious devices, resting on the general principle that the mind can only take into account a certain length of time; we can see far enough before us to realise that vice will be punished in the next world, and not far enough to realise

[71]Tucker, 'Re-enlargement of Virtue,' sec. 5, i. 665.
[72]Ib. 'General Good,' sec. 9, i. 621.   [73]Ib. 'Equality,' sec. 2, i. 597.

that the punishment will be finally compensated after some indefinitely vast lapse of time. A thousand years or so of torment would, he thinks, be enough to deter a man from wickedness, though they might be followed by an eternity of happiness. The strange whim, characteristic of a solitary and half-trained thinker, had the recommendation to him that it enables him to get rid of eternal punishment. He takes a view of our destinies almost as cheerful as that of Hartley. By a queer series of calculations, founded on certain hypothetical statistics as to the vehicular state, he persuades himself that our whole amount of suffering may be equivalent to a 'minute of pain once in every twenty-two years.'[74] The minutes of trouble, however, often come 'so thick toegther' that they prevent us from seeing beyond them to the remoter ages of happiness.

130. Let us hope that this kindly extravagance solaced the good Tucker, when the evil of the world pressed too heavily on his soul; if it rather shakes our belief in his intellectual vigour, it helps to complete the portrait of a singularly innocent, cheerful, and kindly temperament. The moral theory which, in other hands, seems to involve a degrading view of human nature, seems with him to be the natural expression of cheerful common sense.

131. Paley, in the preface to his 'Moral and Political Philosophy,' candidly acknowledges his great obligations to Tucker. Their theories are, in fact, nearly identical. The whimsical fancies which adorn or disfigure Tucker's pages have indeed disappeared. We hear nothing of the mundane soul, the vehicular state, or the equality of all human lives. Paley is a hard-headed North-countryman, whose chief mental sustenance has been a severe course of Cambridge mathematics. He is throughout a systematiser, not an original thinker; and his system begins by expelling as far as possible everything that is not as solid and tangible as a proposition in Euclid. Moreover, his ethical treatise is, in fact, intended for educational purposes. In such works, clearness and order are the cardinal virtues, and originality, if not a vice, is of equivocal advantage. Paley primarily is a condenser and a compiler; though he modestly enough claims to be 'more than a mere compiler.'[75] He gives a lucid summary of the most generally accepted system; and if there is any gleam of originality in his writing, it is, for the most part, such as occasionally results from a rearrangement of old materials. Law, afterwards Bishop of Carlisle, and Waterland, were both heads of houses,

[74]Tucker, 'Divine Economy,' sec. 39, ii. 364.
[75]Works, i. xlix.

and Rutherforth a professor of divinity at Cambridge.[76] Paley was an intimate friend and colleague in the tuition of Christ College of John Law, son of the Bishop of Carlisle, and it was from the Bishop that he received his first preferment. Locke's Essay was the main authority upon which he relied in his college lectures. Thus, the influences under which he was placed were all favourable to that phase of utilitarianism which we are considering; and Paley, with his undeniable merits as a reasoner, was not the man to desert the paths into which he had been guided. He has simply given a compact statement of what may be called the orthodox theory.

132. Thus he attacks the moral-sense theory by the arguments of Locke, with some additions from later writers. Caius Toranius, he says, betrayed his father to the executioners under circumstances of special atrocity. Would the wild boy who was caught in the woods of Hanover have disapproved the action?[77] Paley's answer is that he would not have disapproved it. His reasons are that, in the first place, the moral sense varies indefinitely; that, in the second place, its growth is sufficiently explained by the theory of association, which causes us to transfer to actions generally useful, the sentiment which is excited by actions useful to ourselves; and, thirdly, because there are no moral laws 'absolutely and universally true,' and we, therefore, cannot have an intuitive perception of their truth. Moreover, the moral sense, if it exists, must be justified by some external test, or how can we arbitrate between different moral intuitions? That test, of course, is the production of happiness, and happiness consists, not in the sensual pleasures, or in the mere absence of pain, or in rank and power, but in the exercise of the social affections, in the devotion of our faculties to 'some engaging end,' in the prudent arrangement of our habits, and in health. Happiness, therefore, is equally distributed throughout all ranks, and the vicious have no advantage—even in this world—over the virtuous.

133. Having thus cleared the ground, Paley proposes, with somewhat amazing calmness, his definition of virtue. 'Virtue is the doing good to mankind, in obedience to the will of God, and for the sake of everlasting happiness.'[78] It is characteristic that this doctrine is propounded

[76]Rutherforth's views may be sufficiently indicated by one entry in the index to his 'Essay on the Nature and Obligations of Virtue.' 'Disinterestedness, instance of it, 109; accounted for, 110.' He accounts for it by showing that it does not exist. The obligation to virtue is the future reward or punishment known by Revelation.

[77]Paley's Works, i. 7.   [78]Ib. i. 27.

as though it were a self-evident truth. Paley proclaims it as calmly as if he were giving Euclid's definition of parallel straight lines, as though the statement bore its own evidence with it. To most later thinkers it has appeared to be as palpably false as to him it appeared to be palpably true; and there can be no more curious proof of the firmness with which the doctrine of theological utilitarianism had established itself than the calm enunciation of its most questionable tenet as an ultimate truth by a singularly clear-headed thinker, and that at the very time when he is maintaining the necessity of basing all moral theories on experience. His argument, indeed, betrays a half-conscious sense that some justification of the doctrine is needed; for he proceeds to explain, in the spirit of Tucker, that the thought of divine rewards and punishments need not be present to our mind in every action, inasmuch as we generally act from habit; but that thought must have been the foundation of our habits. The best servants learn to act for their master's interests, without thinking of his wishes; but a regard for his wishes must have been the first motive to the formation of the habit. The doctrine is expanded in the chapter on Obligation. A man is 'obliged,' 'when he is urged by a violent motive resulting from the command of another,'[79] whence it follows that 'we can be obliged to nothing but what we ourselves can gain or lose something by.'[80] To say that we are 'obliged' to keep our words means simply that we shall go to hell if we don't; and 'the difference, and the only difference,' between prudence and virtue is, 'that, in the one case, we consider what we shall gain or lose in the present world; in the other case, we consider also what we shall gain or lose in the world to come.'[81]

134. To complete the ground-plan of Paley's system, one other doctrine must be added. The moral sanction is the theological; what is the criterion? Paley's answer is, that the rule is the will of God. But how is the will of God to be known? First, by the Scriptures; and, secondly, by the light of nature. But how do we interpret the teaching of nature? By the help of the doctrine that God wishes the happiness of his creatures; whence it follows that, to determine the morality of an action, we must enquire into 'the tendency of the action to promote or diminish the general happiness.'[82] In carrying out his system, Paley, of course, makes far greater use of this test than of the Scripture test. The primary duties, such as respect for private property and fidelity to promises, are defended purely and simply on utilitarian grounds. Scripture is only

[79]Paley, i. 37.   [81]Ib. i. 40.
[80]Ib. i. 38.   [82]Ib. i. 42.

invoked where it is necessary to fill up gaps in the code. Thus, for example, Paley, though a keen sportsman, has some difficulty in defending our right over the lives of animals; and he ultimately defends it simply by the permission recorded in the ninth chapter of the Book of Genesis.[83] Wanton cruelty, he says, is certainly wrong; and possibly he would have had some difficulty in defending, on theoretical grounds, his love of fishing.

135. Paley is thus the typical example of the moralists who enjoyed the greatest reputation throughout the eighteenth century. His theology, as we have already seen,[84] is essentially a belief in God as the contriver, not as the ever-present regulating power of the universe. 'The world,' he says, 'abounds with contrivances,'[85] and it is entirely upon those contrivances that here, as in the 'Natural Theology,' he rests his proof of the Divine benevolence. 'The contemplation of universal nature rather bewilders the mind than affects it,'[86] but when we see teeth made to bite and eyes to see, we are convinced of God's love for his creation. He declares, with a higher tone of sentiment, that he sees 'the benevolence of the Deity more clearly in the pleasures of very young children than in anything else.'[86] In one shape or another, however, it is by regarding the world as a collection of cunningly contrived machines that we learn to adore the machine-maker. Theological utilitarianism is essentially connected with this form of theology. Heaven and hell are the weights which work the great machine of the universe, so far as it has any moral significance, and love of pleasure and fear of pain the passions through which they act. Paley, however, is not only the clearest, but the last, representative of the doctrine. The system, in fact, when thus elaborated, was rapidly becoming intolerable. Heaven and hell had retired too far from men's minds, and the authority of Scripture had become too feeble to provide an effectual rule. The characteristic laxity of the contemporary theology, represented by such men as Paley, Watson, and Hey, shows that it was, in fact, a rationalism thinly concealed; and men who wished to affect the thoughts of the world, rather than to compile orthodox summaries for students, hastened to discard the flimsy theological disguises which might do for the schools, but had lost their potency with the mass of mankind. And here, therefore, we arrive at a critical point. The Deism, whether it called itself orthodox or infidel, which had hitherto given a decorous vent to the quasi-scientific systems of morality, was to be thrown aside, and the divorce of ethics and theology openly proclaimed. Hume had already reached

<hr>

[83] Paley, i. 61.   [84] Above, ch. viii.   [85] Ib. i. 44.   [86] Ib. i. 45.

that point; but Hume's speculations were too much in advance of his age, and too far removed from practical application, to give birth to a corresponding movement in the sphere of practice. A thinker of a very different order was to take the next step, and to open a warfare along the whole line of politics, legislation, and morals, which has not yet subsided.

136. When Paley's treatise appeared, a friend wrote to Jeremy Bentham, then travelling in Russia, that the new writer had anticipated the doctrines of Bentham's 'Principles of Morals and Legislation'—then already in print, though not as yet published.[87] The coincidence, he added, was so close that it almost seemed as if Paley must have seen Bentham's introduction. The relation, indeed, of Bentham's ethical doctrines to Paley's may be expressed by saying that Bentham is Paley *minus* a belief in hell-fire. But Bentham, in another sense, is Paley *plus* a profound faith in himself, and an equally profound respect for realities. Benthamism represents a phenomenon common enough in the history of thought. The conditions have changed, and the germs of belief long dormant suddenly develop unsuspected powers of growth. As Rousseau took the doctrine of abstract rights from the schools into the streets, so Bentham transferred the doctrine of utility from the sphere of speculation to that of immediate legislation. The belief in future rewards and punishments was too effete and too little congenial to the tendencies of that party to which Bentham belonged to survive in his teaching. He held to facts, and was scornful of obsolete theological figments as of obsolete legislative principles. For Paley's placid conservatism he substituted an ardent desire to bring every existing institution to the test of immediate practical utility; and though rejecting the principles of the revolutionary party, as represented by French or American[88] declaimers, he applied a method less calculated to produce catastrophes, but equally adapted to effect a thorough reconstruction of the old order.

137. I shall not, however, attempt to discuss Bentham's principles or influence. The history of utilitarianism as an active force belongs to the present century; and an adequate estimate of Bentham's achievements would take me far beyond the scope of this book and of my knowledge. Moreover, it is admitted even by Mr. J. S. Mill, the great writer who has pronounced the best judgment upon Bentham from a disciple's

---

[87]Bentham's Works, x. 163.

[88]The famous American 'Declaration of Independence' was, in Bentham's view, a 'hodge-podge of confusion and absurdity' (Works, x. 63).

point of view, that vast as were Bentham's labours, and great as were their results upon jurisprudence, he effected little or nothing as a philosophical moralist. What he did was to utter, with an emphasis not previously attained, the verdict of common sense upon the flimsy nature of the rival theories; to stimulate the belief in the possibility of basing a moral theory upon observation, and, it may be added, by constantly applying the celebrated 'greatest happiness' formula to bring into clear relief some leading ethical problems, and to help on the emancipation of ethics from theology.

138. All this, however, throws little light upon speculative problems. Bentham, as a moral philosopher, was certainly not in advance of Hume, and is only so far in advance of Tucker or Paley as he abandons the incongruous addition by which they had striven to affiliate their doctrine to the orthodox teaching. The main difficulty remained unaltered. Utilitarianism is an attempt to base morality upon observation, instead of following the *a priori* method. But from the point of view of Bentham, as from that of his predecessors, this was to reduce it to a mere chaos of empirical doctrines. A science of morality presupposes certain principles which belong to the sciences of psychology and sociology. Whilst the very conception of such sciences was scarcely entertained, the attempt to give a scientific account of morality was necessarily imperfect. According to Mr. Mill, Bentham overlooked the 'moral part of man's nature in the strict sense of the term,'[89] and was totally indifferent to historical considerations. That is to say, he was ignorant or careless of the two kinds of knowledge which are most essential to ethical speculation. Naturally, his results were unsatisfactory.

139. Bentham, indeed, attempted to provide a scientific apparatus by a classification of pains and pleasures. Such a classification could not be exhaustive, except as a statement of his own emotions; and, as Mr. Mill fully shows, his life and character made his knowledge of the great springs of action singularly limited. But, in any case, it could not afford a secure base for reasoning. To compare the value to the individual of different classes of pleasures and pains, we must understand something of the nature and relations of the faculties affected. To understand their importance to the community, we must have a clear view of the nature of the social organisation. Otherwise our attempts at calculating the consequences of action leave out the only element by which unity can be given to the resulting system. We may roughly sum up the evil consequences produced by a murder to its victim, and the people more

[89]Mill's 'Dissertations,' i. 360.

indirectly affected. But we cannot treat the question scientifically till we can analyse the nature of the moral disease of which the murderous impulse is a symptom, and of the morbid social conditions which generate murderers. Thus the method is as crude as, in some cases, the results are unworthy. With Bentham the altruistic impulses are still scarcely admitted, as he contemplates society as a mere aggregate of jostling individuals. Virtue is scarcely intelligible, for he identifies the moral with the 'popular' sanction, and says that 'popular' is the best name as most indicative of the constituent causes.[90] That is, virtue means simply the average belief of mankind as to what will produce the greatest quantity of happiness. Though the doctrine may be, in a sense, true, it is but a rough approximation to any tenable theory upon the subject.

140. The attempt to found a scientific system of morality was thus doomed—not indeed to failure, for it stimulated further enquiries—but to remain in the stage of crude empiricism. That it produced so vast an impression is due to the fact that it was in reality a first step towards a more systematic and satisfactory conception, and to the other fact, that the doctrines which it opposed were not really better founded, though put forward with pretensions which, while claiming a loftier origin, were becoming rapidly untenable. Bentham's influence on morality was destructive of many phantoms which were still going about in spite of Hume's more searching scepticism, and if its constructive efficacy was not great in the sphere of speculation, it encouraged the adoption of profounder methods. Mr. Mill describes in his 'Autobiography' the immense effect which the perusal of one of Bentham's treatises produced upon his mind, by holding out prospects of useful effort in the cause of mankind. With all Bentham's faults, he gave a vast stimulus, if only through his disciples, to others who were wearied of the old effete assumptions, and longing for more fruitful methods of enquiry. But here, again, I must pause on the threshold of a new era. To discuss the relations of Benthamism to the scientific morality of which we may hope that later thinkers have at least laid the foundations, is a task not here to be attempted.

[90]See vol. i. 'Principles of Morals' &c. p. 14, and 'Table of Springs of Action,' p. 195.

NOTE TO CHAPTER IX

The principal authorities for the above chapter and the editions cited are as follows:

BALGUY, JOHN (1686–1748), 'Letter to a Deist,' 1726. 'Foundation of Moral Goodness,' 1728.

BROWN, JOHN (1715–1766), 'Essay on Characteristics.' 1751. Third edition. London: 1752.

BUTLER, JOSEPH (1695–1752), 'Sermons on Human Nature,' 1726. Works. Oxford: 1836.

CLARKE, SAMUEL (1675–1729), 'Demonstration of Being and Attributes of God,' 1704–5. Works: 1728.

COCKBURN, CATHERINE (1679–1749), 'Remarks on Foundation of Morality,' 1743. Works. London: 1751. 'Remarks on Rutherforth,' 1747.

FORDYCE, DAVID (1711–1751), 'Elements of Moral Philosophy,' 1754.

GISBORNE, THOMAS (1758–1846), 'Principles of Moral Philosophy,' 1789.

HARTLEY, DAVID (1705–1759), 'Observations on Man,' 1749. London: 1791.

HOME, HENRY (Lord Kames), (1696–1782), 'Essay on Principles of Morality,' 1751. Third edition: 1779.

HUME, DAVID (1711–1776), 'Treatise of Human Nature,' 1740, vol. iii. 'Enquiry Concerning the Principles of Morals,' 1751. 'Four Dissertations,' 1757. Philosophical Works, by Green and Grose.

HUTCHESON, FRANCIS (1694–1747), 'Ideas of Beauty and Virtue,' 1725. 'Passions and Affections,' 1728. 'System of Moral Philosophy,' 1755.

LAW, WILLIAM (1686–1761), 'Remarks on Fable of the Bees.' Works. London: 1762.

MANDEVILLE, BERNARD (1670–1733). 'The Fable of the Bees,' 1714. London: 1806.

PALEY, WILLIAM (1743–1805), 'Moral Philosophy,' 1785. Works. London: 1837.

PRICE, RICHARD (1723–1791), 'Review of Principal Questions on Morals,' 1757. Second edition. London: 1769.

RUTHERFORTH, THOMAS (1712–1771), 'Nature and Obligations of Virtue,' 1744. 'Institutes of Natural Law,' 1754.

SHAFTESBURY, LORD (1671–1713), 'Characteristics,' 1708, &c. Edition of 1723.

SMITH, ADAM (1723–1790), 'Moral Sentiments,' 1759. Tenth edition: 1804.

TUCKER, ABRAHAM (1705–1774), 'Light of Nature,' 1768–78. London: 1834.

WATERLAND, DANIEL (1683–1740), 'Remarks on Clarke's Exposition of the Catechism,' 1730.

WOLLASTON, WILLIAM (1660–1724), 'Religion of Nature delineated,' 1722. Sixth edition: 1738.

CHAPTER X

POLITICAL THEORIES

I. Introductory.

1. At some future day, if the aspirations of philosophers are justified, there will be a science of sociology. We shall unravel the laws of growth of the social organism, and determine the condition of its health or disease. Then, and not till then, it will be possible to present political science as a coherent body of doctrines, deduced from certain axioms of universal validity, but leading to different conclusions according to the varying conditions of human society. We shall be able to say what form of government is most favourable to the happiness of a nation at any given period of its development. Then we shall have at once a firm base for our speculations, and the utmost possible flexibility in their application. We shall see how to reconcile justice and expediency; and establish the rights of man, not as conflicting with considerations of utility, but as logical consequences of the laws of social health. Hitherto, reasoning has been alternately purely empirical and purely abstract. Political machinery, of a more or less satisfactory kind, has evolved itself out of the blind conflict of selfish or patriotic passions. Institutions which enable men to secure the main objects of life have been slowly established; and a few empirical principles have come to be widely accepted, though not yet combined into any satisfactory system. But we are still so far from possessing anything like a science of politics, that most of the current maxims involve conceptions which could hardly find place in a scientific system. Fragments of the old theories by which men endeavoured to explain the origin of government, or to show how it might be best administered, still perplex our discussions, and hinder the attempt to lay a sound foundation of theory.

2. The difficulty of discovering anything approaching to an historical development of political theory is the greater, inasmuch as theories have followed, more than they have guided, events. Happy is the nation which has no political philosophy, for such a philosophy is generally the offspring of a recent, or the symptom of an approaching, revolution.

During the quieter hours of the eighteenth century Englishmen rather played with political theories than seriously discussed them. The interest in politics was chiefly personal. References to general principles are introduced in rhetorical flourishes, but do not form the basis of serious argument. In the mass of pamphlets and speeches which fill our library shelves it is rare to find even a show of political philosophy. The Tory argument is that De Foe has been put in the pillory; the Whig argument is that the French wear wooden shoes. Walpole's friends rail at the Pope and the Pretender; and Bolingbroke's friends abuse the Excise and the Hanoverian subsidies. Generalities about liberty, corruption, and luxury are equally convenient for filling the interstices of either set of arguments. To discover from such materials what are the real political views of the writer would be a difficult task; and the investigation belongs rather to the historian of facts than to the historian of thought. In the earlier part of the century there are but one or two books which fairly belong to the speculative order; and even in the more stirring times which preceded the French Revolution the political philosophy of the time is generally imbedded in discussions of concrete facts. A brief account of the few writers who refer most distinctly to general principles will sufficiently indicate the general set of the currents of political thought.

3. In the absence not only of a science of sociology, but of a belief that such a science was possible, men might fall back upon the old theological synthesis. Here, as in ethical speculations, the hypothesis of a divine interference simplified all questions. If the king was the representative of the Deity in secular as the priest in ecclesiastical matters, all discussion was at an end. In a sense higher than the technical the king could do no wrong; his right to rule could never be impugned. The great convulsions which followed the Reformation had rudely broken down any such theories. The relation between the secular and the spiritual power became perplexed and often opposed; and Jesuits had written in defence of tyrannicide when kings were against the Pope. When Filmer maintained the divine right of kings, he found it necessary to attack the great Catholic theologians, Bellarmine and Suarez. The Church of England, indeed, clung as long as it could to some fragment of the theory. Clergymen rivalled each other in preaching the doctrine of unconditional submission till the Church and king quarrelled, and none but a few Jacobites could adhere to the old creed. The Hanoverian dynasty was too obviously endowed with no divine sanctity. George I. was clearly not the representative of God Almighty; and the disappearance with Queen Anne of the quaint superstition of touching for the

evil marked the extinction of the last fragments of the belief in the special sanctity of kings.

4. But what theory was to replace the old? If we substitute the abstract metaphysical Deity for the personal Ruler of the universe, we have the same difficulty which occurs in the ethical speculations. God, when identified with nature, sanctions all instincts and all forces alike. And thus we obtain the political theories (for the two are strikingly alike) of Hobbes and Spinoza, in which right is identified with might. The moralists who desired an absolute basis of speculation, and yet shrank from the immoral consequences of this identification, thought, as we have seen, that an absolute law of nature might be constructed from certain 'inherent and immutable relations of things.' Applying the same method to politics, we find certain inalienable rights of man corresponding to the immutable laws of morality, and following from the essential relations of human beings to each other and to God. The primary rules have an absolute character, and are discoverable either by intuition or by an *a priori* method of reasoning entirely independent of experience. The difficulty, however, of crossing the gulf which separates such transcendental regions from concrete institutions was greater in the case of political than in that of ethical speculations. The rule, do as you would be done by, might seem to rank with mathematical axioms; any rule applicable to political constitutions, unless indeed Hobbes's theory of the absolute power of the sovereign was accepted, required too many qualifications to be capable of such absolute statement. The passage from the abstract to the concrete was therefore effected by the help of the social-compact theory, which appears to have had its origin in the speculations of Roman jurists.[1] The convenience of the theory is obvious. To obtain an absolute relation between human beings, you may appeal to the law revealed by an authority absolute because divine. When this power is too vaguely conceived to be capable of originating a political constitution, the most obvious legal analogy is that of a compact whose binding force does not appear to be dependent on the will of any superior. Thus, it was possible to find an absolute basis for political theory, whilst the imaginary compact allowed for the development of certain special rules applicable to concrete societies.

5. The social contract theory was indeed necessarily of the most elastic kind. Amongst the absolute thinkers it marked the passage from a supposed state of nature into a social state. The compact into which men entered by abandoning part of their natural liberty in consideration

---

[1] See Sir H. Maine's 'Ancient Law,' ch. ix.

of certain advantages remained unalterably binding upon all subsequent generations, and thus gave rise to those rights of man which have a superior validity to any rights conferred by later legislation. No human legislation could override them; though the widest possible difference of opinion unfortunately existed as to the precise code thus unalterably fixed. The laws had thus the absolute character of a scientific 'law of nature,' and yet were sufficiently specific to afford grounds of distinguishing between different concrete cases. But in the mouths of a different school the same compact was unconsciously used for quite a different purpose. It signified that compact which was assumed to have taken place in any particular nation. It might vary indefinitely according to circumstances, and be the foundation as well of a democracy as of a despotism. It was used, that is, not to preserve the absolute character of certain laws, but to justify the most purely empirical methods. The compact sanctioned any existing constitution, and was at most valuable as appearing to condemn arbitrary and violent changes. It gave a vague but useful sanction to the existing order, whatever that order might happen to be. Thus it might at times be convenient to thinkers who admitted that political theories were to be tested solely by experience. In the absence of any satisfactory conception of political development, that test was necessarily applied in the crudest fashion. Politics, it may be said, were regarded from the statical, instead of the dynamical, point of view. In other words, the forces by which a government was maintained were not held to express the relations between the different parts of a growing organism, but the conditions of equilibrium of a cunningly balanced machine. It had been suddenly called into existence by some mythical legislator, who had pieced it together and determined its character. The ancient generalisation had divided all governments into monarchical, aristocratical, and democratical. Each form had its vices and virtues, its principle of life and of decay, upon which Aristotle was the great authority, and was to be considered absolutely without reference to conditions of time, place, and development. Permanence and not progress was the highest possible merit of a government. As a human machine it was liable to decay, and indeed, at some time or other, decay was inevitable. To arrange the machine so that, when once set going, it might continue to work smoothly as long as possible, was the great problem of legislators. Venice seems to have been the favourite model of such reasoners; but they had an abundant supply of classical instances to illustrate their arguments.

6. Each of these theories thus recognised as important truth. The metaphysical theory of absolute rights recognised the truth that a politi-

cal system should ultimately rest on some surer foundation than the fancy of the day, or the contrivance of politicians. The theory of the three elementary forms of government recognised the necessity of appealing to experience and history, though history was still too little organised to enable the appeal to be made effectually. The two theories are, of course, strangly combined and distorted by partisans of conflicting opinions; and even when any coherent theory was accepted, it was frequently obscured by the personal prejudices of the day. I must endeavour to show how, beneath the shifting sands of party dispute, some deeper foundation was to be found, and how, to some extent, the ultimate logic of the dispute governed the immediate manifestations of personal animosities.

II. The Principles of 1688.

7. Locke expounded the principles of the Revolution of 1688, and his writings became the political bible of the following century. They may be taken as the formal apology of Whiggism. He gave the source from which later writers drew their arguments, and the authority to which they appealed in default of arguments. That authority vanished when the French Revolution brought deeper questions for solution, and new methods became necessary in politics as in all other speculation. But during the eighteenth century Locke's theories gave his countrymen such philosophical varnish as was necessary for the embellishment of political pamphlets and parliamentary rhetoric. Their success was partly due to the fact that, like the revolution which they justified, they are a compromise between inconsistent theories. The characteristic quality of Locke's mind is shown in the tenacity with which he adheres to certain principles which seem to work in practice, though they fit rather awkwardly into any logical framework. His doctrine is explained in the 'Treatises on Government' (1690), and in the letters on 'Toleration' (1689). The 'Treatises on Government' are an answer to poor Sir R. Filmer. In the first treatise he disposes, at rather wearisome length, of his opponent's ingeniously absurd doctrine that kings derive their power by direct inheritance from Adam's personal authority over his immediate descendants. As a specimen of the way in which a powerful mind can tear a flimsy fallacy to pieces, the argument may have its interest. But we tire of seeing a strong man deliberately picking to pieces the minutest reticulations of a web of sophistry long since gone to utter decay, instead of summarily brushing it aside. Merciful critics have seen in Filmer's arguments a distortion of the historical theory of the

patriarchal origin of government. The form which the theory took in his hands was, at all events, so absurd that one wonders at Locke's condescending to a serious refutation. A still more elaborate reply is given in Algernon Sidney's 'Discourses on Government'—a book which shows wide reading and some power of style, but of which we must charitably hope that its incessant repetitions and voluminous insistence upon particular points would have been expunged had the author published it in his lifetime. I need not linger upon an argument which, without the assaults of Locke and Sidney, would have died a natural death at the Revolution. It is enough to note that an incidental remark in this part of Locke's[1] treatise implies that, to his mind, it was an exhaustive division of all theories of government, to say that power must be founded either on a divine grant, on paternal authority, or on compact. As, in Filmer's version of the doctrine, the first two theories are identical, we are reduced to the alternative of regarding government as a matter of positive divine appointment, and regarding it as a matter of compact. Locke, like Sidney, unhesitatingly accepts the compact theory, which, stamped by his authority, became the orthodox Whig doctrine.

8. What, then, is Locke's version of the compact? What are its terms? How are they to be discovered, and why are they binding? Hobbes, to whom it is remarkable that Locke makes no explicit reference, interprets the compact as giving absolute power to the sovereign. Locke's special purpose is to prove that the sovereign's authority is limited by the terms of the compact. He therefore interprets it in such a fashion as to make it almost identical with the utilitarian formula. Since government exists for the good of the people, so his argument seems frequently to run, a law or a constitution must be judged simply by its conformity to that end. But Locke can never divest himself of the belief that the compact is somehow necessary to give a sound basis for his theories. Utility is doubtless, in some sense, the ultimate test; but utility must be embodied in a compact before the test can be applied. He is hampered by the reappearance of this imaginary compact, which occasionally clashes with the purpose for which it was designed. Yet, to defend a system simply as useful, seemed to relegate the whole political theory to the region of pure empiricism; and the compact, however useless in reality, could never be frankly cast aside. A curious complexity is thus introduced into his arguments, characteristic of the strange incapacity of so vigorous a mind to free itself from this relic of a metaphysical method.

[1]'Treatise of Government,' i. sec. 96.

9. Locke, like his predecessors, regards the compact as marking the transition from a 'state of nature,' but his state of nature differs materially from that of Hobbes. So far from being a state of anarchy, it has a 'law of nature to govern it, which obliges everyone;'[2] and that law is reason. According to Hobbes, promises are not binding in a state of nature; according to Locke, they are binding, 'for truth and keeping of faith belongs to men as men, and not as members of society.'[3] Indeed, Locke's state of nature is almost the ideal state; he speaks of the 'golden age'[4] in an apparently historical sense, and regards government as introduced by the 'ambition and luxury of future ages.'[4] The difference is characteristic. With Hobbes or Spinoza, though in very different senses, God becomes an expression for the absolute; he is the equal source of all phenomena, and right is necessarily identified with might. The God of Locke, less severely abstract, is capable of taking a side in human affairs; desiring the happiness of men, he gives them a definite rule; the God-given reason teaches us that we should not harm the 'life, health, liberty, or possessions'[5] of each other, for men are the creatures of an infinitely wise Maker, and the servants of a sovereign Master. Thus God is retained to supply the necessary sanction to the social compact. The terms of the compact are that we should do good to each other; the reason for obeying it that God orders us to cultivate happiness as much as possible. The divine sanction does not apply to any particular form of government; and the will of God is to be inferred, as in the doctrine of the utilitarian theologians, by observing what causes produce the greatest amount of happiness. The imagination is thus satisfied by a supposed absolute basis, though the decision in any given case is left to experience.

10. This doctrine may, of course, lapse into simple utilitarianism. Paternal authority, for example, is justified simply on the ground that the care of parents is necessary for helpless children.[6] The obligations of marriage are defined by purely utilitarian considerations. It ought to be permanent in the human species because the infant does not, as in other species, become independent before another infant is born; and the bond regarded exclusively as a means of protecting the family is prolonged, at least, during the period of childbearing and the infancy of the children. The willingness to take the lower animals into account, and the strict limitation of the validity of marriage by considerations of immedi-

---

[2]Treatise ii. sec. 6.   [5]Ib. sec. 6.
[3]Ib. sec. 14.   [6]Ib. ii. sec. 58.
[4]Ib. sec. III.

ate expediency, indicate the thoroughgoing utilitarian of the empirical school. In the sphere of pure politics, Locke naturally applies the same doctrine to the defence of the principles involved in the Revolution. He insists in the strongest terms on the responsibility of all officials to the community;[7] he justifies the sacred right of insurrection in language which would be fully applicable to the American War of Independence or the French Revolution; and enunciates with vigour the duty of a people whose rulers desert their trust, to make an 'appeal to heaven.'[8]

11. But vigorously as Locke can put the utilitarian argument, we become sensible that it somehow fails to give him complete satisfaction. He wants some binding element to supplement the mere shifting considerations of expediency. We constantly meet with rights of an indefeasible nature, which have somehow obtained an authority independent of the source from which they are derived. He is forced to alternate between simple utilitarianism and an odd system of legal fictions. A general, he says, may hang a soldier for deserting his post, but may not take from him a farthing of his estate;[9] and he gives the simple and satisfactory reason that one power is necessary to, whilst the other has no connection with, the good of the community. But he cannot answer the question: What right has a state to punish an alien for crimes committed in its jurisdiction? without this unlucky compact. Punishment is not right because useful, but because, by transgressing the law of nature, 'the offender declares himself to live by another rule than that of reason and common equity.'[10] Why may I kill a thief who wants only to take my money? Because he 'has put himself into a state of war with me.'[11] In such cases the legal fiction leads us by a roundabout path to the same conclusion as the argument from expediency; but elsewhere the perplexity becomes more intricate. Locke's teaching about slavery, for example, is curiously uncertain for so determined an advocate of human rights. In the Constitutions of Carolina, drawn by him in 1669, though they, perhaps, do not represent his opinions in all respects, the freemen are invested with absolute authority over their negro slaves.[12] In his theoretical discussions he adopts the doctrine that a man cannot make himself a slave, because he cannot give away that which he does not possess—namely, the power over his own life; but adds that slavery must be justified as the continuance of a state of war between a lawful

[7]Treatise, sec. 168, and ch. xix. of the 'Dissolution of Government.'
[8]Ib. sec. 139.
[9]Ib. sec. 152.   [11]Ib. sec. 18.
[10]Ib. ii. sec. 8.   [12]Works, ix. 196.

conqueror and a captive. Here, it is evident that Locke, unable to see through the old metaphysical argument, has entirely abandoned the utilitarian test, and forgets the noblest part of his own theory. The justification of slavery jars strangely with a confutation of claims to arbitrary power. A more elaborate specimen of the same perplexity occurs in the chapter devoted to the origin of government by conquest. A rightful conqueror, he thinks, has power over the lives of the conquered, but not over their possessions—a doctrine which he expects to startle his readers, not as allowing too much to the conqueror, but as putting him under some restrictions.[13] The conqueror, indeed, has a right to be paid for damages; but he argues ingeniously to show that they can seldom or never amount to the fee simple of the land.[14] And he concludes that, at any rate, the descendants of the conquered must be freed from all liability, as every man is born free, and with a right to inherit his father's goods.[15] The social contract is indispensable as a ground for the commonest rights. When it is broken by a state of war, any violence is justifiable; though elsewhere war becomes merely a quasi-legal process for the recovery of damages. He can only try, however, to limit it as much as possible, when it leads to results shocking to his sense of justice.

12. It is strange to see a man of such vast intellectual vigour, and, above all, with so firm a grasp of facts, allowing himself to be trammelled with this vexatious figment. It worries him and perplexes all his reasoning. It has to be alternately stretched and narrowed, and involves the most inconvenient hypotheses. And yet it evidently presented itself to him as the only alternative to a theory of arbitrary power. He is troubled for a time by the obvious suggestion that no such compact was ever made in an historical sense. Locke tries to support himself, as Sidney does with a much greater show of historical knowledge, by referring to special cases, such as Rome and Venice,[16] and to certain persons mentioned by Justin, who 'went away from Sparta with Palantus;'[17] but he admits that, historically speaking, government probably arose from the paternal power, though, in all cases, it implied a trust for the good of the governed.[18] But not only was the contract never made, but it would not, by Locke's own showing, have been binding if it had been made. The obligation could not be inherited. He maintains that every man has an indefeasible right to choose his own sovereign. By the practice of governments themselves, he argues, 'as well as by the law of

---

[13]Treatise ii. sec. 180.   [15]Ib. sec. 190.   [17]Ib. sec. 103.
[14]Ib. sec. 184.   [16]Ib. ii. sec. 102.   [18]Ib. sec. 110.

right reason, a child is born a subject of no country or government.'[19] Here we seem to be led straight to anarchy. If no man can be lawfully governed, except by his own individual consent, all government is a mere rope of sand. The bond, therefore, has to be patched up again by the familiar expedient of a tacit consent. A man who has expressly consented to the rule of any commonwealth 'is perpetually and indefeasibly obliged to be and remain unalterably a subject of it.'[20] But a tacit consent is given by every owner of property; for so long as a man enjoys the protection of the laws which defend his property, he tacitly consents to be a subject of the commonwealth which imposes the laws. He may, indeed, at any time sell his property, and join any other commonwealth, or set up a commonwealth in the desert. The allegiance which in the first case is unalterable, becomes in the second analogous to membership of a joint-stock company.

13. The doctrine is worked out in an elaborate form in one of his most ingenious chapters. In discussing the origin of property we come to the ultimate form of this Protean compact, which seems so strangely to alternate between reality and fiction. Property, according to Locke, exists antecedently to the formation of civil society, which was devised chiefly with a view to its protection. It has a character independent of any human conventions, and, therefore, supplies a base from which they may be inferred. Man has a right to monopolise part of the earth, which has been bestowed upon the race by God, because man has a right to his own labour, and, therefore, to anything 'he hath mixed his labour with.'[21] The savage acquires a right to an acorn by the simple act of picking it up. In cultivated countries the chief value of land is that which has been added to it by labour; and a man has a right to so much as he can cultivate. He has 'annexed to it something' which was exclusively his own property;[22] and in this way 'right and conveniency went together, for as a man had a right to all he could employ his labour upon, so he had no temptation to labour for more than he could make use of.'[23] As before absolute rights seemed to involve anarchy, so here they seem to involve communism; and here again we escape by means of a tacit compact. Money is in this case the outward sign of the agreement. The use of money enables people to hold more land than they can cultivate by enabling them to exchange the surplus products; and as money is not perishable, a man may keep as much as he pleases without injuring society by useless waste. The expedient is in some sense

[19]Treatise sec. 118.   [21]Ib. ii. sec. 27.
[20]Ib. sec. 121.   [22]Ib. sec. 32.   [23]Ib. sec. 51.

arbitrary, as money has but a 'fantastical imaginary value;'[24] and as it has been adopted by 'a tacit and voluntary consent,' that right implies a right to the necessary consequences of the expedient—namely, the inequality of possession. Thus the use of money enables us to escape from the universal equality which would seem to be the teaching of the law of nature. The tacit consent to the division of property becomes the main element, if not the whole substance, of the original contract. Government, he says in one place, has no other end but the preservation of property.'[25] Elsewhere this is 'the great and chief end of men's entering into commonwealths.'[26] The theory, though it runs through the Treatise, is mixed with discordant elements; but the nearest approach to a definite statement of Locke's ultimate conclusions seems to be that this mysterious compact, which is the binding force of the whole social order, is in fact the tacit consent of mankind to the inequality of property, as implied in the use of money, and made necessary by the corruption which followed the golden age.

14. Only in this perplexed manner could the sturdy sense of Locke manage to utter its protest against tyranny. Nothing, one might think, would be easier than to cut away all the factitious bonds which so trammel the strong man. The utility, whatever it may be, which Locke represents as the consideration contemplated in this strange bargain, made nowhere in particular, and which he only avoids calling 'nonexistent' by the simple expedient of using the word 'tacit,' is always, as far as it goes, a valid argument for justifying existing arrangements. On the whole, Locke would have said the acceptance of the complex inequalities of the social order is a necessary condition for avoiding the worse evils of barbarism. But the plain reason seemed to him insufficient till it was twisted into the shape of a bargain. That formula seemed to give a binding force wanting in the naked statement of utility. By Locke's contemporaries the assertion that government rested in some sense on compact or consent was valued for itself, though they cared little for the refinements by which the unreal hypothesis was accommodated to the facts. They were parting company for ever with the divine right of kings. Filmer's theories were read by the light of James II.'s practical expositions, and the king's blundering tyranny crushed them more effectually than the philosopher's logic. Political speculators blundered strangely in trying to frame a theoretical formula for this practical revolt against injustice. The social contract was an importation into the sphere of speculation of the ordinary system of legal fic-

---

[24]Treatise sec. 184.   [25]Ib. ii. sec. 94.   [26]Ib. sec. 124.

tions. As old laws were bent and twisted into pure non-meaning before they were finally cast aside, men clung to this last relic of the obsolete methods before they could resolve to trust wholly to experience. Any analogy would serve which deprived kings of arbitrary power. Regarded as managers of a joint-stock company, or as the tacitly appointed guardians of property, they were at least confined by the terms of their trust within some definite limits.

15. The theory, complex and unsatisfactory as it became when severely scrutinised, gave a temporary resting-place. And thus we naturally find in Locke's ingenious hypothesis curious points of contact, both with the theories from which he borrowed and those which were raised upon his foundation. He continually invokes the authority of Hooker, who had found the compact convenient under somewhat analogous circumstances. The Whigs, in their turn, appealed to Locke as the great supporter of their favourite dogma. At times it takes forms which remind us of his special interpretation. The connection, for example, upon which Locke insists between property in land and the supposed compact appears in a popular shape in various writings, as in De Foe's treatise 'On the Original Power of the People of England.' De Foe argues that the freeholders have a natural right to govern the country, inasmuch as all its other inhabitants live 'upon sufferance;' and if the king were sole landlord, he would be naturally absolute. The revolutionary party found their account in the doctrine as expanded for a very different purpose by Rousseau; and they could quote from Locke very sweeping assertions as to the natural equality and liberty of mankind. The utilitarians again might appeal to him as frequently sanctioning their method. Though he scarcely touches upon constitutional details, some of his incidental arguments, and the importance which he attaches to the separation of the legislative from the 'executive and federative' powers, may remind us of Montesquieu.[27] He was one of the first writers to attack the anomaly of rotten boroughs, a grievance which, in his opinion, could only be remedied by the direct action of the sovereign.[28] But, without descending into minutiæ, his chief influence was in popularising a convenient formula for enforcing the responsibility of governors. The social compact did well enough to oppose to such as Filmer and the little band of nonjurors. We shall soon see what strange efficacy lay in its later developments.

16. Another application of Locke's principles was, in one sense, the most important. The great principle of toleration had been asserted,

[27]Treatise ii. ch. xii.   [28]Ib. sec. 157.

though with characteristic incompleteness, by the English leaders of 1688. Dissent was no longer criminal, though it was exposed to various disqualifications. The admission that the Scottish people had a right to their own form of Church government made it difficult—especially after the Union—to revive the old principles of the duty of the State to support any particular Church as the sole depository of the truth. On one side, therefore, none except the small and declining party represented by the nonjurors could regard the Church of England as a divine institution, authorised to command the support of the State. On the other hand, the modern doctrine of 'a free Church in a free state,' the theory, that is, that a Church is merely a voluntary association, with which the laws have simply no concern, was equally incompatible with facts. Both logical extremes were untenable by anybody who professed, as everybody did profess, to be tolerably satisfied by the existing compromise. The old spirit of ecclesiastical domination was still strong enough to find vehement utterance in the early part of the century, as was shown by the Sacheverel agitation and the Bangorian controversy. The revolutionary party laid down antagonistic principles which should have involved the complete separation of Church and State. But the abstract principles had to be guarded by qualifications and reserves corresponding to the compromise actually adopted.

17. The theory of toleration involves some of the most complex of political problems. The controversy, in fact, lies upon the border between the two great fields of discussion, political and religious, and arouses all the passions involved in either. The protest against the persecuting spirit might embody itself in a religious, a moral, or a political doctrine. There are three main reasons against burning a man for disbelieving in Transubstantiation. In the first place, it may be said, the doctrine of Transubstantiation is nonsense. If, secondly, this be denied, the persecutor, it may be said, is as likely to be wrong as his victim. And, thirdly, even if the doctrine be true, burning its opponents does not prove it to be true, and is therefore not a fair method of propagating the truth. This last gives the moral objection to the practice; but it may well be doubted whether it would ever have prevailed without the help of the sceptical objection. If the general belief in the evil of heresy were comparable in intensity to our belief in the evil of small-pox, one would be stamped out as vigorously as the other; but the most ordinary minds can see the objection to propagating by force a faith which they do not really hold. When toleration, whether founded upon indifference or moral principle, has become part of the political creed, there still remains another series of problems. Granting that the secular power

should not punish heretics, can it, and, if so, should it, assume a position of complete neutrality? Can the spiritual and the secular code work side by side without interfering, and if they must interfere, how can their relative claims be adjusted?

Locke's position is given in the 'Letters on Toleration,' the first of which sufficiently indicates his position. The others, devoted to meeting the cavils of an antagonist, consist chiefly of incessant and wearisome repetitions of the same arguments. As in his other controversies, Locke has no mercy upon the patience of his readers.

18. The main points, however, are obvious. Locke does not say that the Thirty-nine Articles are false, but he makes the modest assumption that they are of human origin. Infallibility, if credible, supplies an unassailable ground for persecution. If the voice of a church be the voice of God, it may equally define theological dogmas, and prescribe the mode of propagating dogmas. For Locke such a theory is out of the question. True Christianity, according to him, is to be found in all the churches, though in all the churches it is overlaid with rites and dogmas varying indefinitely, and therefore uncertain. A man will not be damned, as he urges in the 'Reasonableness of Christianity,' for preferring a black gown to a white surplice, or for losing his head in settling the relative limits of nature and grace. If he will not be damned for going astray on such matters, he ought not to be burnt for it. Persecution by a fallible church, it is generally said, must be illogical. If so, it might be replied, all punishment by fallible men is illogical, for I may be as certain of the falsity of an opinion as of the bad tendency of a practice. But, on Locke's tacit assumption that all the churches—or, at least, all the Protestant churches—differed only in matters of minor importance, and in matters of which one man is as good a judge as another, the argument against persecution is conclusive.

19. The question, however, may be pushed further. A thorough rationalist holds that reason is not merely the sole test of truth, but should be the sole instrument of conversion. Locke's favourite mode of stating this argument is by forcing upon his antagonist the conclusion that, if a Christian ruler may persecute, so may a Mahommedan: if the king of England, then the king of France. As, on any hypothesis, error has a majority on its side, this is to say that truth must generally be persecuted. This argument, again, is not logically unassailable; for it is at least a conceivable theory that persecution is right for the orthodox and wrong for the heterodox. But, from Locke's point of view, the mode of evasion would be hardly worth refutation. The opinion that it was the duty of all rulers in all parts of the world to force men to belong to the Church

of England was scarcely tenable even by the most bigoted of nonjurors. He probably held that the Articles included much error; he certainly held that they included much that was open to fair difference of opinion; and, therefore, the Church was so far from being justified in claiming to force its opinions upon men as an established body of definitive truth, that it was rather the duty of the Church to encourage every sincere enquirer, and, without admitting any given dogma to be wrong, to admit that all required constant and free discussion from every point of view.

20. Locke's argument thus includes a sceptical element; that is to say, a denial that religious certainty had as yet been obtained, or could be attained, so far as to justify the State in using force. But the moral argument is equally forcible if we make a still smaller concession to the rationalist. Grant that innocent error in religious matters is possible; grant also that a man is bound to speak the truth as to his religious beliefs; and it follows that persecution implies punishment of men for an action which the punisher admits to be virtuous. This, indeed, is so far an unassailable ground. Locke's antagonist tries to meet the argument by a foolish distinction, which Locke exposes at far more length than it deserves, as to penalties being intended, not to make men believe, but to make them consider their beliefs attentively. The quibble is too feeble to require Locke's serious reply. Laws must sometimes be enforced in spite of conscientious objections; but it is at least a grave objection to any law that it compels a man to do what the legislator admits to be wrong. Force is no argument; and burning may make a hypocrite, but cannot make a true believer. It may produce 'outward conformity,'[29] but not, in its direct effects at least, inward conformity. Therefore, it is a detestable weapon in religious controversy.

21. Locke thus triumphantly establishes a proposition, already accepted by all the greatest Englishmen of his generation, and never seriously contested in later days; the proposition, namely, that the State should not attempt to propagate creeds by force. The common sense of the laity was emphatically saying through his lips to the clergy, We won't do your dirty work any longer. We don't half believe your creeds; we are quite clear that they are not worth the price of punishing honest men for disbelieving them. You shall have fair play, and trust, like other people, to argument. If you can convert us by reason, well and good; if not, don't think that we will fill up the gaps in your logic by the stake, the prison, or by fines. The sects are harmless enough if left

[29]Locke's Works, v. 323, and elsewhere.

to themselves. Some people combine for trade, others for amusement. 'Neighbourhood joins some and religion others. But there is one thing only which gathers people into seditious communions, and that is oppression.'[30] A noble saying, and backed by undeniable truths. The real quarrel with the dissenters was, as Locke adds, that 'they are ill-used, and therefore they are not to be suffered.'[30] Put them on an equality with their fellow-subjects, and the government will have a far higher guarantee for general content than can be extracted from the most systematic oppression.

22. Locke, as I have said, makes throughout the tacit assumption implied in these words. The various churches are, in fact, harmless, so long as they are not oppressed. Quakers, Anabaptists, Independents, Presbyterians, and the whole series of Protestant sects, will do no harm to you if you will do no harm to them. But suppose that this assumption should not be verified? If there be a creed which preaches mischievous doctrines, are we still bound to be tolerant? The difficulty of the problem is indicated by two remarkable exceptions. Atheists, says Locke, 'are not at all to be tolerated;[31] for they deny the only principle in virtue of which human relations are possible. Nor have papists a right to toleration (though he does not explicitly say that they are not to be tolerated), so far as they hold the doctrine of keeping no faith with heretics, or acknowledge the supremacy of another ruler.[32] The distinction seems to imply the general proposition that an opinion may be rightfully suppressed if it is incompatible with allegiance to the state. This evidently introduces a whole series of political problems, which are not adequately discussed by Locke. Suppose, for example, that a man refuses to obey the law on the ground of a religious scruple. Is he to be excused? No; says Locke, a private person must submit to the punishment, if it is 'within the verge of the magistrate's authority.'[33] Otherwise—as in the case of the magistrate enforcing a strange religion—he is bound to resist. What, then, are the proper limits of the magistrate's authority?

23. This undoubtedly, is amongst the most delicate of problems. It is one, I may add, to which any solution based upon absolute and unalterable principles is necessarily inadequate. The limits of the legitimate application of state authority depend (so, at least, I should maintain) upon the stage of social development. We may say that, under given conditions of intellectual, moral, and social order, the magistrate ought, or ought not, to interfere in such matters, for example, as education,

---

[30]Locke's Works, v. 50.   [32]Ib. pp. 45–7.
[31]Ib. p. 47.   [33]Ib. p. 43.

which implies certain religious assumptions. To draw the line accurately, to say in what cases the magistrate is, or is not, overstepping his proper functions to assume those of the priest or of the private individual, is a matter of great nicety even at the present day. To lay down a fixed rule as equally applicable to all past and present cases, is to sin against the first principles of sound political reasoning. But this doctrine, true or false, was not perceptible from Locke's point of view. Some absolute rule must be discovered to serve as a definite bound to the encroachments of the state. Locke, of course, found it, where he found all other principles, in the social compact. The social compact has long been obsolete, but the doctrines which it covered became the permanent creed of the Whigs, and were accepted more systematically both by the English utilitarians and the French revolutionists.

24. The doctrine may be summarily exhibited. The state rests upon the voluntary consent of mankind to trust the magistrate with powers necessary for the protection of their civil interests, that is to say, their 'life, liberty, health, and indolency of body; and the possession of outward things, such as money, land, houses, furniture, and the like.'[34] A Church is a 'voluntary society of men, joining themselves together of their own accord, in order to the public worshipping of God in such a manner as they judge to be acceptable to him, and effectual to the salvation of their souls.'[35] The magistrate alone may use force, the Church ruler must confine himself to moral suasion. The last possible spiritual weapon must be excommunication,[36] which is simply a separation from the society of the man who refuses to obey its laws. This obviously is to assert expressly the modern principle of 'a free church in a free state.' It seems to be fatal to any establishment of a Church. Locke argues at great length that the use of any force against dissenters logically implies the use of all the force necessary for their conversion.[37] The same argument would seem to tell equally against all disqualification, and therefore against all privilege. If Locke never drew this conclusion explicitly, he was restrained, not by logic, but by policy or by ignorance.

His antagonist accused him, not unnaturally, of begging the question. Nothing is easier than to infer any conclusion from this elastic social compact. You have only to make its terms, and it may sanction anything. Locke replies by substantially bringing forward the utilitarian ground. The compact, according to his version,[38] amounts to an agree-

[34]Locke's Works, v. 10.   [35]Ib. v. 13.   [36]Ib. v. 16.   [37]Ib. v. 262, &c.
[38]Ib. v. 212.

ment of men not to hurt each other; a man is not hurt by my being of
a different religion; therefore the compact does not include a clause for
a common form of worship.

25. If Locke escapes from the charge of arguing in a circle, it is clearly
by making an assumption. The assumption is that which is common to
all his party. It is substantially that a church, like a 'club for claret,'[39]
has no bearing upon men's duties as members of a state. Macaulay, in
our own day, argued against Mr. Gladstone that it was as irrelevant to
exact religious tests from members of a political body as from members
of a canal company. So Locke tells his antagonist that it does not follow
that the state is bound to protect religion any more than the East India
Company.[40] Locke, indeed, sees the difficulty more distinctly than his
successor. The government, like the church, is bound to encourage 'a
good life, in which consists not the least part of religion and true
piety'[41]—indeed, on Locke's showing, nearly the whole of true religion.
Thus, as moral actions come within both provinces, there is a danger of
conflict. Locke thinks, however, that, so long as that state confines itself
to its true duty, the promotion 'of the temporal good and outward
prosperity of the society,'[42] there is little danger of collision. His doctrine is, in fact, based on the assumption that men were in fact sufficiently agreed upon all moral questions to be able to submit to a common rule in regard to all the matters actually regulated by legislative
authority. We can, therefore, pass over the difficult problems which arise
in cases where men's views about the fate of their souls make them
adopt inconsistent modes of providing for their bodies, or in which the
action of the legislators obviously affects more than the body. This assumption, moreover, was sufficiently accurate in regard to the state of
things actually contemplated. Religious distinctions had little influence
upon practice for generations to come, and Locke's doctrine did well
enough for the quiet times of the eighteenth century, though its theoretical basis might be defective. If the social compact was a fiction, men
were, in fact, agreed as to what they wanted from government; and
they did not want any interference with their religious practices nor any
interference with practices indirectly affected by religious beliefs. So long
as this remained true, the social compact did well enough, and when
the compact was forgotten, the doctrine that religious controversies were
controversies about words was equally favourable to the old solution. Let
parsons quarrel about creeds, so long as they support the police, is the
true Whig doctrine, and one which answers very fairly in practice. But

[39]Locke's Works, v. 50.   [40]Ib. v. 118.   [41]Ib. v. 41.   [42]Ib. v. 43.

it does not give a scientific solution of the problem as to the limits of state interference.

26. The sceptical side of such theories is more explicitly given in Tindal's 'Rights of the Christian Church'—a book which earned for its author a foretaste of the indignation afterwards produced by 'Christianity as Old as the Creation.' The social compact, according to Tindal, gives the right to punish the wicked and protect the good. The legislator may, therefore, punish atheists, blasphemers, and profane persons,[43] whose principles or practice encourage crime. He may, further, appoint persons to instruct his subjects to fulfil the duty which he is bound to enforce;[44] but, on the other hand, he has no right to enforce opinions not conducive to this purpose, or to tax his subjects to support those who teach them.[45] Speculative opinions, which apparently means all opinions except the opinion that God will punish murderers and thieves, must be left to individuals and voluntary societies. This amounts to saying that the clergy ought to be state officials, paid to teach the religion of nature. Tindal, if he had spoken out with perfect frankness, would have endowed his own creed, given it state support, and left men to squabble about the Trinity or Transubstantiation as much as they pleased. His theory strongly resembles that afterwards set forth with greater vigour by Rousseau. The greater part of the book, however, is an attack upon the claims of the high-church party to supernatural privileges in the Church. To admit such a doctrine is, as he argues with much vigour, to allow the contradiction of two supreme powers in the state, and has practically led to all the evils generally attributed by the deists to priestcraft. Toleration, therefore, in Tindal's mouth, meant simply that priests should not be allowed to burn heretics, because priests were impostors. It is needless to add that priests did not love Tindal. This book and the 'Independent Whig' (1720, &c.), a series of essays in the 'Spectator' shape, devoted to the abuse of the clergy, are the best illustration of that antipathy to sacerdotalism, generated during the struggles of the seventeenth century, which survived into the eighteenth, and is not yet upon its deathbed. Toleration, however, softened its bitterness considerably after the early years of the Hanoverian dynasty. The best illustration of the prevailing theories is that Bangorian controversy which was once celebrated, if only as an instance of confusion worse confounded.

[43]Tindal, p. 12.   [44]Ib. p. 12.   [45]Ib. p. 22.

III. The Bangorian Controversy.

27. Benjamin Hoadly was probably the best-hated clergyman of the century amongst his own order. His titles to the antipathy of his brethren were many and indisputable. A clergyman who opposes sacerdotal privileges is naturally the object of a sentiment such as would be provoked by a trades-unionist who should defend the masters, or a country squire who should protect poachers. In Hoadly's day the feeling was specially intense. Dissenters had extorted toleration without obtaining equality, and the old persecuting sentiment survived, though compelled to satisfy itself by comparatively impotent legislation or by exhibitions of social insolence. The advocates of the Church still brooded over the memories of the Great Rebellion, and grudged the claims of the sects which had once trampled them under foot. Hoadly again not only supported the political pretensions of the dissenters, but occupied a very questionable theological position. To attack the exclusive privileges of the Church was, of course, to attack the divine law; but Hoadly was also suspected, and with good apparent reason, of extreme laxity in his theology. The intimate friend and admirer of Clarke, he was probably further from orthodoxy than the great latitudinarian leader. Add to this that Hoadly was not merely a traitor, but a successful traitor; that Convocation, for attempting to silence him, was itself doomed to silence; and that, according to the system of the day, he rose by several minor preferments to the great bishopric of Winchester. There he remained for more than a quarter of a century, till the controversies of his early life had become a dim tradition with the existing generation, and died in his eighty-fifth year, in 1761. Hoadly, hated for all these reasons, had not the manner to conciliate antagonists. His style is the style of a bore; he is slovenly, awkward, intensely pertinacious, often indistinct, and, apparently at least, evasive; and occasionally (I am thinking especially of his arguments with his old enemy Atterbury) not free from a tinge of personal rancour. He preached his first lectureship down to 30l. a year, as he candidly reports, and then thought it time to resign. A perusal of his writings renders the statement easily credible. The three huge folios which contain his ponderous wranglings are a dreary wilderness of now profitless discussion. We owe, however, a vast debt of gratitude to the bores who have defended good causes, and in his pachydermatous fashion Hoadly did some service, by helping to trample down certain relics of the old spirit of bigotry.

28. Before the controversy to which his fame is chiefly due Hoadly

had written some political treatises. The most elaborate are the 'Measures of Submission to the Civil Magistrate,' and 'The Original Institution of Civil Government discussed.' In them he once more slays the slain. Following in the steps of Locke, to whom, however, he makes but a grudging reference,[1] he argues that Adam's paternal authority over Cain had not been transferred to the King of England, and would not entitle him, if it had been transferred, to burn Protestants in Smithfield. He attacks the Anglican doctrine of non-resistance, which had become obsolete when Anglicans found resistance convenient. He opposes to the patriarchal theory the alternative and equally flimsy theory of a social compact, and labours hard to show that the historical reality of such a compact, though not necessary to the validity of his theory, may be reconciled with the narrow chronological limits of the Book of Genesis. The details of such a discussion may well be swept to the dustheaps. The general tendency needs alone to be indicated. Hoadly seems to labour under a singular difficulty in this as in the Bangorian controversy. He is too much in agreement with his antagonist. All but a few irreconcilables admitted after the Revolution of 1688 that resistance was in some cases allowable. Everybody again admitted that resistance was only allowable in very serious cases. The true question was therefore one of degree. What intensity of evil would justify resistance? Such a question is obviously not to be answered by laying down absolute rules. The problem by its very nature belongs to the sphere of expediency, not of abstract truth. And yet absolute rules were very convenient as taunts to an adversary. Thus Hoadly seems alternately to relax and tighten the bonds of obedience. At one moment he says that the people are to judge for themselves only when they are 'on the brink of destruction;' they are only 'to defend themselves against certain ruin;' and not in that case to upset all rule, but to put themselves under a better government for the future.[2] Nobody who admitted of resistance at all could draw the line nearer to unconditional obedience. Elsewhere, Hoadly uses language which seems to imply that the subject ought to resist all laws which in his opinion are wrong. To escape from this consecration of anarchy, he introduces qualifications which neutralise his theory. Like most writers of his class, he can only abolish a pope or a tyrant by making every man his own pope or tyrant. He cannot conceive of an authority resting upon reason, or of a power which may enforce its command, and yet rest its titles to command upon reasonable enquiry;

[1] Hoadly, Works, ii. 190.
[2] 'Original Institutions' &c. ii. 184.

and this difficulty, which still besets many minds, greatly perplexes some of the later Bangorian arguments. Meanwhile, Hoadly alternates between assertions which nobody would deny and assertions which nobody would seriously maintain. Each side found its account in this style of reasoning. Everybody must always obey, cried the Tory; but, he added in a whisper, cases may occur which necessitate resistance. Every man, proclaimed the Whig, should resist when resistance conduces to the public good; but, then, he admitted, it must be remembered that in almost every case resistance causes more injury than the evils which it professes to cure. Such arguments, in fact, were well suited to a state of things in which Whig and Tory had an instinctive dislike to each other's principles, but had struck out a very fair compromise in all matters of immediate practical interest.

29. In truth, the instinct was not altogether at fault. Hoadly's dislike to the Tory doctrine rested ultimately on a logical basis which he himself probably did not clearly understand. His whole political and ecclesiastical theories may be summed up in a single formula. He denies the divine-right theory, whether of priests or kings, in the only sense in which it can have any application to a specific political problem. This denial (as I have remarked) is the logical consequence of the deist theory. When God becomes nature, or is so nearly identified with nature that all supernatural interference is incredible, the basis of a divine right of any particular family, caste, or constitution, is destroyed. The divine favour can be no more monopolised by a single form of government than by a single sect or organisation. No man or set of men has received any special commission from the Almighty. That religion is best which is most reasonable, and that system of government which is most useful. Hoadly, in accordance with this view, aims at eradicating all claims to authority which rest upon a basis different from that of utility. There can be no supernatural virtue in kings or priests communicating an indefeasible and paramount claim to authority. Hoadly, indeed, could hardly strike at the root of the theory, whilst asserting that God had taken a direct part in the government of the Jews and the foundation of the Church. His doctrine involves the fundamental inconsistency of all the contemporary rationalisers who admitted previous supernatural interventions, whilst denying their actual occurrence in modern times. But in his clumsy and illogical way Hoadly was attacking a theory, then dying, though not yet dead, which endeavoured to provide certain claims to priestly and royal authority with supernatural sanctions, and therefore to base them on the rock of absolute right, whilst the rest of the fabric was founded only on the shifting sands of expediency. Wherever such

a claim to supernatural authority is made or implied, Hoadly sees the evil thing; and the most spirited fragment which he ever wrote is an attack upon Protestants for virtually making claims inconsistent with their repudiation of supernatural authority.

30. The tract is called a 'Dedication to Pope Clement XI' and was prefixed anonymously to Steele's 'Account of the State of the Roman Catholic Religion throughout the World.' It is written in the ironical style so popular in the days of Swift, Arbuthnot, and De Foe, and claims a close resemblance between Papists and Protestants. All the Protestant sects admit their fallibility, and differ in their conclusions, yet all are ready, within their own limits, to enforce their own opinion by prison or the gallows. The difference is, he says, that 'you *cannot* err in anything you determine, and we never *do;* that is, in other words, that you are infallible, and we always in the right.'[3] And, finally, after summing up various proofs of a persecuting spirit, and of the approximation of the English clergy to Roman superstitions, he concludes the only difference to be that 'ours is Protestant popery, and yours is Popish popery.'[4] Protestantism, with him, means the unrestricted right of private judgment, and that right excludes all claims to priestly authority; but the true bearing of his arguments comes out more clearly in the Bangorian controversy.

31. This controversy, which raged furiously during 1717–8, is one of the most intricate tangles of fruitless logomachy in the language. In the bibliography given in Hoadly's works there is a list of more than fifty divines who joined in the fray.[5] In the course of July 1717 there appeared seventy-four pamphlets.[6] At one crisis, when the controversy took a personal turn, we are assured that, for a day or two, the common business of the city was at a stand; that little was done on the Exchange, and even that many shops were shut.[7] The struggle became more and more perplexed, till the precise issue disappeared in a hubbub of confused assertions, contradictions, qualifications, personal imputations, and retorts which soon ceased to be courteous. There is a bewildering variety of theological, ecclesiastical, political, historical, exegetical, and purely personal discussions. The combatants are so fierce, that blows, which need have caused little irritation, produce angry sores. Besides the more serious disputes, we are invited to consider whether Hoadly was justified in keeping a converted Jesuit in his family, and what was the

[3]Hoadly's Works, i. 535.   [4]Ib. i. 544.
[5]Ib. ii. p. 398. A continuation of the list is given at the end of vol. i.
[6]Ib. ii. 385.   [7]Ib. ii. 429.

Jesuit's character; whether he had or had not taken the advice of a friend to insert certain phrases in his sermon before it was printed or before it was published; whether Sherlock had said something to much the same purpose as Hoadly in a previous sermon; whether it is proper to describe prayer as 'a calm and undisturbed' address to God; whether we may say that Christ's example is more peculiarly fit for slaves than for subjects, and if so, in what sense, and whether Hoadly spoke in that sense; what is the proper interpretation of various phrases in the New Testament; what was the precise history of the Corporation and Test Acts; and what is the right answer to various questions connected only in the most accidental and indirect fashion with any reasonable topic of dispute. Throughout this troublesome wrangling, we have the annoying circumstance that nobody admits himself to be fairly represented, and that the charge which each man brings with the greatest bitterness against his adversary is that of entire agreement with himself. To follow out the minute reticulations of this tangled skein of argument would be waste of time. The disputants themselves must have regarded it, one fancies, in later years, as a lamentable waste of good human passion. The anger has long been cold, and the spoilt paper returned to its primitive elements. Three writers were more conspicuous than the rest, and it will be enough to notice their main positions. Hoadly had the ill-luck to encounter two of the ablest—probably, if Bentley be excepted, the two ablest controversial writers of the time. Sherlock and Law attacked different parts of his argument with singular vigour; and in their writings and Hoadly's we may find whatever deserves to survive the general wreck.

32. Hoadly's theory was first stated in the 'Preservative against the Principles and Practice of Nonjurors' (1716)—a book provoked by the publication of certain posthumous papers of Hickes, the nonjuror. His sermon, preached on March 31st, 1717, which was the immediate cause of the explosion, states it more concisely and distinctly. His various answers to Snape, Sherlock, and the Committee of Convocation, explain his view of certain obvious objections. Hoadly simply applies to ecclesiastical questions the principle already explained in a political connection. He is lowering the priesthood, as he had formerly lowered the monarchy, to the ordinary level of humanity. He is striking at the heart of sacerdotalism. A priest is one who claims divine authority for his words, whose privileges are secured by a divine grant, and who can wield certain powers in virtue of his sacred character. Hoadly substantially denies the validity of these claims. Though forced to admit that Christ and the Apostles enjoyed supernatural powers and privileges,

he denies, like the other rationalists of the time, that those powers had been transmitted to their successors. The expression of the doctrine, as it shaped itself in Hoadly's mind, must be given in his own words.

'As the Church of Christ is the kingdom of Christ, he himself is king; and in this it is implied that he is himself the sole lawgiver to his subjects, and himself the sole judge of their behaviour, in the affairs of conscience and eternal salvation. And in this sense, therefore, his king-dom is not of this world; that he hath in those points left behind him no visible human authority, no vicegerents who can be said properly to supply his place; no interpreters upon whom his subjects are absolutely to depend; no judges over the conscience or religion of his people. For if this were so, that any such absolute vicegerent authority, either for the making of new laws, or interpreting old ones, or judging his sub-jects, in religious matters, were lodged in any men upon earth, the consequence would be that what still retains the name of the Church of Christ would not be the kingdom of Christ, but the kingdom of those men vested with such authority. For, whoever hath such an authority of making laws is so far a king, and whoever can add new laws to those of Christ, equally obligatory, is as truly a king as Christ himself is. Nay, whosoever hath an absolute authority to interpret any written or spoken laws, it is he who is truly the lawgiver to all intents and purposes, and not the person who first wrote and spoke them.'[8] The viceroy of an absolute monarch is himself absolute if the monarch never interposes. Interpreting laws, on the same hypothesis, is but a periph-rasis for making laws.

33. So far Hoadly's logic is unimpeachable, though its relevancy might be disputed. His main arguments would have been far more co-herent if, instead of attacking the 'absolute,' he had attacked the 'super-natural' authority of the priesthood. In the 'Preservative' he assails the fundamental inconsistency of Protestant sacerdotalism, the attribution to fallible men, or bodies of fallible men, of powers intelligible only on the hypothesis of infallibility, and therefore, of the continuous inter-vention of supernatural powers. A church claiming such powers must, as he said, come into conflict with the state; it forms an *imperium in imperio,* and sooner or later one of the rivals must swallow up the other. Resistance to such claims is, therefore, of vital importance to the state. According to Hoadly, the state must have every power necessary for its own preservation; and resistance becomes its imperative duty.[9] This theory, which lies, as we have seen, at the base of his political

[8]Hoadly's Works, ii. 404.   [9]Ib. i. 582, 'Preservative.'

speculations, would find its full realisation when the state and church were placed, so to speak, on the same level. Their claims would then be commensurable, instead of resting in one case on divine and in the other on mere human authority. An equitable distribution of powers might be arranged between two corporations, when both allow an appeal to the common tribunal of human reason, judging by motives of expediency. Though Hoadly does not adopt this theory explicitly, his main arguments are those which would naturally arrange themselves in its support. Since the Church is fallible, he says, its decisions cannot possibly affect the relation of man to his Creator. The power of looking into men's hearts, and therefore of pronouncing the forgiveness of sins, might be granted to Peter along with the equally miraculous power of healing the sick; but Atterbury, who could not cure a pope of one twinge of toothache, could certainly not excuse Chartres one minute of hell-fire.[10] The Church may excommunicate a notorious sinner in the sense of refusing to associate with him, but not in the sense of sentencing him to future punishments.[11] Excommunication is thus 'a mere external thing.'[12] The Lord's Supper, as he argued some twenty years later, in a separate treatise,[13] is a mere commemorative rite, for we must otherwise admit that priests have a power of working miracles. Every vestige of supernatural endowment is stripped off the priesthood; the power of the keys is an absurdity, and no magical influence remains in church ceremonials. A bishop, in short, as Bolingbroke more frankly said, is nothing but a layman with a crook in his hand.

34. With the claim to supernatural privileges goes naturally the claim to a supernatural monopoly of truth, or faith in any church can be no more necessary to salvation than submission to its ordinances. The Church, indeed—for Hoadly could not repudiate the Articles—has 'authority in matters of faith;' but it is the authority of a witness, not of a judge; and an authority consistent with the right, or, rather, with the indispensable duty, of every man to judge for himself.[14] Sincerity, therefore, is the only moral duty connected with faith. A man is not bound to accept certain opinions, but to accept those opinions which commend themselves to his unbiassed reason. God, he argues in the 'Preservative,' cannot favour a man because he belongs to a particular

[10]See specially Hoadly's Works, i. 594, 'Preservative.'
[11]Ib. ii. 456, 'Answer to Representation.'
[12]Ib. ii. 860, 'Answer to Hare.'
[13]Ib. iii. 843, 'Treatise on the Lord's Supper.'
[14]Ib. ii. 862, 869, 'Answer to Hare.'

communion, but because he has chosen his communion honestly. 'The favour of God, therefore, follows sincerity considered as such; and, therefore, equally follows every equal degree of sincerity.'[15] The words led to a good deal of wrangling; as, indeed, they are the contradictory of the doctrine which lies at the bottom of all the theology of the preceding century, and the main justification of all persecutions, the necessity of a certain faith to salvation. Law tries to prove that, in admitting the innocence of error, Hoadly gives up the old standing-ground against heresy. This argument need not be followed out; though one remark may be suggested. So long as the ill consequences of any action are regarded as proofs of divine displeasure, it is impossible to deny that honest error is a sin most severely punished. The doctrine of the innocence of error is, therefore, naturally connected with disbelief in the visible interference of providence.

35. Hoadly, however, did not clearly see the tendencies of his own argument. Law, with his invariable keenness of logical perception, recognised the true key of the position. His second letter to Hoadly is, in fact, an argument that Hoadly ought to be a deist. One passage sufficiently indicates the point. 'Is it,' he asks, 'impossible for men to have this authority' (the authority, namely, of pronouncing absolution) 'from God, because they may mistake in the exercise of it? This argument proves too much, and makes as short work with every institution of Christianity as with the power of absolution. For, if it is impossible that men should have authority from God to absolve in his name, because they are not infallible, this makes them equally incapable of being entrusted with any other means of grace; and, consequently, supposes the whole priest's office to imply a direct impossibility to the very notion of it.'[16] Law, as usual, is applying the *reductio ad absurdum*—a dangerous weapon which is apt to go off at both ends. Hoadly never made a direct answer to Law; a neglect for which Sherlock thought that there could be 'but one good reason.'[17] Hoadly, that is, had no answer to make. Perhaps it would be truer in this case to say that a perfectly frank answer would have been dangerous. Hoadly denied, indeed, the truth of the doctrines of the apostolical succession and its various corollaries, which Law endeavours to support by the usual texts and arguments. But he did not deny outright the existence of any supernatural powers and privileges in the Church,[18] though he constantly used language

[15]Hoadley's Works, i. 593, 'Preservative.'   [16]Second Letter, p. 32.

[17]Sherlock, Works, v. 37.

[18]The point is pretty clearly stated in the 'Answer to the Representation.'— See xvii.; ii. 484.

tending to such a denial. He met his antagonist by a distinction which really raised a false issue, and throws the whole controversy into hopeless perplexity. The central knot of the controversy disappears in a hopeless entanglement of crossing threads. His opponents had charged him with assailing all Church authority. He should have replied: I deny that the Church can send a man to hell; I don't deny that it can and ought to censure him for immorality. But he chose to reply: That he had not denied all authority, but only absolute authority, or authority to which 'the people are indispensably obliged to submit.'[19] His opponents replied that the insertion of the word 'absolute' was a mere evasion intended to conceal his true sentiments; and this charge led, amongst other things, to that episcopal version of the counter-check quarrelsome, which, for a moment, silenced even the roar of London commerce.

36. The charge against Hoadly's honour proved only the extreme bitterness of his antagonists. The assault made upon his logic by Law[20] was more successful. Hoadly's arguments, as Law showed, were as good against authority in general as against absolute authority. They were pointed at the very vital principle of supernatural authority; not to its extent or limitations. He did not really object to a certain degree but to a certain kind of authority; nor could Hoadly escape except by making his doctrine nugatory. All Anglicans admitted that the spiritual authority of the Church, like the authority of the English Crown, was in some sense limited. The Reformation in the one case, like the Revolution in 1688 in the other, was a proof that a blind and implicit obedience to authority was not demanded. If, therefore, Hoadly merely attacked absolute authority, he attacked what no one supported. Law naturally supposed that Hoadly's disavowal was merely intended to cover an anarchical doctrine; though we may more charitably believe that it was rather due to a want of acuteness, which prevented the Bishop from ever attaching a very distinct meaning to the word 'absolute.' If Hoadly had expressly wished to make the whole stream of controversy hopelessly turbid, he could not have acted more skilfully; but, in such cases, natural puzzleheadedness performs all the functions of malevolent design.

37. The confusion of ideas thus introduced perplexes that part of the controversy which seems to come nearest to a direct practical issue. What is the bearing of these speculations upon the great question of toleration? Does Hoadly raise another barrier against persecution? So

[19]Hoadly's Works, ii. 484.   [20]In his first Letter.

far as persecution implies a belief in infallibility or in the sinfulness of intellectual error, he is, of course, opposed to it. When priests admit themselves to be mere fallible men, the great justification for burning other men disappears. But the difficulty still remains of so drawing the line between the spiritual and secular authority that all persecution shall be abolished. Perhaps, indeed, the problem is insoluble. So long as religions affect the same part of our lives which is regulated by legislation, the division of powers cannot be completely carried out; and Hoadly himself approved of measures which show how the old spirit might be reintroduced in a new shape. He declared himself unwilling to exclude a Papist or a Protestant from public offices on account of his religion, 'or on any account but that of his open avowed enmity to the civil government as settled in this land.'[21] The ground of their exclusion from the throne was not, as he elsewhere says, 'their religion considered as such, but the fatal, natural, certain effect of it upon themselves to our destruction.'[22] Law fairly ridicules the ingenious logic of this passage, as, in fact, it would make little difference to a heretic whether he were persecuted for his religion 'considered as such,' or for consequences which the persecutor held to be its inevitable result.

38. Hoadly, indeed, uses language which seemed to his opponents to declare for the most absolute separation between church and state. It was not competent for the state even to add its sanctions to the laws of the church. To apply, said Hoadly, force or flattery, worldly pleasure or pain, as motives for religion, is to act against the maxims on which Christ founded his kingdom. Motives of this world must not be used to support a kingdom which was not of this world. Such a theory appeared to Hoadly's adversaries to condemn every connection between the church and the state. But by one of the odd turns which mark the troublesome controversy, it appeared that his meaning was entirely different. In fact, Hoadly was not talking of the Church of England nor of any visible church. The denial of any supernatural authority inherent in any particular organisation leads him, logically enough, to regard the Church of Christ or the Kingdom of Christ—equivalent expressions, according to him—as consisting simply of all people who 'sincerely and willingly' accept Christ for their ruler.[23] Such a body has, of course, no organs for legislation or jurisdiction. Nobody can speak in its name without usurping its authority. Its laws—for in Hoadly's view Christi-

---

[21]Hoadly's Works, ii. 788, 'Common Rights of Subjects Defended.'
[22]Ib. ii. 422, 'Answer to Snape.'
[23]Ib. ii. 408, Sermon 477; 'Answer to Committee.'

anity meant little else—are the unalterable laws of morality; its king
and judge is Christ; its rewards and punishments are heaven and hell;
and its laws apply to the inward affections, not, like the human laws, to
the outward actions alone. In short, it is plain that Hoadly is really discussing the distinction between the spheres of morality and legislation,
whilst his opponents thought that he was discussing the distinction
between ecclesiastical and civil legislation. No wonder if the whole
argument became hopelessly perplexed!

39. Hoadly, in fact, comes to make the distinction between Christ's
kingdom and human kingdoms coincident with the distinction between
inward and outward. God rules the heart, and man the outward actions.
That, said Sherlock, is to divest the law 'of all its moral rectitude'[24]—a
reply which led to some profitless discussion as to the definition of an
'outward action.' Hoadly's meaning, however, evaporates as usual. All
that he means is that, as the magistrate cannot see into the heart, he
cannot punish vice as such. God alone can damn the man who hates
his brother; the magistrate can do no more than hang the murderer. So
far, too, as a man acts from the fear of the gallows he does not act from
the fear of God. But it does not follow that the magistrate is to be
indifferent to virtue and vice. 'Whatever directly affects the happiness
of public societies, and is within the power of the magistrate, is likewise
within his care.'[25] In support of this doctrine Hoadly not only admits
but declares that the magistrate is to 'encourage the same outward
actions which are commanded by the laws of God upon a higher principle, and to discourage the contrary,' and therefore that he is to 'do
everything in his power and belonging to his office for the encouraging
morality and discouraging the contrary.'[26] The only restriction implied
in such language is that the magistrate is not to do what is impossible
or illegal. Hoadly pushes his principle a step further, and claims to be,
as indeed he seems to be, in full agreement with Sherlock. The magistrate is to punish actions which are injurious to society, whatever the
motive, whether want of principle or perverted principle be at the
bottom of them. He is 'to terrify' men 'from any destructive practices,
whether they themselves think them right or wrong.' If, he adds, all
the robbers and murderers in the world thought it a duty to rob and
murder, 'as many rebels and traitors do,'[27] it would not be the less the
magistrate's duty to suppress them. Louis XIV. might have easily turned

[24]Sherlock, iv. 390.
[25]Hoadly's Works, ii. 512, 'Answer to Representation.'   [26]Ib. ii. 538, ib.
[27]Ib. ii. 543, 'Answer to Representation.'

this into a pretext for the revocation of the Edict of Nantes. Hoadly, no doubt, failed to observe the consequences of his argument, owing to his tacit assumption that virtue and vice were independent of church differences. He allowed the magistrate to act only with a view to the public good, and could not conceive that legislation on behalf of the Athanasian Creed could be brought under that category. The conclusion, however, is in sufficient harmony with his real principles. His whole purpose was to get the church of supernatural claims out of the way; he had disarmed it effectually enough, but had to allow the civil magistrate to succeed to its authority, though with less exalted claims.

40. Sherlock, with his clear legal intellect, has a great superiority over Hoadly in this part of the argument. He arrives at similar conclusions by a shorter road, and expresses them in excellent language. The controversy, as Sherlock substantially says, is whether certain consequences, repudiated by both parties, logically flow from Hoadly's principles.[28] On one definite conclusion, indeed, there was a clear difference, and there Sherlock, if a better writer than Hoadly, is a less straightforward reasoner. Both parties were agreed that religion should not be propagated by persecution; they were agreed that the Established Church might be maintained; and they were agreed, further, that disqualifications might be imposed upon people whose religious opinions were dangerous. But Sherlock maintained, whilst Hoadly denied, that Protestant dissenters should be excluded from certain offices of profit and privilege. And thus a dispute, stated in the most abstract terms, dwindled down to a squabble over the Test and Corporation Acts. Sherlock tries to prove that the sacrament is not desecrated by being used with a test, and that there is a broad distinction between positive penalties and negative disqualifications. The result was characteristic of the whole dispute. The Test Act survived the Bangorian controversy for more than a century, but an Act of Indemnity was regularly passed, after a few years, until its final repeal.[29] The legislature, like the controversialists, affirmed a general principle, and took care that it should have no practical effect.

41. The whole question ceased to be interesting, though some feeble attacks upon the Establishment were made in the last half of the century. When passions are calm, shams flourish. Mere verbal theories which could not stand the strain of a real agitation, pass muster in the calmer intervals. Warburton's theory, set forth in the 'Alliance between Church and State,' is a good specimen of that verbal ingenuity which

[28]Sherlock, iv. 386.   [29]Hallam's 'Constitutional History,' iii. 247.

passed with himself and others for reasoning. It is tempting, though the temptation must be resisted, to take from its pages a few more specimens of the peculiar Warburtonian mixture of sham logic and bluster. It is enough to say that Warburton starts with Locke, and accepts his social compact and general outline of theory. But Locke's theory would sanction pure voluntaryism, or deprive the Church of all 'coactive' power. Tindal's theory, on the other hand, tended to Erastianism or Hobbism; that is, to make the Church a mere department of state. The English practice was a compromise between the two, and Warburton's whole artifice is to represent this compromise as the result of a permanent compact between the two bodies. He has little difficulty in deducing the precise arrangements of a British constitution from an *a priori* necessity; and thus mathematically demonstrates, for example, that the bishops ought to have seats in the House of Lords.[30] 'In a word,' as he says in the 'Divine Legation,' 'an established religion with a test-law is the universal voice of nature'[31]—surely, the strangest of all the utterances of that ambiguous authority. Do you ask how such a bargain could be made?—seeing that, according to Warburton, church and state consist of the same individuals, and it is, therefore, like a bargain made by a man with himself—his answer is easy. Because two societies, composed of the same persons, may have 'two distinct wills and two distinct personalities.' The majority in a 'factitious body' has 'the denomination of the person and the will of the society;' therefore it *is* the personality. Therefore, the two societies can make bargains with each other.[32] This sounds rather like a still deeper mystery. But where, you ask, is this bargain to be found? 'It may be found,' replies Warburton, 'in the same archive with the famous original compact between magistrate and people.'[33] There let us leave it. Stripping Warburton's arguments of these obsolete assumptions, pushed by him, as usual, to the extreme of unreality, we may say that he really asserts that the existing compromise was very convenient. Most people agreed with him, and therefore did not trouble themselves about its theoretical basis.

IV. The Walpole Era.

42. The accession of George I. marked the beginning of a period of political stagnation which lasted for near half-a-century. The country prospered and waxed rich. Harvests were abundant; towns began to grow; and the seeds of much that was good and much that was evil

---

[30]Works, vii. 111.　　[31]Ib. ii. 292.　　[32]Ib. vii. 210.　　[33]Ib. ii. 287.

in our later history were sowed. Nor was it a period of intellectual stagnation. The deist controversy was raging; and in literature Pope, Swift,
Richardson, Fielding, and Thomson were producing some of their best
work. Politically, however, the times were quiet, and, it may be, a
golden opportunity was being lost. The governing classes enjoyed the
power which they had acquired by the Revolution, and were content
to keep what they had gained. They would oppress nobody actively; on
the other hand, they would introduce no reforms. Their highest virtue
was in leaving things alone. The Jacobites represented a vague danger
in the background until their suppression in 1745. But the Jacobites
were unable to put any real pressure upon the country; and a governing
class which has nothing to do except languidly to hold the reins of
power and divide the spoils naturally becomes corrupt. Not one constitutional question of the least importance arose until the reign of
George III. The Church retained obnoxious privileges on the condition
of making very little use of them; and the nation indolently drifted
towards the unknown future, carelessly contented for the most part,
amused as much as scandalised by the intrigues of unprincipled politicians, and only once insisting upon having a war for the benefit of its
commerce.

43. The fitting representative of such a period was Sir Robert Walpole; a statesman of admirably shrewd sense and great force of character, whose favourite motto and sole principle of government was
quieta non movere. Walpole found no exponent of his political theories,
whatever they might be, for the best exposition of such theories was
silence. But opposed to Walpole was a man of no common reputation
for philosophical and literary ability. Bolingbroke supplied the brains of
the party by which Walpole was opposed, and to which Walpole's
greediness of power gradually drove the ablest of his former allies.
Bolingbroke was therefore the natural mouthpiece of that accumulated
discontent which, after twenty years' preparation, at length gathered
force enough to sweep Walpole from office. Exiled from Parliament,
Bolingbroke was forcibly confined to literary modes of expression. A
bitterly disappointed man, he was restrained by no scruples from aiming
at the most vulnerable points of his hated opponent. Whatever could be
said against Walpole was sure to be suggested to him, and his reputation seemed to insure that it should be said as forcibly as possible. In
his writings, then, we might expect to find an expression of the political
philosophy of the time, for Bolingbroke professed to have a philosophy,
carefully digested in solitude, and brought to bear upon a conspicuous
instance. We might expect to find anticipations of the coming outburst

of revolutionary feeling, or attempts to restore the dying energy of the ancient political creeds, of which Bolingbroke was, for a time, the acknowledged representative. What do we find, in fact?

44. Two phrases are generally quoted in regard to Bolingbroke, and their conjunction is significant. The young Pitt, it is said, declared that of all lost fragments of literature he would most gladly recover a speech of Bolingbroke. Burke asked, about the same time: Who now reads Bolingbroke? Who ever read him through? Pitt's remark, thoughtless enough, testifies to the impression made by Bolingbroke upon his contemporaries and preserved in parliamentary tradition. Burke's question indicates the general verdict upon that part of his utterances of which we are able to judge. Possibly the 'Patriot King'—his most finished performance—would have thrilled the House of Commons as a speech. Read in cold blood, the weakness of the substance weakens our appreciation of the undeniable elegance of the style. Bolingbroke was clearly a man of great talents. His brief career as a combatant in the open arena, and his long career as the prompter of visible actors in the struggle when the arena was closed to him, prove that he had the great gift of influencing men. His most brilliant contemporaries expressed for him the warmest admiration. Pope idolised him; and he was in some degree the channel of the inspiration which made Voltaire the prophet of English ideas in France. Voltaire, dedicating to him the tragedy of 'Brutus,' declares that Bolingbroke could give him lessons in French as well as in English, or could at least teach him to impart to his own tongue the force and energy due to a noble liberty of thought. And yet, every reader of Bolingbroke must ask whether this brilliant statesman and philosopher was anything but a showy actor declaiming popular platitudes without himself understanding them?

45. The answer may be given briefly. Bolingbroke had in his youth the vulgar ambition which would combine the inconsistent characters of a devotee of pleasure and a man of business. He was to be the English Alcibiades, dazzling at all hazards and replacing labour by genius. Such affectation generally drops off a man of real power with his early youth. The lesson is quickly and painfully learnt that genius involves, though it cannot be resolved into, an infinite capacity for taking trouble. That simple truth never forced itself upon a mind corrupted to the core by vanity. To the end of his days Bolingbroke fancied that he could take political and philosophical eminence by storm, and surmount all difficulties at a bound.

46. The traditional estimate of his style has sufficient foundation. So far as it is possible to separate words from thought, we may call it

excellent. The mould of his sentences is generally good; and one perceives that they must once have contained glowing thoughts which
have somehow evaporated in the course of time. Here and there a happy
expression testifies to a genuine vivacity of intellect. Such, for example,
is the familiar description of the House of Commons. The members of
that assembly, he says, 'grow, like hounds, fond of the man who shows
them game, and by whose halloo they are to be encouraged.'[1] Nor,
perhaps, is it a bad illustration of the fact that enthusiasm is sometimes
more blinding than dulness, when he remarks that 'Don Quixote believed, but even Sancho doubted.'[2] More frequently he descends to the
mere coxcombry of learning. If, he says, a voluntary exile were a completed proof of guilt, we should often pass false judgments. 'Metellus
and Rutilius must be condemned; Apuleius and Apicius must be justified.'[3] Walpole probably smiled grimly at this undergraduate affectation.
Bolingbroke himself, one would think, must have laughed at his own
reflections on solitude, with their pompous plagiarisms from Seneca,
before the ink was dry. An imaginary dialogue between Swift and
Bolingbroke might suggest the question whether bitterness of soul is
more palpably evident in direct cynicism or in hollow affectation. In
any case, we pity Swift, dying 'like a poisoned rat in a hole;' we can
but despise Bolingbroke, the rake and intriguer, professing to console
himself with the thought that 'the same azure vault, bespangled over
with stars, will be everywhere spread over our heads.'[4] It was hardly
under the roof of heaven that Bolingbroke consoled himself for the
sorrows of exile. We may, however, admire an exiled statesman for
finding some relief in a literary exercise even if the sentiment be not
very deep.

47. To seek in such a writer for a coherent scheme of political philosophy would be like criticising Gothic architecture from the sham
cloisters of Strawberry Hill. His fine phrases are a transparent covering
for personal hostilities, and his affected regard for his country a periph-
rasis for a cynical disbelief in the honesty of his countrymen. Catch-
ing at any taunt which serves his purpose for the moment, he falls into
flat contradiction, and proposes remedies whose natural consequences he
would be the last to welcome seriously. Bolingbroke is interesting as a
representative of the current insincerity of the time. The letter to Sir
W. Windham, written in 1717, but published after his death, draws
aside the veil. He avows with cynical candour the principles which

[1] Bolingbroke's Works, i. 13.   [2] Ib. ii. 320.   [3] Ib. i. 543.   [4] Ib. i. 108.

guided him and his party on their accession to power. The enjoyment of great employments and of great patronage supplied, he says, the animating motives of his own party, as, he adds, it has supplied the animating motives of all parties.[5] He afterwards joined the Pretender under stress of circumstances rather than from design; and the most respectable of his excuses for his conduct is a vague point of party honour.[6] Not even as secretary to the Pretender did he believe in Jacobite theories, and he always speaks of them in terms of the bitterest contempt. A sceptic in religion, he naturally regards the dogma of the divine right as too childish for refutation. The doctrines connected with it were, in his eyes, the causes of all the seventeenth-century troubles, and he thinks them absurd enough to 'shock the common sense of a Samoyede or a Hottentot.'[7] A king is nothing but a man with a crown on his head and a sceptre in his hand, as a bishop is a man who holds a crozier and wears a mitre.[8] The symbols are arbitrary marks intended to designate a responsible official; not the outward signs of an inherent grace. All virtue is gone out of secular and spiritual rulers, and the philosopher sees that they owe their distinction to the tailor and the jeweller. What, then, is to be put in their place? Liberty, according to his most grandiloquent declamations, is the true end of government. Liberty, unfortunately, is a 'tender plant,'[9] only to be preserved by incessant care. The 'notion of a perpetual danger to liberty is inseparable from the very notion of government,' and the danger is especially great in a mixed government. To keep alive the spirit of liberty should, therefore, be the great aim of a patriot, and, so long as it is kept alive, it may save the State even in 'the most desperate cases.'[10] But liberty, taken absolutely, means anarchy. How is government to be made out of the formal opposite to government? Bolingbroke's simple expedient is to call the spirit of liberty the spirit of faction, whenever he dislikes its results.[11] He is a type of the easy-going philosophers who escape from the dilemma of defining the excess of liberty by calling it license, whilst they never condescend to tell us what is liberty and what is license. His nearest approach to a definition lies in the statement that liberty aims at promoting public interests, and license at promoting private interests; but the true theory was, doubtless, that the spirit of

[5]Bolingbroke's Works, i. 9, 'Letter to Sir W. Windham.'
[6]Ib. i. 39.   [7]Ib. ii. 43, 'Dissertation on Parties.'   [8]Ib. ii. 188.
[9]Ib. i. 279, 'Remarks on History of England.'
[10]Ib. i. 289, 'Remarks on History of England.'
[11]Ib. i. 294.

liberty animated Bolingbroke's hostility to Walpole, while the spirit of faction animated Walpole's hostility to Bolingbroke.

48. If we still hunt for a guiding principle, we occasionally come upon the social compact. Hooker's theory that 'all public regiment hath arisen from deliberate advice, consultation, and composition between men' is 'undoubtedly and universally true;' as true, he proceeds to add, in Morocco as in England.[12] But what is the use of a principle which is equally applicable to Morocco and England? Bolingbroke was perhaps sensible of the defect in this argument; and, at any rate, he instinctively inclines by preference to the purely empirical theory of the balance of powers. He comments admiringly on the doctrine that, 'in a constitution like ours, the safety of the whole depends on the balance of the parts, and the balance of the parts on their mutual independency on each other.'[13] The doctrine has been sanctioned by many great names; and elsewhere we find the theory of the judicious mixture of the three forms in English government applied to support another favourite commonplace of great vitality—namely, that absolute democracy, though deviating less from nature than monarchy, is 'tyranny and anarchy both.'[14] It is characteristic of Bolingbroke's hand-to-mouth method of reasoning that he elsewhere declares that a 'perfect democracy' provides the best precautions against tyranny.[15] The inevitable difficulty, however, arises. What is this balance, and what is the test of its being rightly adjusted? Since no English party avowedly desired to extrude any one of the elements, a mere assertion that all are to be present leaves us in the safe region of generalities. Bolingbroke is perhaps nowhere more sincere than when expounding the analogous theory in foreign politics. The whole art and mystery of European policy consisted, according to him, in maintaining an equipoise of the scales of the balance of power.[16] The houses of France and Austria were to be always able to neutralise each other, and neither was to obtain a decisive victory. This theory, which has served the politicians of many generations, is at least clear in principle. But to apply it to the different constituents of a single government was to justify anarchy. If King and Commons were to be as independent as France and Austria, the sovereignty was nowhere. The theory would destroy all rule as decisively as the theory of absolute liberty.

[12]Bolingbroke's Works, ii. 172, 'Dissertation on Parties.'
[13]Ib. i. 338, 'Remarks on History of England.'
[14]Ib. i. 178, 'Dissertation on Parties.'
[15]Ib. i. 280, 'Remarks on History of England.'
[16]E.g. ii. 439, 'Study of History.'

49. The only escape lies in an appeal to history. Experience, properly interrogated, may tell us what are the best relations between bodies so intricately connected. Bolingbroke endeavoured to make that appeal, and we must give him credit for occasional glimpses of a method which, in later and more powerful hands, has shown greater promise of fertility. Bolingbroke's conceptions of history, however, are still in an utterly disorganised state. Pedantic in his style, he has yet an indiscriminating hatred for that laborious investigation of facts by which pedants have laid a sound foundation for more scientific methods. He can draw an argument for English use from the annual election of Roman consuls,[17] and he might be countenanced by the authority of Montesquieu; but, in striking opposition to the spirit of Montesquieu's writings, he begins his 'Letters on History' by expressing a 'thorough contempt for the whole business of these learned lives'[18]—of the lives, that is, of such men as Scaliger, Bochart, Petavius, Usher, and Marsham. Those pioneers of historical enquiry had accumulated a vast amount of learned lumber, which required classification and discrimination from men of greater speculative ability or more fortunate culture. But Bolingbroke characteristically begins by depriving himself of the necessary materials for researches, because it would have required too much labour to turn them to account. He manages with curious infelicity to repudiate the true historical method before it has come into being, and condemns himself to a merely empirical system of guesswork. He adopts, indeed, the old saw, that history is philosophy teaching by examples,[19] and states, with some force, the advantage of widening our mental horizon and providing ourselves with concrete examples instead of abstract dogmas. The events of our own lives appear to us, he says, to be 'unrelative' or '*isolés*'[20] (the English 'isolated' being apparently still unknown), whereas history enables us to trace the series of causes and effects, and witness the evolution of the great drama. But when we interpret these generalities by the special instances alleged, we see that Bolingbroke had not, as indeed he could hardly have, any clear conception of the unity and continuity of history.

50. The knowledge which he contemplates is but an extension of that vague body of empirical generalisations which is called knowledge of the world. He regards events in the spirit of a shrewd diplomatist of the old-fashioned school. He is not a Montesquieu. He does not aim at detecting the working of general laws, but at accumulating a number

[17]Bolingbroke's Works, ii. 154, 'Dissertation on Parties.'
[18]Ib. ii. 261, 'Letters on History.'
[19]Ib. ii. 266, 'Letters on History.'   [20]Ib. ii. 279.

of precedents. A story from classical or mediæval times will serve his purpose, without any allowance made for the change of time and thought, as well as an anecdote from the Court of the Pretender or Queen Anne. History, indeed, is not a mere collection of unconnected anecdotes, but the connection which does exist is of the superficial kind; he would desire a narrative of ministerial intrigues, not a theory of the deeper causes of organic changes. Would you understand the Revolution of 1688? Few men, he supposes, have gone further 'in their search after the causes of it' than the extravagant attempts of James II.[21] We must look deeper, he says; but he is not thinking of the character of the English race, of the long series of causes which determined the relations between the king and the aristocracy, of the growth of free speculation and the origin of Protestantism, or of the social changes which made old theories inapplicable. We must, he says, look back to the maladministration of James I., who produced the Great Rebellion, which made our princes exiles, which brought them back with unsuitable ideas of their position. Nay, we must, perhaps, go back further, 'even to the beginning of James I.'s reign, to render this event a complete example, and to develop all the wise, honest, and salutary precepts with which it is pregnant, both to king and subject.'[22] We do not rise beyond the backstairs theory of politics, though we must apply it with more than the ordinary acuteness. Nor, in fact, could any other theory commend itself to men who were constitutionally incapable of recognising the greatest spiritual forces. Here is the theory of the Reformation in a nutshell. 'Henry VIII. divided with the secular clergy and his people the spoil of the Pope and his satellites the monks; Francis I. divided with the Pope the spoil of his clergy, secular and regular, and of his people.'[23] The ultimate source of all great events is personal intrigue, and the moving force in all intrigues is greed or lust of power.

51. Upon such foundations it is not to be supposed that any sound system of politics could be erected. Bolingbroke's practical conclusions are reduced, for the most part, to a beggarly account of those popular cries, which, having had some meaning in previous generations, had now subsided into mere substitutes for meaning. He declaims against standing armies;[24] advocates triennial or even annual parliaments;[25] and denounces corruption. The evil, indeed, was serious, though Bolingbroke's zeal might have declined had he been the corrupter. The corrup-

[21]Bolingbroke's Works, ii. 280.   [22]Ib. ii. 281, 'Letters on History.'
[23]Ib. ii. 363.   [24]Ib. i. 354, 'Remarks on History of England.'
[25]Ib. ii. 151, 156, 'Dissertation on Parties.'

tion was the symptom of an era of stagnation; when the only effective sense of responsibility amongst the governing classes was of their responsibility to their own families. The ancient party issues, as Bolingbroke truly says, had disappeared. The contest between the advocates of popular sovereignty and of divine right, of passive obedience and of parliamentary authority, had died out; all men of sense were ready to accept the principles which had triumphed in 1688.[26] In this absence of political passion, interest became supreme, and as Bolingbroke delighted to assert, for it is pleasant to call your antagonist fool as well as knave, the dullest might govern by such means as easily as the wisest. 'A chambermaid may slip a banknote into a griping paw as well as the most subtle demon of hell.'[27] Bolinbroke's avowed purpose was to meet the evil by reviving the 'doctrines of old Whiggism.'[28] And yet, according to him, the triumph of those doctrines was secure, and had been coincident with the introduction of the evil. Where was the true source of the evil, and how was it to be interpreted?

52. The most explicit answer to these questions is given in the 'Idea of a Patriot King;' the most laboured, and certainly not the least palpably hollow, of all Bolingbroke's writings. We half wonder that the experienced statesman, now sixty-six years old, who had seen many fortunes, and long guided in secret the plans of an active party, could preserve the gravity with which he enunciates his solution of the riddle. With much solemnity he slays once more the dead theory of a right divine. God himself, 'with reverence be it spoken,' is not an arbitrary, but a limited monarch, for his power is limited by his wisdom.[29] Yet Bolingbroke's monarch is to be neither the burlesque Jupiter of the Tories nor the powerless scarecrow of the Whigs. He will be in his right place, when once the principle is accepted 'that limitations on the Crown ought to be carried as far as is necessary to secure the liberties of the people, and that all such limitations may subsist without weakening or endangering monarchy.'[30] Cynics may doubt whether the reconciliation can be effected, but Bolingbroke believes in human nature enough to hold that barriers may be devised which will restrain a bad prince without shackling a good one. Admirable, we admit; but what is the secret? The secret, replies Bolingbroke, with due solemnity and references to Locke and Machiavelli, is to have a Patriot King. 'He, and he alone, can save a country when its ruin is so far advanced' as (so we may

[26]Bolingbroke's Works, ii. 32, 'Dissertation on Parties.'
[27]Ib. ii. 36.   [28]Ib. ii. 19, and see 'Idea of a Patriot King,' iii. 71.
[29]Ib. iii. 53, 'Patriot King.'   [30]Ib. iii. 54, ib.

interpret his language) is implied by the rule of a Walpole and a George II.[31] Corruption will cease when the patriot reaches the throne, and the 'panacea is applied.'[32] The spirit of liberty will revive, and the devil be exorcised. For, and the reason is slightly discouraging, a patriot king is 'a sort of standing miracle,'[32] so rarely seen and so little understood that his appearance will encourage the innocent, astonish the guilty, and secure universal acquiescence. Bolingbroke tells us how the ideal monarch is to begin his reformation. He is to begin 'to govern as soon as he begins to reign,'[33] and first (and here we may be sure that Bolingbroke is sincere) to dismiss the old ministers, leaving some to be punished, and employ new, who are to be wise, instead of cunning. He is to be for a state, not for a party; to unite instead of dividing; to uphold the constitution where it does not admit of improvement; to redress grievances and punish guilty officials; to gain the hearts of his people by withdrawing favour from evildoers and satisfying just complaints; and thus, though he cannot alter human nature, he may stem the corrupt course of human affairs. He is to encourage commerce, on which power depends, and to cherish the navy, for England is an island. And, finally, the patriot king is not to have a pedantic regard for chastity (so Bolingbroke appears to insinuate in a long and involved passage), but to have a strict regard for decorum. When these expectations are realised, 'concord will appear, brooding peace and prosperity on the happy land;' joy sitting in 'every face, content in every breast;' and, in short, England will be honoured and prosperous.[34] In those blessed days, people will remember, 'with some tenderness of sentiment,' a man who, in all sincerity, 'contributed his mite to carry on so good a work,' and 'who desired life for nothing so much as to see a king of Great Britain the most powerful man in the country, and a patriot king at the head of a united people.'[35] The unconscious irony is not complete unless we remember that this consummation was to arrive when Bolingbroke should be Prime Minister of that 'greatest and most glorious of human beings'[36] (such was to be the patriot king), the poor Prince Fred, who 'was alive and is dead.' All will be well, so Bolingbroke tells us, when we have an angelic ruler, who, by some undefined method, is to provide perfect laws, and carry out an unerring policy at the head of a wise and virtuous people. Bolingbroke's last paper, some unfinished reflections on the present (1749) state of the nation, records his final disappointment, and the meagre results of the downfall of Walpole.

[31]Bolingbroke's Works, iii. 73, 'Patriot King.'   [32]Ib. iii. 75.   [33]Ib. iii. 77.
[34]Ib. iii. 125.   [35]Ib. iii. 125.   [36]Ib. iii. 123, 'Patriot King.'

53. In this mass of insincere rhetoric one genuine vein of sentiment was detected. The disappearance of party, which he professed to desire, meant the advent to power of the 'country party.' The phrase is ambiguous, as country is opposed to party or to court. Bolingbroke, in fact, adopts the theory long held by reformers, which regarded the independent members as the sound part of the constitution, and which prompted Chatham's plan for reforming parliament by adding to the representation of the counties. 'The landed men,' he says in his last reflections, 'are the true owners of our political vessel; the moneyed men, as such, are but passengers in it.'[37] In his earlier days he told Sir William Windham that the Tories represented 'the bulk of the landed interest.'[38] In fact, the moneyed men were regarded as a kind of excrescence, in spite of the recognised and even exaggerated value of trade; and the prevalent corruption was supposed to have its root in the machinations of the growing class. The 'great source of corruption'[39] introduced by the Revolution was the public debt; and it was by dexterously manipulating those mysterious creations—the Funds—that Walpole worked his nefarious schemes. The whole art 'of stockjobbing, the whole mystery of iniquity,' arose from the debt, and 'the mainsprings that turn, or may turn, the artificial wheel of credit, and make the paper estates that are fastened to it rise and fall, work behind the veil of the treasury.'[40] A new power was making itself felt in politics, and Walpole's supposed intimacy with its secrets, and skill in turning them to account, was one great source of his power. The phenomenon, like other novelties, seemed strange and portentous, and the old aristocracy looked askance upon the new plutocracy which was gradually coming into being. The consequences of that change were not then—perhaps they are not even now—fully appreciated.

54. Meanwhile, Bolingbroke's showy philosophy passed muster for a time. Great changes were slowly operating in that political interregnum. Society was slowly heaving and changing. Politicians looked on idly, and squabbled for places; facile theorists neatly vamped up old formulæ left as a legacy from more stirring times, and, on the whole, decided that there was no particular principle in politics beyond preserving a tolerably stable equilibrium, and maintaining (for it would be unjust to overlook the favourable side) a wide toleration, verging only too closely on indifference. Bolingbroke's writings, valuable for little else, contributed in some degree, under the good natured king-of-Cockaigne rule of Walpole, to make the power of the press more distinctly felt, and so

[37] Bolingbroke's Works, iii. 174.   [38] Ib. i. 9.
[39] Ib. ii. 243, 'Dissertation on Parties.'   [40] Ib. ii. 245.

aided the development of a new force side by side with the growing
power of the purse. Yet, of Bolingbroke one can say little, but that he
adds one more instance of wasted talents and unaccepted tasks.

55. A far keener intellect than that of Bolingbroke was pondering the
same questions. The problem which lay before Hume, as well as Bolingbroke, was how to make a rope of sand, and to frame a political theory
out of theoretical and practical scepticism. Hume's power as a destroyer
is contrasted with his weakness as a creator, even more conspicuously
in his political than in his other writings. The old theories are slain at
a blow. The divine right of kings is a futile doctrine, for 'whatever
actually happens is comprehended under the general plan or intention
of Providence;' and thus, 'the greatest and most lawful prince has no
more peculiar sacredness than a usurper or a pirate;' whilst 'a constable,
no less than a king, acts by a divine commission, and possesses an indefeasible right.'[41] The more popular social contract theory vanishes as
soon as it is challenged. The imaginary contract has confessedly no
place in history, and it is easy to show that it can have as little in
philosophy. The duties of allegiance and of fidelity to promises rest on
the same foundation of utility, and to deduce one from the other is
mere logical legerdemain. As soon as the question is asked, Why should
I keep my word? the only possible answer is, Because society could not
otherwise subsist; and the same answer serves for the question, Why
should I obey the sovereign? Wollaston's attempt to convert all sin into
lying was liable, it may be remarked in passing, to the same attack;
for it was substantially an attempt to import into the still less propitious
sphere of ethics that doctrine of the social compact which had a certain
convenience in the more obviously empirical science of politics. Hume's
reasoning is irrefragable, admirably put, and too trite for repetition.
And yet the social-compact theory lived long after the brains were out;
nay, it flourished and became identified with theories which exercised,
and still exercise, a vast influence upon political thought. If we ask why
so clear a refutation produced so small an effect, the answer may be
suggested by the incoherence of the rival doctrine.

56. Divine right and the social compact being exploded, and utility
recognised as the sole and sufficient criterion of all political order, how
are we to construct a definite political theory? What forms of government are useful, and why? Hume's conceptions of the origin and nature
of government are perfectly clear and coherent. All government ultimately rests on opinion; the physical force is always on the side of the

[41]Hume's Works, iii. 444.

governed; the various instincts which bind men together in society enable the few to impose their will on the many; and the opinions which
determine the nature of government are those which men form as to the
public interest, as to the right to power, and the right to property.[42]
What then, we might ask, is the genesis of the various opinions which
have prevailed in the world, and how have they developed themselves,
and given birth to different forms of government? But here we begin to
feel that Hume is, at most, feeling after a method. He does not know
clearly what he would seek, or how he is to seek for it. He writes an
essay to prove 'that politics may be reduced to a science.'[43] In spite of
the disturbing influence of individuals, he holds that laws may be discovered as general and certain 'as any which the mathematical sciences
afford us.'[44] He claims that character for a few conclusions; such, for
example, are the doctrines that 'a hereditary prince, a nobility without
vassals, and a people voting by their representatives, form the best
monarchy, aristocracy, and democracy;'[45] that 'death is unavoidable to
the political as to the animal body;'[46] or that arts and sciences can only
take their first rise under a free government.[47] Hume was, of course,
fully sensible of the crudity and uncertainty of such maxims. The world,
he thinks, is still too young for the discovery of many general and
permanent political truths.[48] But Hume does not perceive the fundamental error which vitiates all such reasoning. His inductions are necessarily futile, because they presuppose a merely superficial classification.
He is arguing like a botanist who should divide the vegetable kingdom
into trees, shrubs, and creeping plants, and search for the properties
common to all the members of each class. As the classification would
turn upon points of external form, observations founded upon it would
only bring to light external resemblances, instead of revealing vital
principles of growth. He is dealing in morphology instead of physiology. He throws into one class Switzerland, Holland, Venice, and the
ancient republics as popular governments, and into another, France,
China, the Roman Empire, and ancient Persia as monarchical governments.[49] The phenomena which are to be found in every member of one
class, and absent from every member of the other, must obviously be of
a superficial kind; and so crude an analysis cannot lay bare the real
principles of national life. Like other writers who adopt the same

[42]Hume's Works, iii. 109, &c.   [43]Ib. iii. 98, &c.   [44]Ib. iii. 99.
[45]Ib. p. 101.   [46]Ib. p. 126.   [47]Ib. p. 177.   [48]Ib. p. 156.
[49]See, for example, part i. Essay xiv., 'The Rise of Arts and Sciences,' which
is yet, in many ways, an admirable essay.

method, Hume endeavours to construct the 'idea of a perfect common-wealth'[50] without reference, tacit or avowed, to the conditions of time, place, or development. He justifies his attempt by the precedent of Huyghens' investigation of the best form of ship for sailing, and argues that his ideal constitution is practicable because it resembles that of Holland.[51] He does not remark that even the form of a ship must depend upon the material, and that the material with which he has to deal is living and changing; nor that the constitution of Holland was developed under a special set of historical, geographical, and physiological conditions. With the help of such aphorisms as these, that the lower sort of people are good judges of their own neighbours, but incapable of electing the highest officials; and that all free governments must consist of a senate and a people to supply respectively honesty and wisdom;[52] he puts together a constitution as absolutely as Harrington, his favourite authority, or as his successor Sieyès; and though appealing to experience, really contemplates that metaphysical man who exists under no conditions of space or time.

57. Hume is indeed full of acute remarks, or he would not be Hume. The weakness of his Essays is characteristic of his time; and it would be well if popular writers of the present day had emancipated themselves from the delusions which perplexed his unsurpassed keenness of vision. Perhaps the most instructive example of his method is the interesting Essay on 'National Characters.'[53] The tacit assumptions which pervade his method are there most distinctly exhibited. Character, he says, may be determined either by 'moral causes,' such as the form of government, the wealth and poverty of a nation and its position towards its neighbours, or by 'physical causes,' by which he understands the insensible influence of the climate.[54] This classification tacitly omits the stage of development of a race; and, in spite of acute incidental remarks upon the difference between ancient and modern, or savage and civilised modes of thought, it is plain that he takes the statical view of history, and thus unconsciously ignores all theories of evolution. Another point is more remarkable. Hume was by twenty-two years the junior of Montesquieu. The younger man sought the acquaintance of the older philosopher, and procured a publication at Edinburgh of an English edition of the 'Esprit des Lois' in 1750.[55] Montesquieu's speculations upon the influence of climate, though not entirely novel, produced a

[50]Hume's Works, iii. 480, &c.
[51]Ib. p. 490.
[52]Ib. 487.

[53]Ib. p. 244, &c.
[54]Ib. p. 244.
[55]Burton's 'Life of Hume,' i. 304.

great impression, and clearly aimed at the discovery of a scientific basis for political enquiry. It is curious to find that Hume's essay (published in 1742, or six years before the 'Esprit des Lois') is specially directed against the theory of climatic influence. His reasons are significant. A single government, he says, has spread a single national character over the vast territories of China, whilst separate governments produced the greatest variety of character within the narrow limits of Greece. In a preceding essay he has noticed the obvious connection between the physical geography of Greece and its division into small governments as favourable to the rise of arts and sciences. He considers it, again, to be an argument against the influence of climate, that similarity of manners may be produced by a simple contiguity. It appears, therefore, that his argument against 'physical causes' implies a very limited view of their mode of action. He contemplates only such direct and tangible influences as the supposed influence of damp weather in promoting drink, or of hot weather in exciting the amatory passions. The more remote physiological effects of climate, soil, and physical conditions generally are beyond his contemplation. But the omission of another element of the question is more significant. National character cannot, he says, be a product of physical causes, because it is often limited by an invisible political frontier; because a particular set of men, like the Jews, maintain their character by association; because 'accidents,' such as differences in language and religion, keep two races apart, like the Greeks and Turks; or because the same national character follows the colonies of a people round the globe. These phenomena would all be now accepted as striking proofs of the influence of race. Nothing is more characteristic than the failure to recognise this as a factor in the problem, even when his logic seems to cast it in his face. Hume observes, in a note, that even the merits of horses seem to depend less on the climate than on the 'different breeds and the skill and manner of rearing them.'[56] Here is the very force required to explain his observations, and he is unable to notice it. Indeed, he explicitly asserts that whilst horses transmit their qualities, a 'coxcomb may beget a philosopher,'[57] and therefore denies the influence of race. In fact, he has tacitly assumed that all men are of one 'breed.' They are but the abstract man —the metaphysical entity, alike in all times, places, and conditions. The 'breed,' being a constant quantity, all differences must arise from 'the manner of rearing,' or, in other words, from the form of government. He points out that the character of a given people varies from age to

[56]Hume's Works, iii. 247, note.   [57]Ib. p. 258.

age, and that the English character is strikingly heterogeneous, even in the same country. From this point of view, as excluding any reference to successive stages of development, the first consideration is a decisive proof that differences in character arise from change of government; and, as he excludes reference to variety of breed, the second consideration justifies the inverted conclusion that the character arises from the mixed form of government.

58. I have said enough to illustrate the natural tendency of the method. Hume having abandoned the old theological and metaphysical synthesis, has reduced the race to a mere chaos of unconnected individuals. He cannot recognise, even when they are brought before him, the great forces which bind men together; a nation is not a living organism, but a temporary combination in various conformations of colourless units. National character results from forms of government; forms of government are the work of chance, though chance, as no one knows better, is but a name for undiscovered causes. History, therefore, is rigidly speaking, an inscrutable enigma. The 'Essay upon the Rise and Progress of Arts and Sciences' opens with some able remarks on the influence of chance, or 'secret and unknown causes,' upon human affairs, and shows that general results for the most part depend upon 'determinate and known causes.' He attaches great importance to the influence of individuals. Freedom causes the rise of arts and sciences, and freedom was, perhaps, favoured by the division into small states due to the physical configuration of certain countries; but, after all, we must often trace the character of a people to the rise of some Brutus, at the early period when their imaginations were still plastic, and forms of government unfixed.[58] Even the great movements of thought present themselves to him as 'accidents.' Religious wars are simple follies, for a controversy about 'an article of faith, which is utterly absurd and unintelligible, is not a difference in sentiment, but in a few phrases and expressions which one party accepts without understanding, and the other refuses in the same manner.'[59] 'Parties from principle, especially abstract speculative principle, are known only to modern times, and are, perhaps, the most extraordinary and unaccountable phenomenon that has yet appeared in human affairs.'[60] When such principles involve a 'contrariety of action,'[60] the case is explicable, but he cannot see why men of different religions should not pass each other like travellers going in opposite directions on the same high-road. Religious wars, therefore, all depend on the 'frivolous' principle that people are shocked by a difference of sentiment.

[58]Hume's Works, iii. 248.   [59]Ib. p. 130.   [60]Ib. p. 130.

59. It is no wonder if history presented itself as a mere undecipherable maze to the eighteenth-century thinkers, of whom Hume is the most complete representative. Ignoring utterly the great forces which move men's souls, unconscious of the differences due to race, climate, or gradual revolution, they saw nothing but a meaningless collection of facts, through which ran no connecting principle. The translation of this heretical scepticism into politics is a cynical conservatism; and Hume, though elaborately candid in his Essays, evidently inclines to the side of authority as the most favourable to that stagnation which is the natural ideal of a sceptic. He anticipates, indeed, some modern writers, in insisting upon the advantage of competition amongst rising states, and points to China as an illustration of the check imposed upon progress by excessive authority.[61] A discontented sceptic worships competition, as a contented sceptic worships calm. But, to Hume, the time for struggling seemed to have elapsed. All elements of disturbance were a mere annoyance to the adult world. We should be above playing with toys, religious and otherwise, which amused our childhood. In his Utopia, the Church is a department of the state, and the clergy rigidly bound under secular authority, for they represented a belief in something, and consequently a possibility of fanaticism. We may guess from various indications in his Essays that his ostensible preference for the British Constitution was already tempered by a decided hankering after an enlightened despotism on the French model. His nearest approach to a definite theory is that popular governments suit the infancy and despotisms the age of a civilised state. 'Absolute monarchy,' he says, 'is the easiest death, the true euthanasia of the British Constitution.'[62]

V. The French Influence.

60. The first half of the eighteenth century had thus produced no English book upon the theory of politics capable of communicating any great impulse to speculation, or of directly affecting the dominant ideas of the time. The English people, waxing fat under a succession of good harvests and the rapid development of commercial enterprise, worried themselves very little about the game played by their governing classes. A growl at some tax upon drink, or at a pacific policy which hurt their national pride, or seemed to endanger their trade, was their only sign of life. Nothing could be further from the mind of the aristocracy than

[61]Hume's Works, iii. 183.   [62]Ib. p. 126.

any real attempt to awaken a sleeping democracy. The jargon about standing armies and annual parliaments was the most transparent of artifices. And meanwhile, philosophers, growing ever more sceptical, were pretty clear that where nothing could be known it was better to make no change. By degrees a new spirit was to awake, but the speculative impulse was not to come from England. About the middle of the century appeared two books, which marked a new era. Montesquieu's 'Esprit des Lois' was published in 1748, and Rousseau's 'Contrat Social' in 1762. Far asunder in all else as the poles, they have this much in common, that both are written in French, and both show strong marks of English influence. Nothing would be easier than to put together a theory showing why the best books upon English politics must necessarily be written by foreigners. The complex organisation of the English political system can, it may be suggested, be most easily studied from without. To a Frenchman, accustomed to the simplicity of a centralised government, this cumbrous mechanism, involving the co-operation of so many heterogeneous elements, and yet working out a fair amount of order, prosperity, and general success, presented an interesting problem. A correct analysis of its boasted checks and balances might throw some light on the mysteries of political science. An Englishman, on the other hand, accustomed from infancy to the hand-to-mouth expedients of intriguing politicians, had generally a difficulty in conceiving how such things as general political principles existed. A generalisation was unintelligible to him till it was interpreted into the technical language of his own constitutional lawyers. The complexity was too familiar to excite his astonishment, and discouraged any attempt at discovering the vital formula. Trial by jury and the Habeas Corpus Act were national idols, by which British liberty was preserved, and he cared not to ask from what higher power they derived their sanctity. Montesquieu, like many of his countrymen in later years, is the scientific observer, struck by the strange phenomena which were so familiar to Englishmen, and endeavouring to account for them by an ingenious apparatus of philosophical theory. Rousseau represents a very different sentiment. Philosophically, he is the rigid logical observer, simply disgusted by elaborate combinations, which suggest dishonest juggling, and seem to be calculated to bewilder simple lovers of truth in their endless labyrinths. Politically, he is the mouthpiece of that new spirit which was to find a stubborn opposition in the English embodiment of ancient prejudice. Yet England, as the land of popular, though abortive, revolutions, had some lessons for Rousseau. Hobbes, the product of the society which witnessed the Great Rebellion, and Locke, the mouthpiece of the Whigs of 1688, had laid down principles susceptible of a wide application, and Rousseau owed something to each of them. Any full consideration of either of these great writers would be beyond my task. A brief notice of their relation to English thought is a necessary introduction to a study of our later political literature.

61. The true claim of Montesquieu to enduring reputation is generally recognised. He is the founder of the historical method. His writings, it is true, are defaced by many faults. The superficial antitheses, the constant efforts to dazzle, the trite allusions to classical precedent in the old style of literary coxcombry, obscured the solid merits of his writings, and seemed to his contemporaries in France to justify the familiar phrase of Mme. du Deffand, that his book should be called not 'L'Esprit des Lois,' but 'De l'esprit sur les Lois.' In truth, his grasp of the historical method is by no means assured. He accepts and gives additional emphasis to many of those hasty generalisations which distinguish the merely empirical school from the school which appeals to organised experience. History is still for him a collection of precedents, all of equal value, instead of the record of an evolution. He is content with superficial analogies, instead of detecting laws of growth. He deserves his place, less by reason of any clear results, than by certain tendencies implicitly contained in his arguments. He recognises, though he does not fully develop, the correlation between forms of government and conditions of climate, soil, and race. He jumps to very hasty conclusions upon those subjects, but he sets an example of accounting for political phenomena by historical research instead of *a priori* guesses. He announces, almost at starting, the doctrine that the government most conformable to nature is that of which the particular disposition is best related to that of the people upon which it is established[1]—a saying which should have dispersed many pestilent errors; and his familiar epigram that the English system was 'found in the woods,'[2] clearly indicates the conclusion that more light is to be thrown upon national constitutions by historical enquiries into the origin of a nation than by abstract theories about states of nature and social contracts. He opens, in short, fertile lines of investigation, though he has not the patience to adhere to his own method.

62. His English admirers, it is said, first taught the French to appreciate the prophet who had gained little honour amongst them. And it

[1] 'Esprit des Lois,' book i. ch. iii.   [2] Ib. book xi. ch. vi.

was natural that Englishmen should feel some gratitude to a writer who had pronounced so glowing a panegyric on their constitution. The remarkable chapter[3] in which he describes the English system as the living incarnation of the spirit of liberty, and that[4] in which he describes the relation between the character and the constitution of the people, are striking in themselves, in spite of their superficial assumptions, and became the precedent for a long series of similar demonstrations, both at home and abroad. Of their intrinsic value I need not speak. To the impression which they produced in England it will be sufficient to produce one splendid testimony. The most eminent of Montesquieu's admirers called him in an early work 'the greatest genius which has enlightened this age.'[5] Long afterwards, in endeavouring to set forth with the full force of his magnificent intellect the true spirit of the British Constitution, the object of his life-long idolatry, Burke called Montesquieu as the most unimpeachable witness to its excellence. 'Place before your eyes,' he says, 'such a man as Montesquieu. Think of a genius not born in every country or every time; a man gifted by nature with a penetrating aquiline eye; with a judgment prepared with the most extensive erudition; with a herculean robustness of mind, and nerves not to be broken with labour; a man who could spend twenty years in one pursuit. Think of a man, like the universal patriarch in Milton (who had drawn up before him in his poetic vision the whole series of the generations which were to issue from his loins), a man capable of placing in review, after having brought together from the east, the west, the north, and the south, from the coarseness of the rudest barbarism to the most refined and subtle civilisation, all the schemes of government which had ever prevailed amongst mankind, weighing, measuring, collating, and comparing them all, joining fact with theory, and calling into council upon all this infinite assemblage of things all the speculations which have fatigued the understandings of profound reasoners in all times. Let us then consider that all these were but preparatory steps to qualify a man, and such a man, tinctured with no national prejudice, with no domestic affection, to admire and to hold out to the admiration of mankind the constitution of England!'[6]

63. Alas! that one must quote such a glowing passage with the sense that it must be pared to the quick before it presents an approximation to the truth! Such, however, was the ideal Montesquieu as he presented

[3]'Esprit de Lois,' book xi.ch. vi.   [4]Ib. book xix. ch. xxvii.
[5]Burke's Works, x. 355 (abridged 'History of England').
[6]Ib. vi. 264, 'Appeal from the New to the Old Whigs.'

himself to the imagination of the first of all English political writers. Translated from rhetoric into blank technical phrases, we may say that Montesquieu is the prototype of all the writers who have admired the English Constitution from the purely empirical ground; the most elaborate expounder of that theory of checks and balances, and of a judicious mixture of political elements, which has so long stood its ground upon English soil. From the same eloquent lips which thus offered homage to Montesquieu we might hear a denunciation of the arch-deceiver Rousseau. Rousseau, they could tell us, is the oracle of Jacobinism; he is the 'great professor and founder of the philosophy of vanity in England;'[7] no other principle influenced his heart or guided his understanding; he was possessed with vanity to a degree little short of madness; his life was not distinguished by a single good action; and he has used a genius, trembling on the verge of insanity, to degrade and pollute all who came within the range of his influence. The portrait omits the great source of Rousseau's power. The man who moves the souls of his fellow-men must be possessed by sympathy for others as well as by love for himself. But Burke's instinct does not deceive him in tracing the genealogy of the revolutionary creed. Rousseau's 'Contrat Social' was as the first blast of the trumpet before which the walls of Jericho were to fall. His doctrines, considered under a purely logical aspect, were probably derived to some extent from Locke,[8] whose treatise on Government, though not explicitly noticed, is recalled in many passages. The contract, indeed, of Rousseau's imagination differs materially from that of his English predecessors. According to Hobbes, the fundamental compact runs thus: 'Every man says to every man, I authorise and give up my right of governing myself to this man, or to this assembly of men, on this condition: that thou give up thy right to him and authorise all his actions in like manner.'[9] In Locke's version, though he abstains from giving any definite formula, the compact would run somewhat in this fashion: I give a tacit consent, by accepting property, to become a member of that joint-stock association called the State, and consequently engage to obey its authority so long, and only so long, as it is exercised strictly for the purposes contemplated in the deed, the chief of which is the protection of property, and in accordance with the fundamental regulations, the chief of which are that my consent, or that of my authorised representatives, should be obtained to all taxes, and that every official should confine himself to his own proper province. Rousseau states the problem thus: 'To find a form of association which may defend and protect

[7]Burke's Works, vi. 32, 'Letter to a Member of the National Assembly.'
[8]See Morley's 'Rousseau,' ch. xii.   [9]'Leviathan,' part ii. ch. xvii.

with the whole common force the person and property of every associate, and by which each uniting with all may yet only obey himself and
remain as free as before.' The form of compact which fulfils these conditions is thus expressed: 'Each of us places in common his person and
his whole power under the supreme direction of the general will; and
we further receive each member as an indivisible part of the whole.'[10]
The comparison is curious. 'Strike the crowned head,' says Mr. Morley,
'from that monstrous figure which is the frontispiece of the Leviathan,
and you will have a frontispiece that will do admirably well for the
social contract.' Or, in Hobbes' version of the deed, identify the 'assembly of men' with the whole body of citizens, and the two contracts
become identical.

64. Rousseau thus lays a foundation for his political edifice as absolute and immutable as that of Hobbes. Politics with him, in spite of
some cursory remarks, becomes a quasi-mathematical science. Its formulæ are deducible by rigorous logic from a fundamental axiom absolutely independent of time and place. History and observation are
simply irrelevant. We have an *a priori* system of politics which would
harmonise with the *a priori* theology of the school of Clarke. Society
will be put together on a geometrical plan, without reference to idiosyncrasies of men and races, or to their historical development. On the
other hand, if the logical framework of Rousseau's system resembles
that of Hobbes, the spirit by which it is animated is caught from Locke,
though marvellously altered in the process. 'Man is born free; and he is
everywhere in chains.' That is the celebrated phrase which opens his
discussion, and strikes the keynote of the treatise. Locke, too, had
asserted that doctrine, and had interpreted the freedom of man as involving equality before the laws, and giving a logical support to the
right of insurrection. But between the spirit of Locke and the spirit
of Rousseau there is the difference which distinguishes Somers from
Robespierre. Locke could reconcile slavery to his theories; Rousseau declares that the words 'slavery' and 'right' are contradictory and mutually
exclusive.[11] Locke applies his social contract to modify the natural
equality of mankind, so far as that phrase implies equality of property,
or even of privilege, in consideration of general security. In Rousseau's
version equality is not only the starting-point but the goal. The two
principal objects of every legislative system should be the establishment
of liberty and equality; and by equality Rousseau carefully explains that

[10]Rousseau, 'Du Contrat Social,' book i. ch. vi.
[11]Ib. ch. iv.

he means—not, indeed, an absolute equality of wealth and power—but such an approximation towards such an equality that no citizen may be rich enough to buy another, nor any poor enough to be bought.[12] Locke's metaphysical spirit is limited by his utilitarianism; and he endeavours to sanction an existing order, sufficiently well arranged, in his opinion, to protect individual happiness by a tacit consent, which abandons the 'state of nature.' Rousseau is a metaphysician pure and simple, and his compact overrides all artificial arrangements—by which he means the whole existing order—to revert to the simplicity of the 'state of nature' itself. A religion, said the deists, which is not the religion of nature, must be an artificial religion, or, in other words, a religion consciously invented for the benefit of priests. A political system, adds Rousseau, which is not prescribed by nature must be an artificial system, or a system consciously invented for the benefit of kings. Away with it! We need only add that the state of nature means a collection of men, regarded as individual units, with only those qualities which belong to man as man, and therefore without the qualities generated by the infinite variety of forces which have slowly moulded the concrete human beings whom we see around us. Rousseau's theory, therefore, implies the sweeping away of the whole elaborate growth of beliefs, superstitions, and sentiments, and the institutions in which they have been embodied, which have been developed during the course of man's life on the earth, unless they can be justified by abstract reasoning. He would annihilate history, and preaches the true gospel of revolutionary fanaticism.

65. Here, then, we have formally embodied the two doctrines which are to be at death-grips for generations to come. Each absolutely repudiates the whole foundation upon which the other is avowedly based. On turning from Montesquieu to Rousseau, we may fancy that we have been present at some Parisian salon where an elegant philosopher has been presenting to fashionable hearers, conclusions daintily arrayed in sparkling epigram and suited for embodiment in a thousand brilliant essays. Suddenly, there has entered a man stained with the filth of the streets, his utterance choked with passion, a savage menace lurking in every phrase, and announcing himself as the herald of a furious multitude, ready to tear to pieces all the beautiful theories and formulas which may stand between them and their wants. How will those dilettanti demonstrations of the universe meet the new force which has suddenly come amongst them like the 'blood-boltered' Banquo, to dis-

---

[12]'Contrat Social,' book ii. ch. x.

turb their decorous ceremonials? The guillotine which we can see in the background gives a sufficiently emphatic answer. If Montesquieu represents philosophy coming into the world from the antiquary's study, Rousseau represents a philosophy which had long been familiar to professors, suddenly descending into the streets and revealing most unsuspected capacities. The political philosophy of Rousseau had indeed a fatal weakness which has revealed itself only too plainly in the attempt to translate its theories into practice. No sound structure could be raised on a doctrine which was the incarnation of anarchy. But the bitter teaching of experience was required to reveal that truth; and, meanwhile, the philosophy had certain advantages in practical warfare. In the first place, it laid down definite and authoritative dogmas. No new creed can be propagated which avowedly rests upon uncertain bases. The dogmas of absolute equality and liberty might be erroneous, but they were dogmas. Their simplicity and their show of demonstration enabled the apostles of the new creed to preach as men having authority, not as vague pedants and theorists. And, in the next place, the time was ripe for the truths which they dimly foreshadowed. It was true that political institutions should be formed in accordance with reason and not in obedience to mere blind prejudice; it was true that sympathy with human suffering and impartial justice between men of the same species should guide the labours of legislators. The notions that obedience to reason involved the rejection of experience, and that justice meant not only the removal of arbitrary privilege, but the non-recognition of actual differences, were unfortunately plausible enough to escape detection.

66. How, indeed, could the revolutionary creed be effectually met by the Humes or even the Montesquieus? Doctrines about the judicious mixture of the three forms of government might be very plausible, but would not still the wrath of men writhing under a sense of oppression, or filled with jealousy of arbitrary privilege. The philosophers, with all their classical quotations and neat theories about checks and balances, were aware that their conclusions were at best provisional. They could appeal to no sentiment capable of meeting fierce popular discontent, and to no conclusions sufficiently well established to oppose to the popular dogmas. On one force, however, more reliance could be placed, and especially in England; where sheer stupidity, unreasoning prejudice, a vigorous grasp of realities, and a contempt, healthy within certain limits, for fluent theories, opposed a powerful barrier to the inroad of the new creed, even when its fallacies were not detected. The social order in England was not ripe for a revolution; but even had it been so, it is

probable that the gospel according to Rousseau would have required some modification to fit it to English tastes. As it was, that gospel never became fairly acclimatised, and never won a proselyte capable, even in a faint degree, of rivalling the influence of the original teacher. Englishmen stuck doggedly to their old ways; they despised the new ideas as much because they were supposed to be French as because they could be shown to be demoralising. With that obstinate unreason which sometimes verges on the sublime, they worked on in their own slow blundering fashion. When discontented, they preferred the traditional twaddle about the various Palladia of British liberty to any new-fangled outcries about the rights of man; and when at last the revolutionary spirit succeeded in obtaining some kind of foothold, it showed itself in a form characteristic of the nation. Bentham was nearly as hostile to the traditional beliefs and institutions as Rousseau; but he expressed his dislike in a very different dialect. But we must approach the study of the later development of English thought through some earlier performances.

VI. The Fermentation.

67. The political torpor had become most profound during the Pelham administration. It seemed as if the English people, so devoted to faction in their earlier days, were sinking into absolute indifference. The only event which occupied a session was the alteration of the calendar; and the nation enjoyed a halcyon period, during which such strange creatures as Bubb Dodington and his like intrigued and disported themselves on the surface of politics for the edification of the universe. The symptoms of a change, however, were manifesting themselves; and the outbreak of the seven years' war had ominous meanings not as yet obvious to the world. In 1757 appeared Brown's 'Estimate of the Manners and Principles of the Times'—a book the popularity of which appeared to contemporaries to be a significant symptom.[1] It is a vigorous indictment against the English nation. Admitting that his countrymen have still some spirit of liberty, some humanity, and some equity, he argues that their chief characteristic is 'a vain, luxurious, and selfish

---

[1] The book went through seven editions in little more than a year; but it is said that the editions are probably factitious. See Burton's 'Life of Hume,' ii. 23. Frequent references in contemporary literature show in any case that the book made an impression. Brown is perhaps best remembered now by the line 'coxcombs vanquish Berkeley by a grin,' which occurs in his Essay on Satire, published by Warburton in Pope's works.

effeminacy.'[2] At our schools the pupils learn words not things;[3] university professorships are sinecures; on the grand tour, our young men learn foreign vices without widening their minds; we go to dinner in chairs, not on horseback, and spend money on foreign cookery instead of plain English fare; conversation is trivial or vicious; for solid literature we read silly plays, novels, and periodicals, though, 'amidst this general decay of taste and learning,' one great writer, to wit Warburton, 'bestrides the narrow world like a Colossus;[4] the fine arts are depraved; opera and pantomime have driven Shakespeare into the background; our principles are as bad as our manners; religion is universally ridiculed, and yet our irreligion is shallow; Bolingbroke is neglected, not because he is impious, but because he fills five quarto volumes, whilst Hume's flimsy essays may amuse a breakfast table; honour has gone with religion; we laugh at our vices as represented on the stage, and repeat them at home without a blush; public spirit has declined till a minister is regarded as a prodigy for simply doing his duty; and if the domestic affections are not extinct, we may doubt whether their survival is not another proof of our effeminacy. The professions are corrupt, with two exceptions; law and physic are still tolerably sound, because directly useful even to the most selfish and effeminate; but our politicians are mere jobbers, and our officers mere gamblers and bullies; whilst our clergy have become and deserved to become contemptible, because they neglect their duties in order to slumber in stalls, 'haunt levees, or follow the gainful trade of election jobbing.'[5] 'Low spirits and nervous disorders'[6] have notoriously increased, and made us incapable of self-defence. Our cowardice appeared in 1745, and was due not to a decay of spirit in the lower orders, but to the prevalence amongst their superiors of the sentiment which led a gentleman to say, 'If the French come, I'll pay, but devil take me if I fight.'[7] Suicide is common, but it is the suicide of ruined gamblers, not of despairing patriots. The officers of the army divide their time in peace between milliners' shops and horse-races; and the officers of the navy, even in time of war, attend chiefly to prize-money. The chain of self-interest, now the only binding chain, extends from the lowest cobbler to the King's Prime Minister; but it is but a rope of sand, and the first shock will dissolve us into an 'infinity of factions.'[8] Our colonies have outgone us in 'fashionable degeneracy,' and if the French take North America, we shall be confronted by a naval power equal to our own. 'Thus, by a gradual and unper-

[2]Brown's 'Estimate,' i. 29. [4]Ib. i. 44. [6]Ib. i. 89.
[3]Ib. i. 31. [5]Ib. i. 85. [7]Ib. i. 93. [8]Ib. i. 112.

ceived decline, we seem gliding down from ruin to ruin; we laugh, we
sing, we feast, we play,' and in blind security, though not in innocence,
resemble Pope's lamb licking the hand just raised to shed his blood.[9]

68. Denunciations of this kind prove nothing less than the truth of
statements on which they are professedly grounded. Brown's readers
might console themselves with the reflection that similar lamentations
have been raised ever since men discovered this world not to be Utopia.
Events which soon belied part of his prophecies might justify the opinion that the whole represented a passing phase of ill-temper rather than
a deeply rooted discontent. 'The French,' he said, 'are now pursuing it'
—that is, a system of military conduct, founded on the assumption that
hardy troops will beat luxurious troops—'on the plains of America, and
if we hold to our dastardly maxim, they will pursue it on the plains of
Salisbury.'[10] The French superiority and Brown's credit received a
death-blow on the heights of Abram; and Englishmen, finding that they
had not become cowards, forgot the alarm or remembered it only as a
good jest.

69. Yet Brown was not a contemptible writer; his style is clear, and
his reasoning often vigorous. If the indignation to which his view of
social evils prompts him is faint and colourless beside the deep passion
which breathes through Rousseau's writings, he may, in a certain sense,
be regarded as another indication of the same current of feeling. Brown,
doubtless, would have disavowed any such complicity with horror. He
was a believer in the British Constitution and the balance of power; a
quoter of Montesquieu, Machiavelli, and Sir W. Temple, and an adherent, though not one of the most abject adherents, of the sham giant
Warburton. A sound utilitarian, he cared nothing for the rights of
man; and was much too willing to accept a good preferment to favour
the absolute equality of mankind. He resembles Rousseau only so far
as he endeavoured to express that vague feeling of unrest which was
beginning to pervade all classes; and he gave pretty much the same
theory as to its origin, though he would have shrunk from Rousseau's
drastic remedy. The evils which afflicted society have taken many forms,
and different names have come into fashion at different times. The cant
of the day used the phrase 'luxury;' and luxury was admitted, on all
hands, to consist in a departure from the simplicity of nature. Brown
works out a pretty little theory, showing how commerce, necessary in
the youth of a nation, and useful in its manhood, becomes in its old age
the cause of avarice, luxury, and 'effeminate refinement.'[11] It was now

[9]Brown, i. 144.   [10]Ib. i. 201.   [11]Ib. i. 153.

depopulating the country, as statistics were supposed to prove,[12] as well as ruining our spirit. The remedy applied in France for forbidding the nobility to engage in trade was scarcely to be hoped for in England.[13] Indeed, his proposals are of the vaguest. Some consolation might be found in the theory, in which Brown tells us that he had anticipated Montesquieu, that our liberty was the natural growth of a soil and climate which produce in us a certain 'spirit of chagrin;'[14] and it might seem that Britons would never be slaves as long as they had their fogs and their 'local spleen.'[15] But the mode of applying this ill-temper had to be left in judicious vagueness. He could not, like Rousseau, propose a summary return to a state of nature. Reform, he thought, must come from above; and it was precisely the governing classes who were most corrupt. 'They who should cure the evils are the very delinquents.'[16] A foreign invasion might startle us from repose,[17] or, in some great emergency, the 'voice of an abused people' might rouse their rulers 'into fear.'[18] Not, however, that Brown contemplated a revolution. The voice of the people was to find utterance through a great minister. A portrait of this ideal personage, the successor of Bolingbroke's 'Patriot King,' closes the second volume, or should close it, but that Brown adds a supplementary portrait of the ideal writer on politics. He was, of course, in no want of an original in the last case; and Pitt, then rising into power on the popular favour, stood well enough for the other.

70. Brown, a clever pamphleteer, though no prophet, was speedily forgotten; but the denunciations of luxury, of which his book is perhaps the best English example, continued to be popular in literature and in society. It is written in Boswell how often they stirred the bile of Johnson; and indeed they are for the most part flimsy enough. They might have some significance when regarded as an implicit answer to a very awkward question. The poor and despised were saying to their masters, through the mouth of Rousseau, Is there any conceivable use in you? And it was the fashionable though very far from sincere reply to confess, On the whole, we are of no use whatever. We are simply a product of corruption. At the close of the seven years' war, ominous symptoms of discontent began to make themselves perceptible. Chatham had won for England the empire of the New World. The hands into which he resigned his power were utterly incapable of discharging so lofty a function. Colonial discontents were echoed by the widespread discontent at home; and the nation entered upon a period of vehement

[12]Brown, i. 187.   [14]Ib. ii. 31.   [16]Ib. i. 220.
[13]Ib. i. 218.   [15]Ib. ii. 35.   [17]Ib. ii. 246.   [18]Ib. i. 221.

agitation such as had hardly been known since the Revolution. The popular excitement was the more dangerous from the vacillation of the rulers; the set of factions who plotted and struggled for power, forming and dissolving alliances with scandalous facility, bullying alternately the king and the people, and combining the faults of courtiers and demagogues, were unable to conceive or execute any decided line of policy. Their folly drove America to rebellion; and, at times, threatened to produce a rebellion at home. And yet, though allusions to the days of Cromwell were frequent in the mouths of agitators, the discontent had not as yet the true revolutionary ring. It is amusing to observe how carefully the popular leaders justified even revolution by precedent; and instinctively appealed to the leading cases of Hampden and Sidney rather than to the abstract rights of man.

71. One literary product of that period has obtained a permanent celebrity, and may stand as a sufficient representation of the contemporary phase of feeling. The famous Letters of Junius owe part of their reputation to the historical enigma as to their authorship; in purely literary merits, they are as inferior to Swift's concentrated satire as to Burke's sumptuous rhetoric. The eloquence is stilted; and the invective suggests rancorous ill-will rather than virtuous indignation. The hatred has not that dignity with which the greatest men can invest the expression of their evil passions. Yet Junius stands high above the mere hack pamphleteer. His polish has, to some degree, withstood the corroding influences of time. 'Once for all,' writes Philip Francis to Burke, 'I wish you would let me teach you to write English. . . . Why will you not allow yourself to be persuaded that polish is material to preservation?'[19] When we remember by whom and to whom these words were written, and on what occasion—the publication, namely, of one of Burke's masterpieces of invective against the French Revolution—their arrogance may help to confirm the ordinary theory as to the authorship of the letters. At any rate, they express the literary doctrine of Junius. Polish was to preserve what was else little worth preservation. For the absence of any speculative thought in Junius's Letters is even more remarkable than in the case of Bolingbroke. Bolingbroke at least aims at being philosophical. Junius makes personal denunciations almost the exclusive substance of his letters. He has no affectation of theory. Avowing his belief that a revolution might be approaching, he never invokes those principles a belief in which should inflame the popular passions, and guide men who have for the time abandoned all conventional formulas.

[19]Burke's Correspondence, iii. 162.

Wilkes writes to him professing his readiness 'to plunge the patriot dagger in the bosom of the tyrants of his country.'[20] Wilkes was a mere comedian; but one may fancy that in some popular tumult Junius could have put on a mask and taken advantage of the confusion to plunge a dagger in some hated antagonist. Each object of his wrath—Grafton, Bedford, Mansfield, or George III.—seems for the time to occupy his whole field of vision and stir the depths of his malignity. But the ferocious onslaught turns generally upon some personal scandal, upon the stories that one duke had been horsewhipped and another had taken his mistress to the opera; whilst constitutional principles are invoked to injure his enemy, rather than defended at his enemy's cost.

72. The principles are of a characteristically narrow kind. Junius strains his powers to the utmost in order to prove, not that all men are free and equal, that monarchy is a delusion and the Church an imposture, but that the legal effect of expelling a member of Parliament is at most to nullify that election, and give the constituents a chance of re-electing him if they please, without disqualifying him so as to nullify all votes given for him hereafter. On that distinction the liberty of England depends. Or, again, Junius assures the livery of London that 'The very being of that law, of that right, of that constitution, for which we have been so long contending, is now at stake.'[21] The law and the constitution depend upon the question whether the livery will or will not adhere to the ordinary system of rotation by which the alderman next in seniority to the Lord Mayor was elected to succeed him. Wider questions are characteristically narrowed in the mode of statement. Junius can only argue the great question of the liberty of the press under form of an attack upon Lord Mansfield for maintaining that a jury is judge of the facts, but not of the law. The general principle must be translated into the concrete, and be thus reduced to a statement to which precedents are applicable, before it comes within the sphere of his intelligence. The Letters of Junius, therefore, whatever their ability, belong rather to the historian of fact than to the historian of thought. The weapon already used by men like Swift, De Foe, or Bolingbroke, acquired fresh power in his hands; but he contributed nothing to the development of political speculation. The British Constitution is his ultimate appeal; Magna Charta and the Bill of Rights were to him what the Bible was to Chillingworth; there was no going behind them; and a man who should appeal to abstract principles would be travelling out of the record into arguments irrelevant, or, at all events, superfluous.

[20]Junius, i. * 302.   [21]Ib. ii. 340.

His political principles, so far as they appear, involve a rigid adherence to precedent, and to purely technical arguments. In the letter to Wilkes, which most fully expounds his opinions, he declares that the 'extermination of corruption' is impossible, and that to propose it is to be ridiculous. He is in favour of triennial, but objects to annual, Parliaments. He opposes Parliamentary reform in its later sense, because he holds that, if Parliament could disfranchise a borough, it could disfranchise a whole kingdom, or elect itself for life.[22] Though approving Chatham's plan for increasing the number of county members, he would not enfranchise the large towns. He would prefer to see merchants and manufacturers becoming freeholders by their industry, to making more boroughs as centres of riot and cabal.[23] Obviously the demagogue is still tied and bound by chains of red tape.

73. One tendency, indeed, which resulted from the peculiar conditions of the struggle has a democratic aspect. The House of Commons was at this time the object of popular distrust instead of the organ of the popular will, and Junius tries to assign limits to the supremacy of the legislature, and asserts in strong language the subordination of the House to the people.[24] The liberty of the press is, of course, the 'palladium of all the civil, political, and religious rights of an Englishman,' and the 'right of juries to return a general verdict, in all cases whatsoever, is an essential part of our constitution, not to be controlled or limited by the judges, nor in any shape questionable to the legislature.'[25] In short, the old constitutional precedents are sacred, and the best means of preserving them is to allow Junius an unlimited right of abusing the king and his ministers, without danger of prosecution to his printers. Granting this, no constitutional change was desirable. Junius's pet statesman was George Grenville, whose masterly portrait by Burke has made him the model and antitype of all constitutional pedants. The new impulse as yet showed no signs of a tendency to desert the old channels. The most powerful representative of popular discontent was an embodiment of personal spite, to whom the mouldy parchments of constitutional privileges were as sacred as the laws of nature. Junius, in virtue of the narrowness of his views, has become antiquated more rapidly than almost any writer of at all equal power; and already has less interest for modern readers than Locke or Hume.

74. Thoughts, however, were slowly fermenting even amidst the

[22]Junius, i. * 289.   [23]Ib. i. * 291.
[24]*E.g.* 'Dedication to English People, and Letter to the King,' i. 62.
[25]Junius, i. 4.

dogged conservatism of the English mind, which were destined to produce work of far more permanent value, or to affect more deeply the
history of the country. As I am only indirectly concerned with the
history of events, I shall quit the order of time in order to give something like a logical scheme of the various phases of opinion. The relation between opinion and practice, the way in which political philosophising governed the expression of political passions, is not easy to trace
in detail, though the general relations are sufficiently obvious. Politicians, in truth, cared little enough for logic, and in the shifting phantasmagoria of English politics down to the revolutionary period, it
would be rash to assign too confidently any definite theory to the
various sections engaged in this partisan warfare. Yet, roughly speaking, we may discriminate four, or perhaps five, separate movements in
the political world, to each of which corresponds, roughly and inco-
herently enough, a certain theoretical impulse. Four factions wrangled
and struggled, and went through almost every possible combination and
permutation during the early years of George III.

75. The king himself was at the head of a party personally contemptible. Stranger irony of fate can hardly be imagined than that which
placed this most narrow-minded of rulers at the head of a great people
during one of its most trying crises; as if to show how much mischief
can be worked by wrong-headed honesty, and how little the stupidity
or the mischief wrought by a ruler can affect loyalty. Poor George III.
became highly popular in later years, partly because he became an object
of very natural compassion. But his popularity was also due in part to
the fact that he represented fairly enough those qualities of dogged
courage and honesty, shading by imperceptible degrees into sheer pig-
headedness and insensibility to new ideas, upon which we are accustomed, rightly or wrongly, to pride ourselves. It was natural enough
that such a man should fail to recognise the fact that his aristocracy
regarded him as, in right, a mere figurehead and bit of State cere-
monial. And therefore, with a courage which was respectable, though
with lamentable incapacity to understand the signs of the times, or to
distinguish between narrow-minded scruples and high-handed principle,
he tried to play his part, and defended the decaying fortunes of kingly
sanctity.

76. Alternately opposed to him and truckling to his wishes was the
purely aristocratic party, upon which had descended the mantle of the
revolutionary prophets of 1688. No more selfish and unprincipled clique
ever clung to power in a great country. Its leaders had, indeed, a dumb
sense of patriotism, regarding the honour of England as more or less

involved in the maintenance of their own privileges. But factions, it is said, are like serpents, whose heads are propelled by their tails. And if the Duke of Bedford was the official representative of a great aristo-cratic connection, its animating spirit was best represented by such a man as Rigby, the embodiment of petty personal intrigue, drawn by a certain blind instinct to the side of oppression, but yet too profoundly cynical to be actively tyrannical.

77. Opposed to these two parties, though at times co-operating, were two sections of the Whigs, who had each a genuine political belief. Each of them possessed one leader of surpassing eminence, though the system seemed to be ingeniously contrived to neutralise the influence of great abilities. The Rockingham party seems to have comprised many men of amiable character, of personal purity, and of high intentions. But they were too weak, or too little skilful in the arts of intrigue, to impress a governing impulse upon the country. It never seems to have occurred to them more than to other aristocratic factions, that the claims of genius were for a moment to be compared to the claims of family. The English nation, which had a Burke and a Chatham amongst its statesmen, had, therefore, to be governed by a North, in humble submission to the stupidity of a George III. The most intelli-gent party thought that it had done ample homage to the man whose genius is their one great title to the respect of posterity, when it gave the chief office in the State to his pupil, Fox, and flung to him the crumbs of subordinate office. Burke, however, accepted his position without a murmur. There are, he says, 'two only securities for the im-portance of the people; power arising from popularity, and power arising from connection.'[26] The last source of power was represented by the Whig families, and Burke took a humble place in the ranks of one of the aristocratic 'rings' which then carried on the government.

78. 'Power arising from popularity' was, of course, represented by Chatham, the head of the last great party in the State. By the energy of his haughty will he stands out above all contemporary politicians. Scorning the wretched intrigues which passed for statesmanship amongst rivals, he placed himself for a brief period at the head of the nation. For a moment England was ruled by its natural king, and had its reward in a blaze of military glory. During his later years, disease, the distrust of his rivals, or his own arrogance, kept Chatham for the most part in melancholy retirement: for another brief period he tried, but failed grievously, to weld together the jarring elements of party

[26]Burke's Works, ii. 239.

into a powerful administration. The popular will could only impose a Chatham upon the king and the aristocracy at a time of fierce excitement. In calmer periods, and when his powers were failing, the politicians were too strong for him. Chatham, as the representative of the popular favour, and by the natural turn of a vehement mind, intuitive rather than discursive, and more eloquent than logical, was inclined towards the absolute dogmas of the revolutionary school. He was not, indeed, a believer in the rights of man in a revolutionary sense; for his ardent patriotism often took the form of almost melodramatic loyalty. But he judged the issues of the time by principles which easily assimilated with those of the revolutionists. Wilkes and the patriots of the City revered him as their natural head, though a head generally wrapped in clouds and darkness. Camden, his favourite lawyer, was the great judicial defender of popular rights. Shelburne, his lieutenant, was the patron of Priestley and Price; and it is not difficult to suppose that, under other circumstances, Chatham might have developed into a Mirabeau.

79. The logical division of sentiments which, as I have said, corresponds, though very roughly, to these party divisions, may be briefly defined. George III., as the last representative of some shadow of divine right, found his Abdiel in the last of the Tories, Johnson. The Bedfords and their like would probably have explained their constitutional theories, so far as they had any theories, in the language of the good 'balance of power' doctrinaires, Blackstone and Delolme. Burke was at once the ablest practical exponent, and incomparably the greatest theoretical exponent, of the doctrines of the more intelligent Whigs. The thinkers who sanctioned those more popular impulses of which Chatham was the great representative must be divided into two classes. Some of them belonged to the purely English or utilitarian school, of which Bentham became in later years the accepted prophet. Others were more influenced by the French theorists, and may be regarded as continuing more or less directly the impulse of Rousseau. I propose to consider the various phases of opinion in accordance with the scheme thus indicated.

VII. The Tories.

80. The best interpreter of the lingering remnant of the divine-right theories was silence. A mute but dogged resistance to all change was the natural policy of men in whom the spirit of absolute rule survived

after its logical groundwork had dropped away. The sentiment, indeed, upon which George III. relied was still vigorous; the selfish factious-ness of the aristocracy gave strength to the ruler who at least professed to represent the national will; a strength which afterwards received a great accession from the revolutionary panic. But it was dangerous to look too closely into the reason of the case. The monarchy obviously rested on a parliamentary title, and claims like those of the Stuarts were too great an anachronism. The only doctrine applicable to the case was that of which Johnson was the natural exponent. Johnson was little fitted for abstract speculation. He was an embodiment of sturdy preju-dice, or, in other words, of staunch beliefs which had survived their logical justification. The depth and massiveness of his character redeem his opinions from contempt. His loyalty was absolutely free from the taint of servility. The man who was so profoundly touched by the condescension of his sovereign in once talking to him for half-an-hour was a moral giant beside the courtiers who enjoyed a backstairs inti-macy. And the pamphlets by which Johnson showed his gratitude for his pension are, at least, sincere utterances of a thoroughly masculine nature. Their philosophy, indeed, if philosophy it must be called, is simple in the extreme. 'In sovereignty,' he says, 'there are no grada-tions. . . . There must in every society be some power or other from which there is no appeal, which admits no restrictions, which pervades the whole mass of the community, regulates and adjusts all subordina-tion, enacts laws or repeals them, creates or annuls judicatures, extends or contracts privileges, exempts itself from question or control, and bounded only by physical necessity.'[1] That is Johnson's whole political theory. Subordination, as he constantly asserts, is an essential condition of human happiness. The appeal to the rights of man was a piece of sickly sentimentalism. Rousseau ought to be transported.[2] All Whiggism is detestable, because it implies simply the negation of all principles.[3] The first Whig was the devil.[4]

81. In these and other more or less humorous utterances, Johnson gives his genuine creed. He felt rather than inferred on speculative grounds that no solid basis for government could be made out of social contracts and abstract rights, and all the flimsy apparatus of constitu-tional theory upon which the Whigs of his day habitually relied. The doctrines of Rousseau tended to sap the foundations of all order; and the best reply was to fasten a determined grasp upon whatever order

[1]Johnson's Works, viii. 168, 'Taxation no Tyranny.'
[2]Boswell, Feb. 15, 1766.   [3]Ib. July 6, 1763.   [4]Ib. April 28, 1778.

remained amongst men, without asking awkward questions. The principle, indeed, which implicitly denied the responsibility of governors,
because the advocates of responsibility were opposed to all government,
might in practice lead to the defence of gross tyranny. But Johnson's
views of life made him insensible to all such arguments. The flimsy
patriotism of the day put forward pretexts contemptible to his strong
common sense. In the civil wars we were fighting for a king and a
religion; under Queen Anne there was an effort to upset a government;
but the point over which noisy demagogues were now fighting was,
whether Middlesex should or should not be represented by 'a criminal
from gaol.'[5] The popular cry was the work of reckless demagogues
upon an ignorant mass. Petitions meant nothing. 'One man signs because he hates the Papists; one because it will vex the parson; another
because he owes his landlord nothing; one because he is rich; another
because he is poor; one to show that he is not afraid; and another to
show that he can write.'[6] The Americans, indeed, alleged some grievances; but what they really meant was, that they would only pay what
taxes they pleased. They believed in the doctrine of 'the fanciful
Montesquieu,' that 'in a free State, every man, being a free agent, ought
to be concerned in his own government.'[7] That doctrine meant simply
anarchy. The 'consent' of which theorists talked was 'anarchy passive.'
Every man is 'born consenting to some system of government.' Anything more than this 'is the unmeaning clamour of the pedants of
policy, the delirious dream of republican fanaticism.'[8] If Americans
still chose to complain, they must be satisfied with the answer that they
had made their bargain and must stick to it. Their ancestors had
chosen, for sufficient consideration, to leave a country where they could
have a share in the government, and must take the consequences. If
they complain that a tax is unprecedented, 'it may be easily answered
that the longer they have been spared the better they can pay.'[9] Meanwhile, American and English patriots alike might console themselves
with the thought which Johnson expressed in his familiar addition to
Goldsmith's 'Traveller':—

> How small, of all that human hearts endure,
> That part which kings or laws can cause or cure!

Though boroughs have changed hands, the general state of the nation
has not suffered. 'The sun has risen, and the corn has grown, and what-

[5]Johnson's Works, viii. 94, 'The False Alarm.'   [6]Ib. viii. 89.
[7]Ib. viii. 173, 'Taxation no Tyranny.'   [8]Ib. viii. 174.   [9]Ib. viii. 189.

ever talk has been of the danger of property, yet he that ploughed the field has generally reaped it, and he that built a house was master of the door; the vexation excited by injustice suffered, or supposed to be suffered, by any private man or single community, was local and temporary; it neither spread far nor lasted long.'[10]

82. It would be unwise to depreciate, perhaps it would be difficult to exaggerate, the value of this steady unreasoning prejudice as a practical force in politics. Its weakness in one sense is indeed obvious. When encountered by an equally vigorous prejudice on the other side, the only appeal left was to force. The Americans replied by bullets when it was useless to invoke the rights of man. And, moreover, such theories could not permanently hold out against assaults of a speculative kind. Rousseau was not treated on Johnson's plan; and his books stirred emotions which will not be summarily repressed by simple denial. A doctrine which might be alleged on behalf of other governments, bad, good, or indifferent, was really, like the extreme doctrine of divine right which was its ancestor, an argument for none. There is, indeed, more truth than politicians willingly admit in the theory of the impotence of governments for good or ill. But it was not a truth which would impress men suffering under actual oppression, and still less could it impart the right impulse to governments decaying from within. Philosophers might console themselves with the thought; but the multitude would reject it as irrelevant; and the rulers be demoralised so far as they came to make it an excuse for inaction.

VIII. The Constitutionalists.

83. I turn, therefore, to the constitutional theorists, who endeavoured to discover some sort of scientific basis for government. In the preface to Junius's Letters the anonymous author quotes with admiration a passage from a book, then just published, which gives the fullest exposition of the Whig theory. Jean Louis Delolme is not a writer of great original power; his creed has that taint of unreality which is common to all the doctrinaires, and seems to leave out of account precisely the great forces which mould all human affairs. Yet he puts into symmetrical shape a set of propositions which long passed current with commonplace thinkers. He expounded the gospel—such as it is—of the fossilised constitutionalists. Though very inferior in acuteness and originality to such writers as Montesquieu and Tocqueville, he may be

[10]Johnson's Works, viii. 85, 'The False Alarm.'

ranked for many purposes in the same class. Like them, he was impressed by the complex machinery of the British Constitution, and tried to frame a comprehensive theory of its nature. His admiration did not meet with the reward to which, in his opinion, it entitled him. He fancied that a book, intended to meet the revolutionary sentiments of the day, should have received some recognition from the rulers whose system he glorified. If, he says, he had told them that he was preparing to boil his teakettle with the English edition, he knows not what they would have replied; but he obviously thinks that the reply would have been 'Boil it.' He was forced to publish by subscription, and the result was not encouraging. One noble lord did not subscribe, but graciously recommended the book to a publisher, and the consequence was that Delolme had to buy off two intending translators for ten pounds. Another noble lord did not pay until Delolme, hearing that he had received a pension of 4,000*l.* a year, applied, after delicately waiting till the first quarter's payment must have been received, and a week afterwards received a couple of half-crowns.[1] The poor man, thus discouraged, seems to have fallen into distress, and led an anonymous existence in London for many years, though he ultimately died in Switzerland in 1807. These anecdotes are but too significant of the painful contrast between the ideal and the real; between the wisdom embodied in our matchless constitution and the manners of the constitutional rulers.

84. Delolme came to England at the time of the Wilkes troubles, and published his work contemporaneously with the Letters of Junius. To most Englishmen of the time the working of our constitutional machinery under a severe strain did not seem to justify very rose-coloured views. Delolme, however, was struck, like other foreign observers, by the amount of liberty enjoyed, and especially by the discovery that in England all things not forbidden are permitted, whereas, on the Continent, all things not permitted are forbidden.[2] His book records his explanation of the phenomenon. It consists of a brief historical sketch of the development of the constitution, followed by a discussion of its general principles.

85. In the preface Delolme states, with a curious *naïveté*, the doctrine which, less clearly formulated, lies at the bottom of the whole constitution-mongering creed. 'A government,' he says, 'may be considered as a great ballet or dance, in which, the same as in other ballets, everything depends on the disposition of the figures.'[3] The form, that is, is every-

---

[1]Delolme, pp. iii, iv.   [2]Ib. p. 453, note.   [3]Ib. p. xi.

thing, the substance nothing; to judge of a government, you must not know what are the men of whom it is composed, what their beliefs, hereditary predispositions, traditions, or social organisation, but simply what is the administrative mechanism. The political quacks of the present day, who would reform human nature by means of patent ballot-boxes, make the same assumption, but they make it tacitly. In the keen controversy between the followers of this school and the followers of Rousseau there was a common ground. Both schools agreed in assuming that the man of their speculations was a mathematical unit, whose qualities might be assumed to be substantially identical in all ages and nations. The dispute arose at the further point, whether the form of government suitable to his wants should be determined by *a priori* reasoning, or by observation of the experiments that had been made by legislators. If Delolme has the merit of appealing to experience, the assumptions implied in the 'ballet' theory render the appeal nugatory. Both schools, indeed, are fond of historical, and especially of classical, precedents. Rousseau and his followers fancied that they could find in the old democrat the free citizen, uncorrupted by feudalism and ecclesiasticism. Delolme regards the ancient history as a useful collection of precedents, directly applicable to modern times. A mob, he tells us, will inevitably produce a Spartacus or a Viriathus;[4] whilst 'Pisistratus and Megacles, Marius and Sylla, Cæsar and Pompey,'[5] give sufficient proof, if proof be required, of the danger of a dictator. The characteristic evil of the ancient republics is their instability; they are always losing their liberties, as a man might lose his purse; the most conclusive proof of the merits of the English government is that Marlborough did not convert himself into a Cæsar,[6] and the security of a state is to be found in a delicate poising of the various springs and balances. 'Ponderibus librata suis' is the motto to his book; the end of legislators should be to discover perpetual motion in politics; a clock which will run on indefinitely without requiring to be wound up is his ideal of a constitution; and the ideal, as he thought, was realised in the British Constitution.

86. This, as we have seen, is the logical result of the purely empirical method. Government regarded as a piece of machinery, instead of a natural growth, is naturally valued in proportion to its stability, instead of in proportion to its capacity for favouring progress. The weights are represented by the different powers in the system. The ruler, whether king or consul, is always trying to increase the strength of the executive,

---

[4]Delolme, p. 306.   [5]Ib. p. 200.   [6]Ib. pp. 214, 409.

and the people to diminish it. The problem is to equalise the two forces. Rousseau's scheme of identifying the ruler with the people is rejected as absurd. 'Nothing is more chimerical than a state either of total equality or of total liberty amongst mankind.'[7] Power, wealth, and position tend to concentrate themselves; but a skilful legislator may reduce the conflict to a perpetual drawn battle, and a perfect constitutional government will resemble the celebrated situation in Sheridan's 'Critic' where the three duellists each threaten each other with drawn swords, and each is unable to strike. The ideal state is a permanent deadlock.

87. The British Constitution, as matters then stood, might be taken to represent this state of things; and some of Delolme's ingenious theories remind us very forcibly of later doctrinaires. Historically speaking, he holds that our liberty was due to the early concentration of the central power, which produced a corresponding concentration of the popular power. The seed of liberty, stamped deeply into the soil, received a richer nourishment, and finally rose with a stronger growth.[8] The Commons, protected by their various privileges, the liberty of the press, the independence of the judges, the power of the purse and the power of impeachment, are able to make head successfully against the concentrated power of the Crown. They enjoy that 'freedom of the constitution which is no more than an equilibrium between the ruling powers of the state.'[9] Meanwhile the concentrated royal power is a precise 'counterpoise'[10] to the popular power. But why does not one power increase at the expense of the other?—a question which implies, by the way, a curious non-recognition of the most obvious facts. Delolme answers by explaining that 'masterpiece'[11] of the British Constitution— the identification of the interests of the legislators with the people. The representatives are a select class, not easily misled by demagogues like the ruling bodies of the old republics, whilst their exclusion from any share in the executive power prevents them from setting up for themselves, and keeps them in strict dependence on their constituents. The king cannot originate laws, nor is his name (a very important point) even mentioned in the deliberations of members.[12] Thus the popular power is unassailable. But how can the king, without a standing army, maintain his compensating power sufficiently to enforce the laws?[13] How is this side of the balance to be maintained? The great secret is the division of the legislature into two bodies, which, as is shown by various cases, brings into play the natural jealousy of the two Houses,

[7]Delolme, p. 489.   [9]Ib. p. 195.   [11]Ib. p. 259.
[8]Ib. p. 21.   [10]Ib. p. 202.   [12]Ib. p. 269.   [13]Ib. p. 391.

and thus induces each to restrain any assaults made by its rival on the power of the Crown.[14] The legislature is thus a complex apparatus— a kind of compensating balance or fly-wheel, in which a too violent motion of one part of the machinery spontaneously sets up a counteracting force in another. King and people are pulling at the two ends of a lever, so contrived that, as soon as one is gaining an advantage, the fulcrum shifts and brings it back to the other. And thus, not to follow into details a speculation of which the general nature is only too familiar, Delolme satisfies himself that 'all the political passions of mankind' find a natural vent in our constitutional forms; and is even able, like Montesquieu, to deduce the system by reasoning from first principles. The English government, indeed, cannot be immortal more than any other piece of human machinery; and, as Montesquieu declared that the constitution would perish when the legislature was more corrupted than the executive power,[15] so Delolme declared that a fatal symptom would be the power of the Crown to raise supplies without Parliament, or the concession to Parliament of a share in the executive authority.[16] Either event would show that the balance was fatally disturbed.

88. Delolme, like other observers from without, was naturally apt to assume that the forms of the constitution accurately corresponded to its real spirit. He was unable to detect the now obvious fact of the gradual encroachment of the legislature upon the executive authority, and the tendency, already sufficiently marked, towards making the ministers of the Crown a committee of the House of Commons. Had he been more behind the veil, he might have been led to recognise the importance of the great social forces which his theories implicitly ignore. Yet it would be unjust to dismiss him without acknowledging that he shows great ingenuity, and that the germ of some useful thoughts may be detected in his crude appeal to experience.

89. It is needless to dwell at length upon other writers who took the temporary stagnation of the English system for a proof of its supreme excellence. One writer of considerable contemporary reputation was Adam Ferguson, who professed to be the follower, and was considered by his friends to be the rival, of Montesquieu. Ferguson himself apologises for dealing with the subject at all after so great a master, and consoles himself with the rather doubtful reflection that, being 'more on the level of ordinary men,' his teaching will be 'more to the comprehension of ordinary faculties.'[17] Drummond, Archbishop of York—a

[14]Delolme, p. 399.   [15]'Esprit des Lois,' book xi. ch. 6.   [16]Delolme, p. 498.
[17]'Essay on History of Civil Society,' p. 108.

prelate whose claims to critical authority have long passed into utter oblivion—thought that Ferguson had surpassed his master. Hume, an intimate friend of Ferguson, and always generous in his judgments of friends, was unable to share in this eulogy. He recommended the suppression of the book, and even after its success, confessed that his opinion remained unaltered. He softened the blame indeed by reporting many favourable judgments, and telling Ferguson that Helvetius and Saurin had recommended the suppression of the 'Esprit des Lois.' Hume, in fact, was an excellent judge of the real merits of such a book, and, as in the case of his own Essays, a very poor judge of the popular taste. Ferguson's book has the superficial merits which were calculated for the ordinary mind. He possessed the secret of that easy Gallicised style, which was more or less common to the whole Scottish school, including Hume, Robertson, and Adam Smith. He makes elegant and plausible remarks, and the hasty reader does not perceive that the ease is gained by the evasion, instead of the solution of difficulties. Here and there we come across an argument or an illustration which seems to indicate greater acuteness. One sentence may be a sufficient, as it is a favourable, specimen of his style. 'The bosom,' he says, 'kindles in company, while the point of interest in view has nothing to inflame; and a matter frivolous in itself becomes important, when it serves to bring to light the intentions and character of men. The foreigner who believed that Othello on the stage was enraged for the loss of his handkerchief was not more mistaken than the reasoner who imputes any of the more vehement passions of men to the impressions of mere profit and loss.'[18] Ferguson was in politics what Blair was in theology—a facile and dexterous declaimer, whose rhetoric glides over the surface of things without biting into their substance. He expounds well till he comes to the real difficulty, and then placidly evades the dilemma.

90. From Montesquieu he has learnt that history and observation are to be consulted instead of abstract theory. The 'state of nature' is everywhere, in England as in the Straits of Magellan;[19] for all men's actions are the results of their nature, and investigation alone can tell us what that nature is. All human institutions have been developed out of the rude devices of savage life;[19] and he makes some good remarks upon what modern observers would call the differentiation of the social organs, or what he calls 'the separation of arts and professions.'[20] But he soon slides into Montesquieu's smart theory about the principles embodied in the forms of government, and his fluent rhetoric does not

[18]Ferguson, p. 53.   [19]Ib. p. 13.   [20]Ib. part iv. secs. i and iii.

give it the substance which it wanted in the more epigrammatic statements of his master. Thus, though he goes for descriptions of primitive
men to Tacitus's 'Germany,' and to the accounts of travellers in North
America, his state of nature is pretty much that of Rousseau. The
Spartan and the Indian appear in their old characters. Brutus and Cato
wear the accustomed drapery of eighteenth-century moralists. The fundamental doctrines of the revolutionists appear in a decorous disguise.
'He who has forgotton that men were originally equal,' he declares,
'easily degenerates into a slave.'[21] Luxury is denounced, though his
vacillation between the two schools lands him in a very hopeless conclusion. Men have denounced luxury in all ages; where, then, is it to
stop? 'It should stop where it is,'[22] he replies. Considered as implying a
preference for 'objects of vanity,' it is 'ruinous to the human race;' but
considered as a disposition to use modern improvements, no definite
standard can be fixed. This is the embodiment in politics of the facile
optimism of the comfortable philosophers of the day.

91. I may add a few words of another writer, whom we shall meet
again—Josiah Tucker, the Dean of Gloucester. He was one of those
sturdy cross-grained thinkers, who are shrewd enough to see certain
truths very clearly, but too short-sighted to grasp their general relations.
Even when in advance of the time, their soundest doctrines appear to
their contemporaries like fanciful crotchets. Tucker was full of pug-
nacity, capable of holding his own against all his adversaries, and willing
to have adversaries on every side. He managed to take up a position in
regard to the American War which had a certain foundation of sound
sense, and which was yet peculiar to himself. He was equally hostile to
Johnson and to Burke, to Lord North, to Chatham, and to Franklin.
On the one hand, he abused the Americans as cheats and liars, and
denied their claims to self-government as peremptorily as Johnson; but,
instead of inferring that they ought to be conquered, he concluded that
they ought to be turned adrift as a punishment. When emigration
stopped and they broke up into fragmentary states—the inevitable consequence of such a policy—they would soon beg for re-admission. Hitherto
they had been a millstone round our necks, and the most preposterous
of all policies, for a 'shopkeeping nation,'[23] was the attempt to bully its
customers into dealing with it. Tucker would, in our days, have been
a sound Conservative, and at the same time an adherent of the Manchester school of foreign policy.

92. His 'Treatise concerning Civil Government' is a vigorous, and

[21]Ferguson, p. 147.   [22]Ib. p. 414.   [23]Tucker's Tracts, ii. 132.

often very shrewd, attack on the school of Rousseau, of which the chief English supporters, in his opinion, were Price and Priestley, and of which Locke was the intellectual ancestor. His object is to show that the 'social contract,' as understood by the 'Lockians,' implied that all government was unlawful, except so far as it rested on the voluntary consent of the governed, or that, in other words, it meant simply anarchy. As, however, he is not quite able to emancipate himself from the notion that some sort of contract was necessary, he invents the term 'quasi-contract,'[24] which means simply that government is to be considered as a trust, but that the trustees cannot be dismissed at the arbitrary pleasure of the governed. He strikes some very shrewd blows at his adversaries, contrasts the real savage of the scalping-knife with the imaginary savage of Rousseau,[25] and attacks the popular nostrums of parliamentary reformers as conducive to riot and corruption.[26] He accepts the theory of the mixture of the three forms of government;[27] and gives an antiquarian discussion of the origin of the English form of government by way of illustrating his views of its advantages, and the proper cure for its evils. He had, however, little hope of persuading his countrymen to take a sensible view of their condition. What would become, he asks, of a demagogue who should tell his best friends, the mob, that Gibraltar and Port Mahon are expensive and useless; that the ocean should be free to all mankind; that colonies had always been a useless drain, that they would only trade with the parent-country as much as their interests required, and would trade so much whether compelled or not, and that, consequently, money would be saved, jobs prevented, and undue influence limited by separating from them at once?—would not the preacher of such salutary truths be hooted as an apostate, and consequently try to gain favour by proposing—not to remedy real grievances—but to reform the king's kitchen or his dog-kennel?

93. This is meant, of course, as a shrewd blow for Burke. I must now approach the writings of that great man, incomparably the greatest man, indeed, who has ever given the whole force of his intellect to the investigation of political philosophy in England. But one remark may be premised. Doctrines, such as those expounded by Delolme and his like, had certain merits, too easily overlooked by political enthusiasts and men impatient of superficial formalities. The whole theory was barren enough, but it served to consecrate that system of compromise

---

[24]'Treatise' &c. p. 146.   [26]Ib. p. 257 *et seq.*
[25]Ib. p. 180 *et seq.*   [27]Ib. p. 242.

which has had its utility, to admit of gradual development in the sphere of practice, and to facilitate the transition to a sound historical method in the sphere of theory. On the other hand, its extreme weakness as a permanent creed may be estimated by attempting to oppose arguments of the Delolme variety to the demands which were being put forward through the mouth of Rousseau. It is a weakness of the whole school which descends from Montesquieu that they overlook the really strong passions of humanity. The very conception of a government which contemplates it as a machine to be put together by skilful devices, assumes that the materials of which it is composed are colourless and lifeless. They are mere draughts on the political chessboard, to be arranged by the fancy of the legislator. Loyalty, patriotism, and the fierce desire for equality or liberty, are disturbing elements to be left out of the calculation. These ingenious and old-fashioned statesmen were helpless when confronted by demands made in the name of justice and sympathy. Men complaining that they were naked, and starving, and oppressed were not to be pacified by the assurance that the machine of government was so delicately balanced that it might be expected to run on for ever. Some justification of the existing order resting on deeper principles and appealing to stronger passions was urgently needed; and the most prominent service of Burke in the eyes of his contemporaries was that he supplied that want when the whole constitutional framework seemed going to pieces. And yet, it is frequently said that his opposition to the French Revolution implies a radical inconsistency in his teaching. To understand his position, and to set forth his true doctrine, however incompletely, requires a somewhat full discussion.

IX. Burke.

94. No English writer has received, or has deserved, more splendid panegyrics than Burke. To do justice to his multifarious activity, or to estimate accurately the influence which he exerted upon contemporary history, would involve a course of enquiry alien to the purpose of this book. I must try, however, to disengage his leading principles from the writing in which they are embedded, and to exhibit their relation to other systems of speculation. Considered simply as a master of English prose, Burke has not, in my judgment, been surpassed in any period of our literature. Critics may point to certain faults of taste; the evolution of his thought is sometimes too slow; his majestic march is trammelled by the sweep of his gorgeous rhetoric; or his imagination takes fire,

and he explodes into fierce denunciations which shock the reader when the excitement which prompted them has become unintelligible. But, whatever blemishes may be detected, Burke's magnificent speeches stand alone in the language. They are the only English speeches which may still be read with more than an historical interest when the hearer and the speaker have long been turned to dust. His pamphlets, which are written speeches, are marked by a fervour, a richness, and a flexibility of style which is but a worthy incarnation of the wisdom embodied in them. It matters little if we dissent from his appreciations of current events, for it is easy to supply the corrective for ourselves. The charge of over-refinement sometimes brought against him is in great part nothing more than the unconscious testimony of his critics that he could see farther than themselves. To a certain degree it is, perhaps, well founded. His political strategy was a little too complex for the rough give-and-take of ordinary partisans. His keen perception of the tendencies of certain politics led him to impute motives to their advocates, for which their stupidity rather than their morality incapacitated them. When, for example, we are told that the Court party persecuted Wilkes in order to establish a precedent tending to show 'that the favour of the people was not so sure a road as the favour of a Court, even to popular honours and popular trusts,'[1] we may prefer the simpler explanation founded on the blunted instincts of obtuse rulers. It was doing them too much honour to attribute to them any design beyond that of crushing an antagonist by the weapons readiest at hand. The keen intelligence which thus sometimes takes the form of excessive ingenuity is more frequently revealed by passages in which profound wisdom is concentrated in a single phrase. We should not ask how we got into the American difficulty, was the cry of the hand-to-mouth politicians, but how we are to get out of it. That is to say, is Burke's comment, 'we are to consult our invention, and reject our experience.'[2] 'Nobody will be argued into slavery'[3] is another phrase from the same speech, which compresses into half-a-dozen words the confutation of the special pleading and pettifogging of antiquarian lawyers, which the so-called practical men mistook for statesmanlike reasoning. 'I know no method,' he says elsewhere, 'of drawing up an indictment against a whole people;'[4] but lawyers thought that nothing was beyond the reach of their art. His

---

[1] Burke's Works, ii. 294, 'Present Discontents.'
[2] Ib. ii. 352, 'American Taxation.'
[3] Ib. ii. 433, ib.   [4] Ib. iii. 69, 'Conciliation with America.'

later writings are equally fertile. 'Art is man's nature'[5] sums up his argument against the Rousseau school of theorists; and here is another phrase which might serve as text for a political treatise. On occasions of this nature, he says, 'I am most afraid of the weakest reasonings, because they discover the strongest passions.'[6] Not to multiply instances, I quote one more passage of great significance in regard to Burke's method. 'From this source,' he says, speaking of history, 'much political wisdom may be learnt; that is, learnt as habit, not as a precept, and as an exercise to strengthen the mind, not as a repertory of cases and precedents for a lawyer.'[7]

95. Such sayings, which occur in profusion, illustrate the most marked peculiarity of Burke's mind—the admirable combination of the generalising faculty with a respect for concrete facts. His theorising is always checked and verified by the test of specific instances, and yet in every special case he always sees a general principle. He explains his method himself in a speech made in 1792. The professor, he says, deals simply with general principles; a statesman applies them to varying circumstances; without 'abstract ideas' all political reasoning would be a jumble, without facts a useless frivolity.[8] Burke was at one time suspected of being the author of 'Junius,' on the ground, not altogether devoid of plausibility, that he was the only living writer of the necessary capacity. Yet, if no other evidence were conclusive against the charge, the internal evidence derived from this characteristic would be convincing to those who have really studied the two writers. 'Junius' never deviates from personality into the higher regions of speculation, even when professedly advancing some general doctrine. Burke never condescends to mere personalities, even when his devotion to principles forces him to attack their assailants. He assails Hastings or the Jacobins, as embodiments of evil tendencies, with fierce animosity, it is true, but with an animosity free from any stain of personal dislike; he attacks the king's friends, but instead of fastening, like 'Junius,' on hated individuals, scrupulously avoids giving countenance even to the popular cry against Lord Bute.[9] And yet it is so much his habit to regard principles as embodied in concrete facts, that it is by no means easy to disentangle his speculative influence from the history of his share in current events. This is the specific quality which gives a unique character to his

[5]Burke, vi. 218, 'Appeal,' &c.
[6]Ib. vi. 345, 'Letter to Langrishe.'   [8]Ib. x. 41, 'Speech on Subscription.'
[7]Ib. vii. 197, 'Policy of the Allies.'   [9]Ib. ii. 257, 'Present Discontents.'

writings, and has led to frequent misunderstandings. Goldsmith's felicitous phrase indicates the nature of the difficulty. One party complained
that so great a man

> To party gave up what was meant for mankind;

for they could not conceive how a philosopher could care for the intrigues of Bedfords and Grenvilles. Another complained that

> He went on refining,
> And thought of convincing when they thought of dining;

for they could not conceive how any political object, except the advance-
ment of Bedfords or Grenvilles, could be worth serious struggle, and
much less worth the devotion of a life. Burke alone felt that even the
machinery of party might be used in the interest of mankind. And,
therefore, if he is at times too visionary and at times too condescending
to the men with whom he was unequally yoked, he contributed the
most elevating influence of contemporary politics, and was the one man
who accurately gauged the breadth and depth, though he may have
partly misunderstood the direction, of the great political movements of
his time.

96. The greatness of Burke as a thinker cannot be adequately appreciated without noticing the nobility of his moral nature. It is not from
want of human feeling so much as from want of imaginative power
that we are generally so dead to the sorrows and sufferings of the great
mass of our fellow-creatures. Beneath the rough crust of Johnson and
the versatile talent of Goldsmith lay hearts as true and tender as that of
Burke. Hume possessed an intellect still more penetrative, though he
had little enough of imaginative power. But Burke stands alone in his
generation for the combination of width of view with deepness of sympathy. Thinking of the mass, he never forgets the individual. His
habitual horizon stretches beyond the purlieus of Westminster and St.
James's to include the American colonists and our Indian dependants;
but the prospect, however distant, is never colourless. The wrongs of
Massachusetts stirred him as deeply as the wrongs of Middlesex; and
years of labour unrewarded, save by a good conscience, testified to his
sympathy with a race which, to most Englishmen, were but a name,
and to most Englishmen to whom they were more than a name, mere
grist for the money-making mill. A noble unselfishness stamps all his
efforts. 'I know the map of England,' he says, with admirable pride, 'as
well as the noble lord, or any other person; and I know that the road

I take is not the road to preferment.'[10] Incomparably the greatest in intellectual power of all English politicians, the life and soul of his party for some thirty years, he was in office for a few months at the age of fifty-two when he declined the greatest part of the customary profits, and he received a pension two years before his death, when all ambition, and almost all hope, was dead within him. Few stories are sadder, to us who are accustomed to estimate a man's happiness by his last days, and to see good fortune only in immediate success, than the story of Burke's bereaved old age, when the son whom he loved most tenderly had died before him, and the cause to which he had devoted a life was tottering. Yet he had the right to remember that, throughout life he had, with one doubtful exception, taken the generous side. The exception—namely, his assault on the French Revolution—placed him for once on the side of the oppressors, and therefore brought him the reward denied to his earlier labours. Yet no opponent will now impute to him, even in that case, sordid motive or blunted sensibility. He had defended the Americans against the blundering tyranny of George III., and the dogged stupidity of that part of the nation of which the dull king was the fit representative. He had denounced the penal laws which nearly drove Ireland to follow the American precedent. He had laboured with surpassing industry in the ungrateful task of curbing English brutality in India. He had defended the rights of his countrymen at home as well as protested against the abuses of their power abroad. He had opposed the petty tyranny engendered by the corrupt government of a servile aristocracy; he had denounced the numerous abuses which flourished under the congenial shade of jobbery in high places. If once or twice an irritable temperament led him to sanction mere factious intrigue, his voice had always been the most powerful and the least selfish on the side of honour, justice, and mercy. It is the least of his merits that his views of political economy were as far in advance of his time as his view of wider questions of policy; but the fact deserves notice as a proof that, if an orator by temperament, he laid the foundations of his intellectual supremacy deep in the driest and most repulsive of studies.

97. Burke's judgments upon Montesquieu and Rousseau, to which I have already referred, are sufficiently indicative of the speculative tendencies of his writings from first to last. His first political publication was directed against a teaching identical with that of Rousseau. The 'Vindication of Natural Society,' published in 1756, is an ingenious imitation of Bolingbroke, intended by the writer as a *reductio ad absurdum*

---

[10]Burke, ii. 440, 'American Taxation.'

of the anarchical principles—so Burke considered them to be—in which the friends of Bolingbroke anticipated the revolutionary school. It is, indeed, very remarkable that Burke's first efforts were directed against the very thinkers who were the objects of his dying protest; and that he detected the dangerous tendencies of doctrines which were to shake the whole world in his old age, whilst they had yet found no distinct utterance, and he was but a youthful adventurer. The argument put into the mouth of Bolingbroke is substantially that all government is bad, because resting upon arbitrary convention. War, tyranny, and corruption are caused by our revolt from the 'state of nature.' Politics, like religious dogma, should be constructed by pure *a priori* reasoning, instead of conforming to the teaching of experience. Some bigots and enthusiasts cherish the 'absurd and blasphemous notion'[11] that popular prejudices should not be disturbed for fear of the consequences. If, after showing all the evils due to those prejudices, you still 'plead the necessity of political institutions, weak and wicked as they are, I can argue with equal, perhaps superior, force concerning the necessity of artificial religion.'[12] If we would have perfect liberty, we must renounce the visions of theologians and the cunning schemes of politicians. The argument—remarkable for the skill with which the reasoning of an opponent is simulated, whilst his principles are covertly attacked[13]—may be easily inverted, so as to give Burke's true meaning. He wishes to expose the mischievous and anarchical tendencies of abstract metaphysical speculation. He desires to point out that, whatever be the evils inherent in government, any government is better than none; and that the substitution of abstract speculation for experimental observation can only lead to anarchy. The excessive value which Burke attached to prejudice as prejudice, and the rightful value which he attached to methods resting on experience, are as manifest as in his later writings. The 'Vindication' contains the germ of the more fully developed doctrine of the 'Reflections,' or of the 'Letters on a Regicide Peace.' The principles thus early grasped guided him throughout his life, and are the backbone of his speculations on English, American, Indian, and French politics.

98. His aversion to abstract reasoning upon politics colours every page of his theoretical discussions. He is never tired of dilating upon this

---

[11]Burke, i. 13, 'Natural Society.'   [12]Ib. i. 79, ib.

[13]It is a curious illustration of the fidelity with which Burke represents the revolutionary arguments that Godwin, in his 'Political Justice,' declared that Burke has proved in good earnest what he professes to prove ironically ('Political Justice,' i. 13, note).

text. 'I do not enter into these metaphysical distinctions,' he says, when speaking of the colonial troubles; 'I hate the very sound of them.'[14] The discussion of abstract rights is 'the great Serbonian bog,' 'twixt Damiata and Mount Casius old, where armies whole have sunk.'[15] 'One sure symptom of an ill-conducted State,' he says, in the same connection, 'is the propensity of the people to resort to' theories.[16] No constitution can be called good or bad in itself. 'The circumstances are what render every civil and political scheme beneficial or noxious to mankind.'[17] Even in the heat of his onslaught upon French revolutionists, he admits that there may be situations in which 'the purely democratic form will become necessary.'[18] Therefore, any absolute system must be erroneous and mischievous. The men who drew the Petition of Right under Charles I. were as familiar with theories about the right of man as Price and Sieyès; but they preferred to appeal to hereditary obligation. The doctrine that sovereignty originated from the people is a mere empty speculation, when in its proper sphere, and therefore asserts 'a position not denied, nor worth denying, or assenting to;'[19] and the whole social contract theory is 'at best a confusion of judicial with civil principles.'[20]

99. When the metaphysical basis of political rights is thus summarily cleared away, the question occurs, what other foundation is to be laid? Passages may be found in Burke's writings where language is used superficially resembling that of his antagonists. He speaks of the 'natural rights of mankind' as 'sacred things,'[21] and even says that all power is 'a derogation from the natural equality of mankind at large,'[22] and therefore to be used for their benefit. Elsewhere men have a natural right to the fruits of their industry, though not to a share of political power.[23] Or, again, 'equity' is ranked with 'utility,' as the sole foundations of law, and equity 'grows out of the great rule of equality, which is founded upon our common nature, and which Philo, with propriety and beauty, calls the mother of justice.'[24] The truth of Christianity itself, he infers, is 'not so clear as this proposition, that all men, at least the majority of men in the society, ought to enjoy the common advantages of it.'[25] These transient deviations into the quasi-metaphysi-

---

[14]Burke, ii. 432, 'American Taxation.'

[15]Ib. iii. 74, 'Conciliation.'

[16]Ib. iii. 186, 'Sheriffs of Bristol.'

[17]Ib. v. 36, 'Reflections.'

[18]Ib. v. 230, ib.

[19]Ib. vi. 147, 'Appeal.'

[20]Ib. vi. 257, ib.

[21]Ib. iv. 8, 'East India Bill.'

[22]Ib. iv. 11, ib.

[23]Ib. v. 121, 'Reflections.'

[24]Ib. ix. 351, 'Letter to Burgh.'

[25]Ib. ix. 364, ib.

cal language, when more closely examined, are easily intelligible. The natural equality of mankind, in Burke's mouth, is simply an expression of the axiom which must necessarily lie at the base of all utilitarian, as well as of all metaphysical, systems. He is protesting against the right of a minority to govern Ireland or India exclusively for its own interest; and to assert the rights of man in this sense is simply to lay down the principle acknowledged by all theorists, and equally evident on all methods of reasoning; that the happiness of the governed, and not the happiness of any particular class, is the legitimate end of government. As soon as the abstract theorist proceeds a step further, and would use his doctrine of 'equity,' or of 'natural rights,' to override the teaching of experience, he parts company with Burke.

100. His theory is admirably given in the 'Appeal from the New to the Old Whigs.' The order in which we find ourselves is not, as the pseudo-Bolingbroke argues, a matter of arbitrary convention, nor is it to be condemned because it does not exhibit the mathematical symmetry of the *a priori* theorists. We may assume, he says, 'that the awful author of our being is the author of our place in the order of existence; and that, having disposed and marshalled us by a divine tactic, not according to our will, but according to his, he has, in and by that disposition, virtually subjected us to act the part which belongs to the place assigned to us. We have obligations to mankind at large which are not in consequence of any special voluntary pact. They arise from the relations of man to man, and the relations of man to God, which relations are not matters of pact. On the contrary, the force of all the pacts which we enter into with any particular person, or number of persons, amongst mankind, depends upon these prior obligations,'[26] and he proceeds to argue that the relations arising from marriage, from the filial relation, and from our membership of a given nation, have an inherent sanctity which we cannot abolish.

101. To appeal, then, to the natural right to equality of mankind, as declaring that the existing order should be made conducive to the interests of all, is a legitimate inference from the divine origin of society. To appeal to it in the sense of proposing to level existing distinctions, and disintegrate the divine order, is a palpable and most mischievous fallacy. If we ask how from these general principles we are to descend to those intermediate propositions which may guide us in particular cases, how we are to justify any given order of things from the sanctity of the social order in general, and to distinguish between the divine

[26]Burke, vi. 206, 'Appeal.'

law and the human corruption, Burke would admit or assert that we must appeal to experience. He would further assert that as yet there is no science of politics, and that the doctrines hitherto discoverable are fitted only for the amusement of speculative men.[27] Are we not, then, thrown back upon that chaotic 'jumble' of merely empirical speculation which is the necessary result of an absence of speculative principle? If metaphysics are a Serbonian bog, if observation presents us with facts too complex to be reducible to definite laws, if theology can only tell us that some order is sacred but cannot tell us what order is sacred, whither are we to turn for guidance? To say the plain truth, no definite logical answer was accessible in the time of Burke, or is even now accessible. Every political system must be more or less of the empirical kind, and we must trust in great measure to guesswork, instead of steering our course by compass and calculation. And yet some principles emerge; and there is an immense value in the conception of the political order as presented by Burke, even when it has as yet led to no definitely formulated conclusions. He indicates the true method, if he does not bring out final results.

102. One doctrine is specially characteristic. In one of his best pamphets, the 'Thoughts on the Cause of the Present Discontents,' Burke notices the alarming symptom that 'rank and office, and all the solemn plausibilities of the world, have lost their reverence and effect.'[28] How was the prestige thus shaken to be restored? The sacred phrase which he habitually opposes to the rights of man is Prescription. 'Prescription,' he says, in a speech on Parliamentary reform in 1782, 'is the most solid of all titles, not only to property, but what is to secure that property, to government.'[29] Prescription, he continues, is 'accompanied with another ground of authority in the constitution of the human mind, Presumption.'[29] There is a presumption, that is, in favour of an established order; the nation is not a mere artificial aggregate of units; it has a corporate existence in time and space. The constitution is formed by the co-operation of ages and generations; and, far from being the product of conscious choice, is slowly elaborated by the play of innumerable social forces. 'It is a vestment which accommodates itself to the body.'[30] The individual is foolish; the multitude blunders at every given moment; but 'the species is wise, and, when time is given to it, as a species it almost always acts right.'[30] Thus, in a philosophical sense, Burke believes in the wisdom—the unconscious wisdom—of our ancestors. In

---

[27]Burke, viii, 'Regicide Peace.'   [29]Ib. x. 96.
[28]Ib. ii. 220, 'Present Discontents.'   [30]Ib. x. 97.

the 'Reflections' he quotes, with approval, the phrase of a great French lawyer, that the doctrine of prescription is 'part of the law of nature.'[31] Elsewhere he says that property must be founded 'on the solid rock of prescription; the soundest, the most general, and the most recognised, title between man and man that is known in municipal or in public jurisprudence; a title in which, not arbitrary institutions, but the eternal order of things, gives judgment; a title which is not the creature, but the master, of positive law; a title which, though not fixed in its term, is rooted in its principle in the law of nature itself, and is indeed the original ground of all known property.'[32] Religion itself rests upon prescription. All the chief religions of Europe, he tells us, 'stand upon one common bottom. The support that the whole or the favoured parts may have in the secret dispensations of Providence it is impossible to tell; but, humanly speaking, they are all prescriptive religions.'[33] He infers that Catholicism should not be discountenanced in Ireland; for, like all other forms of Christianity, it rests upon prescription, and the alternative is not Protestantism, but the infidelity which, in attacking prescription, attacks the vital principle of all the creeds.

103. This doctrine of prescription is susceptible of, and received in the hands of Burke, two every different interpretations. Stated crudely, it resembles but too closely the doctrine of all obstructive politicians. It is a version of the saying, 'Whatever is, is right;' the consecration of the absolute immobility, and the antithesis of a belief in progress. Burke too often inclines to this version of his theory. The doctrine that religion rests upon prescription may simply mean that, as a matter of fact, the overwhelming majority of mankind takes its creed upon trust; but Burke seems to infer that, because men believe without reasoning, their creeds should not be tested by reason. His firm conviction that the stability of the social fabric depended on the vitality of the national religion made him look askance upon the freethinkers. We Englishmen, he says, 'know, and, what is better, we feel inwardly, that religion is the basis of civil society, and the source of all good and of all comfort.'[34] The statement justifies an eloquent defence of the Established Church; and he seems almost to think that the truth of the doctrines preached by so useful a body should never be questioned. Exulting over the fall of the deists, he pronounces it to be the disgrace, not the glory, of the age, that 'everything is to be discussed.'[35] We should beware how we scrutinised too closely claims sanctioned by so long a prescription. Tolerant

[31]Burke, v. 276, 'Reflections.'
[32]Ib. ix. 449, 'To R. Burke.'   [34]Ib. v. 173, 'Reflections.'
[33]Ib. ix. 403, 'To W. Smith.'   [35]Ib. v. 175, ib.

as Burke was in spirit, he draws very distinct limits even to the principle of toleration; he would invoke the majesty of the laws to 'cut up
the very root of atheism;'[36] and though all dissenting churches should
be fully tolerated, he would not relax the subscriptions to meet their
wishes. 'Truth,' he said, in speaking on the petition of the Feathers
Tavern, 'may be far better' than peace; 'but as we have scarcely ever
that same certainty in the one that we have in the other, I would, unless
the truth were evident indeed, hold fast to peace, which has in her
company charity, the highest of the virtues.'[37] Peace will be disturbed
if you once set fanaticism free by needlessly reopening settled questions.
In such case Burke's reverence for prescription leads him into doubtful
alliance with the bigots and the cynics. He would strengthen faith by
stifling the free play of opinion; and forgets that a religion supported
by a dread of awkward discussions must crumble when assailed by
active opponents.

104. Even with this, the weaker side of Burke's teaching, there is
blended much wisdom and eloquence, which distinguishes him from
the allies who could boast of so able an advocate. But the doctrine of
prescription admits of another and a far nobler meaning. Burke had
fully grasped the conception of a nation as a living organism of complex
structure and historical continuity. It is precisely the absence of any
such conception which vitiates all the contemporary political speculation.
He had emancipated himself from the purely mechanical and the purely
mathematical conceptions of politics. The methods of the constitution-
mongers and of the abstract theorists were equally beneath his notice;
and the word 'prescription'—not free from an unfortunate ambiguity—
evidences his recognition of that element which they equally neglected.
Prescription, taken absolutely, may of course sanction anything—the
English tyranny in America as well as English liberty at home. But, in
appealing to 'prescription,' Burke is recognising the fact that ninety-nine
hundredths of men's thoughts and instincts are those which they have
inherited from their fathers, and of the corresponding doctrine, that
reform is impracticable in the sense of an abrupt reconstruction of
society, and can only be understood as the gradual modification of a
complex structure. Prescription in this sense is based on the presumption that every existing social arrangement has been developed by certain
needs, and is the mode in which certain forces operate; and that, therefore, to cut it away abruptly is possibly to inflict a vital injury, and

[36]Burke, x. 37, 'Protestant Dissenters.'
[37]Ib. x. 37, ib.

at any rate implies rash and unscientific surgery. A sound political constitution must be the growth of generations; it must be worked into
the whole fabric of society; it must give play for the harmonious action
of all the private relations by which men are bound together; and if it
requires the utmost watchfulness to prevent parts from becoming obsolete, it is the height of rashness to hack and hew such a system in
obedience to some preconceived theory. Prescription, then, is but a legal
phrase for that continuity of past and present, and that solidarity between all parts of the political order, the perception of which is the
essential condition of sound political reasoning. A combination of respect for existing facts, and of a regard to new requirements, underlies
Burke's practical teaching, as a balanced regard for general principles
and for special applications governs his philosophy. 'When the reason
of old establishments is gone,' he says, 'it is absurd to preserve nothing
but the burden of them. This is superstitiously to embalm a carcase not
worth an ounce of the grains that are used to preserve it.'[38] He adds in
the same speech, 'If I cannot reform with equity, I will not reform at
all.'[39] Those two views are combined in the 'Reflections.' 'All the
reformations we have hitherto made,' he says, 'have proceeded upon the
principle of reference to antiquity.'[40] We have received our liberties as
an 'entailed inheritance,'[41] to be transmitted unimpaired to our descendants; and thus 'a disposition to preserve and an ability to improve taken
together would be' his 'standard of a statesman.'[42]

105. In order to do justice, however, to the force of Burke's perceptions, and to measure the doctrine which separated him from his contemporaries, we must descend to some of the applications of these
generalities. It is easy to profess an anxiety to strike the judicious mean
between revolution and obstruction; and now that Burke has been
followed by two generations of able enquirers, it is not difficult to admit
the truth of his general conception of the statesman's problem. But the
true meaning of his doctrines comes out as he deals with the great
questions of the day. Of his writings upon India I shall say nothing;
not because they are inferior in ability or in morality, but because
cruelty and corruption, as such, are defended by nobody; and therefore
the only question at issue was the truth of Burke's allegation, that
Hastings was a corrupt tyrant. His other writings fall chiefly into three
classes; his writings on the theory of the English Constitution, upon the
American War, and upon the French Revolution.

[38]Burke, iii. 278, 'Economical Reform.'
[39]Ib. iii. 299, ib.   [41]Ib. v. 78, ib.
[40]Ib. v. 75, 'Reflections.'   [42]Ib. v. 285, ib.

106. In Burke's first writings he appears to be the great prophet of Whig principles. He set forth the philosophy which was, or which ought to have been, introduced in their policy. He was, indeed, alive to the many defects which made the actual very different from the ideal aristocracy. His earliest writings, indeed, protested against the meanness of the great nobles; and, in one of his latest, the 'Letter to a Noble Lord,' the vice of the system which could make a Duke of Bedford a great power, because he was descended from a corrupt courtier, and yet render invidious the scraps of reward thrown to a simple man of genius, is depicted with unrivalled vigour. But Burke always seems to have considered such blemishes as the separable accidents of the constitution, not as belonging to its essence. To his eyes the constitution was no makeshift scaffolding, destined to speedy decay, but a venerable edifice of superb architecture, resembling 'the proud keep of Windsor, rising in the majesty of proportion, and girt with the double belt of its kindred and coeval towers.'[43] It was built round, indeed, with filthy hovels, and too often converted into a mart for degrading intrigue; but the buyers and the sellers might be driven forth, and its true majesty would then be apparent. His glowing imagination heightened all that was really impressive in the old order, its reverent antiquity, the chivalrous honour of its best leaders, and the liberty of speech and action which had grown up under its shelter. He would willingly have passed with averted eyes by its many defects, had it not been necessary to attack with his whole force some of the short-sighted and selfish men who were using its shelter for their own contemptible purposes.

107. The ideal aristocracy of his imagination was a body whose privileges rested on the sacred right of 'prescription;' not in the sense that its existence justified itself, but that it was the spontaneous result of the free play of social forces through many generations. The rulers of the country would be the men who enjoyed the greatest social influence, and whose high cultivation and delicate sense of honour would enable them to wield it in the highest interests of the nation. It would be responsible to public opinion, not in the sense that its power would be dependent on every breath of popular favour, but as being acutely sensitive to every imputation of unfairness or corruption, and too proud to stifle the criticisms of its inferiors. It would be divided into parties; but their bonds of union would be a community of political principle, not a common desire for place and profit. To this ideal, he thought, the English constitution approximated in its best moments, though it was con-

[43]Burke, viii. 49.

stantly tending to degenerate under various uncongenial influences. 'Our constitution,' he says, in a passage where, for once, he descends towards the Delolme level of thought, 'stands on a nice equipoise, with sharp precipices and deep waters on all sides of it. In removing it from a dangerous leaning towards one side, there may be a danger of over-setting it on the other.'[44] The danger, in fact, was twofold, though the imaginary equipoise suggests an inaccurate analogy. The aristocracy might become a close corporation on a large scale, and either develop into an oligarchy or sell itself to the Crown. On the other side was the danger, less perceptible during the early period of Burke's activity, of a democratic revolution. To this tendency, it is sufficient to say here, Burke was opposed as decidedly, though not as vehemently in early years, as during the French Revolution.

108. He consistently protested against all the popular nostrums. In his earliest pamphlet he declares that 'it would be more in the spirit of our constitution, and more agreeable to the spirit of our best laws, by lessen-ing the number, to add to the weight and independency, of our voters,'[45] than to produce the reverse effect by adding to them. A trien-nial Parliament, he says in his next pamphlet, would increase the cor-ruption of electors, and the dependence of members of Parliament. A place-bill would only substitute occult for overt influence.[46] The consti-tution, he says in a later speech, would not survive five triennial elec-tions 'even to the wrecks of it.'[47] To the end of his life he denied that any sensible grievance had arisen from the want of symmetry in the constitution. 'When did you hear in Great Britain,' he asks in his 'Reflections,' 'of any province suffering from the inequality of its repre-sentation; what district from having no representation at all?'[48] The demand for such reforms was not as yet threatening. The Wilkes agita-tion seemed to indicate that the balance was tottering in the opposite direction. Reforms were demanded, not to save the House of Commons from dependence upon the king, but to preserve its dependence upon the constituents. By declaring Wilkes incapable of re-election, the Com-mons seemed to be asserting a power of self-election. They were usurp-ing, as Burke said, the power of legislation by the simple vote of the House. 'The circumstance of having no appeal from their jurisdiction is made to imply that they have no rule in the exercise of it.'[49] The

[44]Burke, ii. 323, 'Present Discontents.'
[45]Ib. ii. 135, 'State of the Nation.'
[46]Ib. ii. 319 et seq., 'Present Discontents.'
[47]Ib. x. 81, 'Duration of Parliament.'   [48]Ib. v. 336, 'Reflections.'
[49]Ib. ii. 303, 'Present Discontents.'

danger, indeed, that the House of Commons should ever have formed itself into an oligarchy seems to be chimerical enough; and, perhaps, Burke's language exaggerates this particular risk.

109. The true meaning of the struggle, as he clearly saw, was of a different kind. The House of Commons would have no chance of emancipating itself from the control of its constituents, except by falling under the influence of the Crown. George III., though a man of more courage than Charles I., had little chance of founding a despotism; and the Norths and Seckers were but feeble representatives of the Straffords and Lauds. The references to possible Hampdens and Cromwells were equally premature. But it was possible, as to some extent it actually happened, that the Crown should rule by corrupt influence, that the great families should become mere squabblers for place, and that government should be carried on by a system of personal cliques. Parliament might become a close corporation, with all the characteristic vices of such bodies. Against this evil Burke protested emphatically, and his protest is justified, perhaps by rather too complex an exposition, in the 'Thoughts on the Cause of the Present Discontents.' 'I am no friend,' he says, 'to aristocracy, in the sense, at least, in which that word is usually understood'[50]—a sense which is explained by his criticism on the existing body. The danger which he apprehended is not of the 'austere and insolent domination' of a body of independent nobles, but the degrading rule of a body of nobles reduced to 'abject servility.' 'Would to God that it were true,' he exclaims, 'that the fault of our peers were too much spirit!'[51] He dreads a régime of courtiers and favourites; a cabinet of ministers not appointed on national grounds, but 'on the likings and jealousies, the intrigues and policies of a court.'[52] The Court party, representing this demoralising influence, had gained power as the independent gentry had become more indifferent to politics.[53] Favourites with the souls of valets had pushed aside the old high-spirited gentlemen; and the consequent weakening of the old party connections meant, for Burke, the weakening of independent principle.

110. The fervid panegyrics which close the 'Present Discontents' and the 'Letter to the Sheriffs of Bristol' are eloquent expositions of his doctrine. 'In the way which they call party, I worship the constitution of your fathers;'[54] and the party to which he belonged had redeemed the present age by 'grafting public principles on private honour.'[54] Party,

---

[50]Burke, ii. 246, 'Present Discontents.'
[51]Ib. ii. 246, ib.   [53]Ib. ii. 258, ib.
[52]Ib. ii. 260, ib.   [54]Ib. iii. 197, 'Sheriffs of Bristol.'

therefore, was the true antithesis to clique; the proof that a healthy blood was circulating through the veins of the body politic. The quack medicines prescribed by demagogues would be pernicious, for they would stimulate corruption, instead of increasing the sense of responsibility. The true remedy was not to alter the distribution of power, but to take securities that it should be exercised under the pressure of public opinion, and therefore by means which would bear inspection. To Burke's energy was owing in great degree the system which forced Parliament to debate in presence of the nation, instead of settling matters by private conversations; and that alteration in the libel law, afterwards carried out by his disciple Fox, which set free the rising power of the press. But his greatest effort was the plan for economical reform, which was carried in a multilated shape by the coalition administration. The speech in which he introduced the measure is a most admirable specimen of lucid exposition. Its purpose is defined in the opening sentences. 'What, I confess, was uppermost with me; what I bent the whole force of my mind to, was the reduction of that corrupt influence, which is itself the perennial spring of all prodigality and of all disorder; which loads us more than millions of debt; which takes away vigour from our arms, wisdom from our councils, and every shadow of authority and credit from the most venerable parts of our constitution.'[55] The power of corruption enjoyed under the old system lay at the root of all our political evils. Why was it, he asks, that a previous scheme of economy failed, and that the public debt accumulated? 'It was because the king's turnspit was a member of Parliament. The king's domestic servants were all undone; his tradesmen remained unpaid and became bankrupt —because the turnspit of the king's kitchen was a member of Parliament. His Majesty's slumbers were interrupted; his pillow was stuffed with thorns, and his peace of mind utterly broken—because the king's turnspit was a member of Parliament. The judges were unpaid; the justice of the kingdom bent and gave way; the foreign ministers remained inactive and unprovided; the system of Europe was dissolved; the chain of our alliance was broken; the wheels of government at home and abroad were stopped—because the king's turnspit was a member of Parliament.'[56]

111. Such declamations in the mouths of democratic writers were intended to justify the inference that so rotten a system should be summarily destroyed. Burke would not have touched one recognised branch of the royal prerogative or have removed one privilege of the peerage.

[55]Burke, iii. 232, 'Economical Reform.'   [56]Ib. iii. 284, ib.

He would renovate and strengthen the old system. He would enable
its practice to conform to its theory; and, by enforcing publicity and
sweeping away the malpractices of backstairs intrigue, would stimulate
the leaders of the people to adopt an attitude worthy of their exalted
position. He would cherish most tenderly every institution which tended
to preserve the historical dignity of the constitution, whilst removing
the morbid growths which had accumulated in darkness and stagnation. A different spirit, however, was beginning to stir the political
surface; and the method by which Burke encountered it can best be
expounded by his attitude towards the American and the French Revolutions. The influence of the American War of Independence upon
European politics is an interesting subject, to which, perhaps, full justice has hardly been done. The early leaders of the French movement
were undoubtedly stimulated by the American precedent. The names of
Lafayette and Beaumarchais, of Franklin and Paine, of Priestley and
Price, suggest different links of connection between the American outbreak and the advance of democracy in Europe. The philosophers for
once saw what appeared to be a realisation of their dreams. A great
nation was casting aside the relics of feudalism and monarchy, and
founding a new constitution upon first principles. The social contract
theory seemed to be translating itself into history. And yet the immediate causes of the struggle were in the old-fashioned English creed,
rather than in any new development of doctrine. If men like Franklin
and Jefferson sympathised with the French philosophy, Washington
seemed to be an American reproduction of Hampden, and Hamilton
and the Federalists were believers in Montesquieu, and ardent admirers
of the British Constitution. The social order in America was democratic
enough to satisfy the abstract theorists; but it had developed itself peace-
fully and imperceptibly; and the descendants of the Puritans could
appeal to the immemorial privileges of British subjects. Thus two distinct forces were blended in the general result; and the views taken by
the supporters of the Americans were characteristically different.

112. On the immediate questions at issue, indeed, there could be little
room for dispute amongst men not blinded by the bigotry of patriotism.
The essence of the dispute was simply that the English Government had
managed the colonies in the 'shopkeeping' spirit, and yet were not shopkeepers enough to adopt Tucker's recommendation to treat their customers civilly. The colonies were regarded as factories, whose trade was
retained for English merchants by the elaborate system of navigation
laws. No one thought of protesting against the system; and even the
Americans acquiesced, until English statesmen proposed to tax them

directly as well as to monopolise their trade. That they were justified in protesting was obvious even then to men who could think, 'With the two exceptions of Johnson and Gibbon,' says Wraxall, 'all the eminent and shining talents of the country led on by Burke were marshalled in support of the colonies.'[57] The expensive and wicked blunder of the war was, of course, popular, like other such blunders, with the mass of the country. In 1777 Burke, writing to Lord Rockingham, reckons amongst the opponents of their views, 'the weight of King, Lords, and Commons,' nearly all the loungers, the chief part of the commercial and landed interests, and the whole Church 'in a manner,' besides the army and navy.[58] The mass was decided by passion and by narrow prejudice; and the misfortune of the English people was its incapacity to take a view of affairs commensurate with its position. 'I think,' said Burke in 1788, 'I can trace all the calamities of this country to the single source of not having had steadily before our eyes a general, comprehensive, and well-proportioned view of the whole of our dominions, and a just sense of their true bearings and relations.'[59] Here, as in domestic politics, the governing classes from whom Burke expected so much were miserably contracted in their views. When the rulers of a vast empire treated whole continents in the spirit of petty traders, it was no wonder if they had to write off enormous losses in their ledgers. In this case the attempt to inspire a new spirit by removing abuses was too late. Blunders all but irretrievable had already been committed; and the only hope was to persuade the legislature to retract whilst there was yet time. The abolition of the offensive taxes was of course necessary; but on what principles were the future relations of the empire to be adjusted? This was the problem with which Burke attempted to deal, and his solution brought him into conflict with the other wing of the conciliatory party.

113. His first effort was to clear the whole discussion from the confusion imported into it by the theory of abstract rights. The endless wranglings upon these insoluble metaphysical questions entangled and embittered every part of the argument. Johnson and a host of other writers asserted the indefeasible right of England to govern America. Lyttelton, in the House of Lords, quoted the social compact to prove that the Americans had tacitly consented to the absolute rule of Parliament;[60] Pownall inferred from the theory of 'essential and indefeasible

[57]Wraxall's 'Historical Memoirs,' ii. 79.   [58]Burke, ix. 167.
[59]Ib. iv. 201, 'Nabob of Arcot's Debts.'
[60]Phillimore's 'Life of Lyttelton,' p. 693.

rights' that the Americans ought to have representatives in the English Parliament; Chatham, the most weighty, but the most wayward, defender of the colonies, declared that the colonists had an absolute right to arrange their own internal taxation; but that the mother-country had an absolute right to levy taxes for the regulation of commerce. And, meanwhile, Americans were rapidly learning that they had an absolute and indefeasible right to independence. Burke alone desired to sweep aside the whole controversy as so much frivolous logomachy. If only he could persuade men to see that the question was simply a question of expediency, it would answer itself. Men might wrangle till doomsday over the question of abstract right; nobody but a fool would support a policy of simple oppression, stripped bare of the delusive figment of abstract right.

114. On this ground Burke supported the Declaratory Act, passed by the Rockingham Ministry concurrently with the repeal of the Stamp Act. In a history of events, especially if it included the history of what might have been, it might be worth enquiring whether Chatham's policy would not have been better than that which Burke supported. Possibly the recognition of some right in the matter would have satisfied the popular instincts, when Burke's almost nervous desire to transfer the question from the ground of right to the ground of expediency exposed him to some misinterpretation. Indeed, the assertion of the absolute supremacy of the Imperial Government, coupled with an abandonment of the measures passed in virtue of its supremacy, resembled, at first sight, one of those abstract rights which Burke so intensely hated. But Burke's own view—whether suited or not to the time—was perfectly clear and coherent. Chatham's plan of distinguishing between the legitimate and the illegitimate action of the supreme legislature, of 'parcelling out its powers' by argumentative distinctions,[61] would have raised a host of delicate and indeterminable questions. The Declaratory Act merely expressed the first principle of jurisprudence, the omnipotence of the sovereign. Parliament is omnipotent in England, and yet England is a free country. Parliament might, if it pleased, restore the High Commission Court or the Star Chamber,[61] and once more alter the established religion, without any breach of the constitution. Our security is not that such actions would be illegal, but that they would be mad. The ultimate guarantee in all cases is the common sense of the country; and it is useless to trammel ourselves beforehand by definitions which tie our hands in unforeseen contingencies. Legislative omnip-

[61]Burke, iii. 178, 'Sheriffs of Bristol.'

otence might be necessary for imperial as well as for national purposes; it might be required to coerce negligent or violent members of the empire into measures adopted for the common defence;[62] the power should not be abolished, but should be kept in reserve; 'its repose may be the preservation of its existence, and its existence may be the means of saving the constitution itself on an occasion worthy of bringing it forth.'[63] Thus, to declare the unity of the sovereign power was necessary to the unity of the empire, and was as different as possible from proposing to use those rights for tyrannical purposes. 'I look,' he says, 'on the imperial rights of Great Britain, and the privileges which the colonists ought to enjoy under those rights, to be just the most reconcilable things in the world.'[64] Thus, in Burke's mind, the Declaratory Act was intended to remove the question of abstract right altogether out of the arena of discussion, and to leave all the matters at issue to be settled by expediency.

115. This once granted, the wise mode of treatment was palpable. Without entering into the wretched quibbles about virtual representation and all the hopeless confusion produced by the importation of legal fictions and metaphysical refinements into a plain matter of policy, it was abundantly clear that 'a great people who have their property, without any reserve, disposed of by another people at an immense distance from them, will not think themselves in the enjoyment of liberty.'[65] That was the only question worthy of a statesman's notice. 'If any ask me what a free government is, I answer that, for practical purposes, it is what the people think it, and that they and not I are the natural, lawful, and competent judges in this matter.'[66] The definition excited Johnson's contempt. 'I will let the King of France govern me on those conditions,' he said, 'for it is to be governed just as I please.'[67] The only alternative, according to him and others, lies between other men doing just what I please and doing just what they please. The difference between an arbitrary and a responsible authority, between an authority which imposed its own views upon its subjects and one which held itself rigidly to the test afforded by their contentment, was one which could not be driven into the heads of the English people. So long at least as they were themselves the governors, they could not comprehend Burke's maxim, 'to follow, not to force the public inclination; to give a direction, a form, a technical dress, and a specific sanction to the gen-

---

[62]Burke, iii. 179, 'Sheriffs of Bristol.'   [65]Ib. ii. 170, 'State of the Nation.'
[63]Ib. ii. 436, 'American Taxation.'   [66]Ib. iii. 183, 'Sheriffs of Bristol.'
[64]Ib. iii. 181, 'Sheriffs of Bristol.'   [67]Boswell, Sept. 22, 1777.

eral sense of the community, is the true end of legislature.'[68] In vain he explained to them, with admirable force, the true character of their subjects. The origin of the people, their form of government, their religion, their attitude in presence of a slave population, their love of law, their distance from the central authority, were, he said, so many causes of their 'fierce spirit of liberty'[69]—and 'so many reasons for breaking their spirit,' was the answer of men who could see no difference between claiming supreme power and using it for their own purposes. The incapacity of the sovereign people for appreciating Burke's reasoning should perhaps have been an argument for binding them by Chatham's proposed restriction, however unsatisfactory in theory, instead of inviting them to assume supreme authority and to exercise it wisely. At any rate, Burke's most vivid descriptions of the growing wealth of America, his appeals to colonial loyalty, to English precedents, to the advantages of magnanimity, to the folly of substituting arguments of 'geometrical accuracy'[70] for reliance upon affection stimulated by common interest, were all thrown away as idle 'refining.' England stuck to its rights and the decision was made by the sword.

116. In this case, the abstract rights, against which Burke argued so consistently, were invoked on behalf of the central authority; and Burke had to argue not for the sanctity of authority, but for the necessity of limiting its claims by expediency. A very different application of the metaphysical doctrines was to come before him. He had laid down one great principle in the American controversy. 'When popular discontents have been very prevalent,' he says, 'it may well be affirmed and supported that there has been found something amiss in the constitution or in the conduct of government. The people have no interest in disorder. When they do wrong, it is their error and not their crime. But with the governing part of the state it is far otherwise. They certainly may act ill by design as well as by mistake.'[71] And, in confirmation of this theory, he quotes an admirable passage from Sully's memoirs, in which the great minister says that revolutions are never an effect of chance or of popular caprice. 'Pour la populace ce n'est jamais par envie d'attaquer qu'elle se soulève, mais par impatience de souffrir.' During the American troubles, Burke adhered steadily to this view. The French Revolution exposed the theory to a more trying test. Burke had proclaimed the responsibility of rulers to their subjects, and declared that discontent was a sufficient proof of misgovernment. The French people

---

[68]Burke, iii. 180, 'Sheriffs of Bristol.'   [70]Ib. iii. 112, ib.
[69]Ib. iii. 57, 'Conciliation.'   [71]Ib. ii. 224, 'Present Discontents.'

were about to enforce responsibility by the guillotine, and to justify
their actions as a revolt against intolerable oppression. Would Burke
apply the same test in this case? Would he admit that the force of the
explosion testified to the severity of the previous compression? A people, he had said, was free when it thought itself free. Would that view
justify the French, who showed most unmistakably that they considered
themselves to be slaves? Should Burke, therefore, approve of this as of
the former revolt, and agree with his political friends that a new era
of liberty and happiness was dawning upon the world? The writings
on the eloquence and wisdom of which his reputation chiefly rests gave
an answer to these questions which scandalised many of his former
friends, and have exposed him to the imputations of inconsistency, if
not of political apostasy. And yet they are but expansions of the doctrines which he had previously expounded.

117. The outbreak of the French Revolution affected Burke's imagination with extraordinary force. He saw in it something strange, abnormal,
and tremendous. 'Out of the tomb of the murdered monarchy in
France,' he exclaims in one of the letters on a 'Regicide Peace,' 'has
arisen a vast, tremendous, unformed spectre in a far more terrific guise
than any which ever yet have overpowered the imagination and subdued the fortitude of man. Going straightforward to its end, unap-
palled by peril, unchecked by remorse, despising all common maxims
and all common means; that hideous phantom overpowered those who
could not believe it was possible she should at all exist, except on the
principles which habit, rather than nature, had persuaded them were
necessary to their own particular welfare, and to their own ordinary
means of action.'[72] Burke looked upon the Revolution with that kind
of shudder with which man acknowledges the presence of a being believed to be supernatural. All ordinary rules seemed to be suspended.
The earth trembled, and the strongest barriers gave way. No wonder if,
in presence of the spectre, Burke's whole nature, already worn by many
failures, disappointments, and vexations, reeled under the excitement.
Nowhere, indeed, is his intellectual power more marked than in the
outpourings of his anti-revolutionary wrath. But the eloquence passes
into virulence. The 'Reflections' published in 1790 are still philosophical
in tone, though shot with gorgeous rhetoric; but, as the horror increases,
his passion rises, till, in the letters on a 'Regicide Peace' (1796), he
seems almost to be foaming at the mouth, and to be speaking with the
fury of inspiration rather than with the energy of earthly apprehension.

[72]Burke, viii. 83.

118. In January 1791 he already regards the leaders as mere quacks and impostors,[73] and the people as madmen, who, 'like other madmen,' must be subdued in order to be cured.[74] The Revolution, a few months later, is declared to be 'a foul, monstrous thing, wholly out of the course of moral nature;' it was 'generated in treachery, frauds, and falsehood, hypocrisy, and unprovoked murder.'[75] As he goes on he strains his whole power of invective to gratify the vehemence of his hatred. Jacobinism is incarnate evil; it is atheism by establishment; it makes a 'profane apotheosis of monsters whose vices and crimes have no parallel amongst men.'[76] Jacobins are animated by 'determined hostility to the human race.'[77] They have deliberately established a system of manners 'the most licentious, prostitute, and abandoned that ever have been known, and at the same time the most coarse, rude, savage, and ferocious.'[78] And, after a passage in which he labours to prove that every moral principle is intentionally violated by these monsters, the virtue of the nation designedly corrupted, family affections perverted, and marriage made more degrading than any connection which would be tolerated at a London brothel,[79] he finds the only fitting climax to his furious invective by charging them with cannibalism. He recurs more than once to this epithet. The society thus formed resembles that of a 'den of outlaws upon a doubtful frontier; of a lewd tavern for the revels and debauches of banditti, assassins, bravoes, smugglers, and their more desperate paramours, mixed with bombastic players, the refuse and rejected offal of strolling theatres, puffing out ill-sorted verses about virtue, mixed with the licentious and blasphemous songs proper to the brutal and hardened course of life belonging to that sort of wretches.'[80] The fall of Robespierre only added one brutal and treacherous murder the more. He would rather think less hardly of the dead ruffian than associate with the living. 'I could rather bear the stench of the gibbeted murderer than the society of the bloody felons who yet annoy the world.'[81] One seems to see the face of the orator convulsed; he pants, struggles, and gasps for utterance, and in the whirlwind of his passion tears all propriety and common sense to rags. If words could blast, the French revolutionists would have been scorched and shrivelled by his fury.

[73]Burke, vi. 10, 'To a Member of the National Assembly.'
[74]Ib. vi. 19, ib.   [78]Ib.
[75]Ib. vi. 85, 'Appeal.'   [79]Ib. viii. 175, ib.
[76]Ib. viii. 171, 'Regicide Peace.' [80]Ib. viii. 180, ib.
[77]Ib. viii. 172, ib.   [81]Ib. ix. 67, ib.

119. Why did the wisest politician of the day thus throw the reins on the neck of his eloquence? Something must be set down to the excitement of the struggle; something to the pain inflicted by the sharp severance of all ties; much, in the later writings, to the consequences of the cruel domestic loss which shadowed his declining years with so deep a gloom. The actual atrocities of the Revolution increased his horror, but from the very first he saw the glare of hell in the light which others took to herald the dawn of the millennium. Nor, indeed, can it be doubted that Burke's antipathy to the Revolution was based upon a profound and reasoned conviction of the utter falsity of its leading principles. Good steady-going Whigs might fancy that the French were merely a set of interesting converts to the doctrines of the Petition of Right and the Revolution of 1688. Men like Priestley and Price fancied that reason was revealing itself to mankind, and dispersing the antiquated prejudices of centuries. Burke's insight was deep and truer. He saw with the revolutionists that the phenomenon did not signify a mere adjustment of an old political balance, and the adoption of a few constitutional nostrums. A new doctrine was spreading from the schools into the mass of the people, and threatening the very foundations of the old social order. Moreover, he saw through the flimsy nature of the logic which it was supposed to embody; and recognised the emptiness of the predictions of an instant advent of peace, justice, and goodwill. He had weighed Rousseau's metaphysics and found them grievously wanting; and what to others appeared to be a startling revelation of new truths was to him a fitful rehabilitation of outworn fallacies. There was, indeed, something which he did not see; but to appreciate his error we must first do justice to the width of his view.

120. The influence of a revolution which aims at the upsetting a government may be confined to the place of its birth. A revolution which aims at propagating a new order of ideas has an interest for the whole world. In the 'Appeal from the New to the Old Whigs,' Burke expresses his dread of 'a fashion proceeding upon speculative grounds.'[82] 'A theory concerning government,' as was now plain, might 'become a cause of fanaticism as much as a dogma in religion.'[82] And in such cases, calm cannot be regained by the removal of grievances; for monarchy, not a monarch, is assailed. Rather, indeed, the principles were assailed upon which the whole social order rested. Burke would say, when war had begun, 'it is a religious war'[83]—not a war between dif-

---

[82]Burke, vi. 239, and see vii. 13 ('French Affairs'), where the Revolution is compared to the Reformation.　　[83]Ib. vii. 174, 'Policy of the Allies.'

ferent religious sects, but a war between all the religious sects and the enemies of all sects. He deliberately accepted the consequences and preached a crusade. We were at war with 'an armed doctrine;'[84] and such a war, as he rightly inferred, must be a long one.[85] Indeed it is going on still, for Burke erred in supposing that it could be finally decided by the bayonet and the cannon. Assuming, however, that ideas could be put down by the strong hand of Force, Burke's zeal was but the natural consequence of his creed. The new doctrines, as he understood them, were nothing less than the direct antithesis of all which he regarded as fundamental and sacred axioms. A passage which he quotes in the 'Reflections' from Rabaud de St. Etienne gives the essence of the revolutionary creed: 'Tous les établissements en France couronnent le malheur du peuple; pour les rendre heureux, il faut les renouveler, changer les idées; changer les loix; changer les mœurs; . . . changer les hommes; changer les choses; changer les mots . . . tout détruire; oui, tout détruire, puisque tout est à récréer.' To Burke, with whom prescription was the last word of politics; whose ideal statesman was the man who best combined the old with the new; who would guide every step by precedent, even in the destruction of abuses;[86] who would not reform at all unless he could reform with equity; such a proposal seemed as monstrous as a plan for reforming the Church by abolishing a belief in God. Feebler elements, indeed, blend with his general argument. He verges, at times, upon mere sentimentalism. The celebrated 'purple patch' about Marie Antoinette, and the often-quoted phrase, 'the age of chivalry is gone,'[87] excited the spleen of his cynical friend Francis. 'In my opinion,' says the author of 'Junius,' with characteristic bluntness, 'all that you say of the queen is pure foppery.'[88] To which Burke replied, that the loss of the chivalrous spirit was a serious matter of lamentation; and that he did, in fact, weep whilst composing the passage impugned.[89] Yet the argument savours too much of the mere rhetorician; and his more serious reasonings, founded on the reforms of the preceding years, and on his personal observations in a brief tour in France,[90] are scarcely a sufficient basis for the assertion, doubtless sound enough in itself, that the Revolution was not provoked by intolerable suffering alone.

121. But, whatever the value of these appeals to fact or to sentiment,

---

[84]Burke, viii. 98, 'Regicide Peace.'   [85]Ib. viii. 150, ib.
[86]See, for example, the proposals in the speech on Conciliation with America.   [87]Burke, v. 149, 'Reflections.'   [88]Burke's 'Correspondence,' iii. 130.
[89]Ib. iii. 139.   [90]Works, v. 251, 'Reflections.'

the soundness of his main position is undeniable. The question was not as to the personal merits of a certain set of rulers, nor as to the actual amount of wrongs endured and avenged, but as to the merits of a new order of ideas. The equality of mankind was the fundamental dogma of the revolutionary creed. That dogma was equivalent to justifying the absolute disorganisation of the old society. It condemned all subordination, whether to rightful superiors or to arbitrary despots. It involved the levelling of all the old institutions, however important the part which they played in the social machinery. It explicitly swept aside as irrelevant and immoral all arguments from experience and expediency. It regarded prescription, not as the sacred foundation of all social rights, but as a mischievous superstition. It attacked the historical continuity of the race, and proposed first to make a *tabula rasa* of all existing organisation, and then to construct society anew on purely *a priori* grounds. Pure arithmetic was to take the place of observation, and the constitution to be framed without the least reference to the complex internal structure of the nation. The most valuable part of Burke's writings are the passages, full both of wisdom and eloquence, in which he exposes the fallacy of this fanatical creed. The very simplicity of the new schemes condemned them sufficiently, for it proved them to have been constructed without reference to the primary data of the problem. 'The nature of man,' he says, 'is intricate; the objects of society are of the greatest possible complexity; and therefore no simple disposition or direction of power can be suitable either to man's nature or to the quality of his affairs.'[91] To neglect to take into account the forces by which men are bound together in the constituent elements of society is a fatal error. 'To be attached to the subdivisions, to love the little platoon we belong to in society, is the first principle (the germ as it were) of public affections.'[92] As the revolutionists would merge these 'platoons' into an inorganic mass, they would cut off the ties by which generations are bound together, by assuming that each human being was born without specific privileges and duties. They were pushing to extremes the doctrine of individuality; and he prophesies that 'the Commonwealth itself would in a few generations crumble away, be disconnected into the dust and powder of individuality, and at length be dispersed to all the winds of heaven.'[93] In fact, the revolutionary creed asserted by necessary implication the rupture of all the bonds which unite men to each other in families, or in political or ecclesiastical bodies, or which connect one generation to others. The power framed

[91]Burke, v. 125, 'Reflections.'   [92]Ib. v. 100, ib.   [93]Ib. v. 183, ib.

by crushing the whole internal organisation must be tyrannical and shameless. The people collectively being omnipotent, and the people, as units, amenable to the small share of responsibility which falls to the lot of each, 'their approbation of their own acts has to them the appearance of a public judgment in their favour; a perfect democracy is therefore the most shameless thing in the world.'[94] Its tyranny would be the most cruel, the most searching, and alleviated by the fewest consolations.[95] In fact, the revolutionary ideas embodied the formal contradictory to that truth, the full appreciation of which was Burke's greatest title to speculative eminence, and which guided his wisest reflections. To him a nation was a living organism, of infinitely complex structure, of intimate dependence upon the parts, and to be treated by politicians in obedience to a careful observation of the laws of its healthy development. To them a nation was an aggregate of independent units, to be regulated by a set of absolute *a priori* maxims. In Burke's own language, the 'people' is an 'artificial idea.'[96] It is, he means to say, a complex body whose will is to be determined from its recognised organs, and not a mere mass of individuals, whose will is to be discovered by counting heads.

122. To the charge of inconsistency, therefore, Burke had, up to a certain point, a triumphant and conclusive answer, which is given in the 'Appeal to the Old Whigs.' The revolutionary ideas were radically opposed in every detail to the principles which he had spent a life in proclaiming. His defence of the colonies, even his attacks upon the royal prerogative, were obsolutely free from any revolutionary tendency. His efforts had been directed to maintaining the 'equipoise' of the constitution. It is only on the theory that a man who approves of one is bound to approve of all revolts, or that a man who opposes the corrupt influence of any power must be opposed to its existence, that the charge could be made at all plausible. Burke's horror of the Revolution indeed gives to his later utterances upon the British Constitution an exaggerated tone. When, in his 'Appeal from the Old to the New Whigs,' he invokes the authority of the managers of the Sacheverel trial, one feels a little scandalised by his excessive reverence for those rather questionable fathers of the true political church. His faith becomes superstitious, and his catchword prescription covers something like a defence of absolute stagnation. His favourite revolution of 1688 is justified as a strictly defensive revolution, in which the people and not the king represented adherence to the established order; and Burke

[94] Burke, v. 179, 'Reflections.'   [95] Ib. v. 231, ib.   [96] Ib. vi. 211, 'Appeal.'

ignores the fact that it really involved a transfer of power. But though, under the stress of terror and the influence of old age, Burke's conservatism became stronger as well as more emphatically expressed, the change did not seriously affect the substance of his creed. His whole conception of political science is radically unaltered, and his method shows the same characteristic peculiarities. His position in the narrow limits of political party may have changed, but as a thinker he insists upon the same principles, applies the same tests, and holds to the same essential truths.

123. And yet there is a sense in which Burke may fairly be called inconsistent. Popular instinct sometimes outruns philosophical insight. Burke's theory condemned the French, whilst it justified the American, movement; but the two movements had really a connection not contemplated in his philosophy. The man who is in intention only setting a precedent for maintaining an ancient right of way may be, in fact, encouraging his followers to break down established fences. Burke helped—much against his will—to stimulate the current of feeling which drew fresh strength from the American war, and brought about the crash of the French system. He was the less conscious of this because he was blind to the positive side of the revolutionary creed. A characteristic indication is his incapacity to answer the obvious question, What is the genealogy of this monstrous spectre? Repudiating the hypothesis that it was begotten by the spirit of resentment for intolerable grievances, it seemed strange that a false and degrading doctrine should suddenly attract proselytes enough to upset the strongest thrones. Some sort of answer is given in the 'Letters on a Regicide Peace.' To so unexampled an event, as he truly answers, the concurrence of a very great number of causes was necessary;[97] and he attributes the chief influence to the philosophical atheists and the politicians. The great object of these last, he thinks, was the external aggrandisement of France. They held that a military republic would answer this purpose better than a monarchy, partly, it seems, because they had quarrelled with the Court, and partly because Montesquieu and Machiavelli had infected them with an admiration for Rome.[98] The American alliance, though rather the effect than the cause of their republican principles, helped on the work till the palace of Versailles seemed to be a forum of democracy.[99]

124. This, in fact, comes to the theory, popular with minds of inferior calibre to Burke, that any event for which they cannot account is due to a dark conspiracy. The whole movement, he declares, 'has been the

[97]Burke, viii. 240, 'Regicide Peace.'   [98]Ib. viii. 244, ib.   [99]Ib. viii. 250, ib.

result of design; all has been matter of institution.'[100] It has been a
diabolical plot of the few and a madness of the many. The good professions are a mere impudent throwing of dust in the eyes of the world;
and the commiseration for the lot of the 'labouring poor' which has
become popular in England is a 'puling jargon,' 'not so innocent as it is
foolish.'[101] To a system which is thus uncaused it is, of course, impossible to assign a limit. What has come into being without reason may
flourish beyond any bounds assignable by reason. He repudiates the
optimist belief that so monstrous a system must fall to pieces from
inherent weakness. He argues elaborately at the end of 1791 in behalf
of the propositions, that no counter-revolution can be expected from
internal causes; that, the longer the system lasts, the stronger it will be;
and that, whilst it lasts, it will be its interest to disturb all other
countries.[102] It is a kind of 'dry rot'—a mysterious contagion which
propagates itself. Want of money matters nothing; for, as he very forcibly says, material resources have never supplied the want of unity of
design and constancy in execution; whilst such qualities have never
failed for want of material resources.[103] The whole strength of the
country has been absorbed by the new tyrants who came here to rob
at pleasure, and Europe must destroy them or be itself destroyed.

125. One question might have revealed the weakness of a theory
which seems to have imposed upon him, as upon his readers, more by
the power with which it is stated than by the force of the arguments
alleged. Jacobinism, he said, and with perfect truth, was partly the offspring of philosophical atheism; and to what was the atheism owing?
That question could hardly be answered by a thinker content to rest
the claims of religious, as of political faith, upon prescription. Prescription, once questioned, is but a foundation of sand. Burke could not or
would not see that the old ideas were perishing. So long as men could
be warned off the sacred ground, an appeal to prescription might be in
place. But the attempt had long been hopeless. The creeds were rotten;
and therefore the 'dry rot' could sap the old supports and render the
crash inevitable. And, as Burke refused to face this difficulty in the
sphere of religion, he was equally unsound in the sphere of politics. A
religious creed resting on prescription is analogous to a political creed
which renounces responsibility. The rulers who objected to change
could appeal to no satisfactory ground of reverence. The divine right
theory was dead; and therefore to claim the reverence due only to

[100]Burke, viii. 172, 'Regicide Peace.'   [102]Ib. vii. 56, 'French Affairs.'
[101]Ib. viii. 368, ib.   [103]Ib. viii. 255, 'Regicide Peace.'

divinely appointed rulers was to invite destruction. In the face of this, a power relying upon the mere force of prejudice, the revolutionary doctrines had a tremendous advantage; their dogmas might be erroneous, but they were dogmas. The revolutionists asserted, with the fervour of new converts, that laws ought to be reasonable; that social arrangements should be in conformity with justice; that all power should be administered for the good of the people. True, these doctrines were mixed with an element of utterly delusive metaphysics; and therefore the attempt to carry them into practice led to cruel disappointment. Burke's obstructive creed had not that positive element which was required to meet the destructives effectually. Delivered, indeed, to a people full of stubborn conservatism, comparatively careless of general ideas, and frightened by the catastrophe of France, it served to give courage to the party of resistance. But, as yet, men's minds were left in the hopeless dilemma between doctrines which would destroy all authority and doctrines which would support all authority not flagrantly intolerable. In order to appreciate the full significance of the lesson taught by Burke, it is necessary to examine at some length the doctrine which his last breath was spent in opposing, so far, at least, as that doctrine was embodied in English literature.

X. *The Revolutionists.*

126. The shrewd but crotchety Dean Tucker had attacked Price and Priestley as the main advocates of the obnoxious 'Lockian' system in England. In their writings, in fact, we catch for the first time the true revolutionary tone. The liberal dissenters, whom they both represented, were the backbone of the reforming party in England. The theoretical principles of the two men differed widely, but their conclusions as to political questions of the day were identical. Priestley, the crude materialist, and Price, the cloudy advocate of an *a priori* philosophy, united in condemning the existing order which would satisfy neither the test of utility nor the test of abstract justice. The relation between the utilitarians and the metaphysicians is, indeed, a characteristic peculiarity of English political theory. The doctrine of the indefeasible rights of man has never been quite at home on English soil; but writers, avowedly starting from the opposite pole of speculation, have accepted the conclusions to which it naturally leads. Bentham's hatred of metaphysical methods was at least as keen as Burke's. He objected to the American movement in its beginning, because he thought that the Declaration of Independence savoured of those hated principles. Priestley, as we shall

see directly, was in substantial agreement with Bentham, and it was in
reading the 'Treatise upon Civil Government' that the sacred formula
about the greatest happiness of the greatest number first flashed upon
Bentham's mind.[1] And yet Priestley's doctrine, if utilitarian in substance, easily took the metaphysical form; and his conclusions might
have been avowed by Rousseau as well as by Price or Paine. There is,
indeed, an obvious point of contact in all these theories. Priestley and
Bentham, not less than Rousseau and his followers, altogether ignore
the historical method in politics. They are absolutely indifferent to that
conception of the continuity of the social organism which supplies the
vital element of Burke's teaching. They reject all 'prescription' as
equivalent to blind prejudice. They propose to reform society anew,
without reference to the special traditions and beliefs by which it has
been hitherto bound together. The doctrine of the natural equality of
mankind which is openly avowed by the metaphysicians, is tacitly assumed by the utilitarians as a necessary base for their speculations; and
therefore, however widely their methods may differ, they agree in condemning the whole body of beliefs by which the complex structure of
society was bound together. Priestley's 'Treatise on Civil Government'
first appeared 1768; Price's 'Observations on Civil History' in 1775.
Priestley's main object of attack was the Established Church, whilst
Price assaulted the Colonial Empire; but each writer prefaces his special
argument by asserting, with great emphasis, the revolutionary doctrine
of liberty. Government requires to be restrained, whether it seeks to tax
the dissenters for ecclesiastical purposes or the colonies for commercial
purposes. And in each case the opposition to its claims rests on the
single ground that nobody ought to be made to do what he dislikes.

127. Priestley's versatile and receptive, though over-hasty, intellect
enabled him to adopt any popular language without enquiring too
closely into its meaning. He avowedly accepts Rousseau's line of argument.[2] Government, as he maintains, is founded upon a bargain according to which every man resigns part of his 'civil liberty,' that is, his
right to do as he pleases, in consideration of a certain share of 'political
liberty,' that is, of influence on the government of the country.[3] Hence
follow the ordinary conclusions about popular sovereignty and the
justification of rebellion when the fundamental contract is broken. His
theory is summed up in the maxim, 'than which nothing is more true,
that every government in its original principles, and antecedent to its

---

[1] See note to ch. ix. sec. 62, above.
[2] 'Treatise on Civil Government,' p. 7.   [3] Ib. p. 10.

present form, is an equal republic.'[4] His belief in the imaginary compact prevents him, even when attacking its most grotesque form in
Warburton's 'alliance' theory, from striking at the vital point. Eager
as he is to overthrow his enemy, and forcible as are some of his arguments, he never points out, as any modern writer would begin by pointing out, the utterly fictitious nature of the whole hypothetical
structure.

128. Bentham would have done better, and yet the whole of Priestley's argument, when stripped of its superficial dress, is so much in the
utilitarian spirit as to explain very naturally the impression made upon
Bentham's mind. The elastic compact, in fact, is easily twisted into a
shape in which it becomes almost indistinguishable from an assertion of
the greatest happiness principle. Priestley speaks, for example, of man's
'natural right' as 'founded on a regard to the general good,' and argues
that the 'good and happiness of the members, that is,' he significantly
adds, 'the majority of the members of any state, is the great standard
by which everything relating to that state must finally be determined.'[5]
'This one general idea,' he proceeds to declare, 'properly understood,
throws the greatest light upon the whole system of policy, morals, and,
I may add, theology too.'[6] Though he does not grasp this principle as
vigorously as Bentham, or apply it so systematically, it supplies his most
telling arguments. Arguing the question of the interference of the civil
magistrate in religious affairs, he says that no difference is here to be
made 'between the *right* and the *wisdom* of interference. If the interference be for the good of society, it is wise and right; if it would do
more harm than good, it is foolish and wrong.'[7] But the coincidence
between Priestley and the later utilitarians appears most clearly in his
discussion of the advantages of an 'authoritative code of education.'
Brown had added a kind of corollary to the 'Estimate,' showing that
the torrent of corruption ought to be checked by the introduction of a
national system of education. He held, like Rousseau, that our manners
could only be renovated by saving life from pollution at its source. His
great precedent was the case of Sparta, as he apparently held that a
young man accustomed to a dish of black broth would be superior to
the bribes of a Newcastle or a Bute. Priestley's objections are precisely
those which have been raised by later utilitarians to all government
interference. For the doctrine of the revolutionary metaphysicians, that
government has no right to interfere, is substituted the argument that
its interference would be inexpedient. Priestley, like his successors, holds

---

[4]Priestley, p. 40.   [5]Ib. p. 13.   [6]Ib. p. 14.   [7]Ib. p. 120.

that it would be unadvisable to stereotype any system in our present state of ignorance, and assumes that stagnation would be the necessary effect of interference. 'The great excellence of human nature,' he says, 'consists in the variety of which it is capable,' and he holds that 'the various character of the Athenians was certainly preferable to the uniform character of the Spartans, or to any uniform national character whatever.'[8] Interference with family rights will involve the sacrifice of 'the greatest sum of happiness in the community;'[9] and the evil effects of lodging supreme power in the hands of one set of men may be judged from the reception accorded to Locke's Essay, and to the Newtonian philosophy on its first appearance. A fanciful argument follows as to the incompatibility between a uniform system of education and a mixed form of government; but Priestley is one of the first apostles of that gospel of letting things alone which in a later generation was to be regarded as the cure for all our diseases.

129. One other doctrine, which makes its appearance in the pages of Priestley, is more strikingly characteristic of the new period. His sanguine temperament and his scientific abilities predisposed him to accept that unqualified belief in progress which was to be the religion of the coming generation. The old superstitions and prejudices were disappearing; vast possibilities of future progress were opening out in every direction. However the world may have begun, he thinks himself entitled to pronounce that 'the end will be glorious and paradisaical beyond what our imagination can now conceive.'[10] With an unconscious inconsistency, he adds that government is 'the great instrument of this progress of the human species towards this glorious state,'[10] and then argues that government is to promote progress by letting things alone. Everywhere, however, 'the minds of men are opening to large and generous views of things.'[11] Political and religious knowledge advances as rapidly as knowledge of other kinds; and if only governments will stand aside and leave free play to individual energies, the millennium is at hand. Reason is shaking off the vast superincumbent mass of antiquated prejudice; the fetters are falling from all human limbs, and a new order must be soon created. When the French Revolution came, Priestley saw the realisation of his dreams; and though facts did not quite correspond to theories, he was able to take refuge in the interpretation of the prophecies.

130. Belief in a coming millennium is natural to a party still in the

---

[8]Priestley, p. 91.   [9]Ib. p. 94.   [10]Ib. p. 5.   [11]Ib. p. 296.

proselytising stage. A careful study of the past history of the race is necessary to substitute a well-grounded belief in progress for a crude optimism, which is rather the reflection of the hopes of reformers than the expression of a reasoned conviction. To under-estimate the obstacles to success, and to over-estimate its results, is natural to all youthful parties as to the youthful individual; and the sanguine anticipations of men like Priestley implied but an indistinct apprehension of that belief in progress which corresponds to a scientific theory of evolution. The doctrine was not worked into the substance of his creed, though it was congenial to his habitual mode of thought. Some of his fellow-labourers could dispense with it altogether. Price, in particular, represents the growing discontent, as Priestley represents the growing hopes of the reforming party. The two writers agree in their view of the ideal state; but Priestley thinks that his ideal is about to be realised, whilst Price thinks that we are drifting further away from it. He takes up the tone of lamentation made popular in England by Brown, and thinks that the dreaded evil, luxury, is sapping the national vitality. Indifference is gaining ground; the House of Commons is corrupt, short parliaments are hopeless, standing armies are inevitable, the debt grows, national extravagance increases, the Middlesex election has set a dangerous precedent, and the subjection of the East India Company to the Crown has increased the power of corruption.[12] Price's reputation for statistical knowledge enabled him to give a colouring of systematic proof to these gloomy forebodings. From some imperfect information as to the number of burials and the product of the house-tax, he tried to show that the population was actually declining in numbers, under the influence of the luxury which was ruining our virtue and weakening our physical constitution.

131. The principles by which we were to be saved, if, indeed, salvation was possible, were the principles of Rousseau. Price has some cold approbation for the British Constitution. According to some recent statistics, 5,723 voters elected half the House of Commons, and 364 voters chose a ninth part of it.[13] If voters were not corrupt, nor representatives influenced by the Crown, he thinks that even this inadequate representation would afford a sufficient security for our liberties. But his doctrines fit in rather awkwardly with this concession. His theory is briefly expressed by the phrase quoted from Montesquieu,[14] that in a

[12]Price's 'Additional Observations,' p. 50.
[13]Price's 'Observations,' p. 10   [14]'Esprit des Lois,' book xi. ch. vi.

free state every man is his own legislator.[15] All taxes are free gifts; all
laws established by common consent, and all magistrates are deputies
for carrying out this voluntary agreement. Of such liberty, he says, it is
impossible that there should be an excess.[16] He infers that the people
are absolute; that they never divest themselves of their indefeasible
rights; and that Parliament, their creature, cannot rightfully oppose
their will. Such a theory is the only security against oppression, because
a people will never oppress itself,[17] and cannot safely trust anybody else.
On this theory is founded the only system which can stimulate industry,
by giving due security for its fruits, and the only system compatible
with the 'natural equality of mankind.'[18] 'Mankind came with this
right from the hands of their Maker,'[19] and civil government is but an
institution for maintaining it.[20] Government is thus limited to the narrowest functions. 'It is a maxim true universally that, as far as anyone
does not molest others, others ought not to molest him.'[21] Government,
as he elsewhere says, should never trench upon private liberty, 'except
so far as the exercise of private liberty entrenches on the liberties of
others.'[22] Government, in short, though he does not explicitly state the
proposition, is an evil, and the less we have of it the better. The practical application of these theories implies the condemnation of all despotic
and corrupt governments, and especially of all 'provincial governments.'[23] The relation of England to the American colonies was flatly
opposed to his theory of liberty, and to that corollary from it embodied
in the British Constitution, in which the 'right of a people to give and
grant their own money' is a fundamental principle.[24] The claim to tax
America at our pleasure was, in fact, a claim to despotic power; the
more invidious because, whilst we were corrupt, the Americans themselves were 'in the happiest state of society, or in that middle state of
civilisation between its first rude and its last refined and corrupted
state.'[25] Americans, in fact, both in their corporate and in their individual capacity, were beginning to represent the democratic principle;
and Price, Priestley, and Paine, all of them advocates of American independence, were all identified at a later period with the French
application of the same theories of the indefeasible rights of man.

[15]Price's 'Observations,' p. 6, 'Add. Ob.' p. 9.
[16]'Ob.' p. 12.   [21]Ib. p. 12.
[17]'Add. Ob.' p.   [22]'Ob.' p. 13.
[18]Ib. p. 20.   [23]'Ad. Ob.' p. 37.
[19]Ib. p. 22.   [24]'Ob.' p. 49.
[20]Ib. p. 27.   [25]Ib. p. 70.

132. In America, indeed, as I have already said, both the English constitutional theory and the purely democratic theory were represented by able advocates. The doctrines popular with the party which still cling to English theories, though repudiating the English connection, are best expounded in the 'Federalist.' The series of papers bearing that name appeared in 1788, during the discussions which preceded the acceptance of the present constitution. The chief author was Alexander Hamilton, though a considerable number of articles were contributed by Madison, and a few by Jay. The 'Federalist' is a very remarkable example of the calm and logical discussion of an exciting political question, and is creditable, not only to the sagacity of the writers, but to the intelligence of the readers whom it influenced. Its design, however, does not include the discussion of first principles in politics. The writers are not proposing to build up a new order from its base, but simply to unite political bodies already existing into a more stable confederacy. They are mainly preoccupied with the necessity of conjuring down the unreasonable jealousy of their countrymen, who saw in their proposed President a George III. or a Cromwell. The popular cry about 'loss of liberties' was as loud in America as in the old country. Several gentlemen, we are told, in one of the State conventions called to ratify the constitution, mentioned, as a warning, the fate of those nations which have lost their liberty by lengthening the duration of their parliaments; whereupon another member very sensibly asked what were those nations. He could remember none, and nobody was prepared with an instance.[26] Of such platitudes and of references to the Amphictyonic league, and other commonplaces of political philosophers, there was, of course, an abundance. The 'Federalist' disposes of them with excellent sense, and with pithy and appropriate argument.

133. In a book intended to recommend the greatest product of the constitution-mongering art in modern times, there is, of course, occasionally an undue reliance upon the power of paper regulations. The belief, for example, in the efficacy of the system of double election[27] illustrates the illusion, natural to legislators, that the spirit in which laws are designed will determine the spirit in which they are worked. In a more general sense, the efficacy of the great social forces which determine the destiny of a nation is underestimated in comparison with the efficacy of mere external arrangements and legal compacts. Such weaknesses are natural in men who belong to the school of Montes-

[26]Elliot's 'Debates,' ii. 4.   [27]'Federalist,' No. 68.

quieu[28] and Delolme.[29] But, on the whole, the 'Federalist' is a very remarkable instance of statesmanlike ability, in which a certain amount of pedantry and affectation may well be pardoned in consideration of the clearness with which the conditions of a great political crisis are appreciated. Hamilton, whose influence is most perceptible,[30] was by far the ablest representative of what may be called the English theory of government in the United States; and took no inconsiderable share in carrying into execution the plan which he had so ably defended. But a full account of the 'Federalist' would belong rather to the history of American than of English speculation. Another writer, born, like Hamilton, a British subject, but, unlike Hamilton, brought up in England, and under popular English influences, demands a rather fuller consideration.

134. We have already encountered Paine as an antagonist of the religious beliefs of the time. He was already the most conspicuous English representative of the doctrines of the French revolutionists. Paine possessed in the highest degree the gifts of the born journalist. He had only such education as could be gained in a small country town, and had been doomed to the obscure career of an exciseman. His emigration to America just before the War of Independence had given him an opportunity of which he took full advantage. The pamphlets which he published during the struggle had a vast circulation and a marked effect in rousing the spirit of resistance to the English Government. To himself it seemed that his pen was comparable in efficiency to Washington's sword. The pamphlets assume the principles embodied in the Declaration of Independence. They represent the creed of Jefferson or of Robespierre; and show the first application to actual politics of the ideas which were to be proclaimed as a new gospel in France. Paine was thus preappointed to take up the challenge of Burke. He became the authorised expositor of the views of the English sympathisers with the French Revolution. His books were circulated in thousands by the societies formed to propagate the revolutionary creed; and at a later period, when Paine had himself escaped to France, the sale became a

[28]See *e.g.* 'Federalist,' Nos. 43 and 47, in which Montesquieu's authority is specially invoked.

[29]See *e.g.* remarks in No. 51 on the advantage of dividing the legislature into branches.

[30]Hamilton's share is variously estimated at from forty-eight to over sixty of the eighty-five papers. Jay wrote four or five, Madison the remainder.

service of danger, and government strained its powers to make martyrs in the republican cause. Paine became the object of fierce and often libellous denunciations by anti-Jacobins; while his writings were the more valued by the staunch adherents of his creed.[31] Paine represents a type rarer in England than in France. He has the merits and defects of the uncompromising dogmatist. He was a fanatic, with superabundant vanity and self-confidence; and untrammelled by any of the tenderness for the objects of his assault which sometimes makes inconsistency excusable. But his sincerity is above all suspicion; he was honest and independent; his life was devoted to the propagation of ideas, and not to the pursuit of meaner ends. If he was inclined to take too much credit for his achievements, he was free from hypocrisy, and never sacrificed his principles to mere personal interests.

135. Paine's attack upon the established creed in politics showed the same qualities as his attack upon the established creed in religion. He was confronted, indeed, in his later writings by an opponent of incomparably greater power than the orthodox theologians who shrieked at the blasphemies of the 'Age of Reason.' But though Burke moves in an intellectual sphere altogether superior to that in which Paine was able to rise, and though the richness of Burke's speculative power is as superior to Paine's meagre philosophy as his style is superior in the amplitude of its rhetoric, it is equally true that Paine's plain-speaking is more fitted to reach popular passions, and even that he has real advantages in point of argument. Paine's doctrine may be given in two words. Kings, like priests, are cheats and impostors. The dawn of the 'Age of Reason' implies the disappearance of loyalty from politics as of superstition from religion. Democracy corresponds in the one sphere to Deism in the other. It is the teaching of pure unsophisticated nature, and the new gospel is the effectual counterblast to all the nonsense with which statesmen have for their own base purposes imposed upon the people whom they enslaved. These doctrines are laid down as absolutely and unhesitatingly as the axioms of a geometer; and Paine is, in all sincerity, incapable of understanding that there can be any other side to the question.

136. Paine's doctrine may thus be described as the reverse of Burke's.

[31] The 'Life of Paine' by Mr. Moncure Conway (1892) gives the view of a warm, though candid, admirer, and is the result of an elaborate investigation. I regret to say that I had accepted certain charges against Paine's character, which Mr. Conway has shown to rest upon worse than suspicious evidence. I cannot accept all that he says; but I fully admit that I was entirely misled by a hasty reliance upon worthless testimony.

Both writers would admit that the old social order rested upon prescription; but, whilst in Burke's eyes this implied the sanctity of prescription, Paine inferred that prescription, being simply irrational prejudice, the old social order should be swept away. There are, he says, two modes of government in the world—government by election, and government by hereditary succession.[32] Now an hereditary governor is as great an absurdity as an hereditary mathematician or poet-laureate.[33] The representative system admits of government by the wisest, whilst the hereditary allows of government by the stupidest. The last proposition seemed clear enough in the days of George III. The privileges of an aristocracy are as irrational as the privileges of kings. Burke's catalogue of the constituted authorities whom we are to revere and obey is interpreted by Paine to mean that the 'duty of man is a wilderness of turnpike gates, through which he is to pass by tickets from one to another;'[34] whereas it consists simply in obeying God, and doing to his neighbour as he would be done by. The checks and balances of the British Constitution are a juggle for evading responsibility and enabling corruption to work the machine.[35] A claim to rule by prescription, indeed, means a claim to be irresponsible, and, as Paine forcibly remarks, 'a body of men holding themselves accountable to nobody ought to be trusted by nobody.'[36] Monarchy is therefore a mere 'bubble and court artifice to procure money,'[37] whilst the 'representative system is always parallel with the order and immutable laws of nature, and meets the reason of man in every part.'[38]

137. The doctrines thus vigorously laid down have become tolerably threadbare, and every scribbler can expose their incompleteness. One difficulty is unconsciously indicated by Paine. He accuses Burke of taking up a 'contemptible opinion of mankind' and considering them as 'a herd of beings that must be governed by fraud, effigy, and show.'[39] Burke did indeed perceive the truth which underlies the maxim that most men are fools. The assumption that the age of reason was approaching involved the erroneous opinion that men are reasonable creatures; and that a system, constructed on abstract principles of reason, would be worked in a reasonable spirit. It need hardly be pointed out how far that assumption was from being justifiable. But, meanwhile the man who believed in his race, though the belief was extravagant, had an advantage over the more temperate observer, which could only be

[32]Paine's Political Works, p. 152.
[33]Ib. p. 100.
[34]Ib. p. 85.
[35]Ib. pp. 7 and 153.
[36]Ib. p. 100.
[37]Ib. p. 191.
[38]Ib. p. 190.
[39]Ib. p. 182.

neutralised by the bitter teachings of experience. Paine fully believed, or appeared to believe, in the speedy advent of the millennium. His vanity, it is true, was interested in the assumption. The American Revolution, he thought, had brought about the grand explosion, and the foundation of the American Constitution had given the first example of a government founded on purely reasonable principles.[40] Now the pamphlet 'Common Sense' had led to the Revolution, and therefore Paine had fired the match which blew into ruin the whole existing structure of irrational despotism. Still the belief was probably not the less genuine, though thus associated with an excessive estimate of personal merits, and Paine is at times eloquent in expressing the anticipations of universal peace and fraternity destined to such speedy disappointment. His retort upon Burke's sentimentalism about chivalry and Marie Antoinette has real force and dignity. 'Nature has been kinder to Mr. Burke than he is to her. He is not affected by the reality of distress touching his heart, but by the showy resemblance of it striking his imagination. He pities the plumage, but forgets the dying bird.'[41] Paine really feels for the people, instead of treating their outcry as so much 'puling jargon.' And therefore he gives utterance to sentiments not to be quenched by Burke's philosophy.

138. Paine, however, represents the revolutionary sentiment, and does nothing to develop its theories. The fullest English exposition of the creed which Burke had to oppose is to be found in the 'Political Justice' of William Godwin. Godwin, like many other prophets of revolutionary principles, began life as a dissenting minister. His mind, clear, systematic, and passionless, speedily threw off the prejudices from which Price and Priestley never emancipated themselves. More than any English thinker, he resembles in intellectual temperament those French theorists who represented the early revolutionary impulse. His doctrines are developed with a logical precision which shrinks from no consequences, and which placidly ignores all inconvenient facts. The Utopia in which his imagination delights is laid out with geometrical symmetry and simplicity. Godwin believes as firmly as any early Christian in the speedy revelation of a new Jerusalem, four-square and perfect in its plan. Three editions of his 'Political Justice' were published, in 1793, 1796, and 1798. Between those dates events had occurred calculated to upset the faith of many enthusiasts. Godwin's opinions, however, were rooted too deeply in abstract speculation to be affected by any storms raging in the region of concrete phenomena. Condorcet, whose

---

[40]Paine, p. 192.   [41]Ib. p. 70.

writings show curious parallels to the speculations of Godwin, had shown a fidelity to his creed still more touching because exposed to severer trials. The colleagues of the French philosopher in the great task of regenerating the world had become sanguinary tyrants thirsting for his blood. In his precarious hiding-place, haunted by the constant dread of discovery, he composed his treatise on the progress of the human spirit, setting forth the perfectibility of man and the speedy advent of a reign of peace and reason. Godwin, safe from such dangers, persisted in his creed, in spite of discouragements almost equally trying to his intellectual balance. The dawn had become overcast; enthusiasts were dropping off as their dreams grew faint; the free republic was becoming a despotism; the obsolete British Constitution, the very embodiment of effete prejudice, was developing unexpected strength; peace, if peace was coming, was heralded by wars all over the world, and the reign of reason had been inaugurated by the mad saturnalia of anarchy. Godwin stuck to his creed; added a few corollaries, and went on his way unmoved. He remained a republican Abdiel throughout the long dark winter of reaction, though his unfitness for actual political warfare kept him somewhat aloof from his party. He was essentially a closet-philosopher, and both by principle and temperament an advocate of persuasion rather than of physical force. To a later generation he is chiefly interesting as the teacher from whom Shelley received lessons which, in the poetical imagination of the disciple, acquired a magical colouring, though their texture became still more dreamlike. In later years, the philosopher who would have abolished all human institutions became a quiet bookseller, publishing innocent books for children. He died in the enjoyment of a small pension given to him by one of those aristocrats whose corrupting influence he had striven to undermine. Had England suffered a revolution, Godwin might have been its Condorcet, as Paine might have been its Marat. As it was, Godwin remained to the last a quiet and amiable dreamer, who, whatever his errors, deserves at least the credit of maintaining throughout dark days a fervid belief in the progress of his race and in the possibility of making politics rational. Conservative politicians owe more than they know to the thinkers who keep alive a faith which renders the world tolerable, and puts arbitrary rulers under some moral stress of responsibility.

139. Godwin's intellectual genealogy may be traced to three sources. From Swift, Mandeville, and the Latin historian,[42] he had learnt to regard the whole body of ancient institutions as corrupt; from Hume[43]

[42]Godwin's 'Political Justice,' i. ix.   [43]Ib. ii. 490.

and Hartley,[44] of whom he speaks with enthusiasm, he derived the
means of assault upon the old theories; from the French writers, such
as Rousseau, Helvetius, and Holbach, he caught, as he tells us, the
contagion of revolutionary zeal. The 'Political Justice' is an attempt to
frame into a systematic whole the principles gathered from these various sources, and may be regarded as an exposition of the extremest
form of revolutionary dogma. Though Godwin's idiosyncrasy is perceptible in some of the conclusions, the book is instructive, as showing,
with a clearness paralleled in no other English writing, the true nature
of those principles which excited the horror of Burke and the
Conservatives.

140. The complex organisation of human society can be understood
only by a careful study of the processes of evolution. Its most intimate
structure, as well as each of its superficial peculiarities, bears the traces
of forces which have been operating since the earliest dawn of thought.
The most trifling customs and the most vital laws will only give up
their secret when regarded in the light of history. Man, as we see him,
is the product of innumerable forces; his character has been inherited
from a long series of ancestors; his beliefs are, for the most part, a
tradition from remote ages, modified superficially by his own activity.
To have grasped those now familiar truths, and to have seen their bearing upon political speculation, is the great merit of Burke; the utter unconsciousness of their importance is characteristic of the whole revolutionary school. Godwin is conspicuous for the vigour with which he
repudiates them, but still more for the clearness with which he indicates
the logical grounds of the repudiation. He would have fully sympathised
with D'Alembert's wish that history might be abolished. He would ex-
punge every vestige of tradition from the tablet of the human mind.
He would raze to the ground the whole structure of political and
religious belief, and substitute a new order of things in which the sole
binding force should be derived from pure abstract reasoning. Godwin
shared these views with a whole school, but no other English writer
traces them back so thoroughly to first principles.

141. Starting from the philosophy of Locke and Hume, Godwin
denies the existence of what he calls innate principles[45] and instincts.[46]
He even doubts whether we can be properly said to have a mind, and
explains that he uses the word provisionally to signify the chain of
thoughts which, when linked together, produce the complex notion of

[44]Godwin, i. 400.   [45]Ib. i. 27.   [46]Ib. i. 31.

personal identity.[47] He admits that we may receive a certain bias from 'antenatal impressions and original structure;'[48] but argues that such influences are faint as compared with the various impressions made upon us by our subsequent environment. The differences between one man and another result almost entirely from education, using that word as equivalent to the totality of external influences.[49] 'Compared with the empire of impression,' he says, 'the mere differences of animal structure are inexpressibly unimportant and powerless.'[50] Neither race nor physical constitution has any appreciable effect. If the skull of a wise man should be larger than that of a fool, it is because the ideas have enlarged the brain, not because the larger brain has generated more ideas.[51] He borrows Hume's arguments against the influence of climate,[52] with the view of showing that the mind is the same in all regions as in all races. The 'sheet of blank paper' must be proved to be of the same quality in all times and places. 'Man considered in himself,' as Godwin puts it, 'is merely a being capable of impressions, a recipient of perceptions.'[53] From this it follows that men's notions originate in their opinions;—that is, that the senses and the passions are strictly subordinate to the intellect. Unfortunately, indeed, we do not always act from pure reason—a singular circumstance, which he explains by help of Hartley's analysis of the reciprocal action of the voluntary and involuntary actions. The mind approaches perfection in proportion as all our actions become voluntary, or, in other words, as each action is the result of a fresh train of reasoning.[54] All our opinions should therefore be in a state of perpetual revision.[54] And, far as we may be from the ideal consummation in which all formulas are obliterated, it is already true that the intellect is potentially supreme. Thus Godwin, though he has begun by attacking the old metaphysical theories, has prepared the way for a doctrine as absolute and independent of experience as the most audacious of metaphysicians could desire. He has abolished not only innate ideas, but the mind which should contain them. Nothing is left, one may almost say, but a number of logical processes, of which it is convenient to assume that they take place in a vehicle called the mind, but which are everywhere unaffected by external conditions. The organism and the medium are equally abolished; and somehow the

[47]Godwin, i. 26.   [51]Ib. i. 38.
[48]Ib. i. 35.   [52]Ib. i. 100.
[49]Ib. i. 45.   [53]Ib. ii. 78.
[50]Ib. i. 40.   [54]Ib. i. 68.

reason survives. Thus, in Godwin's hands, the scepticism of Hume is applied to construct a theory which at times reminds us in spirit of Descartes and Spinoza.

142. Godwin's political conclusions are, however, more interesting than his metaphysical speculation. He represents the tendency of the revolutionary school towards the deification of the pure intellect. Five fundamental propositions follow from the principles thus stated: 'sound reasoning and truth, when adequately communicated, must always be victorious over error; sound reasoning and truth are capable of being so communicated; truth is omnipotent; the vices and moral weaknesses of men are not invincible; man is perfectible, or, in other words, suscepti-ble of perpetual improvement.'[55] Men being mere reasoning machines, the right reasons must always prevail if poured in in an unceasing stream, until their minds are saturated with argument. The excellent Godwin had the natural predisposition of speculative minds to exagger-ate the influence of logic as compared with emotion; and the simplicity of his faith is almost touching. Virtue and great abilities, according to him, are naturally allied;[56] as appears even from Milton's ideal hero, or from those political incarnations of evil, Alexander and Cæsar. 'What,' he asks, 'would not men have been long before this, if the proudest of us had no hope but in argument . . . if he were obliged to sharpen his faculties, and collect his powers as the only means of effecting his pur-poses!'[57] The worst criminals might be reformed by reasoning. 'If con-duct be wrong,' he says, 'a very simple statement, flowing from a clear and comprehensive view, will make it appear to be such; nor is it probable that there is any perverseness that would persist in vice in the face of all the recommendations with which it might be invested, and all the beauty in which it might be displayed.'[58] Could Godwin have caught Pitt, or George III., or Mrs. Brownrigg, and subjected them to a Socratic cross-examination, he could have restored them to the paths of virtue, as he would have corrected an error in a little boy's sums. 'Vice,' he says—and the statement may be regarded as his fundamental proposition in moral philosophy—'is unquestionably no more in the first instance than error of judgment.'[59] The theory suggests some anal-ogy with thinkers of a different order; but Godwin was here simply expressing the creed of the revolutionary school. The belief in the per-fectibility of the race was a corollary from the rapid increase of scien-

[55]Godwin, p. 86.
[56]Ib. i. 318.   [58]Ib. ii. 34.
[57]Ib. ii. 334 .   [59]Ib. ii. 197.

tific knowledge, and the indefinite vista of future improvement already perceptible. The intellect breaking its old fetters and rejoicing in the consciousness of its strength, looked forwards to the conquest of the whole physical and moral world. Franklin, as Godwin said, had anticipated a day when 'mind would become omnipotent over matter.'[60] A similar omnipotence might be displayed in the social order, as old errors dispersed and society was remoulded in obedience to the teaching of theory. The only obstacle was the existence of human passions; but as every anti-social passion ought to be regarded as implying, and therefore as consisting in, an erroneous conception of human wants, it followed that, as errors were dispersed, the passions would fall into their right places. The fetters forged for their restraint by the priests and kings of old days were based upon doctrines which would not bear the test of reason. But reason once allowed to have full play, would supply a discipline of its own, and men would act rightly for the same reason that a learned arithmetician would add up a column of figures accurately.

143. Godwin's moral philosophy follows easily, and has at least the merit of simplicity. Since all innate principles have been abolished, he holds with Locke that pleasure must be the supreme good; or that 'good is a general name, including pleasure and the means by which pleasure is produced.'[61] Morality, again, is 'nothing else but that system which teaches us to contribute on all occasions, to the extent of our power, to the well-being and happiness of every intellectual and sensitive existence.'[62] Now as every action in our lives has some bearing upon happiness, it follows that at every instant one action must be right; that, namely, which will produce the maximum of happiness. Our duty, therefore, depends upon what Godwin often calls a 'moral arithmetic.'[63] 'Morality,' he says, 'is nothing else but a calculation of consequences,'[64] and it is, therefore, a contradiction in terms to tell us to do our duty without regard to consequences. As the course of a ship at sea should be at every instant directed along that line which will bring it most quickly to its destination, so our course in life should be steadily aimed at producing the maximum of happiness. Various conclusions follow which might startle any man capable of being startled. 'Virtue,' says Godwin, must 'be placed in a conformity to truth, not to error;'[65] or, on his interpretation, we must always act from an impartial estimate of consequences, without allowing our purely rational view to be clouded

[60]Godwin, ii. 503.   [63]Ib. i. 173.

[61]Ib. i. 440.   [64]Ib. i. 342.

[62]Ib. i. 159.   [65]Ib. i. 133.

by personal prejudices. There is, therefore, no place for such virtues as gratitude and friendship. I ought, for example, to have saved the life of Fénelon, when he was about to write 'Télémaque,' rather than Fénelon's valet; for by saving Fénelon I should be conferring a benefit upon thousands.[66] If I were the valet, I ought still to prefer my own death to my master's. If, again, the valet had been 'my brother, my father, my benefactor,' the reason would have been the same, and therefore my course should not have been altered.[67] You say that I should be grateful to my father for his care of my infancy. So far as that care proves him to have been a good man, it furnishes a reason for preserving one who will probably be useful to others. But the fact of my personal interest is irrelevant in the eyes of pure reason, and should therefore be discarded. This doctrine, which appears in the first three editions of the 'Political Justice,' became afterwards unsatisfactory to its author, and he withdraws it in the preface to the novel of 'St. Leon.'

144. Godwin, however, does not shrink from other conclusions almost equally startling to the common sense of mankind. If you urged that filial instincts were necessary for the welfare of society, he would reply that instincts had no real existence, and that every mind should be filled with arguments founded upon general reasoning. You would urge, again, that, as man's intelligence is finite, it is of the very essence of morality that general rules should be observed, though they may produce injury in given cases. The difficulty meets Godwin when he is endeavouring to establish the universal obligation of truthfulness. Why not lie, when a lie contributes to the general happiness? Godwin is forced to condescend to the obvious reply that we cannot work out sums in moral arithmetic so as to arrive within a limited period at the correct result, and he therefore admits that we must have 'resting-places for the mind,' 'deductions already stored in the memory, and prepared for application as circumstances demand.'[68] But he is more anxious to point out that general rules on morality may be fallacious than to insist upon the importance of observing them. Necessity may compel us, or indolence induce us, to be content with general rules; 'but the true dignity of human nature is, as much as we are able, to go beyond them, to have our faculties in act upon every occasion that occurs, and to conduct ourselves accordingly.'[69] Rules are chiefly useful to remind us of the remoter consequences which we might otherwise overlook. Ordinary moralists exhort us to cultivate habits of virtue. In Godwin's opinion we

[66]Godwin, i. 127.   [68]Ib. i. 344.
[67]Ib. i. 128.   [69]Ib. i. 345.

are unreasonable so far as we are creatures of habit; and our aim should therefore be to discourage the formation of habits as much as possible. Godwin, in his haste to make man a reasonable creature, assumes that he is potentially omniscient, and therefore capable, like the Divine Being, of acting without reference to those intermediate maxims which necessarily imply some admixture of error. He thus quietly passes over, as an unimportant exception, what is really a vital condition of the problem—namely, the limited capacity of man. A perfect being could dispense with rules, for to a perfect being every remote consequence in an infinite chain would be intuitively evident; therefore, a perfectible being may dispense with rules.

145. From Hume and Hartley, Godwin had learned to deny the selfish theory. Man, as an embodiment of reason, may therefore place himself at that abstract point of view in which his personal interests disappear. From the doctrine of necessity, again, taught by the same thinkers, he infers that argument must be omnipotent. The will is not an inscrutable faculty, but simply an act of the judgment, determined by logical impressions. And a conclusion is calmly accepted which has been indignantly repudiated by most necessitarians. A man, like a knife, is set in motion from without; the knife is moved by 'material impulse;' the man by 'inducement and persuasion.'[70] To hate a murderer, then, is as unreasonable as to hate his weapon. We may disapprove, indeed, more strongly because he is more dangerous, or more likely to repeat his evil deed; but the degree, not the kind, of feeling should differ. 'Our disapprobation of vice will be of the same kind as our disapprobation of an infectious distemper.'[71] Such a view will tend, as Godwin says, to generate a placid temper. He 'who regards all things—past, present, and to come—as links of an indissoluble chain, will, as often as he recollects this comprehensive view, find himself assisted to surmount the tumult of passion; and be enabled to reflect upon the moral concerns of mankind, with the same clearness of perception, the same firmness of judgment, and the same constancy of temper, as he is accustomed to do upon the truths of geometry.'[72] Godwin is unconsciously teaching a doctrine resembling that of a very different school. Though a sceptic in metaphysics, and an ultra-utilitarian in morality, his intellectual temperament was congenial to the philosophy which would resolve all reality into pure reason, and which would naturally

[70]Godwin, i. 388.   [71]Ib. i. 392.

[72]Ib. i. 396. Godwin in later years was rather frightened by his own logic in this as in some other cases (see the Essay on Liberty in 'Thoughts of Man,' 1831).

find the highest good in the attainment of an absolute intellectual calm.

146. Godwin, however, in the name of pure reason, thus reached a tolerably destructive conclusion. He has abolished family affections and moral disapprobation, and all but abolished all moral laws, except the one law which promotes the cultivation of happiness. His method as applied to politics is equally sweeping. The omnipotence of reason involves the abolition of all political institutions as well as of moral laws. To one difficulty which besets this part of his writings he is curiously blind. If, as he seems to assume, man is but a passive receptacle for logic, and if, as he infers, truth necessarily prevails, how are we to account for the prevalence of error? Why is the perfectible being so far from perfection? As theologians explain the existence of evil by assuming an evil principle more or less subordinate to the infinite goodness and omnipotence, so Godwin sets up a dark power of imposture which fights, and has hitherto fought, with singular success against the power of truth. The fact—if Godwin cared for facts—would seem to be in singular opposition to theory. The same strange contradiction appears in the writings of Condorcet, though he endeavoured to place himself at an historical point of view. In both writers, kings and priests represent the incarnation of evil. Hume remarks, with his usual acuteness, upon the absurdity of Bolingbroke's doctrine that our constitution was perfect but our actual degeneracy due to the wickedness of our rulers. A constitution, as he said, which allowed one bad man to ruin a country might suit angels, but could not be good for human beings. The same fallacy, however, on a far larger scale, pervades the whole logic of Godwin and Condorcet. The world, according to them, is inhabited by a set of beings quite ready for the millennium, if only they could shake off this monstrous incubus; but no explanation is suggested of the unnatural slavery. Such a doctrine could maintain itself only amongst minds blinded by fierce hatred of the existing order, or in that radically unhistorical stage in which the only alternative to a belief in the divine origin of religious creeds was the belief that they were conscious impostures.

147. Godwin, however, untroubled by the shadow of a doubt, makes short work of all existing institutions. It is, as he calmly observes, a 'first principle that monarchy is founded on imposture;'[73] and he involves in his censure not merely virtuous despots, but elective kings, the 'mixed monarchies' which, indeed, were specially offensive as an embodiment of force and corruption, and even the presidential system of the United States.[74] Aristocracy, 'like monarchy, is founded on false-

[73]Godwin, ii. 48.   [74]Ib. ii. 80.

hood—the offspring of art, foreign to the real nature of things—and
must, therefore, like monarchy, be supported by artifice and false pretence.'[75] Indeed, it involves a still greater sin against the primitive law
of the equality of men. For men, according to Godwin, should not only
be equal before the law, but may almost be said to be equal in capacity.[76] Man, the mere recipient of logical impressions, has been
stripped of all differences to which a plea for inequality could attach
itself; and Godwin apparently regards all inequalities as in some sense
a result of the general system of imposture, though here he admits a
qualifying phrase.[77] Monarchy and aristocracy could in his view be only
justified on the theory which divides men from their birth into the
saddled and bridled and the booted and spurred. As he holds the contrary view, that they are simple units, differing only numerically, the
saddles and the spurs are artificial additions, and therefore to be summarily abolished. The doctrine of equality was susceptible of an interpretation which would allow the aggregate mass of similar units to
exercise a very vigorous pressure upon the constituent atoms. But
Godwin proceeds a step further by help of his moral theory. Hume had
taught him the fallacy of the social contract theory which, with Rousseau and others, supplied the binding force of government.[78] Man,
being a purely reasoning animal, and as such under an obligation
always to follow the course most conducive to the general happiness,
could not pledge himself to obedience; and, indeed, all promises 'absolutely considered' are an evil, as hampering the free action of reason.[79]
All coercion is thus essentially wrong. 'That any men or body of men
should impose their sense upon persons of a different opinion is, absolutely speaking, wrong and deeply to be regretted,'[80] though it may
occasionally be necessary. Now as government is nothing but 'regulated
force,'[81] all government implies evil, and Godwin characteristically
jumps to the conclusion that all government should be abolished. With
the utmost calmness he sweeps away one restraint after another. The
army and the church, of course, vanish at once; but even national as-
semblies involve that 'flagrant insult upon all truth and justice, the
deciding upon truth by the casting up of numbers,'[82] and he decides
that a constitution should consist of little more than two articles; one
containing a scheme for electoral districts, the other a provision for the
meeting of the assembly at stated periods, 'not to say that the latter

[75]Godwin, ii. 103.   [79]Ib. i. 196.
[76]Ib. i. 143, book ii. ch. iii.   [80]Ib. i. 258.
[77]E.g. ii. 87.   [81]Ib. i. 230.
[78]Ib. i. 214.   [82]Ib. ii. 205.

of these articles may very probably be dispensed with.'[83] Even the punishment of criminals is wrong, because a gallows is not an argument; and the only punishment which he can find it in his heart to tolerate, even as a temporary expedient, is transportation, or, as he delicately calls it, colonisation.[84] We have failed, even in this, from forgetfulness that the 'colonists are men for whom we ought to feel no sentiments but those of kindness and compassion.' It is but a short step to propose the abolition of laws altogether. 'We can scarcely hesitate to conclude universally that law is an institution of the most pernicious tendency.'[85] Godwin, indeed, verbally admits that anarchy is an evil, and even, though reluctantly, that it is a worse evil than government. He finally decides that we shall employ just as much coercion as is necessary to exclude anarchy,[86] though it might puzzle us to exhibit the difference between anarchy and that ideal state in which all laws and forms of government have been abolished. Godwin says, truly enough, that he differs from Rousseau in that the state of nature is with him the final, as with Rousseau it was the initial, stage of human development.[87] He would, in fact, pulverise society. All association involves some sacrifice of individual judgment, and 'individuality is of the very essence of intellectual excellence.'[88] Co-operation is so hateful to him, that he even doubts whether musical concerts or theatrical performances, which 'involve an absurd and vicious co-operation,'[89] are not doomed to disappear. Cohabitation prevents an absolute independence, and 'the abolition of the present system of marriage appears to involve no evils.'[90] Godwin merely doubts whether the future plan will be promiscuous intercourse, or the formation of alliances terminable at the pleasure of either party. He inclines to the latter hypothesis, as it is the nature of the human mind to persist in its choice, and therefore 'the parties having acted upon selection are not likely to forget this selection when the interview is over.'[91]

148. Godwin's attack upon marriage may be illustrated by the remarkable declaration in favour of woman's rights by Mary Wollstonecraft, afterwards his wife. The book is curious as an anticipation of the arguments used in a future generation. It is, in substance, an appeal against the whole theory, sanctioned curiously enough by the teaching of the great revolutionary prophet Rousseau, that women were made

[83]Godwin, ii. 292.   [88]Ib. ii. 500.
[84]Ib. ii. 391.   [89]Ib. ii. 504.
[85]Ib. ii. 404.   [90]Ib. ii. 508.
[86]Ib. ii. 372.   [91]Ib. ii. 509.
[87]Ib. ii. 129.

for the pleasure of men, and that their education should fit them to be our mistresses, rather than our companions. It protests against the degrading influences of the false gallantry which lowers women under pretence of raising them, and claims for them a perfect political and social equality. There is, indeed, an absence of those direct attacks upon marriage which have appeared in some later writings, and which were, as we have seen, implicitly adopted by Godwin. For whatever reason, that side of the question is left untouched, and the author is content with a vehement assertion of the general principle of abstract rights, and a declaration that the present evils of society are due to the unjust use of physical force, and to the wicked system of class distinctions. The book is throughout rather rhetorical than speculative; and the fervour and even religious spirit of the writer—for Mary Wollstonecraft, unlike her husband, was a decided theist, though not a Christian—is impressive in spite of a very unfortunately pompous style. No two things can be less alike than her vehement declamation and the frigid egotism of her husband. Mary Wollstonecraft has the zeal of the champion of a proselytising faith, and cares little for enquiries into the foundation of a system which commends itself to her intuitive perceptions of the just and generous.

149. The doctrines thus expounded may seem to be the very lunacy of revolutionary speculation. Godwin deifies the principle of individualism; and differs from the later thinkers who agreed with him in regarding 'the suppression of injustice against individuals in the community' as the only legitimate end of government, by regarding even that amount of compulsion as a temporary rather than a permanent necessity. Like them, he holds that man, though bound by absolute duty in every action of his life, has certain 'passive rights,' or a 'sphere of discretion' within which he should be free from all compulsion.[92] He therefore looks with suspicion upon legislative interference, even when directed towards the equalisation of property. The state may abolish entails, but he doubts whether it should abolish titles or armorial bearings;[93] and he admits powers of bequest and inheritance, even though they may tend to the production of inequalities.[94] In all such matters, in fact, Godwin is willing to trust to the omnipotent and omnipresent force of reason, the great prime mover in all human affairs. He sincerely objects to violent revolutions, for they appeal to force instead of reason, and imply a tyranny marked by peculiar aggravations.[95] The sun of reason, when it rises, will disperse all mists, and dissipate all

[92]Godwin, i. 167.   [93]Ib. ii. 447.   [94]Ib. ii. 414.   [95]Ib. i. 268.

oppression without extraneous aid. All government, as he is fond of repeating from Hume, is ultimately founded on opinion, and therefore, if opinion be set right, all reforms will spontaneously follow. 'The universal exercise of private judgment,' he says, 'is a doctrine so unspeakably beautiful that the true politician will certainly feel infinite reluctance in admitting the idea of interfering with it.'[96] It follows that in any case men's actions should be influenced by an appeal to reason rather than to fear. But, whilst Godwin would limit, or indeed annihilate, the application of physical force, he sets no bounds to the application of argument. If we may not burn a man for heresy, it is our imperative duty to reason him out of his errors. Public opinion should be all-pervading and omnipotent, for truth will always be triumphant, and argument cannot be applied too freely. We must, indeed, be careful never to bow to authority in matters of opinion. If I surrender my understanding to that of another, I 'become the most mischievous and pernicious of aniamls.'[97] 'Confidence is in all cases the offspring of ignorance.'[98] I should not say, Do this, for I think it right; but do this, if I prove it to be right. Parents should not punish their children, but reason with them.[99] It is absurd, again, to punish rebels, for such a course is once more to appeal to force instead of reason. A man should be always ready to say, 'Publish what you please against me; I have truth on my side, and will confound your misrepresentations.'[100] A society is effeminate when its members are not confident in the 'sacred armour of truth.'[101] Perfect sincerity implies perfect liberty of speech on all conceivable subjects. 'If the unrestrained discussion of abstract enquiry be of the highest importance to mankind, the unrestrained investigation of character is scarcely less to be cultivated. If truth were universally told of men's dispositions and actions, gibbets and wheels might be dismissed from the face of the earth. The knave unmasked would be obliged to turn honest in his own defence. Nay, no man would have time to grow a knave. Truth would follow him in his first irresolute essays, and public disapprobation arrest him in the commencement of his career.'[102] '*Vivre au grand jour*' would thus be Godwin's motto as well as Comte's; and reason be the supreme and solitary force in all public and private affairs.

150. Thus mankind is, or ought to be, in Godwin's view, a vast collection of incarnate syllogisms. There might, indeed, be a little difficulty in discovering their major premisses, when mind itself and all

---

[96]Godwin, i. 182.   [98]Ib. i. 237.   [100]Ib. ii. 281.
[97]Ib. i. 232.   [99]Ib. ii. 336.   [101]Ib. ii. 282.   [102]Ib. ii. 275.

innate principles have been destroyed. Still, from the clashing and combination of these arguments, a system of absolute truth would be gradually evolved. That man is not an incarnate syllogism, and that other
forces besides reason would mould society and determine political constitutions, is indeed true; and Godwin can at times assert the truth with
sufficient emphasis, and even force it into his service. 'Nothing can be
more unreasonable,'[103] he says, 'than to argue from men as we now
find them to men as they may hereafter be made.'[103] But to his imagination, the difference, however great in practice, seemed to oppose but a
trifling obstacle to the realisation of the millennium. The exposure of a
few palpable blunders would regenerate society.[104] Government cannot
be justified by the frailty of man, for it tends to increase that frailty.
Punishment is bad, even as a temporary expedient. The true remedy
for vice is the new and simple social order which would remove all
temptations, and make vice almost impossible or entirely subservient to
public opinion.[105] Thus the passage is easy to the state in which everybody will do what he likes and say what he likes; and in which everyone will like to speak the truth and to do justice. A curious speculation
follows, which led to an important controversy. In 1761 Wallace had
argued in favour of a community of goods as a remedy for all social
evils. One obstacle, however, stood in the way. The population, he reflected, thus relieved from all pressure, would multiply too rapidly for
the earth. Godwin meets the difficulty by assuming the existence of a
principle in virtue of which population 'finds its level;'[106] by pointing
to the vast uncultivated area still left, and by suggesting that there may
be remedies of which we have not 'the smallest idea.'[107] He proceeds,
however, to suggest one characteristic solution. The growing power of
mind over matter may lead, he thinks, to the indefinite extension of the
term of human life; and as, at the same time, sensual gratification will
lose its charms, propagation and death will cease together. In that
blessed day 'there will be no war; no crimes; no administration of
justice, as it is called, and no government.' 'Besides this, there will be
neither disease, anguish, melancholy, nor resentment. Every man will
seek with ineffable ardour the good of all. Mind will be active and
eager, and yet never disappointed.'[108] In short, heaven will be realised
on earth.

The time has not yet come.

151. Condorcet had indulged in a similar contemplation of the proba-

---

[103]Godwin, ii. 120.   [105]Ib. ii. 361.   [107]Ib. ii. 519.
[104]Ib. ii. 472.   [106]Ib. ii. 516.   [108]Ib. ii. 528.

ble extension of human existence. The visionary prospect suggested the attack of Malthus; but I shall not follow a controversy which belongs chiefly to the next century. Malthus, indeed, had struck a weak point. Godwin's dreams were but gorgeous bubbles, destined to speedy collapse whenever brought into contact with the hard facts of the actual world. Yet the hope, the belief in justice, and the faith in man's capacity for improvement were not quite thrown away, though they could only become fruitful when allied to a clearer perception of the conditions of human existence.

152. The description thus given of the main currents of political speculation might of course be indefinitely extended, by considering their application to the problems of the day. I hope, however, that I have sufficiently indicated the governing principles. The French principles represented by Paine and Godwin never became fairly acclimatised in England; though their first prophet, Rousseau, may be regarded, so far as his speculative tendencies are considered, as the almost servile adopter of the Deism of Clarke and of the correlative political theories. The social condition of England and the English dislike to sweeping abstract theories—whether related as cause and effect, or associated by force of circumstances—prevented us from adopting the metaphysical or quasi-mathematical mode of political reasoning. When the divine right theory disappeared, the doctrine of the social compact speedily followed it. All English theorists agreed substantially that political truth must be based upon experience. Hence we have the true constitution-mongers of the Delolme variety, who represent mere empiricism; or the abler interpreters of the constitution as the embodiment of the experience of many generations, whose teaching found the noblest mouthpiece in Burke. Burke's magnificent imagination and true philosophical insight led him more nearly than any of his contemporaries, and even than any of his successors in English political life, to a genuine historical theory. Unluckily, his hatred of an unsound metaphysical doctrine induced him to adopt a view which seems often to amount to a denial of the possibility of basing any general principles upon experience. Like the cruder empiricists, he admires the 'rule of thumb' as the ultimate rule, and consecrates mere prejudice under the name of prescription. Godwin's title, 'Political Justice,' indicates the weak side of his great opponent. Burke had not solved the problem of reconciling expediency with morality, though he indicated the road to a solution. The English utilitarians, led by Bentham, applied experience in a different sense. They attacked every institution which could not appeal to a plain practical justification; and whilst denouncing all *a priori* truths, were in danger of deny-

ing the possibility of attaining general principles. They escaped by a logical inconsequence; for, at once appealing to experience, and pronouncing experience to be chaotic, they decided that some kind of deductive method must be applicable to political speculation. The consequences already appear in Godwin, and inspired the speculative conclusions of the two Mills. But I cannot here even indicate the general nature of the results. The problem of constituting a science of politics has not yet been solved; nor are even the appropriate methods definitively agreed upon.

NOTE TO CHAPTER X

The principal authorities for this chapter and the editions cited are as follows:—

BOLINGBROKE, HENRY ST. JOHN, LORD (1678–1751), 'Letter to Sir W. Windham,' 1717. 'Dissertation on Parties,' 1734. 'Letters on History,' 1735. 'Idea of a Patriot King,' 1738. Works. London: 1777.

BROWN, JOHN (1715–1766), 'Estimate of Manners and Principles of the Times,' 1757. Second volume of ditto, 1758. Seventh edition. London: 1758.

BURKE, EDMUND (1729–1797), 'Vindication of Natural Society,' 1756. 'A Late Administration,' 1766. 'Observations on a Late State of the Nation,' 1769. 'Speech on America' &c. 1774–77. 'Speech on Economical Reform,' 1780. 'Various Speeches and Reports on India and Warren Hastings,' 1783–89 and 1794. 'Reflections on French Revolution,' 1790. 'Letter to Member of National Assembly,' 1791. 'Appeal from New to Old Whigs,' 1791. 'Policy of the Allies,' 1793. 'Letters on Popery-Laws in Ireland,' 1792–95. 'Thoughts on Scarcity,' 1795. 'Letter to a Noble Lord,' 1796. 'Letters on a Regicide Peace,' 1796. Works. London: 1808, &c.

DELOLME, JEAN LOUIS (1740?–1807), 'The Constitution of England,' 1775. London: 1788.

FERGUSON, ADAM (1723–1816), 'Essay on Civil Society,' 1766. Sixth edition. London: 1792.

FRANCIS, SIR PHILIP (1740–1818), 'Junius's Letters,' 1769–72. London: 1812.

GODWIN, MARY (Wollstonecraft) (1759–1797), 'Vindication of Rights of Women,' 1792. Second edition. London: 1792.

GODWIN, WILLIAM (1756–1836), 'Political Justice,' 1793. Third edition. London: 1798. 'The Enquirer,' 1797.

GORDON, THOMAS (?–1750), 'The Independent Whig,' 1720, &c.

HAMILTON, ALEXANDER (1757–1804), 'The Federalist' (with Jay and Madison), 1788.

HOADLY, BENJAMIN (1676–1761), 'Origin of Civil Government,' 1709. 'Preservative against Nonjurors,' 1716. 'Tracts in Bangorian Controversy' (besides many tracts and sermons), 1717, &c. Works. London: 1773.

HUME, DAVID (1711–1776), 'Political Discourses,' 1752. Philosophical Works, by Green and Grose.

JOHNSON, SAMUEL (1709–1784), 'False Alarm,' 1770. 'Taxation no Tyranny,' 1775. Works. London: 1806.

LAW, WILLIAM (1686–1761), 'Tracts against Hoadly,' 1717. Works. London: 1762.

LOCKE, JOHN (1632–1704), 'Letters on Toleration,' 1689–92. 'Two Treatises on Government,' 1690. Works. London: 1824.

MACKINTOSH, JAMES (1765–1832), 'Vindiciæ Gallicæ,' 1791.

PAINE, THOMAS (1736–1809), 'Common Sense,' 1776. 'Rights of Man,' 1791–92. Political Works. London: 1821.

PRICE, RICHARD (1723–1791), 'Observations on Civil Liberty,' 1776. 'Additional Observations,' 1777.

PRIESTLEY, JOSEPH (1733–1804), 'Essay on Principles of Government,' 1768. Second edition. London: 1771.

SHERLOCK, THOMAS (1678–1761), 'Tracts in Answer to Hoadly,' 1718, &c. Works. London: 1730.

TINDAL, MATTHEW (1657–1733), 'Rights of the Christian Church,' 1706.

TUCKER, JOSIAH (1712–1799), 'Treatise on Civil Government,' 1781.

WARBURTON, WILLIAM (1698–1779), 'Alliance between Church and State,' 1736. Works. London: 1811.

CHAPTER XI

POLITICAL ECONOMY

I. *Introductory.*

1. The year 1776 is marked in political history by the Declaration of Independence; in the history of thought by the appearance of Adam Smith's 'Wealth of Nations.' It was not an accidental coincidence that the same year should witness the great catastrophe brought about by the English Colonial policy, and the fullest confutation of the principles upon which that policy rested. Men generally discover that they ought to have foreseen an evil just as foresight is superseded by actual experience; and the history of political economy is but a series of proofs that the relation of speculation to practice is more frequently one of effect than of cause. We learn to think in proportion as the want of thought has made us suffer. Smith's teaching was emphasised at every line by the comment of contemporary history. The literary skill of the writer, the comprehensiveness of his knowledge, and the acuteness of his reasoning, stamped the book from its publication as one of those which is destined to mould the thoughts of a generation. To a statesman like the younger Pitt, filled with a lofty ambition, the 'Wealth of Nations' might well seem to be a revelation. For the first time an incoherent mass of empirical maxims was codified into a definite system, and elevated to the dignity of a science. The mysteries of trade were cleared up, and a distinct map laid down of those bewildering labyrinths in which professional experts had too often lost both themselves and the statesmen who trusted to their guidance. Had Adam Smith announced no absolutely new doctrines, the comprehensiveness and clearness of his speculations would have given an entirely new rank to his study in the circle of human knowledge. The English economists, before the appearance of the 'Wealth of Nations,' claimed only to be adepts in the mysteries of commercial accounts. After it, they began to regard themselves as investigators of a new science, capable of determining the conditions and the limits of human progress. Some thinkers will infer that Smith was the first expounder of a new gospel; and others that he was the earliest mouthpiece of the degrading and materialising spirit of modern Mammon-worship. But the previous question must be asked as

to the potency of the influence, whether for good or for evil. Eulogists of the great economist have sometimes spoken as though the science, previously unborn, sprang in full maturity from his parental brain. To appreciate more accurately the real value of his work, we must enquire what had been done already, what still remained to be done, in his favourite science; and, further, what was its relation to the contemporary movements of thought in other departments of enquiry.

2. The claim of political economy to a place amongst the true sciences is still disputed. The language of some thinkers would assign to it a position analogous to that occupied in physiology by a study of the nutritive organs. According to them, it forms part of a complete sociology, requiring, indeed, the complement of other investigations of a different order, but accurate and definitive so far as it goes. By other thinkers, it is denied that such a process of separate enquiry is legitimate. The laws by which the social organism obtains, assimilates, and distributes its nourishment cannot, they think, be studied apart from other laws of growth with which they are inextricably involved. Upon either hypothesis, political economy is important regarded as a preparation for deeper investigations. A nation, it may be said, like an animal, is a highly complex piece of mechanism, though it is also something much more than a mere machine. Its wheels and levers are formed of living tissues, whose growth depends upon processes far too refined and intricate for the rough analysis of the economists. And yet the laws which regulate the mechanical relations of the organism may be worth studying as well as those underlying laws whose existence we must take for granted. We learn something from an accurate description of the skeleton, though we do not understand the physiological law in virtue of which bones are formed, or the processes by which the actual framework has been developed. The economist does not tell us what are the ultimate instincts which hold society together; nor does he say by what historical process society has acquired its actual constitution; but, assuming that constitution to be such as we know it to be, he can disperse many fallacies, can explain the true nature of many phenomena, and he can at least prepare the way for the sociologist of the future. He does not, it may be, pierce to the ultimate laws of nature; for to each of his propositions must be added the tacit qualification, 'So long as society is what it is to-day;' but doctrines which hold good under that restriction are likely to be serviceable for a long time to come, and are at least better than doctrines which were never true at all. Many pestilent fallacies rested on a genuine intellectual confusion, and were sufficiently dispersed by an accurate description of the social machinery. The older

theorists often held doctrines which were virtually not much wiser than the plan for raising the level of a canal by pumping water from one end and discharging it into the other. Such errors vanish so soon as the anatomy of the body politic is properly dissected and described. The knowledge thus obtained helps on a recognition of the truth, implied even in the cruder forms of political economy, that there is a certain fixed order in social phenomena, beyond the power of arbitrary modification by the legislator, and admitting of, or rather imperatively demanding, a study carried out in a scientific spirit. Hitherto, it may be roughly said that the advantages gained have consisted rather in clearing away old errors than in discovering new truths—so far as those processes can be separated—and in familiarising men's minds with the belief that human nature and human society do not lie in the domain of the purely arbitrary.

3. That part of the social order which is determined by the need of satisfying our material wants was naturally the first to which a scientific method could be applied. The various processes through which wealth is procured and distributed were obviously not capable of indefinite modification. The religious, or political, or artistic energies of the race may seem to be regulated by supernatural interference or by the arbitrary volitions of human beings. But in their efforts to wrest subsistence from the earth, men are rigidly bound by palpable material laws, which impose a corresponding uniformity of structure upon the social organism. In a primitive state of society, the structure is too simple to suggest any need of investigation. Each individual, or, at least, each family or community, is an independent unit. And when society has become differentiated into various classes, the distinction may be regarded as of divine and inscrutable or of human and arbitrary nature; and the relations between different classes or castes be, therefore, regarded as determinable by the priest or the legislator, not as developed by the operation of natural laws. But in modern European societies the rapid evolution of the different classes, each discharging a certain function, and spontaneously incorporating itself into the social order, the possibility of discovering some principle in virtue of which their position and their mutual relations were determined, independently of positive legislation, had long been recognised. Though, as yet, there had been no conscious attempt to found a science of sociology, isolated theories had grown up which might ultimately be incorporated in such a science, or supplanted by its fuller truths. Two more or less complete systems had obtained a certain notoriety at the time of Adam Smith, and were discussed in the 'Wealth of Nations.' The first of these theories was determined chiefly

by the growth of commercial interests. The curious phenomenon produced by exchange and the use of money had suggested a set of crude
opinions, rather than definite doctrines, which Adam Smith describes
collectively as the 'mercantile system.' A more coherent and philosophical body of doctrines, erring by an excess rather than a defect of systematic spirit, had been worked out by the French economists, to whom
Smith undoubtedly owed a great intellectual debt. It is called by him
the agricultural theory, as the embodiment of speculations suggested
chiefly by the conditions of French agriculture.

4. A brief examination of the chief characteristics of these two systems
will explain the precise service rendered by Adam Smith. One general
remark must be premised. The errors of political economists are almost
a continuous illustration of a single class of fallacies. We may say, in the
phraseology suggested by Bacon, that economists have been constantly
led astray by the idols of the cave and the market-place. The earlier
writers, in the absence of any definite conception of a science of sociology, even as a future possibility, never rose to a point of view sufficiently
elevated to enable them to grasp the subject as a whole. The mode in
which this defect in generality perplexes their speculations is a curious
study in logic. Even the ablest writers are frequently misled by the
fallacies which imperceptibly creep into their arguments from the simple use of the language of the counting-house or the Exchange. Some of
the ablest economists have been men who had no immediate experience
in the phenomena which they describe, and the reason is that the very
want of experience has preserved them from the illusions which beset
men immersed in the actual conduct of affairs. They have detected the
general movement of the crowd better, because they stood apart from it
and above it. Merchants and financiers fall victims to a natural fallacy.
Observing some series of economical phenomena, they virtually isolate
some special organ, and whilst studying its functions, forget that those
functions are unintelligible except in relation to the whole. They resemble observers who should reason about the rainfall without remembering that the conspicuous phenomenon of rain implies the less conspicuous, but necessarily correlative, phenomenon of evaporation; or they
may be compared to physiologists who should forget that the growth
of tissues implies a corresponding process of waste. The function, thus
isolated, becomes an absolute end, instead of forming part of a complex
play of acting and reacting forces. Sometimes, by a hasty induction, it is
inferred that what is true of the part must be true of the whole; and
that the process by which a nation is enriched must be identical with
that which enriches an individual. Such, for example, was the fallacy of

the mercantile system, which assumed that, as in simpler times a man's wealth might be measured by the number of coins in his purse, the same test might be applied without modification to a whole community; and such was the still stranger fallacy, which may be called after the name of Mandeville, and which assumed that, as a builder might profit by the burning of his neighbour's house, the fire of London increased the wealth of the nation. A substantially similar fallacy is to be found in the more refined theory of the French economists, who fancy that an increase of exchangeable value is synonymous with an increase of wealth, not perceiving that dearness and cheapness are correlative terms, and that the change supposed implies, not an increase in the total power of the community, but an increased power of one part of it over the rest. And hence, again, arose those ingenious schemes which are in political economy what the perpetual motion is in mechanics. An acute but partially trained intellect may fancy that force can be created as well as directed by machinery, because in the attempt to trace out the complex actions and reactions of a particular mechanism, it may lose sight of some of the modes in which force is distributed. And, similarly, political economy swarms with ingenious methods by which wealth is to be created by some magical process of changing crowns into pounds, and altering the total by shifting the places of the items. To disperse all such fallacies, it is necessary in the first place to reach a point of view from which the general laws regulating the growth and the mutual relations of the industrial organism can be distinctly grasped; and, in the next place, to trace exhaustively the exceedingly complex methods by which their application to particular cases is regulated. The errors of economists arise from assuming too great a simplicity, or losing themselves in the complexity of the actual phenomena, from want of a definite clue or systematic method. They disappear in proportion as a more scientific conception of the study displaces the partial guesses and the hasty assumptions of the earlier enquirers. Economists, accordingly, set out from the conception indicated in the name 'Political Arithmetic;' their study afterwards became a theory of exchange, or, as it has been called, of 'catallactics;' it now claims to be a department of sociology. The growth of the conceptions underlying these different views of the study explains the gradual change of which it has been the subject.

II. The Mercantile Theory.

5. Few reasoners were so perplexed as consciously to adopt the doc-

trine, generally represented to be the pith of the mercantile theory, that wealth consists exclusively in gold and silver. That doctrine, indeed, underlies the theories about the Balance of Trade which exercised a great influence upon the earlier commercial theorists. The origin of the fallacy is not far to seek. Sir William Petty, a singularly ingenious writer, gave to the infant science the significant name of Political Arithmetic. 'By political arithmetic,' says his disciple, Davenant, 'we mean the art of reasoning by figures upon things relating to government.'[1] Political economy, in fact, existed only as a branch of statistics. To determine from such materials as then existed the population of the country, the amount of its rents, of its exports and imports, of the revenues of the State, and of private persons, was a problem of real interest to the statesman; and it was taken for granted that the task of drawing conclusions from these data needed only a skilful accountant, and not a scientific enquirer. Difficulties, indeed, had to be surmounted and fallacies exposed before an accurate balance-sheet could be presented; but it was hardly perceived that the statement would still be unintelligible without a clear conception of those complex social processes, of which the mercantile transactions might be taken as, in some sense, the outward and visible symbol. If we could add up all the accounts of all the individuals of whom the nation was composed, we could deduce a fair statement of the accounts of that aggregate of individuals which we call the nation. And as each individual desires to see a pecuniary balance in his favour, the same test should be satisfactory on the larger scale.

6. Adam Smith refers to Locke as an exponent of the doctrine thus reached; and the form which it takes in Locke's writings shows how it presented itself to a mind of unusual power. His view is given in two treatises upon certain plans for lowering the rate of interest, and 'raising the value of money.' The obnoxious doctrine is there explicitly stated in these words: 'Gold and silver, though they serve for few, yet command all the conveniences of life, and therefore in a plenty of them consist riches.'[2] Smith is so far justified in attributing to Locke a doctrine which scarcely requires any other refutation than a clear statement; a doctrine, indeed, which has become notorious because later economists have found the refutation so easy, that they are fond of imputing it rather too unreservedly to their antagonists. And yet the statement is not only made by a man of Locke's intellectual force, but is associated in his treatise with the vigorous demolition of certain contemporary

[1]Davenant, Works, i. 128.   [2]Locke's Works, iv. 12.

fallacies not more foolish, though less dexterously concealed, than many modern devices for making something out of nothing by a piece of currency legerdemain. Locke shows excellently that the stamp upon metal has no magical efficacy; and that you do not cheat your creditor the less when you give him half the silver you promised, but call your sixpence a shilling. He explains too, very clearly, the futility of various quack devices by which the legislator has often tried to fix prices and rates of interest without altering the social conditions of which the transactions in question are the natural product. He partly anticipates Bentham's assault upon the usury laws; and, though he grasps very imperfectly the mode in which economical forces operate, he speaks of the laws of supply and demand, though not in the modern phraseology, yet with a conviction of the certainty of their operation equal to that of a modern declaimer of economical platitudes. Even whilst sanctioning the confusion between wealth and money, he sees that the absolute quantity of the bullion possessed by a nation does not matter, so long as there is enough for purposes of circulation,[3] though he argues that, as between nations, that will be the richest which has the greatest share of bullion;[4] and therefore, as he infers, the greatest amount of purchasing power. The heaviest purse will incline the balance of wealth towards its proprietor, though the absolute weight in all the purses is a matter of indifference.

7. The source of his error is given in a single phrase. 'A kingdom,' he says, 'grows rich or poor just as a farmer does, and no other way.'[5] The phrase admits of two interpretations; and Locke's error consists in unconsciously identifying them. It is a truth, and a most important truth, that a farmer and a nation both thrive by frugality, industry, and honesty; and, in the long run, thrive in no other way. Locke enforces the doctrine with his usual vigorous sense. All the rigorous laws of Spain, as he observes, could never retain the precious metals in the country; and his reason is, that riches stay only with 'the industrious and frugal.'[6] The moral is admirable, though the test by which it is confirmed is fallacious; and he applies it for the best purpose in assailing the quacks who proposed to enrich the nation by cheating its creditors and playing tricks with its currency instead of stimulating industrious habits. But, unluckily, the doctrine admits of another interpretation. A farmer grows poor, says Locke, if he spends more than he receives; and a nation must grow poorer in the same way. Now, spend-

<hr />

[3]Locke, iv. 48.   [5]Ib. p. 19.
[4]Ib. p. 14.   [6]Ib. p. 72.

ing generally means parting with bullion; and therefore a drain of bullion impoverishes a nation as a constant excess of expenses over receipts would impoverish a farmer. A certain reservoir of money, he thought, was necessary to drive 'the wheels of trade;'[7] and this reservoir was unduly lowered when the stream set into foreign parts. He inverted cause and effect, and failed to perceive the law, afterwards expounded by Hume, in virtue of which the stream would spontaneously find its own level. He was, therefore, haunted by a chimerical fear, resting on the assumption that a drain of bullion implied a diminution of saving. He mistook, that is, the true nature of the phenomenon from a hasty and imperfect analogy. A closer enquiry might have suggested that, even in the farmer's case, saving did not necessarily imply hoarding; and that exchange of bullion for other goods might be a necessary incident of accumulating productive power. But, regarding all expenditure as the antithesis of saving, he took that for a diminution of natural resources which was merely an exchange of superfluous commodities. He did not see that, if the Spaniards had been the most frugal people in the world, they would still have exported the commodity which they produced at the greatest advantage. And therefore he declared that 'spending less' (that is, incurring a smaller debt in money) 'than our own commodities will pay for is the sure and only way for a nation to grow rich.'[8] The error of confounding wealth with money was thus inextricably associated in Locke's mind with the valuable truth which asserts that capital has its origin in saving. The weak and the sound sides of his reasoning become alternately predominant, and he might be quoted by the advocates as well as by the opponents of a sound commercial system.

8. Another form in which the Balance of Trade theory represented itself is given by Charles Davenant, the most conspicuous writer on economical subjects during the first years of the eighteenth century. Davenant, a writer very inferior to Locke in robust common sense, had the equivocal advantage of an official position (he was Inspector-General of exports and imports at the time of his death in 1714), which gave him much acquaintance with the details of commerce. The advantage was equivocal, because it enabled him to lose himself more systematically in statistical labyrinths. Yet Davenant sees through the simpler forms of the fallacy, though he unconsciously slips back so soon as he takes to his ledgers and his tabular returns. He protests steadily against the doctrine, expounded by his antagonist, Pollexfen, that 'gold

[7]Locke, iv. 21.   [8]Ib. iv. 72.

and silver is the only, or most useful, treasure in a nation.'[9] His view
is the inverse. 'Gold and silver,' he says, 'are indeed the measure of
trade, but the spring and original of it in all nations is the natural or
artificial products of the country; that is to say, what their land or
what their labour and industry produces.' Money, he adds, 'is at bottom
no more than the counters with which men in their dealings have been
accustomed to reckon,'[10] and he presently defines wealth in the widest
phase to consist of everything 'which maintains the prince and the general body of his people in plenty, ease, and safety.'[11] Even 'perishable
goods' form part of the national wealth, if convertible, though not converted, into gold and silver.[12] Industry and skill are more truly wealth
than the possession of gold and silver mines. Nay, as it is 'not the taking
in of a great deal of food,' but a 'good digestion and distribution,' that
nourishes the body, so a people may have a surfeit of the precious
metals, if they be not properly assimilated. The nations which have the
most of them, like Persia, may be the poorest; for trade and industry
may produce incomparably more wealth than can be dug out of mines.[13]
Adam Smith could hardly have denounced more pointedly the fundamental fallacy of the mercantile system. And, like Adam Smith,
Davenant infers the general inutility of high duties and prohibitions.[14]
And yet we find him intermingling his sounder views with the most
grotesque fallacies. He estimates, for example, that the Dutch by simply
raising the price of pepper might enjoy an annual income of 2,498,836l.,
and infers that if they monopolised the East India trade they could
'drain the rest of Europe of six millions annually.' If France became
their masters, this vast revenue in the hands of our natural enemies,
'must prove our ruin.'[15] Whatever country enjoyed that trade must
'give laws to the rest of Europe.' And thus the fate of the world hung
upon pepper.

9. Davenant, in fact, is unable to shake off the illusions of the
counting-house. The cash balances must be the barometer which shows
success in trade. His essay upon the East India trade, for example, is
directed against a proposal, which was then very popular, for excluding
Indian silks from the market for the benefit of our manufacturers. Some
of his reasoning is sound enough; such as the argument that we had
better get our silks in exchange for the wool which is our natural
product, than make worse silks by greater labour,[16] or the argument

[9]Davenant's Works, i. 354.   [13]Ib. i. 383.
[10]Ib. i. 355.   [14]Ib. i. 387.
[11]Ib. i. 381.   [15]Ib. i. 123.
[12]Ib. i. 382.   [16]Ib. i. 111.

that to prohibit Indian silk will only lead to our buying dearer silk elsewhere.[17] But he prefers the favourite method of reasoning, which amounted in substance to giving a forged discharge to a forged bond. He tries to prove not that the test of a balance of trade is fallacious, but that it tells upon his side. He admits that the East India trade is on the whole a loss to Europe at large, because we export solid bullion in return for perishable goods.[18] But it is practically impossible, though it might be theoretically desirable, to staunch the drain; whilst, by taking part in the trade, we may contrive to divert into our own coffers some part of the stream of precious metals which flows from the Continent towards the East.[19] In fact, we make up for our own losses by re-exporting some of the Indian goods, and to such purpose that our whole trade produces an annual return of 2,000,000*l*.[20] The various currents of this trade are so mutually interdependent that we cannot venture to cut off any one, which, considered by itself, might appear to involve a loss.

10. By such arguments as these, which long passed current in economical discussions, believers in the Balance of Trade frequently evaded some of the awkward consequences of their own opinions, and even appeared as consistent opponents of prohibition. Merchants easily assumed their own balances to be a sufficient test of the national prosperity, but when the theories thus framed were applied to limit their own dealings and to prevent them from importing the most advantageous articles of commerce, they naturally found more or less ingenious modes of meeting the awkward inference. It was better, they admitted, to import gold than silk; but by some dexterous manipulation it must be shown that the importation of silk would enable them to get more gold. And such arguments had the merit in theory of at least calling attention to the complexity of the commercial operations which it was sought to regulate by rash empirical measures. The stream of gold, it was true, could not be directed hither and thither at the arbitrary pleasure of the legislator. Unluckily, however, there were other questions of more importance in which the merchants' theories coincided only too well with the selfish prejudices of the time. Davenant accepts without hesitation the protectionist theory which justified the English colonial policy. To prevent English merchants from importing what they pleased was a grievance which no abstract theory could be permitted to justify; but a theory which justified restraints upon colonial planters and merchants was doubly welcome. If, he says, the colonies 'fall into the practice of

[17]Davenant, i. 115.   [19]Ib. i. 90, 91.
[18]Ib. i. 90.   [20]Ib. ii. 18, and elsewhere.

trading independently of England, the plantations which now are a main branch of our strength may come to be turned against us.'[21] In a tract on the plantation trade he considers at length our American policy, and some of his political views are enlightened and liberal. He proposes, for example, a scheme for the colonial union which might have placed the imperial relations of the country on a sounder footing.[22] It is his fundamental principle that the colonial trade must be made to centre in England; but there was as yet little danger that the American colonies should rival us in manufactures, which, as he says, are the natural product of a rich and numerous people on a limited territory;[23] and thus, whilst approving the principle that we should not encourage a possible rival, his argument is chiefly directed against excessive restriction.[24] There was, however, a colony nearer to our shores (he argues elaborately that it is rightfully regarded as a colony) in regard to which his policy was narrower and more acceptable. He had gradually, he says, been forced to the conclusion, from which his general dislike to restrictions had for some time withheld him,[25] that England ought to prohibit the exportation of Irish woollens. His reason, given with unconscious effrontery, is simply that Ireland is naturally adapted for the woollen manufacture, and might therefore supplant us in foreign markets.[26] Now, as the balance of our trade depended chiefly upon our exports of woollens, we should thus be ruined for the benefit of Ireland. English capital would speedily flow into that country, and our poverty be coincident with Irish wealth. When the doctrine of the Balance of Trade came into conflict with the immediate interests of the English merchant, it could be evaded under a dexterous manipulation of figures; when it appeared to fall in with his interests, it could sometimes be so manipulated as to conceal its injurious effect upon the rest of the nation, or upon our customers; but when it sanctioned the practice of national robbery, it was put forward most audaciously as a justification for undisguised selfishness. Ireland was to be ruined for the profit of English manufacturers and merchants. A policy begotten of ignorance and rapacity bore its natural fruits before the end of the century both in Ireland and America; and the revolt of the injured was probably more efficacious than the protest of speculative observers.

11. I must, however, confine myself to the speculative opposition to these doctrines. The Balance of Trade theory was confuted by more

---

[21]Davenant, i. 395.   [24]Ib. ii. 37.
[22]Ib. ii. 41.   [25]Ib. ii. 239.
[23]Ib. ii. 22.   [26]Ib. ii. 251, &c.

than one acute reasoner, whose arguments fell dead upon his contemporaries. In the same year with Locke's 'Considerations' appeared a pamphlet by Sir Dudley North, called 'Discourses upon Trade.' It was speedily suppressed, for some reason which does not appear. North's main argument is a significant one, which was afterwards applied more fully by Hume and Tucker. The whole world, he says, may be considered for purposes of trade as a single country. Now, any argument which would be good for limiting trade as between France and England, would be good for limiting it between Yorkshire and Middlesex. If it would be palpable injury to any given town to cut off its intercourse with its neighbours, the injury must be the same in the case of a whole district or nation. This confutation is perfect considered as an *ad hominem* argument; it throws the burden of proof upon those who advocate restriction; and forces them, at least, to mould their reasoning in such a form that it shall not be as applicable to the restrictions which they condemn as to those which they defend. It illustrates, too, the spontaneous disappearance of many commercial fallacies so soon as the field of observation is widened. Look at the restrictions from both sides, and the illusions, generated so long as they are contemplated simply from the merchants' or the national point of view, vanish by the simple change of perspective. North, moreover, adds some very good arguments against the usury laws[27] and other quackery of State influence. Money, he says, is a commodity like any other,[28] and attempts to keep it to ourselves are 'labours to hedge in the cuckoo'[29]—a phrase used in the same connection by Locke in the same year.

12. A still more remarkable argument, however, appeared in the 'Considerations on the East India Trade,' published by an anonymous author[30] in 1701. The singular acuteness displayed in this tract may entitle the writer to the credit of having anticipated the doctrines of a later generation with a clearness very seldom exhibited in any sphere of speculation. It seems as if he required nothing but a greater command of style, a greater confidence in his powers, and a higher estimate of the importance of his speculations, to have anticipated Adam Smith by

[27]'Select Tracts,' p. 522.   [28]Ib. p. 528.   [29]Ib. p. 542; Locke, iv. 17.

[30]Mr. M'Culloch suggests—though he admits that it is a mere guess—that the author may have been a Mr. Henry Martyn, who wrote a paper or two in the 'Spectator.' As Martyn was a contributor to the 'British Merchant,' which was meant to support the very principles confuted by the author of the tract, the conjecture seems to be very doubtful (see Chalmers's biographical preface to the 'Spectator,' and M'Culloch's introductory discourse to the 'Wealth of Nations,' p. xxxv).

just three-quarters of a century. He is not content with the sufficiently conclusive argument advanced by North, but takes the further and more difficult step of thoroughly working out the mode in which Free Trade operates. Beneath the fallacy of the balance of trade and the identification of money and wealth lay another fallacy, apparently more transparent, and yet so obstinately persistent, that its roots must clearly strike very deep in the minds of most observers. The fallacy is that which was made celebrated by Mandeville, or the assumption that the more labour is required to produce a given quantity, the greater will be the 'demand' for it, and therefore the greater the amount of wages paid to labourers in general. The argument of North implicitly recognises the fact that the value of Free Trade consists essentially in increasing the general efficiency of human labour. It tends to the best distribution of the forces of the race by encouraging each nation to devote itself to producing the articles in which it has the greatest advantage. But even whilst admitting this truth, most writers, till a much later period, and many at the present day, allow the old fallacy to reappear. For one moment they reach an elevation from which they can contemplate the planet as a whole, and at the next moment their vision is confined to the horizon visible from an English shop-window. They cannot bear some of the corollaries, though they can assert the general proposition. Commerce, they admit in general terms, implies a reciprocity of advantages; but in each particular case they fancy that one side must lose and the other gain. That both sides to a bargain should be gainers sounds like a silly paradox. Commerce is regarded not as the means by which forces may be redistributed, and therefore applied more efficaciously, but as the shifting of a burden from one side to the other.

13. At the root of the whole system of fallacies lies a confusion between the true relations of exchange and production—a confusion which, as we shall presently see, the French economist endeavoured unsuccessfully to clear up. There is a vague conviction that to destroy the demand for any particular commodity is to destroy the demand for the labour which produces it, instead of to alter the distribution of the national energy. It is not perceived that the capital employed constitutes the demand for labour, and that it need not, in the long run, be diminished when a change is effected in its application, which makes labour, in general, more efficient. Foreign commerce, in short, is taken for a process of direct nutrition or waste, when its real character is a reciprocation of advantages which indirectly facilitates nutrition. The removal of restrictions is regarded as analogous to the opening of a sluice which enables the wealth accumulated on one side to drain

off to the lower levels, instead of being analogous to the removal of a ligature which facilitates the process of nutrition on both sides. The confusion might be abundantly illustrated from the writings of many authors who could at times grasp the general principle. Thus, for example, a later advocate of Free Trade, Dean Tucker, who fully appreciates North's argument, begins his first tract upon the trade between England and France, published about 1750, by this curious inversion of argument. If, he says, 10,000 people in England make goods for the French, and 40,000 Frenchmen make goods for England, we must pay the 30,000 French in gold and silver, 'that is, be at the charge of maintaining them.' 'This,' he goes on to say, 'is the clearest and justest method of determining the balance between nation and nation; for though a difference in the value of the respective commodities may make some difference in the sums actually paid to balance accounts, yet the general principle, that labour, not money, is the riches of a people, will always prove that the advantage is on the side of the nation which has most hands employed in labour.'[31] The conclusion of this ingenious and often sound thinker is, therefore, that a nation will be richer in proportion to the amount of labour employed on a given product, which is, in fact, nothing else than Mandeville's doctrine that the fire of London was useful, because it caused a demand for labour; and which would make it an advantage to turn our fields into a wilderness, and grow cotton in England in defiance of the climate.

14. The fallacy, though so palpable in such extreme conclusions, is, as I have said, one of the most persistent in Political Economy, and it is important to notice it in view of some theories still to be considered. Meanwhile, it is the special merit of the anonymous author of the 'Considerations' that he exposes it thoroughly and irrefutably. He had to meet the inference that the manufacture of English silk would be destroyed by the admission of Indian silk. Most writers, like Davenant, tried to shirk this difficulty, or to meet it by erroneous reasons. The author shows that the apparent injury really meant nothing more than the diversion of labour to functions which it could more efficiently discharge. Not only does he show this conclusively, and meet all the objections which could be suggested, but he is led to explain the advantages of machinery and of the organisation of labour. His illustration, taken from the many processes involved in watchmaking, is as clear and striking as Adam Smith's pins, and the few errors which are mixed with his sound arguments are not more conspicuous than in the case of

[31]'Tracts of Pol. Economy Club,' p. 315.

his greater successor. No economical writer of the century showed more of that power of close reasoning which is so admirably displayed in the writings of Ricardo. Unfortunately, the oblivion in which his name and essay are buried is a sufficient proof of the futility of clear argument when brought into conflict with the sheer stupidity and selfishness of mankind.

15. Between the time of Davenant and the time of Adam Smith, various writers, of more or less ability, dealt with economical questions; but none of them worked out a general theory of sufficient coherence to make an epoch in the study. There is a mixture of palpable error with occasional glimpses of sounder principles. An essay, for example, upon the 'Doctrine of Foreign Trade,' published in 1750 by a Mr. Richardson, and erroneously attributed by Adam Smith to Sir Matthew Decker, has been noticed for its unqualified demonstration of the evils of monopoly generally. Yet it begins with a statement of the Balance of Trade theory, and is full of economical errors. Franklin, in whom the acuteness of the philosopher was curiously blended with the cunning of the trader, has left some keen remarks upon the evils of protection.[32] He adopts the formula said by him to have been used by some French merchants to Colbert: *Laissez-vous faire* (*sic*);[33] but in the same breath he adduces a palpable fallacy in favour of a system of bounties.[34] In a few essays devoted to economical questions Hume shows his usual perspicuity. He was little likely to be deluded by the gross sophistry, or seduced by the narrow prejudices, of the supporters of the mercantile system. His point of view was too elevated, and his logical sensibility too acute, for him to sanction blunders worthy of a tradesman in a country town. He saw with perfect clearness, and explained with admirable precision, that domestic commerce meant simply an 'intercourse of good offices' between the different classes of a people, and the different districts which were fitted by nature to supply each other's wants.[35] The principle was as applicable to nations as to provinces. The mercantile theory, in prescribing the accumulation of money as an ultimate end, aimed at a result as chimerical as the attempt to heap up water above the proper level.[36] From such principles, he says, 'we may learn what judgment we ought to form of those numberless bars, obstructions, and imposts, which all nations of Europe, and none more than England, have put

[32] See *e.g.* 'Note Respecting Trade and Manufactures' (Works, vi. 61), which is identical nearly with an argument in Richardson's tract ('Scarce Tracts,' p. 255).

[33] Franklin, vi. 87.   [35] Hume's Works, iii. 324, 'Interest.'

[34] Ib. vi. 88.   [36] Ib. iii. 333, 'Balance of Trade.'

upon trade from an exorbitant desire of amassing money which will never heap up beyond its proper level whilst it circulates; or from an ill-founded apprehension of losing their specie, which will never sink below it. Could anything scatter our riches, it would be such absurd contrivances. The general ill effect, however, results from them that they deprive neighbouring nations of that free communication and exchange which the Author of the world has intended by giving them souls, climates, and geniuses so different from each other.'[37] He denounces the silly jealousy to which these restrictions pandered; and ventures to acknowledge that 'not only as a man but as a British subject' he prays 'for the flourishing commerce of Germany, Spain, Italy, and even France itself. I am at least certain,' he adds, 'that Great Britain and all those nations would flourish more did their sovereigns and ministers adopt such enlarged and benevolent sentiments towards each other.'[38]

16. Even Hume had not emancipated himself from some characteristic errors. He has an odd impression, though nobody had explained so clearly the true functions of money, that a State ought to aim at keeping its cash on the increase.[39] He could see the effect, that is, of rising prices in stimulating production, whilst the effect on discouraging demand escaped his notice. Similarly, whilst attacking the Balance of Trade theory, he is yet in favour of some protective duties.[40] His keen insight required to be corrected and checked by the general principles which only revealed themselves on a more systematic treatment of the whole subject. But, in spite of these errors, Hume's acute remarks, appearing, as they did, in his most successful book, should have dissipated some of the prejudices which he asserted had never been governed in such matters by reason. It may, indeed, be taken for granted that they had a considerable effect upon Adam Smith, who is said to have taught similar doctrines at Glasgow in 1753, the year, that is, after the publication of these essays. Smith speaks of Hume with affectionate reverence, and must have been confirmed, if not indoctrinated, in the new principles by the authority of his master.

17. One writer already mentioned demands some further notice before we pass to a different school. The doctrine of Free Trade was generally associated with the new philosophy of the time. Prohibition was not merely injurious economically, but was an infringement of the rights of man. Yet one sturdy opponent of the new ideas must be reckoned

---

[37]Hume, iii. 343.   [39]Ib. iii. 315, 'Money.'
[38]Ib. iii. 348, 'Jealousy of Trade.'   [40]Ib. iii. 344, 'Balance of Trade.'

amongst its advocates. Josiah Tucker was given to odd combinations of theory. Nature had designed him for a shrewd tradesman; fate had converted him into a clergyman. His residence at Bristol, then the second city in the kingdom, had stimulated his commercial tendencies. He was chosen by one of the tutors of George III. to write a treatise called the 'Elements of Commerce and Theory of Taxes,' for the instruction of the heir to the throne. He found, however, that his principles were not adapted for the shelter of royal patronage; and he could have had few less promising pupils for the reception of new ideas. Tucker, however, pursued his studies; and Warburton spitefully said of him that the Dean's trade was his religion, and religion his trade. There was enough truth in the epigram to make it stinging, but there seems to have been nothing sordid in Tucker's character. If his religion was not of the most spiritual kind, he was at least honest and independent. Objecting to North's plan for raising an American revenue, he says, in a pamphlet addressed to Burke, 'I trust you will have more generosity than to tell the Prime Minister that this is my opinion; lest he should deny me a bishopric, which you say I am aiming at; and which certainly is not likely to be obtained by this mode of proceeding.'[41] Burke's insinuation,[42] indeed, seems to have been rather unjust; for Tucker's arguments exposed him to the contempt of Johnson,[43] as decidedly as they brought him into conflict with Franklin, Priestley, and Burke himself. Adopting in politics Johnson's sound Tory view, and bitterly ridiculing the rights of man, he agreed on the other hand with Paine's revolutionary view that America ought to be at once declared independent. The consummation, indeed, which the Americans regarded as a privilege to be won was regarded by him as a punishment to be inflicted. His economic argument, in fact, is given in a single phrase, which has since become proverbial. What are we to gain, he asks, by conquering America? 'Not an increase in trade; that is impossible; for a shopkeeper will never get the more custom by beating his customers, and what is true of a shopkeeper is true also of a shopkeeping nation.'[44] A parallel argument appears in Adam Smith. 'To found a great empire for the sole purpose of raising up a people of customers may, at first sight, appear a project fit only for a nation of shopkeepers. It is, however, a project altogether unfit for a nation of shopkeepers, though extremely fit for a nation whose government is influenced by shopkeepers.'[45]

[41]'Letter to Burke,' p. 52.   [44]Tucker's Works, ii. 132 (written in 1766).
[42]Burke's Works, ii. 413.   [45]'Wealth of Nations,' i. 276.
[43]Johnson, viii. 200.

Tucker, indeed, was rather too much of the shopkeeper; though shrewd enough to see and to expose with great clearness the folly of the war, even when regarded from that point of view. A war for commerce between different parts of the same empire was as absurd as a war between Manchester and Norwich,[46] and he declared that 'our posterity may regard the present madness of going to war for the sake of trade, riches, or dominion, with the same eye of astonishment and pity that we see the madness of our forefathers in fighting under the peaceful Cross to recover the Holy Land.'[47] Our trade will be carried on just so long as we can offer the Americans the best market, and no longer, and will therefore be independent of political connection.[48] He answers the taunt about trade and religion by the very fair argument that a system of universal commerce is the plain teaching of the divine constitution of the world.[49] Almighty Providence has made different nations to supply each other's wants instead of cutting each other's throats; and therefore to preach Free Trade is to preach pure Christianity.

18. Tucker is everywhere a shrewd writer, and he discusses many economical problems in the same general spirit. He is, indeed, rather intricate in his reasoning, and a hot-headed conservatism does not blend very felicitously with his commercial liberalism. He blunders a good deal in his theories about population,[50] regarding an increase of numbers as the proper end of a statesman—to be pursued by such doubtful methods as a tax upon bachelors[51]—and emigration as simply a pernicious drain. But he is full of acute remarks, and may be credited with the rare glory of having made a political prophecy which was actually fulfilled. In half a century, he says, writing in 1774, two great and right measures will have been adopted—a separation from America 'and a union with Ireland;' and perhaps that which happens to be first accomplished 'will greatly accelerate the accomplishment of the other.'[52] Tucker stood too much apart from all parties to receive much credit for his perspicuity; but he lived long enough to see one prediction verified and the other on the verge of verification.

19. An elaborate 'Enquiry Concerning the Principles of Political Economy' (1766), by Sir James Steuart, requires a word of recognition, as probably the most elaborate attempt which had hitherto been made to give a systematic account of economical principles. Steuart is a candid,

---

[46]Tucker's Works, ii. 68.
[47]Ib. ii. 89.
[48]Ib. ii. 200.
[49]See 'Two Sermons.'
[50]E.g. Tract iv. 214.
[51]'Select Tracts,' p. 404.
[52]Tucker's Works, ii. 214.

patient, and original thinker; on some topics, such as population,[53] he anticipates later writers; and he is not wanting in logical ingenuity. On the other hand, his style is awkward and his method intricate. He becomes hopelessly confused by the complexity of his subject-matter; and argues himself into elaborate blunders in attempting to refute Hume's lucid and satisfactory account of money and the balance of trade. He is, therefore, amongst the most tiresome individuals of that most tiresome of all literary species—the inferior political economists. He is interesting only as a product of the two chief schools of economical speculation. Having been more or less involved in the rebellion of 1745, he was forced to pass many years in France and elsewhere. He employed himself in studying social questions, and was obviously much impressed by the French writers. From them he learnt to take a wider view of the study than was common amongst the English rivals, and to go beyond questions of trade into more important questions of social welfare. On the other hand, instead of imitating their logical simplicity, or adopting their conception of a fixed social order, he exaggerates the ordinary complexity of the mercantile theories, and believes implicitly in the indefinite modifiability of mankind. The 'statesman,' according to him, is not only to direct hither and thither the flow of commerce according to very erroneous principles, but to mould the character and regulate the social organisation of his subjects. Thus, though he breaks ground upon many important questions, he rather perplexes than clears the subject; and we may pass, without further notice of his conclusions, to the school from which he, like Adam Smith, received a powerful impulse.

III. The French Economists.

20. Writings, such as those which I have noticed, show that the simple principle of Free Trade lay but one degree removed from the sight of unprejudiced observers. Cosmopolitans, like Hume and Franklin, and shrewd reasoners, like the worthy Dean Tucker, could disperse many of the fallacies, though they could not quite shake off the inveterate prepossessions of the time. Political economy had become in their hands something more than a branch of statistics, though it was not yet more than a theory of commerce. No attempt had been made to solve some

---

[53]*E.g.* Works, i. 24. 'Thus the generative faculty resembles a spring loaded with a weight, which always exerts itself in proportion to the diminution of resistance,' &c. See also i. 201, 208, &c.

of the deeper problems of social organisation. Here and there the sound sense of men, like De Foe or Franklin, had called attention to such questions as the effect of poor-laws upon population. Their remarks, however, are rather specimens of good homely morality than of scientific reasoning. The advantages of frugality and independence, and the evil effects of paying people to be paupers, are fortunately perceptible without any deep scientific theory. The very notion of discussing, in a scientific spirit, such questions as the relation between labourers and capitalists, which are incomparably the most important topics with which economists can deal, had not yet dawned upon the economical speculators. Now it is impossible to frame a satisfactory theory of trade between nations without understanding the industrial organisation of the nations themselves. The disturbance produced in a nation by the opening or closing of a foreign trade can only be traced when we begin to appreciate the general conditions of the production of wealth. A discussion of the effects of protection naturally led, as we have seen, to an investigation of the perplexing question as to the real effect of different forms of expenditure. By what process and to what extent did foreign trade really enrich a nation? Was it an advantage to a people to get perishable materials in exchange for solid gold? Was it an advantage that many labourers should be employed in producing a commodity at home instead of a few in raising the materials which could be exchanged for the same amount abroad? Such questions inevitably suggested themselves; and most writers shrank from the difficult task of answering them satisfactorily. Hume glided over the subject with suspicious lightness, and able advocates of Free Trade, like Tucker, fell into gross errors in dealing with such knotty points. A school, however, was rising which endeavoured to supply an answer to such difficulties, and whose endeavours, though not supplying a satisfactory theory, for the first time led to the conception of political economy as a theory of social organisation instead of a mere generalisation of mercantile maxims.

21. The French school of economists struck out a doctrine remarkable for its ingenuity and simplicity, and for a logical symmetry which covered some radical confusion of ideas. It was expounded by a number of able writers, such as Quesnay, its inventor, the elder Mirabeau, and especially by Turgot, who tried to carry some of its teachings into practice. Turgot's treatise, 'Reflections on the Formation and Distribution of Wealth,' was called by Condorcet the germ of Smith's 'Wealth of Nations;' and, though the justice of the name may be disputed, it is at least a compendious statement of principles by which Smith was materially influenced. The French economists illustrate the general tendency

of their nation, and of the school of thought to which they belonged, to frame a coherent and over-rigid logical system. They aimed at the discovery of a few simple formulæ which should determine the industrial relations, as the dogmas about the rights of man determined the political relations, of mankind. The cumbrous system of restrictions by which statesmen of the Colbert school had sought to regulate industry were to be superseded by a few clear laws, framed on a rational basis, as the old political order was to give place to a symmetrical constitution based upon principles of abstract justice. In England, reformers found themselves in conflict with an apparatus of tariffs and navigation laws produced by commercial jealousy. In France, the new school had to attack a series of regulations by which the internal development of the country was hindered and trammelled. The French economists naturally inclined to a system which traced all national wealth to agriculture, as the English writers were inclined to assume that foreign commerce was the only mode by which a nation could acquire wealth. In England, speculation confined itself almost exclusively to the interests of the foreign merchant. The French economic theories were the work of men who had before them a highly centralised government, and whose aim it was to simplify the administrative system. They opposed cumbrous restrictions, but were generally of absolutist tendencies, for the central power was to be invoked in order to overpower the obstacles of local prejudice and corrupt interest. The direction of their enquiries towards an investigation of the primary sources of wealth rather than the mere ebb and flow of foreign trade, their intellectual tendencies and their position in a centralised government, encouraged them to treat the subject on a more systematic method, and to raise profounder questions than those which occupied their English contemporaries. We are in presence of men who are not merely treating upon some external conditions of commercial prosperity, but have their fingers upon the main arteries through which the life-blood of the country is propelled from the centre to the extremities. They are not asking whether the ports should be open to more or less silk and tobacco, but what is the nature and distribution of the wealth by which the whole nation is supported.

22. There is—such is their most fundamental and valuable proposition—a certain natural order of society, independent of all legislation, and the recognition of which is the essential condition of all sound legislation. The 'Natural and Essential Order of all Political Societies' is the title of a treatise published by Lemercier de la Rivière in 1767; and the same doctrine is assumed, though less pretentiously expressed,

in all their writings. To explain this order we must determine what is the true nature of the various industrial functions of the social organism. For, as they saw, the complexity of modern society had, in fact, given rise to the most complete misconceptions of the real tendency of many operations. Political economy, as I have said, begins with the division of labour, and the consequent differentiation of classes; and Turgot, like Adam Smith, begins his treatise by pointing out the nature of this process. But so soon as the various functions are distributed amongst different classes, it becomes easy to misunderstand their true nature. Hasty observers had confounded operations productive of national and of merely personal wealth—between labour which adds to the total amount of valuable articles existing in the world, and labour which only enables a man to appropriate part of the wealth which would have existed without him. One form of this confusion, as we have seen, was the fallacy connected in England with the name of Mandeville. In France, the contrast between the luxurious or profligate expenditure of the government and the upper classes, and the poverty of the producers of wealth, had made the problem one of vital interest. Was the rich consumer really a benefit to the country? Who were to be rightfully regarded as mere parasites upon society, and who as contributors to its resources? If in some cases the line could be easily drawn, in others the question presented a real complexity. In an estimate of the national wealth, to count both the revenue of the master and that of the menial servant who depended upon him would obviously be to count the same portion twice over. To avoid such errors it was desirable to mark off the different classes of labour as unmistakably as possible. Practical consequences of immense importance would result from a clear theory. We may regard the national revenues as a reservoir which is being constantly filled and then flowing through innumerable channels to each of the numerous units of which society is composed. We have to distinguish between the perennial springs which fill the reservoir and the streams by which it is steadily drained. To solve this problem is to discover the natural order of society. The system of taxation had hitherto—so the economists taught—been grounded upon a false anatomy. The simplest and best plan would have been to draw the needed supplies directly from the head fountain. The actual practice was to collect them by driblets from the channels through which the wealth afterwards percolated. The plan involved not merely a cumbrous machinery, but an injurious system of vexatious restrictions. All manner of sluices and stops had to be provided to facilitate the collection of taxes; subsidiary interests were set up conflicting with the true interests of the nation,

and illusory theories invented to justify arbitrary interference with the
natural order. To sweep away the whole system, to leave the greatest
possible liberty to the natural development of industry, to take away the
grasp of the tax-gatherer from the minute vessels of circulation, and to
send him directly to the original sources of wealth, was the object of
the economists. Such an attempt indicates an advance in the philosophical conception of the study, as it harmonised naturally with their other
theories of a philosophical reconstruction of the political order. Unluckily their method was still erroneous, and the error which vitiated
Quesnay's arguments was indorsed with curious unanimity by his able
followers.

23. What is the distinction, they asked, between productive and un-
productive, or, as Quesnay called it, 'sterile' labour? The answer seemed
to follow from some obvious reflections. Political economy begins with
the division of labour: the division of labour implies exchange of the
products of labour; and an article which is exchangeable is said to have
value. Political economy, then, must be the science of value, value
being the common quality of all the objects with which it deals. But in
this simple theory there already lurks a fallacy. One of Adam Smith's
most important remarks consists in the distinction between intrinsic
value and exchangeable value. The worth of anything, according to one
definition, is what it will fetch; its worth, according to the other, depends upon the number and importance of wants which it will supply.
Things which have the highest value in one sense may have the lowest
in the other. Air, according to the familiar illustration, has no exchange
value, because everybody can get as much as he wants; and has the
highest intrinsic value, because nobody can do without it. The two conceptions are radically distinct, though most intimately connected; and a
theory of political economy which neglects the distinction must be defective in essential points. The French economists constantly overlook the
difference, and the error is characteristic of the stage of speculation. The
economists had seen through the vulgar fallacy which identified wealth
with money. Gold and silver, they perceived, were merely articles of
commerce, and formed but an insignificant item in the whole wealth
of a nation. But when for money they had substituted the abstract conception, value, the statement, though apparently more philosophical,
and leading to very simple conclusions, was still tainted by the old fallacy.
An increase of value, like an increase of money, might be significant not
of a real increase of national resources, but of an increased power of
one part of the community over another. The French reasoners had
ceased to regard the world through the eyes of shopkeepers. They had

not yet risen to a thoroughly scientific point of view. A complete sociology, in fact, would exhibit the relations of different parts of the organism as ultimately determined by the external conditions to which it is subject, or, in other words, by the mode in which the wants of men must derive satisfaction from the external world. It must, that is, take into account the intrinsic, as ultimately determining the exchange, values of commodities. Men who regard political economy not as a branch of sociology, but as a theory of 'catallactics,' implicitly assume that it is unnecessary to look outside of the organism itself to determine the conditions of exchange. They, therefore, take the relative term to have an absolute value; and hold that the value, which is merely an index of the difficulty of obtaining a certain useful commodity, is a sort of inherent quality, indicative of a certain natural 'pre-eminence' of that commodity over others.

24. The confusion manifests its nature so soon as we endeavour to determine a law of value from this conception. Turgot, for example, states with perfect clearness that theory of the relation of supply and demand which had been given in his own phraseology by Locke, and which is, in fact, nothing but a generalisation of the familiar truth, known in the days of Joseph, that scarcity and plenty correspond to dearness and cheapness. The inadequacy of the statement to supply a true law of price is obvious from a simple consideration. The formula, in fact, that price must equalise supply and demand gives a condition of equilibrium, but does not fix the point at which equilibrium will be established. It tells us that, given a certain demand, the supply and the price will regulate themselves accordingly; but it does not help us to determine what the demand will be under any given circumstances. To solve this problem we have to take into account another order of conditions, and, in fact, to consider the intrinsic value of the various commodities under consideration. We must pass, that is, from the 'catallactic' to the sociological point of view. Locke, for example, had already pointed out the very important fact that a diminution of supply would generally raise the price of necessaries more than the price of luxuries.[1] Since everybody must have bread and water, the effect of straitening the supplies will be much more conspicuous in such cases than in the case of some luxury with which men can dispense at the cost of a little vanity instead of actual starvation. The remark leads the way to a whole series of observations, which lie beyond the sphere of pure catallactics.

[1] Locke, iv. 31. See the same principle well stated by Sir J. Steuart, i. 388, and elsewhere.

We have to examine the limitations imposed upon the growth of a given population by the limits of its territory, the alterations of its internal constitution by the appropriation of certain parts of that territory, the varying difficulty of raising different kinds of produce, and, in short, to solve a number of problems which imply that the doctrines of Smith already require to be supplemented by those of Malthus and Ricardo.

25. In the absence of any clear perception of this want, the French economists seem to be studying the action of the several forces without considering them as limited by a certain base of operations. They seem to assume that the internal laws of growth may be treated satisfactorily apart from any reference to the medium from which it derives its existence. Thus the organism appears to be, so to speak, in the air, and capable of extending with equal facility in every direction. Hence follows the peculiar dogma with which their name is generally associated. Locke and Davenant[2] had thrown out the opinion that all taxes fall ultimately upon the land. In their writings this merely indicated a vague perception of the solidarity of all industrial interests, and an impression that, as land was in some sense the basis of all wealth, and the ownership of land the base of political power, the landowners must be affected by every burden imposed upon other classes. By the French economists the doctrine was worked into the foundation of a system. They tacitly assume that the distinction between productive and 'sterile' labour coincided with the distinction between labour which did or did not add value to its products. Taking value in the sense of utility, the definition might coincide sufficiently with that sanctioned by later writers. But the confusion already indicated vitiates their application of the test. Commerce, for example, appeared to them to be non-productive. The condition of exchange is equality of value; if we should not rather say that equality of value means that articles will exchange for each other. Commerce, then, cannot possibly add to value, or, in other words, is sterile. The error, it may be remarked, is the converse of that involved in the mercantile system. The English writers assumed that, as commerce was the only means by which a nation without mines could get money, it was the only means by which such a nation could gain the wealth which was identical with money. It followed that commerce was profitable only to the party which got most money, that is to say, to which the balance of trade inclined. The French economists, seeing that it was as advantageous to get money's worth as to get money, pro-

[2]Locke, iv. 55; Davenant, i. 77, 269.

nounced commerce to be profitable to neither party. The true theory, of course, is that commerce is useful to both parties, because by putting things where they are wanted it increases the efficiency of labour. The economists, indeed, admitted that commerce was in some sense useful, and should not be restricted; but, blinded by their prepossessions, they failed to see that the labour by which men weave bread on their looms, or hammer it on their anvils, may really increase the returns to labour as distinctly as the process by which they dig it out of the ground.

26. Commerce was thus regarded as analogous to the labour of menial servants, or as a mode of expenditure rather than a mode of production. At the opposite extreme was labour applied to land. Here it seemed there was an absolute creation of value. The seed was converted into bread partly by human labour, but partly also by the co-operation of natural forces. The part played by the earth and the air was more conspicuous than the analogous service rendered by natural forces in manufacturing operations. The substance, as well as the forces, seemed to be altered. A certain quantity of corn being inserted into the social mill, three times as much comes out at the other end; but when a raw mass of iron is inserted, the same mass comes out changed in shape alone. As the direct products of the earth are essential to all men, it seemed that, in this respect too, agriculture had a certain natural 'pre-eminence' over other forces of industry. And the proof of these propositions lay in the really important fact, that the price of agricultural products supported two classes, both the actual labourers and the landlord, who contributes nothing directly to the result. The existence of the 'unearned increment' of rent, so frequently discussed by later economists, was thus recognised, though the explanation given implies a curious inversion of later theories. The supposed pre-eminence really indicates a defect rather than an excellence. In fact, the agriculturist depends upon the labour of other classes as they depend upon his. They co-operate in a total result, and though the intrinsic importance of the wants which they supply may be different, any attempt to measure the importance by the exchange value of products is necessarily illusory. Rent, in fact, is merely the result of a partial monopoly, the most important of all monopolies, but not specifically different from others in its operation. The economists, regarding value as a kind of inherent quality, comparable to a chemical property of the products exchanged, attributed to some natural peculiarity what they would have seen on a closer analysis to be merely a result of the limited quantity of fertile land. In other words, they thought that a flow of the stream of wealth in

one direction signified, not the existence of a certain obstacle, but a positive increase in its volume.

27. Here, then, in Turgot's language, was a 'disposable' revenue, a fund differing in kind from the wealth of other classes, and representing, in fact, the reservoir from which all others were supplied. Some difficulty was felt in regard to other parts of the national revenues. The artisan, like the merchant, might be regarded as a menial servant, simply paid for his labour, though his wages took the form of payment for its products. The profits of the capitalist might seem to be part of the disposable revenue; but, after explaining with great clearness the mode in which capital is produced, and the services which it renders, Turgot finds a reason for denying that its profits are fairly to be called disposable. He argues, as Locke and North had already argued, and as Bentham afterwards argued with greater completeness, and from a more purely utilitarian point of view, that the interest paid for money should be determined by the will of the parties without State interference. Now, a revenue with which the State may not tamper is not to be called disposable. The test thus accepted seems to be different from the one previously applied, but its meaning is sufficiently obvious. Turgot, in fact, saw more or less distinctly that the owner of the land enjoyed a monopoly, whilst the capitalist is exposed to free competition; and hence it follows that the State might appropriate parts of the rent of land without setting up any ulterior action; whereas, an interference with the free play of competition will necessarily propagate its effects to classes not immediately affected. The distinction rests upon a real difference; and though it cannot be easily brought into harmony with other parts of the system, it shows that Turgot, at any rate, sometimes approximated very nearly to the theory of rent as established by later English writers.

28. It would, however, be out of place to enquire into the details of a system, the general tendencies of which are sufficiently apparent. The French economists, whatever their errors, had impressed an entirely new character upon the study. For a series of detached, though often acute, speculations upon the nature of commerce, they had substituted a coherent theory of the industrial aspect of society. They had recognised the necessity of studying the social organism as a whole instead of attempting explanations of detached series of phenomena. They had shown how intimately the interests of different classes were connected, and had even exaggerated the certainty and rapidity with which any action upon one part of the body politic would be transmitted to others.

Their misconceptions, indeed, had led them to state this principle in far too absolute and one-sided a fashion. The doctrine that all taxes must fall upon land is, of course, a very crude solution of a highly complex problem, and overlooks a whole series of intricate reciprocal actions. Indeed, an excessive love of logical simplicity and symmetry gave some plausibility to the popular objection that their doctrine was rather theoretical than practical. That accusation, though often meaningless enough, rested in this case upon a real weakness. In their anxiety to frame a premature synthesis, they overlooked too much the necessity of checking their speculations by constant reference to facts. Confident in the conclusions to which they had leaped, they did not condescend to trace out the process by which the phenomena would be brought to correspond with the general laws enunciated. A more careful analysis was necessary before theory could be brought into due contact with observation; and it was the great work of Adam Smith to apply this essential correction. Meanwhile the economists deserve the glory of having recognised the existence of a certain natural social order, the comprehension of which was an essential preliminary to intelligent interference. If they drew their lines rather too sharply, and conceived of society as bound by a kind of rigid geometrical order rather than as promoting the complex relations of vital growth, they at least gave prominence for the first time to a conception which must underlie all sound social theories. They applied it chiefly to justify the widest application of Free Trade principles; and were thus brought into direct collision with the chief commercial prejudices of the time. For a brief period they succeeded in influencing the administration of the country, and thus gave the first important example of the relation of scientific principles to actual legislation.

IV. Adam Smith.

29. Adam Smith passed a year in France in 1765–66. He there made the acquaintance of many of the new school, and especially of Turgot and of Quesnay, the author of the economist system. To Quesnay he owed intellectual obligations, which would have been acknowledged by a dedication of the 'Wealth of Nations,' had not the French philosopher died before its appearance. For ten years after his return, Smith devoted himself to solitary study at Kirkcaldy. In 1776 the result of his labours appeared; welcomed by all intelligent contemporaries, and described long afterwards by an eloquent panegyrist as 'probably the most im-

portant book which has even been written.'[1] We shall, perhaps, be slow
to agree with that enthusiastic phrase, when we remember one or two
other masterpieces of the human intellect. We may, however, admit
that no more important book than the 'Wealth of Nations' was published in Great Britain during the last half of the eighteenth century.
Few writers have ever done for any study what Smith did for Political
Economy. If he did not found a science, he brought a great body of
theory into close relation with facts, and may be said to have first
brought about a union between abstract reasoners and practical statesmen. To marry science to practice is the great problem of politics; and
from the appearance of the 'Wealth of Nations' the main outlines and
the chief methods of one important branch of political science were
distinctly marked out. Much had been done, and much still remained
to do; but Smith took the significant step, and is rightly regarded as the
intellectual ancestor of a race of theorists, whose influence, though not
uniformly beneficial, has at least been of great importance towards constituting the still rudimentary science of sociology.

30. The peculiar merits of the 'Wealth of Nations' may appear from
this point of view. If the value of a book be measured simply by the
number of definite propositions which it states for the first time, we
should find some difficulty in assigning a very high place to Smith's
great work. He was by no means the first author to expose the fallacies
of the mercantile theories; he was not the first to advocate complete
freedom of trade, and to trace the evil influence of commercial restrictions. He did not discover the true nature of rent, or state with any
completeness the laws of population, or detect the relation between price
and the cost of production; and the formulæ which express those
theories may be said to lie at the base of the modern doctrine of Political Economy. If at frequent intervals he catches a glimpse of the doctrines expounded more fully by his successors, it is still true that any
adequate commentator upon the 'Wealth of Nations' would have to
pause at every chapter to point out erroneous assumptions and arguments, the fallacy of which has been explained by his successors. But
Smith's vast superiority to all who previously treated of the subject, and
even in some respects to all who have treated of it since his day, is still
unquestionable. He differs from his English predecessors by completing
and correcting their detached remarks, and by mapping out, though not
with complete accuracy, a vast field of enquiry, of which they had only
examined a few detached fragments. He differs from the French econo-

[1] Buckle's 'Civilisation,' i. 194, ii. 443.

mists, not merely by pointing out some of their fallacies, but, more conspicuously, by tracing out in detail the operation of the laws which they had summarily described in far too absolute a fashion. He differs from both in the vast variety and extent of the information which he brings to bear upon the problems discussed. Nothing is more remarkable in the book than the fertility of illustration and the immense stores of knowledge which it embodies. It was inevitable that he should sometimes commit the error, common to all economists, of laying too much stress upon the economical aspect of phenomena which cannot be adequately understood without calling in the aid of considerations of a higher order. We see that everything which he observes, from the Christian Church to a passing shoeblack, suggests to him some association with supply and demand. But his remarks upon the historical development of societies, upon the condition of contemporary European affairs, upon the industrial circumstances of the British Empire, and upon the minuter facts which had come within his own observation, show a mind of extraordinary width and ingenuity, well able to master a vast accumulation of materials, always dwelling upon them with a lively desire to discover their lessons, and able to expound those lessons in the most effective manner.

31. Comparing Smith with the French economists, one might be inclined to say that his merit lay in substituting an inductive method for *a priori* theorising. The statement would be inaccurate; for, as is often remarked, the vast complexity of the phenomena under consideration prevents a direct application of simple induction. But Smith fully appreciates, and it is one of his chief merits, the part which should be assigned to actual experience in such enquiries. He invariably tests the general theories by their application to particular facts, and avoids many of the errors produced by a too great facility in admitting convenient assumptions. He never takes leave of the solid ground in his most daring flights. Every general maxim is stated in language applicable to cases of actual occurrence. And, therefore, in the hands of Adam Smith, Political Economy passed from the professor's study to the market-place and the exchange. Men who were indifferent to general demonstrations of the futility of commercial restrictions, and thought, with some justice, that the French speculations savoured of metaphysical refinement, were forced to listen respectfully to a man who had all available statistics at his fingers' ends, and was able to show to them in black and white the mode in which the English commercial system had generated certain definite and assignable evils. All Smith's critics have remarked upon the felicity of his illustrations. A man whose mind is always on

the alert ends by finding the precise embodiment of a general principle which brings out the particular aspect desired. Other writers, the anonymous author already noticed, Mandeville, and Turgot, had recently illustrated the advantages of division of labour. Smith's illustration of the pins struck the popular imagination, to use Burke's phrase, 'between wind and water.' His illustrations generally imply an argument. The often-quoted comparison, for example, of paper money to a 'waggon road through the air,'[2] not merely expresses his meaning with admirable neatness, but incidentally clears up a confusion which had imposed upon the acute understanding of Hume. The ingenuity with which his conclusions are brought out gives at times a pleasurable shock of surprise like that which we receive from a witticism. Facts which seemed to be anomalous fall suddenly into their right places. It is obvious enough, when it has once been explained, that the contempt to which certain employments are exposed is the cause of their being highly paid. But the first time that we read Adam Smith's statement, by which things are simply put in their right places, we seem to be dexterously unravelling a paradox. We follow him through the whole treatise under the influence of a similar charm. We are under the guidance of a discoverer who has found the clue to a previously unexplored labyrinth, and leads us through its windings with unflagging interest, delighting and causing us to delight in the exercise of an ingenuity which finds at every fresh turn a fresh illustration of some simple general principle.

32. Adam Smith's popular fame is that of the first prophet of Free Trade—a doctrine which in the popular opinion is supposed to be the essence of all Political Economy. It would be nearer the truth to say that he was the first writer who succeeded in so presenting that doctrine as to convince statesmen that there was really a great mass of intelligible argument in its favour. It is indeed remarkable that some of Smith's reasoning upon the subject contains some of his worst Political Economy. He was, however, the mouthpiece through which the philosophy of his time succeeded in making itself audible to the world. The old industrial barriers, which had split Europe into unconnected fragments, were giving way along with many political and ecclesiastical barriers. Here, as in the political world, reformers regarded themselves as returning to a simple order of nature from the artificial complexity introduced by a selfish tyranny. Smith's preference of a minute analysis to a sweeping enunciation of general principles, prevents him from appeal-

[2] A. Smith, p. 141.

ing to the natural rights of man so distinctly as his French contemporaries. But the theory, though seldom explicitly stated, is everywhere in
the background of his arguments. He admits that considerations of general security should overrule in these cases a respect for abstract rights,[3]
and is always anxious to corroborate the argument from justice by the
argument from expediency.[4] Yet his conclusions generally coincide with
those of the abstract reasoner, though he ostensibly bases them upon
empirical grounds. The doctrines of the 'Wealth of Nations' have thus
a certain moral aspect which must be compared with the theories expounded in the ethical treatise. In his ethical treatise, it has been said by
his warmest admirer, he confines himself to the consideration of the
sympathetic emotions; in his economical treatise he regards man as an
exclusively selfish animal. The last statement is certainly true so far as
it must be agreed that Smith preaches that gospel of individualism
which was the natural product of the philosophy of the time. 'The
natural effort of every individual to better his own condition'[5] is, according to him, a principle powerful enough to make a society rich and
prosperous, and restrictions upon it are therefore impolitic. He explains
the moral standard,[6] and the political creed,[7] popular at a given time,
by the working of this all-pervading principle, and the same theory
generally accounts for the development of any specified institution.

33. The apparent inconsistency between this view and the view which
resolves the moral sentiments into sympathy has been explained as a
legitimate application of the analytical method. We may fairly isolate
the action of any particular force, and trace its consequences, whilst admitting that, in any concrete example, the results thus obtained will be
blended with those due to other forces. We may regard men first as
selfish and then as sympathetic, and combine our results, as in mechanics
we may investigate the nature of a centrifugal and centripetal force,
and then determine the effect of their united action. But, in truth, the
inconsistency is less than would appear from this mode of statement.
The moral theory expounded in Smith's other treatise may be regarded
as an answer to the question: given man as a predominantly selfish
animal, how does he come to condemn actions which are prompted by
his selfishness? The answer is substantially that morality is a kind of
reflected selfishness. Owing to what may be almost called an illusion of
the imagination, we cannot help seeing ourselves as others see us. And
thus that reflex selfishness which we call morality exerts a regulative

[3] A. Smith, p. 143.
[4] Ib. 236.   [6] Ib. p. 356.
[5] Ib. p. 241.   [7] Ib. p. 280.

power which restrains purely mischievous actions; and we may admire the ingenious arrangement by which Providence has produced a certain compensating action from passions which would otherwise render us mutually destructive. But it by no means follows that the reflected motive is as strong as the original, or that a sympathy thus derivative in its nature can be an animating principle of life in the same sense as the feelings on which it is grounded. My sympathy with others may make me condemn myself as I should condemn my neighbour for cutting a throat or picking a pocket; but it will not make me attend to my neighbour's interests more energetically than to my own. The great impelling force which drives the wheels of life is a man's desire for his own comfort. The regulative, rather than the antagonistic, force, which keeps his energy within certain bounds, is sympathy with the same desire in others.

34. The view implicitly adopted in the 'Wealth of Nations' is in perfect harmony with this. By the beneficient arrangements of Nature (Providence, I think, does not appear in the 'Wealth of Nations'), the pursuit of the individual's own selfish interest is made to coincide with the pursuit of the greatest happiness of the race. In both treatises we are called upon to trace the workings of a kind of pre-established harmony. It is the fundamental proposition of the 'Moral Sentiments' that our natural sympathies impose upon us certain restraints. It is the fundamental proposition of the 'Wealth of Nations' that so long as those restraints are obeyed (for the existence of such virtues as honesty and peacefulness is as much assumed in one treatise as the other), the happiness of mankind will be promoted by allowing each man to obey his own instincts without authoritative interference. If I buy in the cheapest market and sell in the dearest, I really contribute to the general comfort; for, in each case, I supply the strongest wants of my neighbours. So long as I do not steal or cheat, I in no way disobey the promptings of sympathy; unless sympathy could be pushed to the self-contradictory excess of declaring that each man should give his own property to his neighbour. An altruism, which would be inconsistent with the general principle that each man should generally look after himself, was never contemplated by Smith. Smith's philosophy of life, which is thus tolerably consistent, is substantially a corollary from the principles which he shared with the French philosophers generally. Its main propositions may perhaps be thus stated. There is a certain natural order in society. The final cause of this order is the happiness of mankind. The main condition for securing its natural fruits is the liberty of each man to follow his natural instincts. So long as those instincts do not bring men

into collision, the artificial interference of government is unjust, because it disregards the natural rights of mankind, and impolitic, because it hinders the natural development of the agencies by which men's wants are supplied. The sympathetic instincts are valuable as suppressing the tendency of each man to invade his neighbour's equal rights to life, liberty, and enjoyment. Where they are not sufficiently strong, there and there only government may rightfully interfere.[8] These doctrines do not often come to the surface in Smith's writings, because he aims everywhere at dealing rather with facts than with these primary principles. But they are so definitely implied that the 'Wealth of Nations' may be regarded as one continuous illustration of their value, as regulating principles in all the industrial relations of mankind.[9]

35. The merits and the shortcomings of Smith's theory may be indicated from these reflections. The tendency to regard government in general as a kind of artificial restriction imposed from without, and as mischievous because in some sense not 'natural,' was perhaps less defective in economical than in purely political speculation. The restrictions actually in existence were calculated to defeat their own object, and were merely a disguised method of plundering mankind for the benefit of a particular class or country. Denunciations of government interference might be perfectly right as applied to the actual system, though needing qualifications as absolute universal propositions; and Smith, at least, cannot be charged with falling into revolutionary extremes, for his treatment—always tempered by respect for facts—leads him to err chiefly on the side of moderation. He permits the legislator, for example, to fix the rate of interest;[10] an error which gave occasion to Bentham's crushing assault upon the usury laws. But though Smith dealt over-delicately with some existing restrictions, his conclusions could in such cases be refuted from his own principles. His view, when logically developed, implied the unreserved adoption of the let-alone doctrine. The exceptions which he admits are remnants of old prejudices rather than anticipations

[8]See, for example, an interesting passage in which the Marquis de Chastellux expresses the theory in a few words. Man, he says, is born for liberty; and 'si l'on ajoute que cette liberté est indéfinie par sa nature et qu'elle ne peut être limitée dans chaque individu que par celle d'un autre individu, c'est encore exprimer une vérité qui trouvera peu des contradicteurs dans ce siècle éclairé.' Quoted in Lavergne ('Economistes Francais,' p. 287).

[9]The French economists, indeed, differed from the revolutionary school by their absolutist tendencies; but, so far as trade was concerned, they were equally in favour of reducing government interference to a minimum.

[10]Smith's 'Wealth of Nations,' p. 204.

of any new principle. The sole remedy for the evils which he describes was the thorough demolition of restrictions which had long lost whatever justification they might have once possessed, and which were doomed to destruction by the force of events still more than by the force of his arguments.

36. Economists, indeed, are generally condemned for a different failing. That they should condemn the arbitrary regulations by which a statesman sought to hamper the free play of men's instinctive desire to attend to their own interests was right enough. It was better that sellers and buyers should be allowed to meet each other's wants without having to pay toll to the greediness of their rulers. The instinct of barter, which Smith rather oddly treats as possibly a primitive element of human nature, or that self-bettering instinct of which it is one manifestation, were at least respectable impulses; and, if duly restrained, all moralists who do not belong to the most ascetic type would propose rather to regulate than suppress their development. But when economists proceed a step further, and declare this self-regarding instinct to be the only force which governs, or ought to govern, human relations, a moralist of less exalted views may begin to be suspicious. Adam Smith, as I have already hinted, assigns to supply and demand a more extensive dominion over conduct than can be altogether admitted. He is a philosopher after the fashion of his day; and we can see that he had sate at the feet of Hume. The chapter, for example, upon Church establishments is curious and significant. He quotes the authority of Hume, 'by far the most illustrious philosopher and historian of the present age,'[11] for the opinion that rich endowments supplied the best means of keeping the clergy quiet. Smith appears to support the opinion that a number of small competing sects, without endowments or privileges, would be the ideal arrangement. But the end which he contemplates is the same—the production, namely, 'of philosophical good temper and moderation with respect to every religious creed.'[12] The religious sentiments, in fact, were a troublesome and expensive force, which could not be kept too quiet. An equilibrium of forces, general indifference, and room for every man to do his work and earn his wages in peace, was the most desirable continuous motive.

37. And thus the peculiar doctrine of the economists receives an interpretation which has been too common in later times. The natural order of society which they proclaimed, and which they held to be injuriously affected by every application of government interference,

[11]A. Smith, p. 354.   [12]Ib. p. 356.

was identified with the actual industrial structure of society. Smith would abolish all restraints upon trade; but nobody would be less inclined to sanction any theory for reconstructing society, or substituting any new principle for the régime of universal competition. He implicitly adopts the doctrine of some modern economists that the existing order is the only order conceivable. He would abolish all monopolies and all endowments, and leave religious and educational needs to be satisfied, like industrial needs, by the free action of supply and demand. The laws which he announced were to be regarded not only as determining the actual order from which any future development must proceed, but also as fixing conditions which could never be materially altered. It had been already assumed by some writers,[13] and it was systematically assumed by later writers, as, for example, by Ricardo, that the lowest classes must always receive the smallest remuneration consistent with the bare support of life. The assumption, which is highly convenient as simplifying many arguments, takes for granted that the most important aim of all sound economics is for ever impracticable. Smith takes a more historical view of the question than his predecessors, and his remarks upon the varying rate of wages are valuable and interesting. But in the 'Wealth of Nations' he assigns but a very small space to the discussions which rightly fill a principal part of all modern enquiries. He does not discuss the policy of the poor-laws, though such an investigation might seem to come naturally within his scope; and he is not troubled by any of those discussions as to the necessary limits of population, which were already coming to the surface, and were presently to provoke a vehement controversy. In the whole sphere of speculation to which these topics belong Smith is still a stranger. He represents the calm intellect which has seen through the superstitions of the antiquated restricted system, but is not prescient of the troubles that were to come with the bursting of the ancient barriers.

38. Here, too, we come upon the main speculative defect of the 'Wealth of Nations.' We are sensible, after reading his always lucid and ingenious, and often most acute, though rather too discursive enquiries, that there is something wanting. The arguments are not properly clenched. The complexity of Smith's enquiries has prevented him from drawing them to a focus. Price, he tells us, is fixed by supply and demand; supply and demand act through the 'higgling of the market;' the buyer wants the things cheap, and the seller wishes them to be dear; and so at last an agreement is struck out. But, if we go a little further,

[13]*E.g.* Locke, Turgot, sec. 6.

if we ask what general causes determine the precise rate of exchange, how it happens that a certain weight of yellow metal exchanges for a certain bulk of the seeds of a vegetable, we can get no definite answer, though here and there are glimpses of an answer. There is a whole side of the question which is left in obscurity. Roughly speaking we may say that Smith's conclusions are satisfactory if we assume that a certain social equilibrium has been somehow established, and seek to trace the process by which slight disturbances are propagated from one part to another. But to the further questions, what are the forces that are thus balanced? what is the true nature of the blind struggle which rages around us? and what are the ultimate barriers by which its issues are confined? we get a rather cursory and perfunctory answer. The difficulty is analogous to that which meets us in the 'Moral Sentiments.' We there follow the play of sympathy till we are perplexed by the intricacy of the results, but we do not perceive what is the ultimate ground which determines the limits and the efficacy of sympathy. And here, after tracing hither and thither the complex actions and reactions of supply and demand, we somehow feel that we have gone over all the ropes and pulleys by which force is transmitted, but have not fairly come in sight of the weights by which the force is originated.

39. The point to which Smith had thus pushed the enquiry is that at which 'catallactics' passes into sociology. Omitting a few errors, he has done all that can be done without bringing a theory of commerce into actual contact with the underlying social problems. He has explained with great clearness the ebb and flow of markets, the curious mechanism of paper money and credit, the manner in which the effects of taxation are propagated to different classes, and many other phenomena of which a good Chancellor of the Exchequer should take an intelligent view. But he illustrates once more the truth so frequently noticed, that theory generally lags behind experience. Society was heaving with new passions, and forces were being generated which were to try the strength of its most intimate structure. As they began to manifest themselves, economists found themselves confronted by new and more difficult problems. To the theory of exchange was to be added a theory which should determine how the wealth acquired by society was to be distributed amongst its different classes, and to what extent the efforts of well-being were confined by irremovable limits. The new doctrines of socialism or communism, tending to a regeneration or a disintegration of society, were beginning to stir in men's minds, and the doctrines of the later investigators begin to take a different colour and to centre round more vital problems. It becomes more evident at each step that a mere theory

of commerce, though such a theory may be useful in its place, cannot answer the serious difficulties which are beginning to present themselves to the legislator and the social reformer. The doctrines enunciated by Adam Smith refer chiefly to the superficial phenomena presented by a society of which it has hitherto been the greatest triumph to preserve a decent amount of fair-play between individuals and classes immersed in a blind struggle for existence. Is that struggle always to continue on its present terms? Is it always to be blind? Must starvation and misery be always in the immediate background, and selfishness, more or less decently disguised, and more or less equitably regulated, be the one great force by which to determine the conformation of society? What are the conditions which we can hope to modify by combined effort, and what are the irrevocable conditions imposed upon men by virtue of their position in the planet, by accommodating themselves to which they can minimise the evils of their lot, but of which it is in vain to seek the absolute removal? In the coming years such problems were to assume continually greater prominence; and, as yet, we are only on the threshold of the speculations which they suggest. On one side were to range themselves the Utopians, who hoped for an extemporised regeneration of society; on the other, the rigid and sometimes cynical observers who proclaimed too unequivocally the impossibility of ever delivering ourselves from the tyranny of our fate.

40. The two schools found themselves opposed when Godwin announced the perfectibility of man, and Malthus opposed to him the limits presented by the invariable conditions of human existence. This controversy once opened, it was plain that political economy could no longer be regarded as an isolated science. Its assumptions entered into all the great political and social questions of the day. Whatever might be its methods, and whether or not the industrial organisation could by a logical artifice be studied apart from other problems, it was evident that it had a common ground with wider speculations. It must henceforth be regarded not as a separate study, but as a department of sociological theory. Here, as in the history of political speculation, I must stop at the opening of a new era. In the gradual process of generalisation which I have attempted to describe, the true character of problems, which had been attacked only in detached fragments, was beginning to make itself evident. The new theories which were to be introduced are all significant of the wider scope of the dawning science. If Malthus called attention to the limits produced by the struggle of the whole human race against natural forces, Ricardo, and Malthus himself, showed how individuals who had posted themselves in advantageous

positions obtained the largest share of its profits; and Ricardo discussed the general connection between the phenomena of exchange and the conditions under which labour is applied to different objects. The doctrines of rent and of population had been partly anticipated, as later writers have pointed out, by various authors; but, as in so many other cases, their observations did not attract general attention until the times were ripe, and the special struggle to whose conditions they referred was making its nature evident in the convulsions of a great revolution.

NOTE TO CHAPTER XI

The following are the chief authorities for this chapter and the editions cited:

BENTHAM, JEREMY (1747–1852), 'Defence of Usury,' 1787.

DAVENANT, CHARLES (1656–1714), 'Various Tracts on Trade' &c. 1695–1712. Works. London: 1771.

HUME, DAVID (1711–1776), 'Political Discourses,' 1752. Philosophical Works, by Green and Grose.

LOCKE, JOHN (1632–1704), 'Considerations on Value of Money' &c. 1691. Works. London: 1824.

NORTH, SIR DUDLEY (1641–1691), 'Discourse upon Trade,' 1691. Collection of 'Select Tracts,' by Political Economy Club.

SMITH, ADAM (1723–1790), 'Wealth of Nations,' 1776. Edinburgh: 1863.

STEUART, SIR JAMES (1713–1780), 'Enquiry into Principles of Political Economy,' 1767.

TUCKER, JOSIAH (1712–1799), 'Essay on French and English Trade,' c. 1750. 'Scarce and Valuable Tracts,' published by Lord Overstone.

Richardson's 'Decline of Foreign Trade,' 1744, is in the 'Scarce and Valuable Tracts;' the 'Considerations on the East Indian Trade,' in the 'Select Tracts.'

CHAPTER XII

CHARACTERISTICS

I. Introductory.

1. The literature of a people may be divided into three classes: the historical, that of which it is the primary purpose to record facts, and to summarise or amplify existing knowledge; the speculative, of which it is the primary purpose to discuss the truth of the various theories by which our knowledge is bound together; and the imaginative, of which it is the primary purpose to utter the emotions generated in mankind by the conditions in which they are, or believe themselves to be, placed. With the historical literature—taking that word in the widest sense—this book has little direct connection. The views which men take of history are indeed very significant of their speculative opinions; but I have not ventured to enlarge my plan sufficiently to include such indirect evidence. Hitherto I have dealt with the speculative literature, or rather with that part of it which deals directly with the highest problems of human thought. And here I might stop, but that it seems desirable to touch briefly upon the reflection of the prevalent theories upon the world of the imagination. The doctrines which men ostensibly hold do not become operative upon their conduct until they have generated an imaginative symbolism; the reaction of the emotions upon the intellect is again of primary importance; and too great a gap would be left in this account of English thought if I were to omit all consideration of the influences, not less effective because exerted through extralogical channels, which were due in different directions to such men as Law, Wesley, Pope, Swift, Fielding, Johnson, Cowper, and Burns. It is desirable, however, to explain with some care the limits within which my remarks must necessarily be confined.

2. The character of an imaginative literature is a function of many forces. It depends not only upon the current philosophy, but upon the inherited peculiarities of the race, upon its history, its climate, its social and political relations, and upon individual peculiarities of mind and temperament which defy all attempt at explanation. Thus, in our English literature of the eighteenth century, we can see the reflection of the

national character; its sturdy common sense; the intellectual short-
sightedness which enables it to grasp details whilst rejecting general
systems; the resulting tendency to compromise, which leads it to acquiesce in heterogeneous masses of opinions; its humour, its deep moral
feeling, its prejudices, its strong animal propensities, and so forth. Or,
again, the social development affects the literature. The whole tone of
thought is evidently coloured by the sentiments of a nation definitely
emerging from the older organisation to a modern order of society. We
see the formation of an important middle-class, and of an audience
composed, not of solitary students or magnificent nobles, but of merchants, politicians, lawyers, and doctors, eager for amusement, delighting in infinite personal gossip, and talking over its own peculiarities
with ceaseless interest in coffee-houses, clubs, and theatres. Nor, again,
are the political influences unimportant. The cessation of the fierce
struggles of the previous century, culminating in the undisputed supremacy of a parliamentary oligarchy, led to a dying out of the vehement discussions which at other periods have occupied men's minds
exclusively, and made room for that theological controversy which I
have described, and which itself disappeared as the political interests
revived in the last half of the century. Foreign influences, again, would
have to be considered. French literature was to Dryden and Pope what
Italian had been to Spenser and Milton; the influence of Bayle may be
traced in the earlier criticism, as at a later period Montesquieu, Rousseau, and Voltaire profoundly affected English thought. The attempt,
then, to deduce Pope from Clarke, or to connect Swift with Butler, to
the neglect of the many conflicting influences, would be necessarily
illusory. It is not the less true that remarkable analogies may be traced
between the speculative and the imaginative literature. The complex
conditions to which I have referred affected both modes of thought; and
sometimes we may best regard the two manifestations as springing from
the same root, sometimes as directly influencing each other. My attention, even in discussing the speculative literature, has been chiefly confined to what I may call the logical relations of different intellectual
creeds. I have considered the successive controversies as of a continuous
debate, in which each writer starts from positions determined by the previous course of discussion. I have only referred incidentally to other conditions which, so to speak, dislocated the logical series. I now propose to
touch briefly upon the mode in which the logical confusions affected the
imaginative embodiment of thought. From such a point of view much
that would otherwise be of the highest interest must be overlooked.
That which gives the special value to a work in the eyes of the literary

critic is often due to some idiosyncrasy of the individual writer; whilst the historian will be interested in the light which it throws upon the social and political conditions of the time. Though I shall have to touch such topics incidentally, my primary purpose is to suggest some answer to the problem: How far, and in what way, was the imaginative literature of the time a translation of its philosophy in terms of emotion?

3. We can conceive of a state in which all growth should be consistent with equilibrium, and involve no destruction. We may imagine a society growing in wealth, intelligence, and order, without the need of revolutionary disturbance. Its creeds, we may suppose, would be thoroughly assimilated, and therefore be in perfect harmony with each other, with the social order, and with facts. The religious impulse would receive its form from the philosophical, every moral doctrine would be the application of some admitted social law, and every poetical conception be the imaginative reflection of some scientific truth. No near approximation has hitherto been made to such a condition; fatal errors have always lurked in philosophy, and the seeds of disorder been germinating in the most stable social order. There have, however, been periods at which some common convictions and passions have so dominated mankind as to suggest an impression of the possible harmony. Those have been the creative periods, when forces, at other times wasted in endless wrangling, have been available for a common co-operation. Philosophers can at times combine to work out new truth instead of attacking each other's principles; preachers can speak boldly and eloquently, delivered from the bondage of paralysing doubts, and animated by an uninterrupted circuit of sympathy; artists can work effectively, for the common faith generates a symbolism universally understood, and appealing to genuine beliefs; leaders of men can advance without needing at every step to entrench themselves against open enemies and insidious friends. But it is to be feared that equilibrium generally implies, not harmony, but stagnation. Improvement first shows itself by introducing discord; and periods of comparative repose are interrupted by confused epochs of jarring chaos, in which the noblest imaginative work reflects the passions of the sincerest combatant, not the combined impulse of a united people.

4. The beginning of the eighteenth century was a period of comparative quiescence. Society was not in a state of furious ebullition, and the conflict of ideas was not manifestly internecine. There existed, therefore, a kind of relative harmony. It was a harmony of compromise rather than reconciliation; a truce, not a definite peace. The deist controversy scarcely led more than two or three daring thinkers to question ulti-

mate assumptions. And a common theological philosophy was very widely accepted by men who denounced each other heartily for comparatively trivial differences of opinion. In politics, Whiggism and Toryism were little more than names, and both parties agreed to accept, with little modification, that body of doctrines which afterwards came to be known as Revolution principles. In literature and art we shall find an analogous disposition to agree upon certain accepted canons. An academy of the reign of Queen Anne might have laid down a code upon such matters which would have been accepted with little disagreement, and which would have corresponded to what is called the classical theory. We shall have to consider some of its principles in greater detail.

5. Starting from the theological doctrine, we may say that the dominant creed was either the pure or the Christian Deism worked out by the rationalism of the day. As we have seen, the philosophy tended to identify God with nature, though with a reserve and hesitation which stopped short of thoroughness. By nature was meant a metaphysical entity, whose existence was to be proved by mathematical reasonings; and yet not proved too clearly lest it should lapse into Pantheism or become independent of Christianity. This intellectual attitude corresponds to an imaginative difficulty. The old vivid mythology was rapidly fading. The distinct realisation of a supernatural Being constantly intervening in the actual affairs of life was no longer possible. Nor, on the other hand, could the pantheist adopt the more genial conception of a later philosophy, and frankly regard nature as animated by an all-pervading force, breathing in every plant and moving the whole choir of heaven, and bringing the whole universe into a loving unity. A greater scientific development and a livelier realisation of the continuity and order of the world are required to give force to such a conception. The metaphysics of the day placed all reality in certain abstract substances and empty forces, and the whole phenomenal world was made up of independent fragments which were yet in some sense illusory. So frigid and mechanical a conception could scarcely afford a point of support for the imagination. Laboriously as philosophers might establish the divine attributes, the deity remained obstinately lifeless. He was but an idol made of heterogeneous fragments of the old traditions, and of half-hearted and chilling metaphysics. The difficulty of reconciling such a conception to admitted facts was, as we have seen, met in two ways. One set of thinkers retained theological language, but made it studiously vague. They found God in nature, but they found an impalpable essence. They clung to a vague optimism, generated by the attempt to transfer to this abstract being the creations associated with

the vivid because anthropomorphic type, and talked vaguely of harmony and unity, without caring to translate phrases into facts. Their morality tended to degenerate into vague sentimentalism, or mere prudence thinly varnished over with traditional grandiloquence.

6. Others still retained the old conception, but reconciled the imaginative difficulty by remembering that God had shown himself a long time ago, and in a very different country. He became the almost grotesque deity of Warburton—the supernatural chief-justice whose sentences were carried out in a non-natural world—the constitutional monarch who had signed a social compact, and retired from active government. These thinkers would join with the sceptics in contemptuously assailing deistical rationalism as too flimsy for actual life. To the optimism of their rivals, they opposed a vigorous assertion that vice, misery, and corruption still existed in the world. The sentimental morality was met by a downright statement of the tangible motives of a selfish prudence. And, even in artistic questions, the correct and classical school was encountered by an unflinching realism which showed things as they are in their whole deformity. The two tendencies are intricately blended. Appeals to experience mingle with appeals to *a priori* demonstration. Common sense, in the vulgar acceptation of the word, is confused with the philosophical appeal to innate ideas and universal intuitions. The imagination confounds the two really distinct deities, and, indeed, is shocked at a plain statement of the inconsistencies involved. Men, who are really working with the forces of disintegration, believe in the most entire good faith that they are supporting the established order. It is not an easy task to unravel these opposing currents of thought and feeling, or to discover the logic implied in unreasoning impulses, and the unconscious tendencies which would have been disavowed if plainly brought before the consciousness. Heterogeneous elements are so united, that it is not only difficult to discover their existence, but almost impossible to indicate it plainly in a continuous narrative. I propose, however, to describe the most obvious phenomena as well as I am able, by first considering that series of writers who seem to represent what may be called the most characteristic product of the eighteenth century; and then to trace the second series, who represent the growing element of reaction or development. But though the line may be thus drawn for the present purpose, it does not correspond to an equally marked division in reality. We shall find, for example, amongst the religious writers, the poets, the novelists, and the essayists, tendencies analogous to those which are represented in speculation by the ontologists, the sceptics,

and the school of common sense. But amongst men who felt rather
than reasoned, or who reasoned by feeling, the logical divisions will be
less distinctly marked, and one man may often represent the resultant
of various forces, rather than the impulse of a single force. The poet
may naturally seek to bring into unity all the strongest impulses of his
time, and sometimes he fuses into a whole very inconsistent materials.

II. The Preachers.

7. I will begin with that system of practical theology which corresponds more or less distinctly to the speculative theory of Clarke. How
could the theistic doctrine, vague, frigid, and artificial as we have seen
it to be, be applied to influence human conduct? That was the problem
presented to the dominant theological school. They should, therefore,
give us the best clue to the solution of the problem which we have to
consider. Two things, it may be said, were conspicuously absent from
that form of religious doctrine—faith and poetry. What remains when
they are taken away? Common sense and candour. Without a distinct
doctrine and without any warmth of feeling, what guides are to be
found? Substantially those empirical guesses which provide for the
ordinary affairs of life, although there must be an ostensible connection
of such guesses with a foundation of demonstrated truth. An alterna-
tion, then, of high-sounding appeals to reason with dexterous appeals
to obvious motives must be the general tendency of such theology.
Sometimes the preacher will lose himself in abstract reasoning, and
sometimes descend to the dead level of homely common sense. Rhetoric,
in its full sense, becomes almost impossible. The first condition of
effective oratory is given in the words 'this man speaketh with authority.' English preachers, since the seventeenth century, have never
possessed this secret, and have therefore never commanded their hearers.
The demonstrations which are so frequent in the sermons of the eighteenth century are obviously not demonstrative, or they would not be
used. The preacher can take nothing for granted. He is always bound to
encourage himself and his hearers by once more repeating a series
of proofs which he knows to generate at most probabilities, though he is
forced to give them the air of certainties. He can never advance, because his base is never beyond the reach of attack. It would be well, it
is sometimes said, if every preacher felt that there was an opponent in
his congregation. It might be well for his logic, though it would be of
doubtful benefit to his rhetoric. But in these sermons we often feel that

the opponent must not only by present as the butt of the preacher's arguments, but that he has got into the pulpit, for we feel that the preacher is too often arguing with himself.

8. And, again, the preacher, uncertain of his position, is obliged to be arguing as much against the extremes of his own party as against his avowed antagonists. He is in constant fear lest he should be thought to believe too much or too little. The aim of every orthodox or rationalist preacher is to keep to the *via media* between superstition and fanaticism. Superstition is the belief that God ever reveals himself to external experience in the modern world; and fanaticism the belief that he reveals himself by internal experience. The preacher, in denouncing these extremes, shows himself as much afraid that we should believe in God too much as that we should believe in him too little. The deity whose existence is established by abstract reasoning must never be allowed to place himself in contact with the concrete facts. He appears, at most, under the colourless shape of Providence—a word which may be taken to imply a remote divine superintendence, without admitting an actual divine interference.

9. Thus the preacher, uncertain, as it were, of his equilibrium, and with his hands tied by a strict bondage, is unable to give way to any spontaneous bursts of emotion. We have none of Taylor's flashes of fancy, or of Barrow's masculine reasoning, or of South's wit, or of Baxter's earnestness. The positive element, which replaces all these, is good commonplace morality, defended by ordinary common sense, and supported by appeals to the ordinary facts of daily life. Don't get drunk, or you will ruin your health; nor commit murder, for you will come to the gallows; every man should seek to be happy, and the way to be happy is to be thoroughly respectable. That is the main substance of such preaching as is not controversial, backed by the argument that it is decidedly probable that there is another world in which the bad will be turned into hell. Every man of sense would admit a certain force in such arguments; though no man of imagination could be moved by the rhetoric, and no human being, at the present day, not forced by some external consideration, could ever read the literature thus produced.

10. Yet the literature of the pulpit should give us the most characteristic indications of contemporary thought. What, the preacher should ask himself, are the true roots of the religious faith of his countrymen? What was it that the ordinary Englishman of the Georgian period really believed? What arguments satisfied his reason, and what emotions clothed themselves in his forms of worship? Pedants in the schools, and

controversialists in their professional literature, might wrangle over matters for which the ordinary merchant or lawyer cared not a farthing. The preacher has to move the masses, and must dwell upon the topics which are really capable of sending a sympathetic thrill through the ordinary bosom. The mere dead forms of extinct thought are useless in a form of literature which men judge by their spontaneous feelings and not by deliberate reflection. In the pulpit we should hear the living voice, not the mechanical echoes of departed centuries.

11. The study of eighteenth-century sermons, however, is not exhilarating. We know from sufficient testimony that they really impressed our forefathers. We can discover on reflection that in some cases they represent genuine thought and emotion. But no one, unless he were confined to a desert island with no other form of literature at hand, could really affect to read them with pleasure. Dull, duller, and dullest are a sufficient critical vocabulary to describe their merits; or, if one would fain discover some less damnatory form of description, it may perhaps be said that they are but one degree superior to the average sermon of the succeeding century. If less emotional, they have a greater appearance of sincerity. There is in them, too, a certain vein of common sense, which may be prosaic, but is in its way respectable. There is no effort to stimulate the imagination of the hearers, to raise them above the turmoil of daily life into a higher region of thought, and still less to provoke anything like a passionate outburst of emotion. But there is a sincere wish to stock the ordinary mind with a due provision of common-sense maxims, which may serve to keep its proprietor out of mischief, and make him a respectable member of society. To dip very deeply into such literature would be superfluous as well as wearisome. A few brief characters of the most distinguished performers will be amply sufficient for my purpose.

12. Let us take, for example, Clarke, the typical rationalist divine. Warburton commends his sermons as the best model for a young preacher, especially for their abundant illustrations of Scripture,[1] and Johnson, though with a due reservation on the score of orthodoxy, seems to admire them equally.[2] The most obvious criticism upon these performances is, that they are, for the most part, not sermons at all, but lectures upon metaphysics. They are generally fragments of the arguments in the Boyle lectures, illustrated by quotations of texts, profuse enough to prove Clarke's powerful memory, and to explain Warburton's eulogy. To believe in God is to have 'worthy and honourable apprehen-

---

[1]Warburton, x. 373.   [2]Boswell (Fitzgerald's edit.), ii. 268.

sions of his nature and attributes;'[3] that is to say, fully to appreciate the arguments of the Boyle lectures. A thorough assimilation of that thrice-sifted essence of reasoning will naturally generate virtue and lead to a reception of the corollaries added by Revelation. The belief may be commanded on pain of damnation; for being reasonable in itself, and proved by 'the strongest evidence in the world,' the only cause of its rejection must be 'a love of vice.'[4] As demonstration is the basis of our belief, appeals to the reasoning faculty are everywhere substituted for addresses to the imagination or the emotions. The glowing imagery of poetical writers suggests to Clarke's mind a legal .fiction to be carefully defined and analysed. He gives a mathematical diagram where Taylor would have drawn a picture. His twentieth sermon, for example, is on the text, 'Call no man your father on earth, for one is your father which is in heaven.' We have first a careful statement of what is precisely meant by the Fatherhood of God—the sacred phrase which to some later writers has appeared to be the perfect embodiment of the central thought of Christianity. Clarke tells us that it has two meanings. It means, in the language of natural religion, that God created us, whilst, in the language of revelation, it is used to express a legal metaphor. The process by which sinners are restored to virtue, and therefore to the favour of God, 'is elegantly styled by St. Paul, God our Father's adoption of children by Jesus Christ to himself.'[5] Secondly, we are told why God, though really omnipresent, may be fairly said to be in heaven. Thirdly, it is argued that, to call any man father on earth would be to admit human authority in matters of faith; 'which thing is altogether inconsistent with true Christianity.'[6] And therefore, fourthly and lastly, the ground of the prohibition is that such language would imply the setting up of other conditions of salvation than those which God has 'clearly and fully presented to us.'[7] To modern ears the text is associated with the soothing doctrine that all earthly evil is but the transient mask of universal benevolence. To Clarke's clear mathematical intellect the mysticism which seeks to turn the metaphor into a truth is not so much uncongenial as simply inconceivable. He calmly strips off the illusion, and presents us with a frigid metaphysical conception instead of a glorified person.

13. In the twenty-sixth and twenty-seventh sermons, again, he deals with the love of God to sinners—a topic which might justify some

[3]Clarke's Works, i. 177.

[4]Ib. i. 330.   [6]Ib. i. 128.

[5]Ib. i. 125.   [7]Ib. i. 129.

momentary burst of rhetorical fervour. In fact, they are a careful exposition of the mutual claims of man and his Maker, as cleared up by
Clarke's theory of free-will. The demonstration leads up to the practical
conclusion that all truths—as, for example, the truths that God is just
and that he is merciful—are perfectly consistent when properly explained, and that it is of the highest importance 'to frame right and
worthy notions concerning the attributes of God.' When everything can
be so satisfactorily explained, there is little room for those deeper emotions which accompany a strong perception of the great mystery of evil.
Nominally, the world is corrupt; but the corruption is proved chiefly by
the stupidity which prevented people from anticipating the demonstrations of scientific theology. Since the problem has been solved, we can
get on pretty comfortably. The old dark days of persecution are over.
We are now required 'only to retrench our vain and sinful expenses;
not to sell *all* and give to the poor, but to be charitable out of the
superfluity of our plenty; not to lay down our lives, or even the comfortable enjoyments of life, but to forsake the unreasonable and unfruit-
ful pleasures of sin,'[8] and so on. Who would not accept so light and
easy a yoke? The statement is a common one in the comfortable days
of Queen Anne and the early Georges. Christianity was delightfully
easy when it imposed no severer checks upon life, and studiously appealed to common sense. If a more heroic note occurs at intervals, it is
when Clarke is dwelling upon the love of truth. His sixty-eighth sermon
deals with that awkward virtue, Christian zeal. It has, of course, to be
discriminated from its hated counterpart. True zeal aims at the practice
of virtue; and right practice can only be built on the foundation of
truth. 'Therefore, the object of zeal first in the order of nature is the
knowledge of truth.'[9] Such zeal, he says, can never be excessive; and
the cause of all corruptions in religion is the lukewarmness of men as
to whether their beliefs be true or false.[10] Elsewhere the unpardonable
sin against the Holy Ghost is characteristically explained to mean a
malicious and perverse refusal to be convinced by the 'greatest and
highest evidences'[11] which God has condescended to give to men;
inasmuch as a man so obstinate as to resist the strongest arguments can
never be brought to repentance, for he can never be persuaded of his
errors.

14. Love of pure truth—that is with Clarke the foundation and the
superstructure, the beginning and the end of all true religion. All virtues
are but corollaries from this fundamental virtue; and, naturally, logic is

---

[8]Clarke, i. 212.   [9]Ib. i. 421.   [10]Ib. i. 422.   [11]Ib. i. 540.

the one mode of converting men to Christ. The doctrine is, however, inadequate, though perhaps natural in a passionless age. At any rate, it is honourable, and is sincerely held by Clarke. We should be, perhaps, a little more impressed if we felt that his confidence in his logical apparatus was more unhesitating; and Clarke, though his preferment was injured by his honesty, somehow suggests to us the existence of unconscious mental reservations.

15. If Clarke represents the Latitudinarian, Sherlock may be taken as the best representative of that characteristic wisdom of the Church of England which delights in keeping the mean between two extremes. He hits the taste of his age 'between wind and water,' for the common sense which was worshipped by his contemporaries was his most prominent faculty. It receives, however, a peculiar flavour from the strong legal bent of which I have spoken elsewhere. Sherlock is a lawyer in a cassock, and a thoroughly masculine lawyer. He does not condescend to the special pleading which irritates us as much in the sermons as in the ponderous treatise of the sham colossus Warburton. He is a vigorous advocate, convinced of the substantial soundness of his case, though not too candid to his adversaries; massing his arguments upon the vital points, instead of frittering them away in minute details; and at rare intervals rising to such eloquence as is produced by sheer strong sense, without much imagination or abstract thought. He is no philosopher, and takes for granted the primary doctrines which Clarke labours to demonstrate. The legal analogy pervades all his sermons. The religion of nature according to him resembles the common law of England, a traditional body of doctrine, which at some early period was sufficient for the government of an uncorrupted race.[12] No religion has a right to be considered which contradicts one of the plain principles of this fundamental code.[13] The fall of man, however, necessitated the promulgation of a body of statute law, re-enacting the old code, but adding to it a set of provisions under which sinners may obtain the favour of God. Reason proves the law of nature, and miracles prove the law of revelation. Remorse is the only punishment under the first code; the sanctions of heaven and hell have been added by the second.

16. The doctrine is perfectly clear and coherent in itself, and Sherlock does not trouble himself about its ultimate basis. He starts from the conception of the supernatural chief-justice. To him Christianity is not

[12]Sherlock has a peculiar theory as to the convenant with Noah, which places the Golden Age just after the Flood ('Discourses on Prophecy,' No. 4; Works, iv. 76).   [13]Ib. i. 175.

the advent of a new spiritual force moulding men's hearts, nor the withdrawal of the veil of sense from the awful realities of the universe; it is simply the authoritative and duly authenticated statement of a new code for the discouragement of vice. There is no question of bowing in reverence before the inscrutable mysteries of the divine will. Sherlock treats the Jewish covenant as respectfully as a lawyer might speak of Magna Charta; and considers that the Gospel is the embodiment of perfect wisdom, as Blackstone might attribute the same excellence to the British Constitution. He expounds the relations of the codes, and extols their practical working, but is as little anxious as an ordinary constitutional lawyer to go into the ultimate philosophical questions. His argument against the deists is substantially the strong one that Christianity has worked better than the pure religion of nature. When the deist is out of sight, and he is not settling the limits of our moral and religious obligations, he discourses sensibly upon ordinary duties; he proves that the poor ought to work rather than steal; that idle words are wicked and the heart deceitful; that excessive discouragement and excessive confidence are equally wrong, and antinomianism equally contrary to Christianity and common sense.[14] The morality is for the most part of the prudential variety, and teaches us to make the best of both worlds. Sometimes the effect is unpleasant. The old argument against which Chillingworth had protested was that Catholicism was the safest creed, because Protestants were all damned on the Catholic theory, whereas Catholics might be saved on the Protestant theory. This appeal to cowardice had now been transplanted into the Christian argument against deists. The safety of staying in the old paths is the natural argument of all conservatives against reforms; but it has not an elevating effect. If—so Sherlock says frequently to the deists—there is a hell, we are far better off than you; if there is none, we are at least no worse off.[15] 'It is ten to one,' he says elsewhere, 'against you, that if you follow the world you get nothing or little by it; and therefore there are the same odds on the other side, that if you follow religion you lose little or nothing by it; so that, supposing religion to be uncertain, yet a man does not venture much for it, or put himself in a much worse condition than he was in before, by reason of the uncertain condition of the world.'[16] It is thus but common prudence to be virtuous.[17]

[14]Sherlock, ii. 323.   [15]Ib. iii. 43.   [16]Ib. iii. 182.

[17]The oddest statement of this argument is to be found in the conclusion of Price's 'Review,' where he says that, assuming the chances against the truth of the doctrine of a future retribution to be ten to one, it would still be worth while to sacrifice the whole happiness of our lives for the chance of receiving

17. Yet Sherlock was at times really eloquent. Of a Letter which he published on the occasion of the earthquakes in 1750 it is said that over 100,000 copies were circulated. It now reads like a commonplace diatribe against vice and Deism, in which Sherlock has forgotten not only philosophy, but his own common-sense remarks about the error of supposing that the world is growing worse. Earthquakes suggested very different thoughts to Voltaire. We are told that this letter produced a temporary show of outward decency. Perhaps Walpole spoke more accurately when he described Sherlock as 'running a race' with Secker 'for the old ladies.'[18] Another anecdote of Sherlock's powers is more remarkable. When he presented the collected edition of his sermons to Lord Hardwicke, it is said that Hardwicke repeated to him *verbatim* a passage from one of them which had been published separately thirty years before. We need not enquire too closely whether this proves that Hardwicke had learnt it at that distant period. But the passage is short as well as eloquent, and may be quoted as giving Sherlock at his best. The sermon is an answer to the deist objection founded on the multiplicity of revelations; and attempts to retort the argument by saying that the fact proves the incompetence of natural religion to repress superstition. The Gospel alone survives all other attempts at framing a universal creed, and was without competitor until Mahomet. In this case, he says, there can be no difficulty. 'Go to your natural religion; lay before her Mahomet and his disciples, arrayed in armour and in blood, riding in triumph over the spoils of thousands and tens of thousands who fell by his victorious sword; show her the cities which he set in flames, countries which he ravaged and destroyed, and the miserable distress of all the inhabitants of the earth. When she has viewed this scene, carry her into his retirements; show her the prophet's chamber, his concubines and wives; let her see his adultery, and hear him allege revelation and his divine commission to justify his lust and oppression. When she is tired with this prospect, then show her the blessed Jesus—humble and meek, doing good to all the sons of men, patiently instructing both the ignorant and the perverse. Let her see him in his most retired privacies; let her follow him to the mount, and hear his devotions and supplications to God. Carry her to his table to view his poor fare, and hear his heavenly discourse. Let her see him injured, but not provoked; let her attend him to the tribunal, and consider the patience with which he

---

a reward eleven times as great as that happiness. But the reward is infinitely greater; whence the wisdom of virtue is obvious (Price's 'Review,' p. 453, &c.).

[18] Walpole's 'Correspondence,' ii. 201.

endured the scoffs and reproaches of his enemies. Lead her to his cross, and let her view him in the agony of death, and hear his last prayer for his persecutors: "Father, forgive them, for they know not what they do!"

'When natural religion has viewed both, ask, Which is the prophet of God? But her answer we have already had; when she saw part of the scene through the eyes of the centurion who attended the cross; by him she spoke and said: "Truly this man was the Son of God." '[19] This marks the highest level of eighteenth-century eloquence. It is terse, vigorous, and really to the point.

18. Atterbury may represent the High Church as Clarke the Low, and Sherlock the judicious mean. His contemporary reputation would justify lofty expectations. He had come off with momentary honour from his assault upon Bentley. Pope listened respectfully to his tolerably keen criticisms, and was encouraged to take to satire by his judicious, if not very Christian, appreciation of the famous lines upon Addison. His warm admiration for Milton is a proof of his literary taste. In the pulpit he was equally famous. The complacent dissenter, Doddridge, called him the 'glory of English orators' and 'the model of courtly preachers.'[20] The meteoric Duke of Wharton went further. In a copy of panegyrical verses he compares the preacher to Christ at Emmaus, and to Jove still-ing the tempest, and ends with this joint compliment to Atterbury and Kneller:—

> As in him another Paul we view,
> Another Raphael may we find in you.

Neither aspiration has been quite fulfilled; though Atterbury's last biog-rapher declares that, except Pope and Samuel Wesley, 'none of the bishop's contemporaries have left so agreeable and so vivid a recollection of him.'[21] A less hyperbolical compliment is perhaps more impressive. Steele, in one of his 'Tatlers,' describes Atterbury as an exception to the general indifference of the English clergy to the art of speaking. The dean, he says, is an orator. We are told further that he learnt his ser-mons by heart, neglected no graces of manner, had an attractive person, and had the special virtue of never attempting the passions before he had convinced the reason.[22] The eulogy accounts for the disappearance of the charm which it commemorates.

[19]Sherlock's Works, i. 179, 180; and see the comparison between Paul and Socrates in the same spirit, i. 105 *et seq.*

[20]Williams's 'Life of Atterbury,' i. 70.

[21]Ib. i. 315.   [22]'Tatler,' No. 6.

19. Reading the sermons in cold blood, and deprived of all the charm of delivery, we find them in substance wonderfully like other sermons of the time. The deists are refuted, and virtue is recommended in the ordinary method; though Hoadly discovered traces of the hated sacerdotal taint. The style is not unworthy of the friend and critic of the most brilliant writers of the day; and here and there, as in the sermon on the death of poor Lady Cutts, at the age of eighteen, the pathos has not entirely evaporated. But there are no traces of real power of thought or depth of emotion. They are the performances of a very able man, who is a politician before he is an ecclesiastic, and a Tory more distinctly than a High-Churchman. In other times, Atterbury might have been a Laud or a Wolsey; in the eighteenth century his ambition could end only by sacrificing his talents and energy to the most contemptible of all pretenders. The spirit of the age enervates his religious thought as well as his political principles. He has the objection to being righteous overmuch, common to nearly all his contemporaries. He warns us that even charity may lead us into folly if we go as far as some Catholic Saints;[23] and he points out that we are not bound to spread Christianity at the risk of our lives, when we have no longer the power of working miracles; though, on the other hand, we need not deride men whose honest zeal had carried them further.[24] The flame of priestly devotion was burning low when the most high-spirited of its leaders found it necessary to qualify his exhortations by these prudential provisos. These writers may be a sufficient specimen of a literary product which has become the rightful property of the library moth. A few other names might be mentioned which once enjoyed a certain celebrity. In Smalridge, the ordinary materials are coloured by academical pedantry; Foster's moral essays contain a still weaker infusion of Christian sentiment than Clarke's; and Seed has a certain smartness which might have made him a useful contributor to some of the successors of the 'Spectator,' whilst Secker pours forth a continuous stream of prosaic moralising.

20. But enough has been said to illustrate the general tone of thought. As the century went on, the eloquence became feebler; for all warmth of sentiment had passed to the side of Wesley and Whitefield. A preacher in the land of Knox obtained a great popularity, and the sermons of Hugh Blair may represent the last stage of theological decay. Five volumes appeared during the last quarter of the century; for the first he received 200*l.*, for the second 500*l.*, and for the third 600*l.*—a sufficient proof that he enjoyed a considerable popularity. He was

[23]Sermons, i. 62, iv. 52.　　[24]Ib. i. 169.

praised by Johnson, who seems, however, to have doubted the permanent interest of his work;[25] and George III. wished that every youth in
the kingdom might possess a copy of the Bible and of Blair. And yet it
is hard to say anything of Blair, except what Johnson said of Dodd's
sermons, when somebody asked whether they were not 'addressed to the
passions.' 'They were nothing, sir, be they addressed to what they may.'
They are not so much sermons as essays, composed by a professor of
rhetoric to illustrate the principles of his art. For unction there was
mere mouthing; instead of the solid common sense of earlier writers, an
infinite capacity for repeating the feeblest of platitudes; the style seems
to be determined by an attempt at the easy flow of the Addisonian
period, disturbed by a recollection of Johnsonian grandiloquence; the
morality can scarcely be dignified by the name of prudential, unless all
prudence be summed up in the great commandment, be respectable; the
theology is retained rather to give a faint seasoning to the general in-
sipidity of moral commonplace than seriously to influence the thought;
and the nearest approach to philosophical argument is some feeble echo
of Pope's 'Essay on Man.' Blair, in short, is in theology what Hayley
was in poetry—a mere washed-out retailer of second-hand commonplaces, who gives us the impression that the real man has vanished, and
left nothing but a wig and gown. Such was the phantom devised by the
goddess Dulness in the 'Dunciad':—

> All as a partridge plump, full-fed and fair,
> She formed this image of well-bodied air;
> With pert flat eyes she windowed well its head;
> A brain of feathers, and a heart of lead;
> And empty words she gave and sounding strain,
> But senseless, lifeless! idol void and vain!

21. Is it worth while to dip into the pages of this solemn trifling? to
quote prosings about adversity and prosperity, and the happiness of a
middle station, or eulogies upon that most excellent of virtues, moderation; and warnings against ever running into extremes, or proofs that
religion is, on the whole, productive of pleasure? 'We call you not to
renounce pleasure,' he says to the young, 'but enjoy it in safety. Instead
of abridging it, we exhort you to pursue it on an extensive plan. We
propose measures for securing its possession and for prolonging its
duration.'[26] Christ, Blair says, is our great example; and Christ's special
merit seems to have been that he indulged in 'no unnatural austerities,

[25]Boswell, ch. xxxiv. (1777).   [26]Blair, p. 111.

no affected singularities,' but practised the virtues 'for which we have most frequent occasion in ordinary life.'[27] Christ's deportment was unimpeachable. Yet, at due intervals, Blair invites us to a higher strain. He knows that a preacher ought to have his rhetorical flights as well as his calm levels of moral advice. And here is a specimen. 'To thee, O Devotion! we owe the highest improvement of our nature, and the merit of the enjoyment of our life. Thou art the support of our virtue and the rest of our souls in this turbulent world. Thou composest the thoughts, thou calmest the passions;' and, in short, givest me an excellent opportunity for finishing a paragraph with an admirable prosopopœia, according to the approved rules of art.

Nothing more need be said, unless, indeed, it may be as well to repudiate the hasty conclusion that Blair was a mere hypocrite. His creed, obviously, was a mere thing of shreds and patches; but, fortunately for us, men are frequently better than their creeds.

III. The Poets.

22. The preacher of an age should, I have said, find utterance for the real belief of their hearers, instead of the mere sham relics of extinct beliefs. The penalty for shortcoming is that the hearers will not be moved. But, unfortunately, this penalty has been so generally incurred, that the value of sermons as indications of the contemporary currents of thought is materially diminished. For a less questionable evidence we should turn to the natural channels of spontaneous emotions. The imaginative literature of an age must express the genuine feelings of the age, or it will perish stillborn. From Pope, and Swift, and Addison, we can often learn more safely than from Clarke, or Waterland, or Bentley, what were the deepest convictions of their age.

23. Many circumstances, I must once more repeat, contribute to determine the character of a literature, besides the logical relations of its dominant ideas. That which was once called the Augustan age of English literature was specially marked by the growing development of a distinct literary class. It was a period of transition from the early system of the patronage of authors to the later system of their professional independence. Patronage was being changed into influence. The system of subscription, by which Pope made his fortune, was a kind of joint-stock patronage. The noble did not support the poet, but induced his friends to subscribe. The noble, moreover, made another discovery. He

[27]Blair, p. 520.

found that he could dispense a cheaper and more effective patronage than of old by patronising at the public expense. During the reign of Queen Anne, the author of a successful poem or effective pamphlet might look forward to a comfortable place. The author had not to wear the livery, but to become the political follower, of the great man. Gradually a separation took place. The minister found it better to have a regular corps of politicians and scribblers in his pay than occasionally to recruit his ranks by enlisting men of literary taste. And, on the other hand, authors, by slow degrees, struggled into a more independent position as their public increased. In the earlier part of the century, however, we find a class of fairly cultivated people, sufficiently numerous to form a literary audience, and yet not so numerous as to split into entirely distinct factions. The old religious and political warfare has softened; the statesman loses his place, but not his head; and though there is plenty of bitterness, there is little violence. We have thus a brilliant society of statesmen, authors, clergymen, and lawyers, forming social clubs, meeting at coffee-houses, talking scandal and politics, and intensely interested in the new social phenomena which emerge as the old order decays; more excitable, perhaps, than their fathers, but less desperately in earnest, and waging a constant pamphleteering warfare upon politics, literature, and theology, which is yet consistent with a certain degree of friendly intercourse. The essayist, the critic, and the novelist appear for the first time in their modern shape; and the journalist is slowly gaining some authority as the wielder of a political force. The whole character of contemporary literature, in short, is moulded by the social conditions of the class for which and by which it was written, still more distinctly than by the ideas current in contemporary speculation. Whilst tracing, therefore, the connection between the philosophy and the artistic literature of the time, it is necessary to bear in mind that we are dealing with only part of a highly complex phenomenon.

24. Pope is the typical representative of the poetical spirit of the day. He may or may not be regarded as the intellectual superior of Swift or Addison; and the most widely differing opinions may be formed of the intrinsic merits of his poetry. The mere fact, however, that his poetical dynasty was supreme to the end of the century proved that, in some sense, he is a most characteristic product. Nor is it hard to see the main sources of his power. Pope had at least two great poetical qualities. He was amongst the most keenly sensitive of men, and he had an almost unique felicity of expression, which has enabled him to coin more proverbs than any writer since Shakespeare. Sensitive, it may be said, is a polite word for morbid, and his felicity of phrase was more adapted to

coin epigrams than poetry. The controversy is here irrelevant. Pope, whether, as I should say, a true poet, or, as some have said, only the most sparkling of rhymesters, reflects the thoughts of his day with a curious completeness. Some of his thoughts are, of course, the outgrowth of his own special idiosyncrasies; others are common to the poet of all ages; but Pope also resembles a plastic material, which has taken the impress of the main peculiarities of the time with singular sharpness and fidelity. The works which are specially instructive are, in the first place, the 'Essay on Man,' which is a poetical version of the religious creed of the age; secondly, the translation of Homer, which exemplifies some of its chief poetical theories; and, thirdly, the various satires, which are significant of its social structure. He has numerous followers and rivals in each of these capacities. Yet, as a translator and a satirist, and even as a didactic poet, he was scarcely approached by any writer of his own school, and will, perhaps, survive some writers who have been exalted above him by modern taste. The satires are on the borderland between prose and poetry. The characteristics of the loftier species of contemporary poetry must be sought chiefly in the other writings.

25. The 'Essay on Man' is Pope's most ambitious, though not his most successful, work. One great, and indeed insuperable, difficulty which made it unsatisfactory from the first, shows the radical unfitness of the philosophy of the time for poetical, and therefore for religious purposes. The 'Essay on Man' aspires to be, like Leibnitz's celebrated work, a 'Theodicæa.' The first paragraph ends, like the first paragraph of 'Paradise Lost,' with the statement that the poet hopes to 'vindicate[1] the ways of God to man.' Elsewhere,[2] Pope boasts, in a phrase adopted from the first stanza of the 'Faerie Queen,' that

> Not in Fancy's maze he wandered long,
> But stoop'd to truth and moralised his song.

The relation between the three poems is, indeed, characteristic. Milton and Spenser could utter their deepest thoughts about man's position in the universe and his moral nature by aid of a symbolism intelligible to themselves and their readers. But where was Pope to turn for concrete symbols sufficiently expressive of his thought? The legends of the Bible claimed too little reverence. Even in the majestic poetry of Milton we are unpleasantly reminded of the fact that the mighty expounder of Puritan thought is consciously devising a conventional imagery. The

---

[1]In Milton the word is 'justify.'   [2]'Epistle to Arbuthnot,' l. 341.

old romance which had fed Spenser's imagination was too hopelessly
dead to serve the purpose. It had left behind a wearisome spawn of so-
called romances; it had been turned into mere ribaldry by Butler; and
Pope wisely abandoned his cherished project of an epic poem, though
feebler hands attempted the task. The 'Essay on Man' is substantially a
versification of the most genuine creed of the time; of that Deism which
took various shapes with Clarke, Tindal, and Shaftesbury, and which
Bolingbroke seems to have more or less put into shape to be elaborated
into poetry by his friends. But the thought had generated no concrete
imagery. It remained of necessity what it was at first—a mere bare
skeleton of logic, never clothed upon by imaginative flesh and blood. As
in Clarke's sermons, we have diagrams instead of pictures; a system of
axioms, deductions, and corollaries instead of a rich mythology; a barren
metaphysico-mathematical theory of the universe, which might satisfy
the intellect, but remained hopelessly frigid for the emotional nature.

26. Pope's poetry is thus forced to become didactic, and not only
didactic, but ratiocinative. It consists of a series of arguments, and,
what is worse, of incoherent argument hitched into rhyme. The emotion is always checked by the sense that the Deity, whose ways are
indicated, is after all but a barren abstraction in no particular relation
to our race or its history. He never touches the circle of human interests. We believe in a mathematical proposition without caring whether
it was known to Archimedes or to Newton; and the God whose existence is proved like a proposition in Euclid brings us into no sympathy
with the saints and heroes of old. Primitive imaginings as to the nature
of God had become for Pope a meaningless jargon like the speculations
of Ptolemaic astronomers. Theology divorced from history does not take
us back to the Garden of Eden, but to some conventional age of which
we know, and the poet knows, that it never existed except as a metaphysical hypothesis. We have no visions of heaven and hell, regions
which obviously lie beyond the range of philosophy; and though Pope
was of course attacked for omitting them, their appearance in his poem
would have been æsthetically discordant as well as logically absurd. He
deals with demonstration, not with tradition. History is a miscellaneous
collection of precedents more or less applicable to modern times, but not
the record of earlier stages of processes still at work. The new enlightenment had made men more conscious than their ancestors of the difference between the thoughts of succeeding ages, and made them incapable
of the old naïve identification of classical, mediæval, and modern types;
it had not yet revealed the identities which produce a new interest in
the ancient forms as containing the germs of the new. Thus limited to

the sphere of abstract logic, only one practical conclusion emerges in the doctrine to which the essay finally leads us, 'that whatever is is right.' Nothing is less poetical than optimism; for the essence of a poet's function is to harmonise the sadness of the universe.

27. Pope, it must be added, might have been more successful even under these conditions if he had been more consistent. Unfortunately, his logic is spoilt by his timidity or his real absence of speculative power. A consistent pantheism or a consistent scepticism may be made the sources of profoundly impressive poetry. Each of them generates a deep and homogeneous sentiment which may utter itself in song. Pope, as the mouthpiece of Spinoza or of Hobbes, might have written an impressive poem, if he had not attained to the level of Lucretius. But the age was not favourable to consistency and thoroughness. The 'Essay on Man' remains radically unsatisfactory, considered as a whole, though there are many brief passages marked by Pope's special felicity of touch; many in which the moral sentiment is true and tender; and many in which he forgets for a moment the danger of open heterodoxy, and utters with genuine force some of the deeper sentiments which haunt us in this mysterious universe.

28. Another side of Pope's genius is illustrated chiefly by the translation of Homer. That translation undoubtedly produced a more powerful influence upon the age than any other which has ever been executed. Bentley, doubtless, expressed the opinion of all qualified readers, even at that time, when he said that it was a pretty poem, but not Homer. And yet, if the authority of competent critics may be trusted, it enjoys, in virtue of a certain width and vigour of style, a stronger vitality than that of recent performances of incomparably better scholars. The artistic theory, however, which is assumed throughout the work, is all that need attract our attention. Pope's view of Homer illustrates the peculiar classicism of the time. The merit at which Pope specially aimed— according to the often-repeated anecdote—was that described by the technical phrase 'correctness,' and to be correct was the same thing as to be classical. Warton, like Macaulay long afterwards, ridiculed the artificial code of criticism in which this formed the universal term of commendation. It is, however, worth while to endeavour to perceive its meaning a little more distinctly.

29. In religion, or morality, and in politics, the thought of the age recognised a system of abstract rules, mathematically precise and coherent, which, as regarded from various aspects, gave rise to the conceptions of the religion of nature, the law of nature, the social contract, and other allied hypotheses. A similar code was supposed to exist in the

sphere of imagination. Obedience to that code constituted correctness, though deviations might sometimes be excused under the name of irregular greatness. The political creed was then, as afterwards, a 'religion of nature,' taking that phrase in the sense of Clarke, rather than the sense of modern pantheistic or poetic mysticism. The imagination was to work within the limits prescribed for it by the cool and impartial reason. Superstition and enthusiasm—the dreaded diseases in the religious world—were equally abhorrent in the sphere of poetry. The poet was never to throw the reins upon the neck of his passion, or to abandon himself to a fine frenzy in defiance of mechanical laws. No sane critic will deny that there was a core of truth in these assumptions. The desire for correctness, so far as correctness implies symmetry, a continuous reference to the general effect in working out subordinate details, temperance in expression, and careful polish of style, is a sentiment indispensable to the creation of great and permanent work. The weakness of the Pope school consisted chiefly in the assumption that such a code of laws could be laid down in a series of mathematical propositions. The essence of poetry is to be spontaneous, and the laws obeyed by the imagination must, so to speak, be imbedded in its structure, not imposed from without. In the great ages of art the creative imagination is instinctively shocked by defects of harmony. In the more conscious and less passionate periods the instinct disappears, and the place is ill supplied by rules which can never be adequate, and which, therefore, appear to be artificial. The fine sense which enables a painter to draw an exquisite curve cannot be compensated by a pair of compasses, which enables a mechanic to draw a perfectly accurate and perfectly monotonous circle. The rules of Pope's period sanctioned the attempt to do by rule and compass what ought to be done by the eye. That is the natural result of reason intruding into the place of imagination, which makes poetry prosaic, as it lowers morality to a set of prudential maxims, and forces the religious instinct to abandon ideal symbols for a system of abstract laws.

30. But how were these rules to be framed? Where were men to look for that poetical code which was to take a place analogous to that of the 'law of nature'? The classical models, as interpreted by French critics, had the appearance of giving just the system of abstract rules founded on common sense which was required by the artist. There were difficulties, indeed, in accepting the French empire. The old English tradition remained throughout the century. Hume and Gibbon might prefer Racine to Shakespeare; but English writers in a blind way continued to protest against the chains imposed upon them. The rules of

epic poetry and the law of dramatic unities never fairly established themselves. Addison, indeed, criticised Milton by the help of Aristotle and Bossu, with all the correct jargon about the machinery, and the episodes, and the fable, and composed 'Cato' as a model of dramatic propriety. The old national vigour struggled against the imposition of these handcuffs, and Dennis, worst of critics though he might be, ridiculed 'Cato' effectively enough. But though the code of rules never became satisfactorily formulated, its potential existence was more or less tacitly assumed. The classical poets and their commentators occupied a poetical status precisely analogous to that of the Bible in theology. The once living forces were paralysed but not dead. The critic had succeeded to the commentator, but had not yet become openly sceptical. Similarly the classicalism of the time was midway between the taste of the Renaissance and that of modern times. The poet, down to the time of Milton, could avail himself freely of classical types, and mix the Christian and heathen mythology without any perception of incongruity. In our own day the growth of an historical sense has enabled us to understand classical art more perfectly, but has forced us to recognise the impossibility of reanimating the dead bones. The modern revivals are free from the old daring anachronisms, but the old fire is quenched. They can exhibit at best a momentary play of the poetic fancy, or the painful industry of the antiquarian. The transitional period presents a compromise between these opposite points of view. The old incongruities had become shocking. Lycidas appeared to be simply a monstrosity when tried at the tribunal of common sense. St. Peter, it was plain, belonged to a different family from Phœbus and Comus, and the herald of the seas, and they ought not to be brought together. Milton, no one could deny, was guilty of the grossest anachronism. But, meanwhile, an incongruity of a different, and to us more vexatious, kind passed without notice. The old mythology was regarded as dead, but it was still to be employed.

31. How was the difficulty to be surmounted? By accepting as a principle that poets might deal in consciously devised figments, so long as they took care not to break the illusion by figments belonging to different categories. The old spontaneous symbolism thus passed imperceptibly into an arbitrary conventionalism. What passed with ancient poets for divine inspiration was taken to be a process of conscious and deliberate invention. The process was precisely that which we have seen exemplified in theological and political controversies. Ancient prophets and legislators were no longer regarded as supernaturally inspired, but they were thought to have invented at one blow the mythologies and

religious rites and political institutions which we now see to have been the slow growth of uncounted ages. In the same way the poet was thought to have consciously devised the legends and the imagery which formed the subject of his song. When the poetical writers personified abstract qualities by the help of capital letters, they fancied that they were simply repeating the process by which the pagan pantheon had been originally filled. And as the classical poetry had thus been constructed by a consciously artificial process, there was no reason why the same plan should not answer as well in the eighteenth century. It never occurred, apparently, to the writers of the time that the old gods could ever have been the objects of a genuine and spontaneous belief. The theory is very clearly expressed in Pope's preface to his translation.

32. Homer, he says, is specially distinguished by the strength of his 'invention,' and by this he meant something quite different from exuberant vigour of expression or intense glow of imaginative insight. 'Homer,' says Pope, 'not only appears the inventor of poetry, but he excels the inventors of all other arts in this, that he has swallowed up the honour of those who succeeded him.' Homer 'invented' poetry as, according to the deists, ancient legislators invented heaven and hell, or as Watt invented the steam-engine. He sat down deliberately to invent a story with a proper set of characters, which should be in conformity with the best canons of criticism. He invented allegorical personages, moreover, in which he wrapped up 'secrets of nature and physical philosophy.' 'How fertile will that imagination appear which was able to clothe all the properties of the elements, the qualifications of the mind, the virtues and vices, in forms and persons, and to introduce them into actions agreeable to the nature of the things they shadowed!' Then Homer, though he did not exactly invent the gods, turned them to account for the first time. 'He seems the first who brought them into a system of machinery for poetry, and such a one as makes its greatest importance and dignity.' Nobody has been able to improve upon his invention, and after all changes of time and religion 'his gods continue to this day the gods of poetry.' This indeed is, unluckily, too near the truth. The gods now became mere theatrical properties, which did not even affect to be more than cunningly devised masks, the secret of whose destruction was fully understood by all. Unable to excite any true sentiment, the old spontaneity was to be replaced by the judicious code of rules about the fable and the 'machinery'—a most characteristic phrase—which recent critics defended by the authority of Aristotle.

33. The change was, in fact, the same which was taking place, though not so avowedly, in religion. There, too, the old supernatural agents

were becoming part of a cunningly devised machinery, intended to keep the wicked in order. The more cultivated classes did not wish to part with the old conceptions, but were content to use the old phrases, and explain them more or less distinctly to be merely conventional and allegorical. The palpable artificiality of these devices gave a hollowness and pomposity to the whole poetical school, which was faithfully reflected in the formal diction which excited Wordsworth's indignant rebellion. The poet, unable to use the vivid language of downright passion, lest the poor ghosts of old superstitions should be shrivelled into nothingness, was forced to distinguish his work from prose by the adoption of conventional phrases. Like the ancient actors, he wore a mask which produced the effect of a speaking-trumpet, and gave a certain factitious dignity to his empty words. A man of real genius like Pope still might preserve, amidst his conventionalities, some genuine sense of large effects and vigour of style; but in the succeeding generation the pseudo-classicalism became hopelessly effete, and could oppose no resistance to the new reaction. The epic poems of the latter part of the century, which still obeyed the old canons, such as Glover's 'Leonidas' and Wilkie's 'Epigoniad,' have sunk irrecoverably into the deepest gulfs of oblivion. Pope, however, though he struts and mouths, is not yet puerile or affectedly simple. He is not consciously trying to ape the manner of simpler ages; and though his theory as to ancient poetry is grotesquely wrong, it still leaves him a certain freedom of motion. If he has not the independent daring with which the great poets of the Renaissance use the old materials where they find them, he is not a mere imitator of extinct forces of thought. There is just a flutter of life in these dying conventionalities. By the side of Pope's 'Homer' we may, perhaps, place Addison's 'Cato,' as the most successful attempt to transplant to the English stage something of the contemporary classicalism. Addison, however, was trying an unfortunate experiment. He had to lay aside that exquisite humour in which he was unrivalled, and had not the fire which could have given some animation to his lay figures. A few familiar quotations have survived the decay of the general fabric, to show that his elegance of style had not quite deserted him; but his characters are scarcely even shadows; they are nonentities.

34. Pope's influence remained, in a certain sense, predominant until the revolutionary era. His versification became the common form for all poets of the second order. He was placed by ordinary critics in the front rank of English poets; and the poetical revolution led by Wordsworth and Coleridge took the form of a protest against his authority. It must, however, be observed that the supremacy was never complete, as is

sometimes assumed. There were many symptoms of revolt from the very beginning of the dynasty, and Pope is to be considered more accurately as marking the culmination of the tendencies which his writings embody than as inaugurating a new period. Like the Deism with which his poetical doctrines are correlated, the poetry of the true Pope school was a rather evanescent phenomenon, and was in full vigour for his own generation alone. The chief poetical writers of the century all deviate more or less from Pope's peculiar model. The divergence of form is significant. Thomson, Young, and Akenside, for example, discard the monotony of the heroic couplet in favour of blank verse, though their blank verse is of a stilted and constrained character. Collins and Gray express themselves in the lyrical form which is least adapted to Pope's calmer and more reasoning temperament. Another significant circumstance is the fashion of imitating Spenser, denounced by Johnson in the 'Rambler.' 'Life is surely given us for higher purposes,' says that incarnation of strong sense, 'than to gather what our ancestors have wisely thrown away, and to learn what is of no value but because it has been forgotten.'[3] Spenser's poetry is indeed the precise antipodes of Pope's, and its tender romance aimed against all those canons of common sense in which Johnson was the sturdiest of believers. For that reason his fairyland was a delightful retreat for poets weary with the prevailing rigidity of form and coldness of sentiment. Steele had tried to bring Spenser into notice in the 'Tatler' and 'Spectator.' Thomson's charming 'Castle of Indolence' and Shenstone's 'Schoolmistress' were popular echoes of Spenser's style; Beattie makes his 'Minstrel' confute Hume in Spenserian stanzas; William Thompson, Gilbert West, the defender of the Resurrection, Lloyd, the friend of Colman, Wilkie, of the 'Epigoniad,' Mickle, the translator of Camoens, and Cambridge, best known by the 'Scribleriad,' all wrote imitations of more or less elaborate kind. Collins loved Spenser, and Gray paid him a more discriminating homage than that of sheer imitation, for he never wrote a line himself without attuning his mind by first reading Spenser for a considerable time. Pope himself, it may be noticed, was a lover of Spenser in his boyhood, though a coarse burlesque seems to imply that he regarded him with no particular reverence. In fact, the poets of the eighteenth century, with one or two exceptions, show a disposition to edge away from the types which they professed to admit as ideally correct.

35. In spite, however, of such instinctive deviations towards a differ-

[3] 'Rambler,' No. 121.

ent type, the general characteristics so prominent in Pope are strongly marked upon all the chief poetical works of the time. Prior's 'Solomon' might be compared to Pope's 'Essay on Man,' to which it was greatly preferred by Wesley, as more in harmony with his theories of human corruption. The design, indeed, is more poetical, because less tending to the argumentative; though the inferior execution has prevented Prior from attaining the occasional success which redeems parts of Pope's poem from oblivion. Blackmore's 'Creation' gives a system of natural theology in several thousand lines of blank verse, of which no phrase has survived, though Johnson's orthodoxy caused a reprint of the portentous mass in collections of English poets. Three poems not written by Pope, and of comprehensive design, made a considerable impression in the first half of the century, and two at least have still a certain vitality. Thomson's 'Seasons' appeared in 1726–30, Young's 'Night Thoughts' in 1742–46, and Akenside's 'Pleasures of the Imagination' (in its first form) in 1744. Each of these has a didactic purpose.

36. Thomson is generally noticed as an exception to the general tendency of eighteenth-century poetry, by reason of his original descriptions of natural scenery, and is, in this capacity, the forerunner of Cowper and Wordsworth. This part of his poetry has survived the rest, as genuine work must always survive mere second-hand conventionalities. It may fairly be said, too, that the power with which he represents nature—and there are few poems in which we can more distinctly hear the wind stirring the forests, and feel the sun striking upon the plains—makes him, in some degree, exceptional. He was an outsider of that brilliant society which delighted in the life of towns as in a new-found pleasure, which looked upon fox-hunting squires as the embodiment of rustic brutality, and could never sincerely prefer a hillside to a coffee-house. But the judgment probably exaggerates the indifference of the age to descriptive poetry, and certainly exaggerates the indifference of Thomson to the general thought of his time. The love of nature was not with Thomson, as with Cowper, a sign of any revolutionary tendency. He was a Whig, not a Radical, in poetry as in politics. He was given to pompous declamations about liberty, simplicity, integrity, and various excellent abstractions, such as fell in well enough with the general tone of the opponents of Walpole in the days of the long opposition. His poem upon 'Liberty,' which Johnson confesses that he had never read, appears—so far as I have inspected it—to be a series of such sounding commonplaces as Bolingbroke was in the habit of embodying in his political essays. Doubtless there was some sincerity in such declamation, but clearly there was little passion. It implied contempt for

priestcraft, and dislike to the absolute rule of a despot; but not the least desire to upheave and reconstruct society. It is the sentiment of a British Whig, not of Rousseau or Voltaire. The poem on 'Liberty' and the plays, in which he indulged the same vein, are as dead as Blackmore. The 'Seasons' survives by virtue of that genuine eye for open-air sights and sounds which excited Wordsworth's sympathy. But if we ask what was Thomson's conception of nature, we shall see that it was substantially that of his age. The old pastoral poetry which filled the country with fauns and satyrs and semi-mythological rustics was extinct; its last breath was uttered in the faded sentimentalism of Phillips and Pope, and the dead form was only available for such pleasantry as that of Gay and Lady Mary Wortley Montagu. In the previous century, Thomson would probably have adopted the form of Jonson's 'Sad Shepherd,' or Fletcher's 'Faithful Shepherdess,' or Milton's 'Comus.' But the mythology which they assumed in the Renaissance spirit was too extinct for serious poetry. In the succeeding century he might have adopted Wordsworth's lofty mysticism, and seen in nature the living embodiment of the great forces which pervade the universe, conformity with which constitutes the highest happiness of man, and a true insight into which makes him a genuine poet. Or, again, nature might have suggested to him that kind of misanthropy, or perhaps soured philanthropy, which breathes in the sentimentalism of Rousseau and Byron, and implies the revolt of passion against the ossified organisation of an effete society.

37. Thomson shared with such men, and indeed, with poets of all ages, a vivid enjoyment of natural beauty, but it suggested to him a different set of reflections. He learns, as all thoughtful men must learn, the advantages of quiet and contemplation as a relief to the restlessness and excitement of town life. Contemplation with the true Thomson perhaps meant lying in bed till mid-day and enjoying his bottle at night. In his poetical capacity, however, it meant an indulgence in the ordinary philosophising of the period. In 'Winter,' for example, he follows in one passage the general design of Milton's 'Allegro;'[4] but, instead of indulging the romantic visions which seemed congenial to the retirement of the elder poet, he proposes to find time to discuss moral philosophy with Lyttelton, and to talk commonplaces about corruption with Chesterfield. Nature is not so much regarded as itself a living power, or animated by the forms projected from a poetic imagination, as the series of judi-

---

[4] See passage beginning:—
        Thus in some deep retirement would I pass.

cious arrangements which enabled the theologians of the day to confront sceptics. And, therefore, Thomson, though a most genuine lover of natural scenery, sees in it a comparatively lifeless series of phenomena. The pompous style is still more significant of the contemporary tendency; but it would be doing Thomson gross injustice to force him into the framework of a theory, or to overlook the fact that some men in the first half of the eighteenth century could feel the beauty of nature as deeply as Milton before them, or as Wordsworth afterwards. The rapture and the mystic glow is not, indeed, to be found, and too often we are jarred by conventional sentiment and mere prosaic argument. But a good healthy delight in natural beauty was never quite absent from our literature.

38. If Thomson's unfortunate tendency to didactic and bombastic declamation led to a lamentable waste of his powers in 'Liberty,' and injures parts of the 'Seasons,' it is unfortunately far more prominent in the other two writers I have named. Young was one of the cleverest men who ever wrote English verse, but the cleverness extinguishes the imagination. The 'Night Thoughts,' owing in great measure to its subject, has enjoyed a vast popularity, in spite of its offences against all literary canons of taste. It was intended by its author as a supplement to the 'Essay on Man:'

Man, too, he (Pope) sung; immortal man I sing.[5]

Young expresses, that is, those supplementary doctrines which constituted the difference between the religion of nature and Revelation. The design and form are equally characteristic of the time. Young sees no visions, but he argues with overstrained energy; he sets up an infidel man of straw in the ordinary fashion of the orthodox preacher; denounces him through several nights, and finally reclaims him by a battery of arguments for immortality. There is as little of really deep sentiment as of sincerity; for, in fact, Young's hatred of the world revealed the disappointed patronage-hunter, rather than the religious enthusiast; and, instead of a uniform flow of poetry, or even of rhetoric, he lashes himself into a never-ending series of antitheses. The unnatural strain is felt in every line; each paragraph bristles with a number of points; witty epigrams take the place of imaginative images; and he resorts to an exuberant use of italics to enforce every smart saying upon the reluctant hearer. His ingenuity is so great, that we may fancy that he could have rivalled the far-fetched conceits of Donne and Herbert;

[5]Night the First.

but the quaintness is not redeemed by simplicity, or a substratum of genuine earnestness. Every line shows us a very clever man labouring to be more clever than nature has made him, and eager to win applause by the skill with which he exposes the worthlessness of applause.

39. The substance is everywhere commonplace; and Young shows his inferiority to Pope by inventing phrases for copybooks, where Pope coins proverbs for cultivated thinkers. The love of gloom, of the imagery of the grave, and the awful mysteries of life, which animated our older writers, is not absent, but it is turned to account by this clever man of the world with such ingenuity, that we become aware of the shallowness of his feeling. How hollow are the enjoyments of this world, and how deep the surrounding mystery! is the ostensible sentiment. What a clever fellow I am, and what a shame it is that I was not made a bishop! is the sentiment plainly indicated in every line. Can I not say as many smart things about death and eternity as anybody that ever wrote? Am I not a good orthodox reasoner, instead of a semi-deist like that sinner Pope? We see, as we read, the very type of the preacher of a period when the old mythology, no longer credible or really imposing to the imagination, is still regarded as capable of, at least, an ostensible demonstration, and may afford a sufficient excuse for any quantity of intellectual ingenuity. To serious minds, one would have thought, the exhibition must always have been repulsive, were it not that serious minds seem specially liable to be imposed upon by an affectation of religious unction; and are willing to admit for genuine poetry, if disguised by a thin mask of orthodoxy, a kind of writing which reminds us of Pope's

> Dissonance and captious art,
> And snip-snap short and misconceptions smart,
> And demonstration thin, and theses thick,
> And major, minor, and conclusion quick.

Indeed, if Young is not capable of a noble melancholy, he is in a thoroughly bilious condition. This preacher among the tombs cannot rival the grim pathos of Hamlet with Yorick's skull; but he could have turned as many epigrams about it as would have thoroughly astonished the gravediggers, and excited the envy of Rosencrantz and Guildenstern. If he cannot show Lorenzo heaven and hell, the angels harping in 'unexpressive quire,' and the devils defying the Almighty despot from the ocean of fire, he can fairly triumph over him when he exclaims

> Hence a fifth proof arises, stronger still;

for poor Lorenzo is not allowed to have an innings—otherwise he might have remarked that a poet who no longer sees, but argues, has ceased to be either poetical or convincing. Young's parody of 'Othello,' called 'Revenge,' is a curious illustration of the view taken of the Shake-spearian drama by the poets of the eighteenth century; and his satires, called 'The Love of Fame,' are a proof, to any one who needs it, that something more than extreme cleverness was necessary to give to Pope's writings their enduring brilliance. And yet Young has talent enough to have made a mark in any age as a writer of the second order.

40. Akenside is a man of very different stamp. A certain force and dignity of thought is perceptible beneath a rather cumbrous style; he is prompted to write by a full mind instead of an empty purse. He has a certain message to deliver to mankind, and the difficulty of his utter-ance is characteristic. For, in fact, he is wrestling with the difficulty which perplexed Pope in the 'Essay on Man.' He has to make bricks without straw; to turn a philosophical system into poetry without the help of any symbolic imagery except a few hollow abstractions such as the Genius of the Human Race, Happiness, Virtue, and Remorse. The vision in which these personages appear and declare their sentiments with amiable frankness displeased Akenside himself in later years, and he swept them away in recasting his poem, to be able to philosophise at his ease. The doctrine which Akenside undertook to expound had some natural charms for a poet. He stood in nearly the same relation to Shaftesbury which Pope occupied to Bolingbroke, though the inspiration was less direct, and the coincidence not so close. Parts of this philosophy —the doctrine especially that ridicule is the test of truth—were as little suited for poetical treatment as can well be imagined. But the general theory, the identification of the good, the true, and the beautiful, the belief in an all-pervading harmony revealing itself to the purified intel-lect, was calculated to generate a poetical philosophy, if not a philosophi-cal poetry. Akenside says[6] that the separation of philosophy from the imagination has been an injury to both; and congratulates himself on their closer approximation in recent years. At the time of the Revolu-tion, he says, Locke was at the head of one party, Dryden at the head of the other. Now poets have taken to 'subjects of importance to society;' and philosophy must 'borrow of their embellishments, in order even to gain an audience with the public.' It would not be very easy to translate these generalities into particular instances; but the sentiment is charac-

[6]See Argument of Book ii. on the first form, and note.

teristic. Akenside judged well in desiring a harmony between poetry and philosophy; but the attempt at a fusion was unfortunate. His formulas suffered a fate analogous to that of his master's writings. The rather stilted style and not very lucid thought have in both cases rendered the difficulty of penetrating to the real thought too great for cursory readers; and a poet suffers more than a philosopher for wrapping his meaning in sententious obscurity.

41. Thomson and Young had each their followers, though I do not know that anybody imitated more than the title of Akenside's poetry. Blair's 'Grave' is a kind of corollary to Young's 'Night Thoughts;' Mallet's 'Excursion' and Savage's 'Wanderer' are attempts to follow Thomson; and perhaps we might put in the same class such poems as Falconer's 'Shipwreck,' Somerville's 'Chase,' or Dyer's 'Fleece,' so highly praised by Wordsworth. The second-rate performances are dead, while even the best have but a feeble vitality. The general source of weakness is abundantly evident. The philosophy and the passions of an age should be projected into concrete symbols by the poetical imagination. But the passions were too cool, and the philosophy too abstract and frigid, to be capable of symbolic representation. Nothing remained but didactic, or rather argumentative poetry, in which the feeble 'machinery' of mere abstractions, galvanised into some faint semblance of vitality by the free use of capital letters, mere shadows of shades, phantasmal images of ghosts long since laid, wandered dreamily through the mazes of con-sciously constructed allegories. No wonder that such a poetry gradually collapsed, after feebly trying to support itself above the solid ground of prose by help of an inflated phraseology. As the philosophy itself ceased to be interesting after the middle of the century, the poetry, which was but the philosophy versified, decayed still more rapidly, and expired altogether at the first touch of real passion. There are still imitations of Pope's satires, some of them of considerable force; there are some pon-derous attempts at epics and classical drama by Glover, Wilkie, and Mason, but the didactic or philosophical poetry becomes extinct. Two poets, indeed, of very remarkable quality, may be regarded as in some sense belonging to the earlier school. The exquisite felicities of Gray's 'Elegy' and Goldsmith's 'Traveller' and 'Deserted Village' show the true polish desired by the disciples of the correct school. But Gray is more than half romantic in his temperament, and Goldsmith is deeply tinged with the sentimentalism of Rousseau. The influence of the older canons of taste is chiefly perceptible in diminishing the productiveness and stimulating the fastidious taste of these two admirable poets.

IV. General Literature.

42. There is, however, another wide province of literature in which writers of the eighteenth century did work original in character and of permanent value. If the seventeenth century is the great age of dramatists and theologians, the eighteenth century was the age in which the critic, the essayist, the satirist, the novelist, and the moralist first appeared, or reached the highest mark. Criticism, though still in its infancy, first became an independent art with Addison. Addison and his various colleagues set the first example of that kind of social essay which is still popular. Satire had been practised in the preceding century, and in the hands of Dryden had become a formidable political weapon; but the social satire of which Pope was, and remains, the chief master, began with the century, and may be said to have expired with it, in spite of the efforts of Byron and Gifford. De Foe, Richardson, Fielding, and Smollett developed the modern novel out of very crude rudiments; and two of the greatest men of the century, Swift and Johnson, may be best described as practical moralists in a vein peculiar to the time. I have already pointed out, more than once, that the causes of the great development of this kind of literature must be sought chiefly in social conditions. The rise of a class of comparatively educated and polished persons, large enough to form a public, and not so large as to degenerate into a mob, distinct from the old feudal nobility, and regarding the life of the nobles with a certain contempt as rustic and brutal, more refined again than that class of hangers-on to the Court, of merchants and shopkeepers stamped with the peculiarities of their business, which generated the drama of the Restoration, and, on another side, beginning to despise the pedants of colleges and cathedrals as useless and antiquated encumbrances, accounts for many of the most obvious phenomena of the time. After the long struggle of the end of the preceding century, the society called 'the Town' in the language of the essayists, definitely emerges, and is inclined to identify itself with the nation. Poets, novelists, essayists, and satirists consult its tastes, and consider Temple Bar as the centre of the universe. What are the characteristics in its intellectual relations of the literature which emerges?

43. Three tendencies, strongly marked in all this crowd of writers, may be noticed as sufficiently indicative of the contemporary modes of thought. The first is a speculative, the second an ethical, and the third an æsthetic tendency. They are intimately connected, and may be plausibly deduced from the working of the dominant ideas which have been expounded in previous chapters. The first half of the century was a

period of vehement discussion; the deists and their antagonists fought over questions of the deepest importance with an energy proportional to the interests at stake. But there is a tendency, strongly marked on both sides, which determines the limits of the controversy. Neither party wishes really to push matters to an extremity. The deists attack priest-craft with fierce hostility; but they do not wish to destroy theology. The priest once deprived of his exaggerated pretensions may be allowed to remain as a useful member of society, and the natural religion which is desired is to be but a modified and emasculated version of the old creed. The orthodox, on the other hand, have no inclination to attack the vital principles of their opponents. They admit the duty of free thought; they claim to be thoroughgoing rationalists, and they only desire to embody the teaching of reason in the old formula. Both sides tacitly evade certain crucial questions. Even Butler refrains from search-ing into the fundamental difficulty; and Hume alone dares to suggest the logical answer. This kind of intellectual indolence is revealed in the sphere of direct controversy by a general superficiality and readiness to put up with flimsy theories; and it is naturally connected with the cardinal fact that, in attacking the religious theory of the time, the deists were not animated, like their French successors, by any decided discon-tent with the social order. They were not seriously persecuted, and did not wish to inflict serious injury. To keep the clergy well under the heel of parliamentary authority would describe the ultimate limit of their political aspirations, as in a philosophical sense they wished generally to preserve theology, whilst getting rid of the supernatural. In literature the same tendency is marked by a stronger feeling. The strongest intel-lects of the day perceived, or felt instinctively, that the tendency of the deist speculations was to undermine the whole social order, and to undermine it in the interests of a flimsy creed. To any man with a strong sense of the practical needs of the time, the deists appeared to be superficial theorists who were gratifying their vanity at the expense of the most important institutions. They were insisting upon asking questions which had better not be asked, and to which they were prepared with no satisfactory answer. To stir the very foundations of society, a man must be prompted either by a passionate love of speculation, or by a distinct prospect of some fruitful result, or by a conviction of the abso-lute necessity of social reconstruction. Neither of the last two elements was present; and the pure love of enquiry is at all times the rarest of endowments. The hidden fear of dangerous consequences, which kept the deists to half-truths, led men of strong, but not really speculative, intellects to object to speculation altogether.

44. This sentiment is curiously expressed in the ablest writing of the time, down to the very end of the century, when it takes a rather different colouring. Why can't you let things alone? is the unanimous cry of the intellectual leaders. The old theology is effete; but a creed which is effete (an unlucky but a plausible doctrine!) is harmless. The deists are almost uniformly mentioned with a mixture of contempt and dislike. Addison dislikes them as much as he can dislike any one. Swift dislikes them, also, as much as he can dislike any one; and the phrase in his case represents, perhaps, the greatest intensity of aversion of which the human soul is capable. With the whole body of essayists, from Steele downwards, a deist is a futile coxcomb, to be ridiculed like the 'virtuoso' and the fine gentleman. The novelists are equally clear. De Foe makes Robinson Crusoe preach sermons fit for a dissenting pulpit. Richardson has so great a contempt for infidels that he will not contemplate the possibility that even a Lovelace should disbelieve in a future state of rewards and punishments. Fielding, laughing over his beer and pipe at Richardson's namby-pamby sentiment, still has as hearty a contempt for a deist as for a Methodist. Johnson turns the roughest side of his contempt to any one suspected of scepticism, and calls Adam Smith a 'son of a bitch.' When Burke endeavours to blast the deists with his fiery rhetoric at the end of the century, it is only that the wrath which had been smouldering whilst the Deism was comparatively masked bursts into flame as soon as the concealment vanishes. The common sense of the country was entirely on the side of Revelation as against Deism, and the ablest writers were but the mouthpiece of the common sense. The result, however, of this sentiment was not to give an actively orthodox tone to the writing of the time; for theology was for the most part almost as deistical as the deists.

45. A hatred for enthusiasm was as strongly impressed upon the whole character of contemporary thought as a hatred of scepticism. And thus the literary expression of the feeling is rather a dislike to all speculation than a dislike to a particular school of speculatists. The whole subject was dangerous, and should be avoided by reasonable men. A good common-sense religion should be taken for granted, and no questions asked. If the philosophy of the time was unfitted for poetry, it was, for the same reason, unfitted to stimulate the emotions, and therefore for practical life. With Shakespeare, or Sir Thomas Browne, or Jeremy Taylor, or Milton, man is contemplated in his relations to the universe; he is in presence of eternity and infinity; life is a brief dream; we are ephemeral actors in a vast drama; heaven and hell are behind the veil of phenomena; at every step our friends vanish into the vast abyss

of ever-present mystery. To all such thoughts the writers of the eighteenth century seemed to close their eyes as absolutely as possible. They do not, like Sir Thomas Browne, delight to lose themselves in an Oh! Altitudo! or to snatch a solemn joy from the giddiness which follows a steady gaze into the infinite. The greatest men amongst them, a Swift or a Johnson, have indeed a sense—perhaps a really stronger sense than Browne or Taylor—of the pettiness of our lives and the narrow limits of our knowledge. No great man could ever be without it. But the awe of the infinite and the unseen does not induce them to brood over the mysterious, and find utterance for bewildered musings on the inscrutable enigma.

46. It is felt only in a certain habitual sadness which clouds their whole tone of thought. They turn their backs upon the infinite and abandon the effort at a solution. Their eyes are fixed upon the world around them, and they regard as foolish and presumptuous any one who dares to contemplate the great darkness. The expression of this sentiment in literature is a marked disposition to turn aside from pure speculation, combined with a deep interest in social and moral laws. The absence of any deeper speculative ground makes the immediate practical questions of life all the more interesting. We know not what we are, nor whither we are going, nor whence we come; but we can, by the help of common sense, discover a sufficient share of moral maxims for our guidance in life, and we can analyse human passions, and discover what are the moving forces of society, without going back to first principles. Knowledge of human nature, as it actually presented itself in the shifting scene before them, and a vivid appreciation of the importance of the moral law, are the staple of the best literature of the time. As ethical speculation was prominent in the philosophy, the enforcement of ethical principles is the task of those who were inclined to despise philosophy. When a creed is dying, the importance of preserving the moral law naturally becomes a pressing consideration with all strong natures.

47. I have coupled Swift and Johnson as the two most vigorous representatives of this tendency. Between them there is a curious analogy as well as a striking contrast. They are alike in that shrewd humorous common sense which seems to be the special endowment of the English race. They are alike, too, in this: that they express the reaction against the complacent optimism of the Pope-Shaftesbury variety. They illustrate the incapacity of that system of thought to satisfy men of powerful emotional nature. The writings of each might be summed up in a phrase embodying the most uncompromising protest against the optimist

philosophy. Swift says, with unrivalled intensity, that the natural man is not, as theorists would maintain, a reasonable and virtuous animal; but, for the most part, a knave and a fool. Johnson denies, with equal emphasis, though with inferior literary power, that the business of life can be carried on by help of rose-coloured sentiments and general complacency. The world is, at best, but a melancholy place, full of gloom, of misery, of wasted purpose, and disappointed hopes. 'Whatever is, is right,' say the philosophers. Make up the heavy account of suffering, of disease, vice, cruelty, of envy, hatred, and malice, of corruption in high places, of starvation and nakedness amongst the low, of wars, and pestilences, and famines, of selfish ambition trampling on thousands, and wasted heroism strengthening oppression by its failure, of petty domestic tyranny, of lying, hypocrisy, and treachery, which run through all the social organism like a malignant ulcer, and see how far your specious maxim will take you.

48. That is the melancholy burden of the teaching of each of these great men; and it was echoed in various tones by many who felt that the grain of a sham philosophy consisted chiefly of unprofitable husks. Between Swift and Johnson, indeed, there was a wide difference; and the sturdy moralist had a hearty dislike for the misantropist whose teaching was so far at one with his own. The strong sense of evil which, in Johnson's generous nature, produced rather sadness than anger, had driven Swift to moody hatred of his species. He is the most tragic figure in our literature. Beside the deep agony of his soul, all other suffering, and especially that which takes a morbid delight in contemplating itself, is pale and colourless. He resembles a victim tied to the stake and slowly tortured to madness and death; whilst from his proudly compressed lips there issue no weak lamentations, but the deep curses of which one syllable is more effective than a volume of shrieks. Through the more petty feelings of mere personal spite and disappointed ambition we feel the glow of generous passions doomed to express themselves only in the language of defiant hatred. The total impression made by Swift's writings is unique and almost appalling; for even the sheer brutality suggests some strange disease, and the elaborate triflings remind us of a statesman amusing himself with spiders in a Bastille. If we ask what were the genuine creeds of this singular intellect, the answer must be a blank. The 'Tale of a Tub' is the keenest of satire against all theologians; 'Gulliver's Travels' expresses the concentrated essence of contempt for all other classes of mankind; the sermons and tracts defend the Church of England in good set terms, and prove beyond all question his scorn of dissenters, deists, and papists; but it would be an insult to

that fiery intellect to suppose that his official defence of the Thirty-nine Articles represents any very vivid belief. He could express himself in very different fashion when he was in earnest. Jove's address, in the 'Day of Judgment,' shows the true Swift:—

> Offending race of human kind,
> By nature, learning, reason blind;
> You who through frailty stept aside,
> And you who never fell—from pride;
> You who in different sects were shammed,
> And come to see each other damned
> (So some folks told you, but they knew
> No more of Jove's designs than you)—
> The world's mad business now is o'er,
> And I resent these pranks no more—
> I to such blockheads set my wit!
> I damn such fools! Go, go, you're bit.

That is genuine feeling. The orthodox phrases are no more part of Swift than his bands and cassock.

49. Swift's idiosyncrasy would doubtless have made itself felt at any time. The special direction of his haughty passions and intense intellect is determined by the conditions of the time. In a time of strong beliefs he would have been a vehement partisan. But what to an intellect contemptuous of all shams were the specious varnish which Clarke and Shaftesbury spread over the hard facts of life, or the lifeless exuviæ of dead creeds which satisfied conventional theologians, or the pompous phrases with which the politicians of both sides disguised their struggles for the division of the spoils? Mere tawdry frippery, incapable of satisfying a man with brains fit for something more than the manipulation of extinct formulæ. Swift called himself an old Whig and an orthodox churchman; but he cared little enough for the Thirty-nine Articles, or the platitudes about standing armies or social contracts. He felt to the depths of his soul the want of any of the principles which in trying times take concrete shape in heroic natures; and he assumed that the whole race of the courtiers of kings and mobs in all ages were such vile crawling creatures as could sell England or starve Ireland to put a few thousands in their pockets. He felt the want of some religion, and therefore scalped poor Collins, and argued with his marvellous ingenuity of irony against 'the abolition of Christianity;' but the dogmas of theologians were mere matter for the Homeric laughter of the 'Tale of a Tub.' He had not the unselfish qualities or the indomitable belief

in the potential excellence of human nature to become a reformer of manners, or the speculative power to endeavour to remould the ancient creeds. He stands in fierce isolation amongst the calmer or shallower intellects of his time, with insight enough to see the hollowness of their beliefs, with moral depth enough to scorn their hypocritical self-seeking, and with an imagination fervid enough to give such forcible utterance to his feelings as has scarcely been rivalled in our literature. But he had not the power or the nobility of nature to become a true poet or philosopher or reformer. When a shallow optimism is the most living creed, a man of strong nature becomes a scornful pessimist.

50. Johnson escaped from the hell of Swift's passion by virtue of that pathetic tenderness of nature which lay beneath his rugged outside. If Swift excites a strange mixture of repulsion and pity, no one can know Johnson without loving him. And what was Johnson's special message to the world? He has given it most completely in 'Rasselas;' and the curious coincidence between 'Rasselas' and 'Candide' has been frequently noticed. Voltaire, the arch-iconoclast, Johnson, last of the Tories, agree in making the protest against optimism the topic of their most significant works. Besides the vast difference in style between the greatest master of literary expression and the powerful writer whose pen seems to be paralysed by his constitutional depression, there is another striking difference. The moral of 'Candide' is, in one sense, speculative. The result, it is true, is purely negative. Optimism, that is Voltaire's thesis, will not fit the facts of the world. Johnson, on the other hand, is exclusively moral. A disciple of Voltaire would learn to 'cultivate his garden' and abandon speculation; but then, with speculation, he would abandon all theology. A disciple of Johnson learns the futility of enquiring into the ultimate purposes of the Creator; but he would acquiesce in the accepted creed. It is as good as any other, considered as a philosophy, and much better considered as supplying motives for the conduct of life. Johnson's fame amongst his contemporaries was that of a great moralist; and the name represents what was most significant in his teaching.

51. He was as good a moralist as a man can be who regards the ultimate foundations of morality as placed beyond the reach of speculalation. 'We know we are free, and there's an end on't,' is his answer to the great metaphysical difficulty. He 'refutes' Berkeley by kicking a stone. He thinks that Hume is a mere trifler, who has taken to 'milking the bull' by way of variety. He laughs effectually at Soame Jenyns's explanation of the origin of evil; but leaves the question as practically insoluble, without troubling himself as to why it is insoluble, or what

consequences may follow from its insolubility. Speculation, in short, though he passed for a philosopher, was simply abhorrent to him. He passes by on the other side, and leaves such puzzles for triflers. He has made up his mind once for all that religion is wanted, and that the best plan is to accept the established creed. And thus we have the paradox that, whilst no man sets a higher value upon truthfulness in all the ordinary affairs of life than Johnson, no man could care less for the foundations of speculative truth. His gaze was not directed to that side. Judging in all cases rather by intuition than by logical processes, he takes for granted the religious theories which fall in sufficiently with his moral convictions. To all speculation which may tend to loosen the fixity of the social order he is deaf or contemptuously averse. The old insidious Deism seems to him to be mere trash; and he would cure the openly aggressive Deism of Rousseau by sending its author to the plantations. Indifference to speculation generates a hearty contempt for all theories. He has too firm a grasp of facts to care for the dreams of fanciful Utopians; his emotions are too massive and rigid to be easily excited by enthusiasts. He ridicules the prevailing cry against corruption. The world is bad enough, in all conscience, but it will do no good to exaggerate or to whine. He has no sympathy with believers in the speedy advent of a millennium. The evils under which creation groans have their causes in a region far beyond the powers of constitution-mongers and political agitators.

> How small of all that human hearts endure
> That part which laws or kings can cause or cure![1]

52. These words sum up his political theory. Subordination is the first necessity of man, whether in politics or religion. To what particular form of creed or constitution men are to submit is a matter of secondary importance. No mere shifting of the superficial arrangements of society will seriously affect the condition of mankind. Starvation, poverty, and disease are evils beyond the reach of a Wilkes or a Rousseau. Stick to the facts, and laugh at fine phrases. Clear your mind of cant. Work and don't whine. Hold fast by established order, and resist anarchy as you would resist the devil. That is the pith of Johnson's answer to the vague declamations symptomatic of the growing unrest of European society. All such querulous complaints were classed by him with the fancies of a fine lady who has broken her china, or a fop who has spoilt his fine clothes by a slip in the kennel. He under-estimated the signifi-

---

[1] Lines added by Johnson to Goldsmith's 'Traveller.'

cance of the symptoms, because he never appreciated the true meaning of Hume or Voltaire. But the stubborn adherence of Johnson, and such men as Johnson, to solid fact, and their unreasonable contempt for philosophy, goes far to explain how it came to pass that England avoided the catastrophe of a revolution. The morality is not the highest, because it implies an almost wilful blindness to the significance of the contemporary thought, but appropriate to the time, for it expresses the resolute determination of the dogged English mind not to loosen its grasp on solid fact in pursuit of dreams; and thoroughly masculine, for it expresses the determination to see the world as it is, and to reject with equal decision the optimism of shallow speculation, and the morbid pessimism of such misanthropists as Swift.

53. The moralising tendency thus directly expressed by poets and preachers, both lay and professional, may be traced through many other forms. The essayists preach a series of sermons, varying indefinitely in grace and power, upon every conceivable text, from the shortness of life to the extravagant size of feminine petticoats. The same material, treated in verse, and mixed with more or less poetical feeling, supplies the satires of Swift, Pope, Johnson, Young, Churchill, Mason, Cowper, and their innumerable imitators and rivals. The novelists have a similar didactic tendency. De Foe preaches incessantly; Richardson is ostentatiously and supereminently a moralist; Fielding, though his morality is of a rather different type, moralises as persistently as any contemporary preacher, and a good deal more forcibly. The theatre which had excited the indignation of Collier was partly occupied by the moralists, and sentimental comedies took the place of the cynical dramas of the Restoration. The morality, whether inculcated by direct precepts, or pompous allegory, or fictitious narrative, is much of the same stamp. Everywhere it expresses the remarks upon human life and conduct made by shrewd and sensible men, living in a society defaced by much coarseness and corruption, and stirred by no very strong passions or deep speculations; but yet comfortable, growing in wealth and mechanical knowledge, and profoundly impressed with the importance of the domestic virtues.

54. Fielding, it is true, has a contempt for Richardson as a milksop and a straitlaced parson out of the pulpit. But Fielding has a very decided morality of his own. He does not, like the old dramatists, describe all passion with equal sympathy; nor, like Byron, express the indignant revolt against the whole system of effete respectability. He spares no pains to express his theory. He despises the Pharisee, and has

a considerable compassion for the sinner; but then there are sins of different degrees of turpitude. The doctrine of male chastity, expounded in 'Pamela,' struck him as simply ridiculous; but though a man was not bound to be a monk, he was not to be a seducer or a systematic voluptuary. He would be the last man to attack marriage, and his ideal woman, though made of very solid flesh and blood, is pure in conduct, if tolerably free in speech. His view reflects the code by which men of sense generally govern their conduct, as distinguished from that by which they affected to be governed in language. His respect for facts is, in this sense, as marked as Johnson's. He refuses to be imposed upon by phrases. The ecclesiastical type of morality, with its tendencies to the ascetic theory that passions should be eradicated rather than regulated, or that, at best, they are necessary evils to be kept within the narrowest bounds, produced that fierce reaction in France which seemed to assail not only theology, but all the virtues associated with it. In England, where theology was diluted instead of rejected, the reaction against the theological virtues was proportionally less intense. The ideal man of Fielding's novels is as far from being a libertine as from being an ascetic. He is a full-blooded healthy animal, but respects the Church so long as the Church does not break with common sense.

55. Parson Adams—probably his finest conception—drinks beer and smokes pipes, and when necessity compels, takes to the cudgels with a vigour which might have excited the envy of Christopher North. He scorns the unborn Malthus, and is outrageously impecunious in his habits. He is entirely free from worldliness, and is innocent as a child in the arts of flattery and timeserving. But it is not because he is an enthusiast after the fashion of Whitefield, or has any highflown views of the sacerdotal office.[2] Common sense is the rule of his life, or, in other words, the views which commend themselves to a man who sees the world as it is, who has no visionary dreams, and who has a thoroughly generous nature. Fielding would have Christianity freed from all extravagances—that is to say, from those vivid imaginings which subordinate the world of sense to the supernatural; he thinks that a man should be a gentleman, but laughs heartily at the extravagances of the fire-eating descendants of the old romantic cavaliers;[3] he is for a stringent enforcement of the moral laws, which actually keep society together, but has no patience with those who would attempt any radical reform,

[2]See 'Joseph Andrews,' ch. xvii., where Parson Adams gives his opinion of Whitefield, and expresses his admiration for Hoadly's book on the Sacrament.
[3]See especially Colonel Bath, in 'Amelia.'

or draw the line higher than ordinary human nature can endure. Richardson is more of a sentimentalist; De Foe is simply commonplace; and Smollett content to observe the eccentricities of his race without preaching about them. Fielding, though hardly an exalted moralist, expresses the genuine sentiment of his time with a force and fulness which make his works more impressive than the whole body of contemporary sermons, because untrammelled by conventional necessities.

56. The æsthetic tendency of the time is precisely in harmony with this moral sentiment. I have endeavoured to show how the poetry, in which the deepest thoughts of human beings should be reflected, had become merely argumentative, and had then died of inanition. A new form of art was developed which expressed more easily and fully the prevalent emotions of the time. The English novel, as the word is now understood, begins with De Foe. Though, like all other products of mind or body, it was developed out of previously existing material, and is related to the great family of stories with which men have amused themselves in all ages, it is, perhaps, as nearly an original creation as anything can be. The legends of saints which amused the Middle Ages, or the chivalrous romances which were popular throughout the seventeenth century, had become too unreal to amuse living human beings. De Foe made the discovery that a history might be equally interesting if the recorded events had never happened; and Richardson that a series of letters did not require real correspondents. Fielding, though his first novel was a parody of Richardson, was, no doubt, influenced, like Smollett, by the example of Le Sage, and, therefore, indirectly by the Spanish stories from which Le Sage drew his inspiration.

57. But, whatever the origin, the instinct gratified by the novels, and the conditions of the time, sufficiently determined the form. The world of legend and of ideal grandeur had grown dim. A new social form was developing itself. What could men do more natural than talk about themselves? And thus, since the days of De Foe, we have derived unceasing amusement from looking into the mirrors which reflect, with more or less fidelity, the incidents and manners of our daily life. As the essayists were never tired of discussing the social phenomena of the time, from the most trifling to the most serious, the novelists were never tired of portraying the same phenomena, coloured by some favourite moral or sentiment. From Sir Roger de Coverley and Robinson Crusoe down to the appearance of a new type in Waverley, we have a vast family of fictitious characters, who are the most faithful reflection of the originals. Indeed, as the novel is substantially the embodiment of remarks made by the ablest observers upon their contemporaries, we may

in some sense admit Fielding's claim to be a writer of history more faithful than the elaborate fictions generally known under that name. No enchanted light of old romance colours or distorts his fictions; we do not feel that his characters are puppets in the hands of an irresistible destiny, or constituent atoms of a vast organism slowly developing under the action of gigantic forces; there is no tender regret for past forms of society or passionate aspirations for the future. But for insight into the motives of his contemporaries; for a power of seeing things as they are; for sympathy with homely virtues; and contempt for shams and hypocrites, Fielding is as superior to some later writers of equal imaginative force as they are superior to him in width of sympathy and delicacy of perception. His art is thus the most faithful representative of his age; he gives its coarseness and its brutalities, and sometimes with too little consciousness of their evils, though no one ever satirised more powerfully the worst abuses of the time. But he also represents the strong healthy common sense and stubborn honesty of the sound English nature, with a certain massive power of grouping and colouring which is peculiar to himself.

58. In Fielding and his beloved Hogarth we have the 'prosai-comi-epos'—I use Fielding's phrase—of the middle class of the time. Richardson, though a greater artist, is far inferior in sheer intellectual vigour; and Smollett is comparatively but a caricaturist. Fielding announced that his object is to give a faithful picture of human nature. Human nature includes many faculties which had an imperfect play under the conditions of the time; there were dark sides to it, of which, with all his insight, he had but little experience; and heroic impulses, which he was too much inclined to treat as follies. But the more solid constituents of that queer compound, as they presented themselves under the conditions of the time, were never more clearly revealed to any observer. A complete criticism of the English artistic literature of the eighteenth century would place Fielding at the centre, and measure the completeness of other representatives pretty much as they recede from an approach to his work. Others, as Addison and Goldsmith, may show finer qualities of workmanship and more delicate sentiment; but Fielding, more than anyone, gives the essential—the very form and pressure of the time.

V. The Reaction.

59. How does the advent of a new creed announce itself to the world? If we were to frame a conjectural account of a revolution of

thought from our preconceived notions, we should perhaps be inclined to some such anticipations as these. The man, we should say, of greatest intellectual power will be the first to catch a sight of the new principles, and will most correctly appreciate their consequences. Some Descartes or Kant will lay down a new philosophical system, correcting and supplementing the old. The primary axioms having been modified, all the subsidiary consequences will gradually undergo a corresponding change, until the whole system of thought is gradually wrought into harmony. The religious conceptions, as being rightly felt to be of the greatest importance and exciting the strongest interest, will be the first to show the influence of new methods. As men come to take a different view of their position and destiny, they will gradually learn to subordinate their moral and political views to the new teaching, and the artistic expression of sentiment will mould itself upon the new framework of thought. The change impressed upon the vital principle of the organisation will gradually propagate itself to the remotest extremities.

60. Whether such a theory would fit any other revolution which has happened in the world is a question to be decided by other enquirers. It certainly does not fit that revolution in ideas which is the most striking phenomenon of the eighteenth century. The change does not follow any purely logical order. The greatest thinkers of the century are not the first to show the working of the new leaven. Hume was, in one sense, far in advance of his time, and indeed of the average opinion of the present time. But the change may in many respects be described as a revolt from Hume's opinions much more than a development of them. Nor could we say that the change in the speculative tendencies of the time preceded those other correlative changes which may be described as its logical consequences. The history of philosophical and of theological opinion in England is a history of gradual decay down to the revolutionary era, when a new impulse was received from France and Germany. But a revival of practical theology, that is to say, of devotional feeling and vigorous belief, had been developing itself in what may be called the subterranean channels of society from a period antecedent to the first publication of Hume's philosophy. Still less does it appear that any conscious logical process connected the various movements of thought, which we can now see to have been in some sense symptomatic of a new growth of ideas. Tendencies which display the working of processes destined at a later period to acquire a great importance in connection with a changed philosophical movement showed themselves sporadically and in curious combination with heterogeneous forms of opinion. We may find, for example, indications of the modern

tendency to mediæval revivalism in such a man as Walpole, who, in a philosophical sense, was the very embodiment of the Voltairean scepticism; and for certain purposes we might put him into the same class with Wesley, the religious reformer; with Richardson, a representative of the driest orthodoxy; and with Sterne, a representative of pure indifferentism. The particular mode of change may be more intelligible when we have examined it in greater detail; but a general conclusion may be at once indicated. The nature of the process is, in fact, misrepresented in our conjectural description. The change was not due to the gradual growth from below of a new order of ideas displacing the old, as the buds in spring push off the dead leaves of the previous season. A creed dies first at its extremities. Every creed decays, or certainly the creed decayed in this instance, as it became incapable of satisfying the instincts of various classes of the population, and the perception of its logical defects was the consequence, not the cause, of its gradual break-up. It was not that men perceived a new method of meeting Hume's scepticism, or the deistical arguments of Shaftesbury or Tindal; but that the Deism and the scepticism were unlike unable to supply satisfactory answers to the questions which men asked or a satisfactory language in which to clothe their emotions. The old creed met certain wants of the time sufficiently for the moment; but as society developed, as knowledge extended, and the instincts shaped themselves into new forms, the doctrine broke down at different and apparently unconnected points. One class required a more highly coloured symbolism for its religious emotions; another became weary of the old artistic forms which persisted after they had failed to correspond to any vivid beliefs; a third required a political theory which would gratify a stronger feeling of discontent; a fourth, and much smaller class, might be impressed by the growth of scientific or historical knowledge, and perceived the inadequacy of the old theories to explain the various phenomena; a fifth, again, might simply have a vague sense of weariness with the process of marking time without advancing, characteristic of contemporary philosophy and divinity. And thus, according to the general law, the old theory broke down by actual experiment before any perception of its logical invalidity disturbed men's minds. Men's sentiments became daily more heterogeneous, until at last the necessity of reducing the chaos by a reconstruction of the underlying philosophy forced itself upon the acutest minds.

61. Here, therefore, more than in preceding chapters, it would be a hopeless task to present the actual process as conforming to any logical method. We have to observe the unconscious co-operation of many

different minds, guided far more by instinct than by reason; and urged to the embodiment of their thoughts and feelings in new formulæ by a vague unrest, of which they did not themselves possess the secret. The men of strong feeling or delicate perception precede the men of stern intellect. The instinct outruns the reasoning power. And the cause of this priority seems to be simple enough. The love of intellectual truth is the weakest of all passions with the overwhelming majority of mankind; and though the errors of a creed may be the hidden cause of its decline, men become conscious that it will not satisfy their feelings before they discover that it is unsatisfactory to their intellects.

VI. The Religious Reaction.

62. It has become a common practice to denounce the frigidity and formality of the eighteenth century. We always think our grandfathers fools because we value inordinately the changes which have been effected in our own times. For our great-grandfathers we can make allowances, for they are at a distance which levels all petty jealousies. Whatever the correctness in some respects of the judgment passed upon the eighteenth century—and I have tried to show at length why its creed should strike us as irretrievably effete—the general condemnation is far too sweeping. Many of the clergy, as of other classes, were undoubtedly worldly and timeserving, and some of the noisy controversialists of the time suggest little confidence in their honesty or their depth of feeling. But I do not feel certain that we could mention in the first half of the nineteenth century three bishops whose characters make upon us a greater impression of purity and devotion than those of Berkeley, Butler, and Wilson; I doubt whether amongst those of less dignity we should find men more honest and manly than Clarke, or with a finer glow of devotional sentiment than William Law; and if the dissenters, freed from persecution, could no longer boast of Baxters and Bunyans, it is impossible to think without sincere respect of the honourable and laborious lives of such men as Watts, Doddridge, and Lardner, by whom the chances of preferment were voluntarily rejected for conscientious reasons. Wesley is generally represented as having been the first man to struggle against the indolent frigidity which had stolen over the Church. The statement, as we shall see, was true enough; but it is also true that, during the first half of the century, there were many religious leaders, whose devotion has not been exceeded in more recent times. I have already had occasion to mention incidentally some of the

eminent men just noticed. Butler stands by himself as a thinker, and
Berkeley is, of course, chiefly remarkable in literature as a metaphysician; Law was admirable as a controversialist, though he was something more than a mere controversialist; Lardner devoted his whole life
to composing a refutation of Deism; and I have already described
Clarke sufficiently as the typical rationalist of the time.

63. Wilson, Watts, Doddridge, and Law, who are chiefly remarkable
as devotional writers, occupy positions of varying importance in relation to the contemporary speculation. Of the first three it may be said
that they represent rather the survival of old methods of thought than
any fresh development. Wilson, the 'Apostolic,' was a man of the old
sacerdotal type, full of simplicity, tenderness, devotion, and with a
sincere belief, inoffensive because alloyed by no tincture of pride or
ambition, in the sacred privileges of the Church. Amongst his scattered
reflections there are many of much beauty in expression as in sentiment.
They imply a theology of that type of which à-Kempis is the permanent
representative; less ascetic, inasmuch as Wilson had the good fortune
to be a married man instead of a monk; and, of course, less vivid, as he
was one born out of due time. His superstitions—for he is superstitious
—no more provoke anger than the simple fancies of a child; and we
honour him as we should honour all men whose life and thoughts were
in perfect harmony, and guided by noble motives. To read him is to
love him; he helps us recognise the fact that many of the thoughts
which supported his noble nature in its journey through life may be
applicable in a different costume to the sorrows and trials which also
change their form rather than their character; but we see with equal
clearness that he has little or nothing to say upon the speculative difficulties of the time. He may be passed over with the remark that his
example proves conclusively that a genuine Christian theologian in the
most characteristic sense of the term might still be found under the
reign of George II. in the Isle of Man.

64. Watts and, in a less degree, Doddridge, are to the dissenters of
the preceding generation what Wilson was to its best Anglican divines.
The name of Watts, associated with certain hymns still dear to infancy,
has contracted a faint flavour of the ludicrous, though other poems of
greater pretensions are still preserved in the lower strata of literature.
The hymns, indeed, of Watts, Doddridge, and the Wesleys, whatever
their literary merit, have been popular enough to show that they are not
inadequate expressions of a strong religious sentiment. It is said that for
many years 50,000 copies of Watts' 'Psalms and Hymns' were annually
printed; and if there be any truth in the commonplace about songs and

laws, Watts' influence must have been greater than that of many legislators, and, indeed, many more distinguished writers. But such an
influence is too intangible in its nature to be easily measured. Watts,
however, was a voluminous writer in prose. The last thirty-six years of
his long life was passed in valetudinary retirement in the family of a
London merchant and his widow. In this retreat he wrote nearly all
those works which—as a biographer says[1]—'have immortalised his name
as a divine, poet, and philosopher.' The philosophy and the divinity,
however, would appear to have been chiefly buoyed above utter oblivion
by the poems. His philosophy was the expression of a desire to preserve
part of Descartes' theory about the soul, whilst accepting Newton's
physical philosophy, and a good deal of Locke's metaphysics.[2] Such a
crude amalgam could have no great value in itself, and occasionally he
descends to mere childishness, as in some remarks upon the awkward-
ness of a complete resurrection of the body of a dropsical patient.[3] We
need not trouble ourselves with such speculations, nor with his views
about the Trinity, which seem to have shown traces of the Unitarian
tendencies which affected the old dissenters. In his doctrinal writings
there are signs of the diffuse sentimentalism which not unfrequently
accompanies a feeble constitution.[4] We may grant to his biographer
that there is not an expression in his sermons 'that could raise the faint-
est blush upon the cheek of modesty, or irritate the risibility of the
most puerile.'[5] The more positive merits discovered by the same admirer will, perhaps, hardly keep the modern reader from somnolency.
The sermons, however, show something of the old unction. They appeal
strongly to the inward witness of the spirit, with a comparative indifference to the ordinary evidential argument. Unlike most of his contemporaries, he addresses the heart rather than the intellect; and in his
hands Christianity is not emasculated Deism, but a declaration to man
of the means, by which God pleases to work a supernatural change in
human nature. The emotional current is still running strongly, though
combined with a rather heterogeneous collection of speculative opinions.

65. Doddridge, the admiring friend of Watts, exercised a considerable
influence as the master of a dissenting academy, in the days when the
right of dissenters to teach schools was still exposed to some legal difficulties. His position is best defined in a tract contributed in 1730 to a

---

[1] See notice in Chalmers's 'Biog. Dic.'
[2] See 'Philosophical Essays,' vol. viii. of Works.
[3] Watts' Works, viii. 422.
[4] *E.g.* Watts, i. 182, where he apologises for the warmth of his colouring.
[5] Ib. i. p. xiii.

controversy about the 'most probable means of reviving the dissenting interest.' The difficulty, which increased as the century went on, was already sensible. The dissenters, no longer forced into unity by serious external pressure, were showing symptoms of approaching disruption. The more educated classes among them—steeped in traditions of intellectual liberty, and not confined by definite tests—were ripening for Unitarianism. Rationalism was sapping the old dogmatic stringency. The more ignorant classes were complaining of the diminished fervour of their spiritual guides. Latitudinarian 'demonstrations' flew above their heads, and they were lapsing into indifference, or ready to welcome the fresh impulse of Wesley. The first nucleus of the Methodists which was formed in 1729 might have suggested a better solution of the difficulty than that which satisfied Doddridge, and Doddridge's contemporary difficulties show what was the field provided for their energy. The general spirit of his advice was that the dissenting minister should try to please everybody. His antagonist seems to have hinted at the propriety of a separation between the bigots and the persons of 'generous sentiments.'[6] Doddridge wished the minister to become 'all things to all men.'[7] That was rather too markedly the leading principle of his own life. The eminent dissenter was on friendly terms with the established clergy, and corresponded with bishops; he had relations with Wesley and the Methodists; he was a spiritual adviser of Lyttelton,[8] and of the converted rake Colonel Gardiner; and his academy, once, at any rate, was honoured by the presence of a duke's nephew.[9] Such intimacies, cultivated by the dissenting schoolmaster in a country town, indicated considerable powers of attraction. His life was honourable, independent, and laborious; but we may, perhaps, surmise, without injustice to a good man, that his emotions were rather facile, and that his temptation was to err on the side of complacency. There is a want in his writings of that firmness which is produced by the bracing air of more vigorous times; they show a tendency to flabbiness, and the enthusiasm has but a hollow ring.

66. His chief work, the 'Rise and Progress of Religion in the Soul,' is an exhortation to a change of life, conceived in what would now be called the evangelical spirit, but apparently tempered by a dread of the rational critic. His energy is restrained by unseen chains. Whilst insisting on the value of conversion, he has an eye to the possible charge of

---

[6]Doddridge's Works, iv. 216.   [7]Ib. iv. 218.
[8]In Phillimore's 'Life of Lyttelton' there are some curious letters.
[9]Doddridge, v. 542.

'enthusiasm.' Christianity is more than an intellectual change, but it is still—as he maintains against Dodwell—'founded on argument.' We are to break with the world, but not too decisively; for it may be necessary to indulge ourselves in 'the elegancies and delights of life,'[10] for the good of trade and the poor. There is much dwelling upon the horrors of hell-fire; but we feel that he is lashing a jaded imagination rather than overpowered by an awful vision. When, in one of his sermons, he comforts the parents of the damned by the reflection that in the next world they will be without their natural affections,[11] we are not in presence of a seer oppressed, like Jonathan Edwards, by his tremendous faith, but of an ingenious special pleader too much pleased with a neat argument to realise its atrocity. His dogmas have passed from the stage of intuitive conviction to that of orthodox positions capable of logical defence. It would be unfair to regard Doddridge as in any degree insincere. The zeal is a reflection, though a faint reflection, from the older Puritans; and if the fire no longer communicates much heat, it produces amongst the respectable the sensation of a good comfortable glow. His favourite authors seems to have been Leighton, of whose works he published an edition, and the choice is creditable to his insight. Of his most ambitious work, 'The Family Expositor,' a dilution of the Gospels and St. Paul's Epistles into five volumes quarto, it can only be said that it consists of 'words, words, words.'

67. Towards the middle of the century the decay of the old schools of theology was becoming complete. Watts died in 1748; Doddridge in 1751; the good Bishop Wilson died in his ninety-third year in 1755. A new religious impulse was beginning to exhibit its strength, though regarded with intense dislike and suspicion by the whole body of the orthodox, and heartily despised by the philosophers and men of the world. Wesleyanism is, in many respects, by far the most important phenomenon of the century. Here I have only to enquire what were the intellectual aspects of the movement, so far as they are reflected in the writings of its most eminent men. Wesley himself appears to have been influenced at the most critical period of his life by three great writers, Thomas à-Kempis, Jeremy Taylor, and Law. If the two former were the greatest men, Law had the indefinite advantage of still being alive. The 'Imitation of Christ' has influenced more minds than any book outside the sacred canon; but for that reason we could not discover from its contents what was its special aptitude to Wesley. A

[10]Doddridge, i. 444.   [11]Ib. ii. 179.

similar remark may be made in a degree of Taylor's 'Holy Living and Dying.' It was Law who, alone of living writers, materially influenced Wesley's mind; and gave to universal principles that special form which rendered them suitable at the moment. From him and the Moravians came the external impulses which chiefly affected Wesley; and the fact would be enough to give an interest to Law's writings. But he is himself a man of remarkable power and originality, and, indeed, very superior as a thinker to his more active disciple. I have already noticed his controversial eminence. It remains to study the writings by which he exercised his chief influence upon the time.

68. The name of William Law will recall to most readers a passage in Gibbon's Autobiography. The cynical historian is thought to have shown little insight into the loftier motives of the earlier Christians. Yet he spoke with affectionate tenderness of the man who, almost alone amongst his contemporaries, might stand for a primitive Christian come to revisit a strangely altered world. 'In our family,' says Gibbon, 'he left the reputation of a worthy and pious man who believed all he professed, and practised all that he enjoined.' Gibbon's respect for the purity and tenderness of Law's character is mixed with admiration for his intellectual vigour. As a controversialist, according to Gibbon, he showed himself, at least, the equal of the Whig champion, Hoadly; and in his practical writings, his fervid emotion is seconded by a power of satire displayed in portraits 'not unworthy of the pen of La Bruyère.' Were it not for his mysticism, he 'might be ranked with the most agreeable and ingenious writers of the times;' and even 'a philosopher must allow that he exposes with equal sincerity and truth the strange contradiction which exists between the faith and practice of the Christian world.'

69. Gibbon's Autobiography is a very delightful specimen of one of the most generally delightful of all forms of literature. Nobody ever laid bare his own character with more felicity; and there is something curiously dramatic in the contrast between the two men thus brought into momentary contrast. Gibbon is as perfect an incarnation of the worldly thinkers of the eighteenth century, with their placid contempt for all the higher spiritual influences, as Law of the counteracting forces which were gradually stirring beneath the surface of society. The life of the teacher is as characteristic as his writings. The son of a country grocer, he had obtained a fellowship at Emmanuel in 1711, and became an ardent High Churchman. He seems to have been suspended from his degree for a tripos speech, in which he defended, amongst other things, the objectionable doctrine that the sun shone

when it was eclipsed.[12] The eclipsing body, of course, was the parliamentary monarch, which intercepted the rays of divine right. At any rate, he refused to take the oaths enforced upon the accession of George I., and thus became one of the second generation of nonjurors. After having thus sacrificed all worldly prospects for a crotchet or a creed, he became the tutor of Gibbon's father, and when his pupil was grown up, remained for some years an inmate of the family. There, though apparently respected by all its members, he found types of the great division between the Church and the world. Two of the portraits in the 'Call,' which represent the worldly and the converted woman, are said by Gibbon to stand for his two aunts. Hester Gibbon, the Miranda of the 'Call,' was to the end of a long life Law's spiritual support. Catherine, the 'Flavia,' married a man of fortune, and her daughter, afterwards Lady Eliot, grievously offended her pious aunt Hester by an intimacy with the Mallets—Mallet being that 'beggarly Scotchman' who, according to Johnson, fired off Bolingbroke's blunderbuss against religion and morality for half-a-crown. A curious correspondence is preserved[13] between this lady and her aunt:—'If this were the last sentence I should speak,' says the spirited young woman, 'these would be my words, that the aspersion' (that is, Miss Gibbon's aspersion on the Mallets) 'is as false as heaven is true;' and Miss Gibbon replied to her rebellious niece in a letter animated with such holy unction, that Law substituted a more courteous document. 'Talk not of gratitude to infidel friends,' says this softened version; 'their friendship is of no better a nature than that which kindly gave thirty pieces of silver to Judas, and both you and your unhappy uncle' (the historian's father) 'sooner or later must find that falseness, baseness, and hypocrisy make the whole heart and spirit of every blasphemer of Jesus Christ. It would be less a pain to me, or to your deceased friends, whom I have mentioned, to see

[12]If, that is, I am right in identifying him with a 'Mr. Laws,' mentioned in Hearne's Diary, as quoted in Mr. Christopher Wordsworth's interesting book on 'University Life in the Eighteenth Century' (see pp. 40, 231). See also Byrom's diaries.

[13]In a book called 'Memorials of Mr. Law,' privately printed, which consists, for the most part, of an exposition of the doctrines of Jacob Behmen, drawn chiefly from the MSS. of a disciple, unfortunately preserved in the British Museum for the bewilderment of ordinary intellects. The author, however, fearing, not irrationally, that his readers may weary of the theosophical quagmires through which they are dragged, inserts a gigantic footnote from p. 334 to p. 628, in which are imbedded a few facts about Law's life and a good many letters.

you attending a dung-cart for the sake of bread, than riding in a coach of your own crowded with beloved infidels.' It does not exactly appear how the niece received this vigorous bit of plain speaking, or what Miss Gibbon thought in after years of a certain pair of chapters in a celebrated History. Gibbon, at any rate, could write to her affectionately in her old age. She died in 1790 at the age of eighty-six, and two years earlier she received a letter from the historian, touching with tenderness on the old lady's prejudices. 'Your good wishes and advice,' he says, 'will not, I trust, be thrown away on a barren soil; and, whatever you may have been told of my opinions, I can assure you with truth that I consider religion as the best guide of youth, and the best support of old age, and that I firmly believe there is less real happiness in the business and pleasure of the world than in the life which you have chosen of devotion and retirement.' Was there some slight expression of pious equivocation in these sentiments, or did Gibbon perhaps reflect that middle age is a tolerably elastic period?

70. The 'retirement and devotion' to which Miss Gibbon had devoted herself had lasted since 1740, about which time she and a rich widow, a Mrs. Hutcheson, had taken a house in Law's native village of King's Cliffe. There, with Law for their director, they gave themselves up to the course of devotion and charity described in the 'Serious Call to a Devout and Holy Life.' Three times a day the family assembled for prayers and religious exercises. Law himself rose at five, and spent many hours in a little study, four feet square, furnished only with a chair, a writing-table, the Bible, the works of Jacob Behmen, and a few other mystic writers; and, according to his biographer, prostrated himself, 'body and soul, in abyssal silence, before the interior central throne of the divine revelation; and, according to his high supersensual science, presented the now passive, desireless, resigned, mirror-eye of his purified will and intellect to the free, active, gladsome, supercogitative researches of the Spirit of Wisdom and openings of the Divine life.' When, descending from these celestial regions, he presented himself at his frugal meals, he could talk pleasantly and fluently; he delighted in playing with children, and could never, we are told, see a bird in a cage without trying to release it. As his controversies pretty plainly show, there was a certain choleric element in the good man, which manifested itself in private life when the soup had not been properly made for distribution to the poor. He took care to taste it himself, and, moreover, to try on his own person the shirts which were to accompany it. The charitable energies of such a man are not likely to be directed in accordance with the strict rules of political economy. In fact, it seems that King's

Cliffe gained so bad a reputation for attracting the idle and worthless, that some of the richer inhabitants protested. The protest, however, dropped when the little household threatened to withdraw themselves and their money. The united incomes of the two ladies amounted to nearly 3,000*l.* a year, of which much the greatest part was given away. Law himself had founded a school in his native village by means, as was reported, of a hundred pounds presented to him in gratitude by an anonymous reader of the 'Call.' Nineteen poor girls were to be taught reading, knitting, and needlework. They were to learn the catechism, and to go to church regularly, and to curtsey 'to all ancient people, whether rich or poor.' Mrs. Hutcheson added another school and alms-houses; and the superintendence of these foundations appears to have been Law's principal external employment. He died in 1761, at the age of seventy-four, almost in the act of singing a hymn.

71. Certainly, this is a curious picture in the middle of that prosaic eighteenth century, which is generally interpreted for us by Fielding, Smollett, and Hogarth; the period of Squire Westerns and Parson Trullibers, and the boisterous humours of ponderous well-fed masses of animated beefsteak. Since the time of the holy Mr. Ferrars, commemo-rated by Isaak Walton, there had been few parallels in the Church of England. The fine gentlemen, the worldly dignitaries, and the coarse, full-fed squires who were scandalised at the obtrusive preaching of his disciple Wesley, could afford to look with compassion upon the gentle quietist and the pair of old ladies who were saying their prayers at King's Cliffe; here and there some eccentric persons asked Law's advice in cases of conscience; and a few disciples corresponded with him upon the depths of the divine mysteries. The only one who may deserve a moment's notice is the poet, shorthand writer, and clergyman, John Byrom. Byrom may be still remembered by a few epigrams,[14] and a poem upon the great fight between Figg and Sutton, which is done into prose in Thackeray's 'Virginians.' But these rather incongruous per-formances were only one manifestation of an almost morbid faculty of rhyming. One of his longest so-called poems is a minute piece of scrip-

---

[14]That, for example, sometimes ascribed to Swift on Handel and Buonon-cini; and the well-known lines about the King and the Pretender, ending:

> But who Pretender is, or who is King,
> God bless us all—that's quite another thing.

Byrom, too, tells the excellent apologue of the 'Three Black Crows.' His curious Journals have been published by the Chatham Society.

tural exegesis in answer to Conyers Middleton, in refutation of a particular text. Others propose and discuss emendations in the text of
Horace. Four epistles enquire into the exact nature of the miracle on
the day of Pentecost, in such verses as these:—

> 'Are not these,' said the men (the devout) of each land,
> 'Galileans that speak? whom we all understand?'
> As much as to say, by what wonderful powers
> Does the tongue Galilean become to us, ours?
> Whilst the good were unjustly astonished, the bad,
> Whose hearts were unopened, cried out, 'They are mad.'
> Unaccountable charge, if we do not recall
> That, in one single tongue, the apostles speak all.

If these marvellous productions be intentionally facetious, Byrom
was perfectly serious in versifying Law's sentiments with a closer fidelity than Pope exerted in turning Bolingbroke's philosophising into
poetry. The poem which is pronounced to be his best, 'On Enthusiasm,'
is simply a fragment from one of Law's works; and the people who like
their theology done up into neat couplets may read him in place of his
original.

72. Law, however, will be to most tastes the best exponent of his
own principles. His masterpiece, the 'Serious Call,' which seems to have
superseded the similar book on 'Christian Perfection,' may be read with
pleasure even by the purely literary critic. Perhaps, indeed, there is a
touch of profanity in reading in cold blood a book which throughout
palpitates with the deepest emotions of its author, and which has
thrilled so many sympathetic spirits. The power can only be adequately
felt by readers who can study it on their knees; and those to whom a
difference of faith renders that attitude impossible, doubt whether they
are not in a position somewhat resembling that of Mephistopheles in the
cathedral. When a man is forced by an overmastering impulse to lay
bare his inmost soul, the recipient of the confession should be in harmony with the writer. The creed which is accepted by Law with such
unhesitating faith, and enables him to express such vivid emotions, is
not exactly my own; and, if I do not infer that respectful silence is the
only criticism possible, I admit that any criticism of mine is likely
enough to be inappreciative. One who has yielded to the fascination
would alone be qualified fully to explain its secret. And yet no one,
however far apart from Law's mode of conceiving of the universe,
would willingly acknowledge that he is insensible to the thoughts interpreted into his unfamiliar dialect. In one sense, not only the Apostles

on the day of Pentecost, but all great movers of mankind, speak a universal tongue. Law, indeed, requires a tolerably lax interpretation to be turned to account by a complete outsider; and many within the sacred pale would more or less explicitly disavow his definite conclusions. The dominant idea in each book is the contrast between the Church and the world; or, as we might say, between the morality taught by Jesus of Nazareth and the morality practised by a Walpole or a Warburton. It requires no belief in the supernatural origin of any religious doctrine to admit the force of much of his teaching. The 'world,' if the world is the aggregate of petty and selfish motives, is 'too much with us, late and soon.' The nobler impulses are in constant danger of being stifled under the crust of petty cares and subservience to the meaner social conventions. Not to be galled at times by the harness in which the world drives us is to be dull to all the finer feelings, and to have a blunted intellect and imagination. But a divergence appears so soon as we attempt to lay down the boundary between the kingdoms of light and darkness. Which are the sentiments which can be rightly cultivated? and which are those which require to be restrained or extirpated? In Law's dialect, which is the divine and which the carnal element of our lives? As the answer to that question varies, we pass from one end to the other of the scale of moral teaching. Is everything good which is 'natural'? and all pleasure, so far as it is pleasant, deserving of cultivation? Or are we to say that every natural impulse is tainted by some mysterious corruption, and that all that the unregenerate man agrees to call pleasant is so much outward show, and turns to ashes in the mouth?

73. Law, one might say, takes the specifically Christian view of it, were it not that Christian has become one of the vaguest epithets in the language. It must be added, therefore, that he was one of those peculiar thinkers who refuse to allow a commonplace to lie in a merely dormant state in their minds. Most men blandly accept formulæ which appear to condemn not only their practice but their most settled convictions, either because an illogical state of mind is not painful to them, or because they have tacitly put some conveniently rationalising interpretation upon the familiar words. Law, whose sensitiveness to logic is as marked as his sensitiveness to conscience, is incapable of any such compromise. He not only believes what he professes, but he believes it in the most downright sense, and he is not content till it is thoroughly worked into his whole system of thought. He accepts unhesitatingly the literal meaning even of those passages which the fairest commentators may take to be intended as hyperbolical expressions of one aspect of the truth. Law, for

example, feels none of the difficulty which perplexed some contemporary divines in expounding Christ's precept to the young man to sell all he had and give it to the poor. In the treatise on 'Christian Perfection,' he energetically assails the various devices by which the duty imposed by Christ's command could be represented as of temporary or partial obligation; though he maintains, of course, that the spirit of the command is more important than the letter. If we sincerely humble ourselves, we need not be particular as to literal sackcloth and ashes; and it may be right to hold our estates for the good of the poor instead of parting with them; but all that is not distinctly necessary for health is part of that encumbrance which prevents the rich man from entering the narrow gateway of the kingdom of heaven. Good, easy-going divines considered that rules of this inconvenient severity were made exclusively for the early Christians. The Church and the world had become tolerably reconciled. A strict training was necessary in the early days of warfare; and miracles were required to keep up the spirits of expectant martyrs. But good living might now serve the turn. The profession of the Christian faith, as Warburton naïvely remarked, was now attended with ease and honour; patronage would produce quite as much zeal as was necessary or desirable; and why should we reject the good things of the world when they were thus the natural reward of virtue?

74. Law's logic will admit of no such temporising. The very essence of Christianity is the production of a certain temper: that temper must be good now which was good in the first century; then, as now, it can only be gained by systematic sanctification and self-denial, and a stern discipline is to the full as necessary to meet the cajolery of the world as to encounter its hostility. Phrases such as these may run glibly enough from the lips of some preachers, who at most consider sackcloth and ashes to be a picturesque dress in the great masquerade of sanctity; but Law applied them with the uncomfortable thoroughness of simple sincerity. All pursuit of money, of power, or of pleasure is vicious when it implies delight in pleasures for their own sake. 'Our bodies,' he says, 'and all bodily pleasures are at one dash struck out of the account of happiness' by the Christian doctrine. It teaches us that 'the whole race of mankind are a race of fallen spirits, that pass through this world as an arrow passes through air.'[15] We are pilgrims who stay here but for an instant, but in that instant we are upon our road for eternity. Descriptions of earthly pleasures should interest us as little as descriptions of the world in the moon. The honours which a king can give are

[15]Law's Works, iii. 37.

literally no more than the toys with which a nurse amuses a child. The contrivances which we break our peace to acquire are as worthless as the staff or money which some nations bury with a corpse. It is no more a hardship upon Christians to be restrained from such pleasures than for a man crossing a river upon a rope to be forbidden to walk in silver shoes, or to look about at the beauty of the waves.[16] From such a point of view most pleasures are frivolous, or playing with forbidden things. Law was ridiculed for the very trenchant application of his maxims to the stage. He summarily declares that it is as unlawful for a Christian to go to a theatre as to be a drunkard, a glutton, or a swearer. 'The playhouse,' he says, 'is as certainly the house of the devil as the church is the house of God.' The entertainment there offered is as bad as the worship of the lewd deities of paganism, and differs from gladiatorial shows only because Christians are risking their souls as well as their bodies. You should remember that the laughter which you hear there is a laughter among devils, and that you are upon profane ground, and hearing music in the very porch of hell. It is to be feared that the laughter was not quenched by Law's onslaught. To do him justice we must of course remember what was the state of the stage which had provoked Collier's attack; and to confess the truth, I must say that, in spite of all ingenious defences, it seems to me that pruriency and cynicism are qualifications for a thorough enjoyment of the Congreve school of comedy. Law, at any rate, took for granted that the one ultimate end and aim of all plays was to stimulate lust and facilitate debauchery. He assumes that, as a matter of fact, all actors and actresses were immoral by profession. 'Perhaps you had rather see your son chained to a galley, or your daughter driving a plough, than getting their bread on the stage by administering in so scandalous a manner to the vices and corrupt pleasures of the world.' If Law had rightly gauged the contemporary prejudice, he might fairly denounce people who, by their own showing, paid men and women to debase themselves for the amusement of their spectators.

75. Yet Law's logic would scarcely discriminate between the vilest ribaldry of Wycherley and the purest creations of Shakespeare's fancy. What is poetry or art or learning to the divine essence of the soul? 'When we are at the top of all human attainments we are at the bottom of all human misery, and have made no further advance towards true happiness than those whom we see in the want of all these excellences. Whether a man die before he has writ poems, compiled histories, or

[16]Law, iii. 193.

raised an estate, signifies no more than whether he died an hundred or a thousand years ago.'[17] If human learning be not bad, and even in his mystical period Law disclaimed an absolute antipathy to it,[18] it is good only in so far as it may be the instrument of the religious emotions. To the outsider it often seems as though the acceptance of such doctrines would fill the deserts with hermits, and gradually depopulate the world. Law, of course, like other ascetics, stops just short of such a conclusion. If virginity, retirement, and a life of mortification be the best, they are not the sole means of cultivating the pure spirit. The world may be condemned, but the world must continue; and therefore room must be allowed for a certain amount of eating and drinking, marrying, and giving in marriage.

76. No man can free himself from the habits of thought of his time. Little as Law resembles the contemporary essayists and schools, his portraits remind us that he was in fact a contemporary of Addison, Steele, and Swift. Miranda and Flavia and Lucius and Mundanus might, with a little expansion, have made admirable papers in the 'Spectator.' If he has not the delicate humour of Addison, he has a vigorous touch, which reminds us more closely of Pope's spirited sketches than of any other writer of the time. Like Pope, he delights in exhibiting the logical inconsistency embodied in the ordinary ideals of conduct; and coincidences in language suggest that Law was amongst the various authors from whom Pope borrowed. 'Meat, drink, and clothing are the only things necessary in life,' says Law, for example; and Pope wrote a few years later—

> What riches give us let us then enquire:
> Meat, fire, and clothes—what more? meat, clothes, and fire.

Law's satire, though more serious, is scarcely less pointed than the poet's. His special objects of attack are the Pharisee, who takes the form for the substance, and the worldling, who forgets the warning, 'Thou fool, this night shall thy soul be required of thee.' There is Calidus, who seems to have anticipated some modern complaints. Every hour is passed in business; his meals are hurried, though hearty, and he would say grace if he had time. He can't get to his tavern till nine, when he drinks a hearty glass to make him sleepy. His prayers are a short ejaculation or two, which he never misses in stormy weather, because he has always something at sea. He tells you that his business would have

[17]Law, iv. 438.   [18]Ib. vii. 93.

killed him if he had not made Sunday a day of quiet and refreshment in the country. He is afraid that he would grow melancholy if he gave up business, and says with great gravity that it is a dangerous thing for a man that has been used to get money ever to leave it off. His religious thoughts consist in the reflection that he was never a friend to heretics or infidels, that he has been civil to the clergyman, and has always given something to charity schools. Then we have Flavia, or Miss Gibbon, who is very orthodox, and often takes the sacrament. She had been known to praise a sermon against vanity in dress, and thought that it was very just upon Lucinda. If you ask her for charity, she may perhaps give you a crown, and add that, if you knew what a long milliner's bill she had just paid, you would think it very handsome. The next time she hears a sermon on charity, she congratulates herself on having given a crown when she could so ill spare it. She knows that the poor are cheats and liars, who will say anything to get relief. Her conscience is admirably tender in regard to the guilt of giving amiss. She buys all the books of the wits and poets, for she says that you cannot have a true taste of any without being conversant with all; and she will read a book of piety, if it is short and well written, and she knows where to borrow it. She would be a miracle of piety if she took as much care of her soul as of her body; and is as much disturbed as Pope's Celia by the rising of a pimple in her face. You will always find the best company and hear the latest gossip in her house on Sunday; she thinks that only atheists play at cards on that day, but after church she will tell you the details of all the games of the past week, mixed with the latest anecdotes about the bad behaviour of Lucius to his wife. She respects the day, however, so much that she turned a poor old widow out of her house for having once been found mending her clothes on a Sunday night. If she lives thirty years in this way, she will have spent fifteen in bed, and fourteen in eating, drinking, dressing, visiting, reading plays and romances, and going to the theatre. She will have spent 6,000*l*. on herself, and a few odd crowns upon charity. It cannot be said that she will not get to heaven, but she is hardly cultivating the temper which the Gospel declares to be necessary for salvation.

77. Then we have Fulvius, who is very proud of his conscientious refusal to undertake any duties, and even to be godfather to his nephew, because he is not holy enough in his temper; and Flavus, who tries every variety of amusement, from dress to architecture, and by the last account was going into training to try to rival the wind of a running-footman; and Lucius, who, when he is serious, studies a treatise upon ancient cookery, and is an enemy to all party politics, having remarked

that there is as good eating amongst Whigs as amongst Tories; he is always ready to drink the King's health, and will never be a rebel, unless there should be proclamation against eating pheasants' eggs; he denounces the town rakes, and his bitterest saying is that he believes some of them to be so abandoned as not to have a regular meal or a sound night's sleep in a week. Cognatus is a parson, universally respected by the farmers for his judgment in selling corn; and hopes that, in spite of the hard times, his good management will enable him to leave a fortune to his neice out of the riches of his two livings. Mundanus is a profound authority upon trade, who never took up a book without thinking how it could be improved; but is quite content with the prayers which his mother taught him at six years old. Classicus is an elegant scholar, who knows all the commentators upon Cæsar, Horace, and Ovid, but tells you with great complacency that he will have no other book of devotion but the Holy Scriptures; and Cæcus, a rich man, who can't bear contradiction, and insists upon having the best of everything, but specially plumes himself upon his humility, because he admires it so heartily in his companions.

78. The predominantly logical character of Law's mind may be noticed in these sketches; and it is perhaps too prominent in writing which appeals rather to the emotions than to the intellect. His exhortations run naturally into the form of a *reductio ad absurdum*. If you admit this or that duty, you must admit all; if you must pray to God in words, you must pray by actions; if any earthly pleasure is frivolous, the same rule is equally applicable to all earthly pleasures. There is no logical resting-place between a life devoted exclusively to sensual enjoyments and a life devoted exclusively to spiritual enjoyments. No action or habit is good which is not consciously determined by the desire to please God. The mode of forcing people to accept one of two horns of a dilemma has the practical disadvantage that it may change a qualified submission into unlimited revolt. To preach that Christianity condemns as equally worthless all intellectual and artistic and worldly and sensual pleasures is either to force the majority of mankind into a rejection of Christianity, or to force them to challenge the authority of its advocate. By what right, they might say substantially, do you order us to give up all that makes life beautiful and refined? What is the value of your peremptory denunciations of all that our souls delight in? A messenger from heaven may venture into Vanity Fair, and order its inhabitants to put on sackcloth and ashes, and raise hermitages on the site of its warehouses; but his credentials should be unmistakable. Who are you who come hither to turn the world up-

side down, and ruin the silversmiths and the priests of the Great Diana of the Ephesians? To such a challenge Law conceived himself to have a decisive answer; but the answer changed at different periods of his life, and the change explains the development of his religious theories.

79. I have noticed in previous chapters Law's attacks upon Hoadly, Mandeville, and Tindal, and I may briefly recall the logical position which they indicated. In answering Hoadly, Law had planted himself upon the ordinary High-Church theory. A permanent corporation endowed with supernatural attributes was the rock upon which his faith reposed. We do not know by what process of thought this creed became unsatisfactory to Law as the ultimate basis of his religion. Perhaps it was not a very tenable position when the embodiment of the divine element in human affairs was to be identified with the church of the Georges. Perhaps his resistance to Mandeville and Tindal, and to the theories which they represented, forced him to seek for some more satisfactory standing-point. Mandeville, as I have said, represents the sceptical pessimism of the day, as Tindal represents the deistical optimism. In replying to Mandeville, Law had vindicated human nature from the charges of that shrewdest of cynics, and denied his analysis of all virtue into a superficial disguise of selfishness. In replying to Tindal's theory of the supremacy of human reason, he had stated in vehement language the utter incapacity of human reason to frame a theory of the universe, or to divine without supernatural aid the mysterious purposes of the Creator. But how were these two theories to be reconciled? Mandeville had, in fact, done little more than give a legitimate development to that doctrine of the corruption of human nature which was the central tenet of divines, and of none more decidedly than Law. If Tindal's attempted construction of a rational theology was to be repudiated on the score of the utter helplessness of the human intellect, what answer could be opposed to Mandeville's scepticism? The corruption of human nature has not only tainted the passions and weakened the will, but obscured the intellect. How then is this corrupt, ignorant, and foolish being to escape from the labyrinth of mystery in which he appears to be hopelessly lost? How can he even distinguish between a true and a false revelation? Tindal had argued, in fact, that the legitimate consequence of such a theory would be to force us to rely entirely upon the external evidences; and Law seems to accept the conclusion. We were, that is, to accept Christianity on the strength of the miracles and prophecies. Tindal's argument, he said, would lead to Atheism; for, if we may reject a divine revelation on account of its imperfections, we may on the same grounds reject the divine origin of the world. The difficulty which

pressed upon Butler when applying this argument pressed equally upon Law. If any one refuses to be frightened by Atheism, how is he to be opposed? Is he not simply carrying out your own logic?

80. This central and ever-recurring difficulty was scarcely felt by most contemporary theologians. To a man of Law's spiritual depth, the attitude which they adopted could not be satisfactory. Standing alone against the world, denouncing all its faiths and practices, declaring the utter incapacity of the natural reason and the corruption of the natural passions, Law could appeal to no authority except the historical evidence of certain events which had once happened in Palestine. Against such a position Hume's logic was absolutely unanswerable. How should a story prove the existence of God and be a sufficient support for the whole superstructure of religious faith which, told in any other connection, would simply prove its narrator to be the inventor or the victim of a lie? Law must have felt this difficulty, and he certainly felt that other difficulty which was the ultimate outcome of the Deist controversy. The evidence upon which Christianity was based might possibily satisfy the learned, especially when backed by patronage; but it was not of that kind which could carry vivid conviction into the ordinary soul. Where were those letters of light, legible alike to the wise and the ignorant, the poor and the rich, which alone could justify the demands of theologians for the implicit faith of all believers? Dodwell, as we have seen, replied ironically that they must be written upon the soul of every man. Law accepted the same answer seriously, and the acceptance determined the remainder of his career. Nature is corrupt, but the primitive nature is recoverable by the divine grace. Reason is impotent, but we have a faculty of spiritual insight which supersedes reason, and enables us to catch glimpses of divine mysteries through the veil of sense. The connection of ideas is distinctly given in several of his writings.

81. His object is to give a 'short method' on a new pattern, 'yea, the shortest, and, at the same time, surest of all methods,'[19] and the difference between the method of Leslie, at the opening of the controversy, and that of Law, in its decline, is sufficiently characteristic. It is the tacit confession of the most religious mind of the time of the futility of the favourite argument of his contemporaries. The ordinary apologists had endeavoured to meet the difficulty by staking the whole of Christianity upon one point—the proof of Christ's resurrection. Law, in his later writings, says also that deists are to be confuted by reducing Christianity to a single point; that point is the redemption of man from

[19]Law's Works, v. 238.

the earthly to the divine; and the proof, lying in each man's consciousness, is altogether independent of external evidence. 'I had frequently a
consciousness rising up within me,' says a speaker in one of his dialogues, 'that the debate was equally vain on both sides, doing no more
real good to one than to the other; not being able to imagine that a set
of scholastic, logical opinions about history, facts, doctrines, and institutions of the Church, or a set of logical objections against them, were of
any significancy towards making the soul of man either an eternal
angel of heaven or an eternal devil of hell.'[20] Twenty years' experience
in this dust of debate had taught him, he says, that the more books were
written in defence of the Gospel on the ordinary plan, the more new
objections were suggested. The change in Law's mind followed soon
after his attack upon Tindal. Tindal's book was published in 1730, and
Law began his studies of Behmen about 1733. All his later writings are
more or less expository of Behmen, or applications of his principles to
special questions. The impression was natural. Law shows the mystical
temperament even in his earlier writings; he is always ready to withdraw from the external world into rapt contemplation of celestial things,
when the fighting instinct is not stirred by some external impulse; and
Behmen professed to give him the key to the invisible world, just when
he most wanted it. Behmen's theosophy is admitted to have anticipated
many of the leading principles of Schelling and Hegel; though the
relation may be regarded as creditable to Behmen or discreditable to his
followers. It is intelligible, therefore, that Behmen should be to Law
what the later German speculation was to men like Coleridge in a succeeding generation. It seemed to him that a new spring of truth was
gushing up in the wilderness of arid criticism and futile logomachy.

82. This, however, is not the place to touch, even in the briefest manner, upon the theological ontology which Law derived from his master.
I shall say nothing of the glassy sea, of that primary struggle and contrariety from which all materiality is derived, or of the seven resultant
properties of nature. Law, it is said, gives a clear exposition of his
master's principles, and is a useful guide to a labyrinth which few care
to penetrate. But a great part even of Law's later writings expounds
doctrines which may be disentangled from this mass of technical phraseology; they strikingly anticipate the teaching of the later school of
theology, which traces its origin to Coleridge, and has a natural affinity
for the mystical element. The chief difference is that in Law their tendency is less obscured by heterogeneous elements. Law starts, it may be

[20]Law, vii. 'Way to Divine Knowledge,' p. 16.

said, from a conviction of the utter futility of the external evidences of
Christianity, and of the whole theological conception to which they
were congenial. Arguments may alter the deist's opinion about facts,
but cannot change the state of his soul.[21] We know the fall by our
own direct consciousness; and need not go to Moses for it; he does not
prove the fact, but only tells us the how and the when.[22] If God's goodness were no more than equal to human goodness, he would have made
man better than he is; therefore we have an 'infallible demonstration'
that we are creatures fallen from a better state.[23] The God whose existence was proved by evidence was necessarily an external being; and, as
analysed by metaphysicians, instead of pictured by the spontaneous
imagination of mankind, he had gradually become the supernatural
judge, who administered and was bound by the law of nature. Law
pointedly repudiates this theory, so popular with his contemporaries,
which took the analogy as a literal truth, and arranged the terms of
salvation from the precedent of pardons uttered under the great seal.
When the subject derives his life and breath from his prince, says Law,
pardon can no longer mean a legal transaction, but an inward effect
wrought upon his inmost nature.[24] In short, the God who is revealed to
us by the heart is an entirely different being to the God who is built up
by external demonstration. He is not the judge nor the artificer, but the
all-pervading and immanent force, from whom all nature is an emana-
tion. We recognise him by a sensibility of our nature which reveals the
spiritual world, as the senses reveal the visible world; and reason is an
'impotent spectator' which only receives its materials from this supreme
faculty.[25] Reason is thus 'pulled out of its usurped throne, and shown
to be a powerless idle boy, when compared to the royal strength of the
heart, which is the kingly power, that has all the government of life in
its hands.'[26] When the heart thus displaces reason, rightfully or wrong-
fully, we can tell what God it will recognise. 'God is love, yea, all love;
and is so all love that nothing but love can come from him: and the
Christian religion is nothing but an open full manifestation of his universal love towards all mankind.'[27] Elsewhere, in language reminding us
of another modern formula, we are told that God is only 'an eternal will
to all goodness.'[28] The heart recognises his power as the eye perceives
light, or the body feels heat.

83. Religion, then, with Law, becomes subjective and emotional, when

[21]Law, vii. 11, 'Way to Divine Knowledge.'   [22]Ib. p. 41.
[23]Ib. v. 241, 'On the Sacrament.'   [24]Ib. v. 167–201, ib.
[25]Ib. v. 527, ib.   [26]Ib. vii. 164, 'Spirit of Prayer,' part ii.
[27]Ib. v. 46, 'Regeneration.'   [28]Ib. viii. 5, 'Spirit of Love,' part ii.

to almost all his contemporaries it was historical and rational. A sovereign faculty of intuition sets aside the common sense which they took to be the only judge in all controversies. Or, in different phrase, the mechanical is superseded by the dynamical view, and we contemplate the forces by which the heart is transformed, not its arbitrary relations to an external being. The most appropriate metaphor—which, indeed, he takes to be a literal truth instead of a metaphor—is that God acts upon the soul as magnetism upon the needle. 'There is nothing in the universe but magnetism and the impediments of it.'[29] In a state of perfection the impediments would disappear, and the whole universe be a harmonious manifestation of this all-pervading force. We see heaven breaking through the veil of the world, wherever there is order and beauty; and hell is to be seen in all discord and wrath, showing that the current has been broken by some mysterious jar. Heaven and hell, therefore, are states actually dividing all our thoughts and actions, not a mere future palace and prison-house.[30] The ordinary theory of the Atonement, 'the philosophy of debtor and creditor,'[31] of a satisfaction made by Christ to the wrath of God, is a vain fancy of human reason. The Atonement is the process by which the jarring elements are brought back to unity; it is the birth of a heavenly life within us, not the settlement of an account by a transference of balances of merit. Christ is within us in the sense that his power produces an inward life, as the light of the sun is a force which incorporates itself in a growing plant.[32] The Last Judgment is not a legal decree, but what may be called the spontaneous arrangement of all things which takes place when temporary nature disappears, according to the affinities already manifested.

84. The heart thus resembles a needle conscious of the magnetism which moves it, and is able to recognise the efficient force instead of the mere superficial change. Newton dealt only with the phenomenal, or, as Law says, only with 'facts and references, whose ground is not pretended to be known.' But Behmen's divine philosophy has to do with the noumenal, and shows us the ultimate principles from which, for example, Newton's three laws of motion spring.[33] Thus we see the utter vanity of the human reason, which Law is fond of denouncing. It deals with mere appearances instead of realities; and in religion leads us to mere 'notional conceptions,'[34] instead of opening our eyes to the divine

---

[29]Law, v. 209, 'On the Sacrament.'

[30]Ib. vi. 130, 'Appeal.'

[31]Ib. viii. 94, 'Spirit of Love,' part ii.

[32]Ib. vii. 49, 'Spirit of Prayer,' part i.

[33]Ib. vii. 38, 'Spirit of Love,' part i.

[34]Ib. vii. 237, 'Way to Divine Knowledge.'

source of light. All the ordinary dogmatic theology belongs to the lower faculty. In the language of a modern school, it does not express God's revelation of himself to us, but consists of our theories and notions about him. The letter of the Scriptures is either unconsciously spiritualised, or may be set aside if it conflicts with our intuitions; for a man who is face to face with God can dispense with any of these external wrappings of belief.

85. Here, then, Law finds a sufficient escape from the superficial controversies of his time; and an unassailable fortress from which to denounce the world and its ways. He has appealed from the intellect to the heart. He gets rid of many revolting theological figments, and forms a coherent, though, in its phraseology at least, a quaint and fanciful system. Whether it has less intrinsic value than some more pretentious systems of later growth may possibly be doubted. That such a system should be sterile was of course inevitable. The English soil seems to be averse to mysticism; and in any soil it is a plant of tender growth. Few men can find satisfaction in the cultivation of theopathetic emotions; or sincerely discover that their hearts do in fact teem with those glorious revelations of the dark secret of the universe which excited Law's ecstatic meditations. The church which a man can find in his own bosom turns out to be a church limited by the walls of his hermitage. The system must be adulterated by coarser elements before it can be adapted to ordinary consumption. In Law's devotional creed we can only expect to find some of the strong wine which gives a flavour to weaker, but more generally acceptable, growths. The Wesleyans and Evangelicals, who were most immediately influenced, were, of course, repelled as much as attracted. The philosophy flew above their heads. They loved that popular mythology which seemed to evaporate into mere sentiment in Law's hands. They would not give up their anthropomorphic conceptions of the Deity; they loved the 'debtor and creditor scheme,' which Law denounced; and feared, not without reason, that the Christ who was said to be within them would cease to be an historical character at all. Thus the circle of Law's adherents was almost confined to King's Cliffe; and even those who have adopted some of his language in later days, would shrink from the imputation of being in any fuller sense his disciples. The very fact of his unique attitude in the English theology of the time gives him a peculiar interest; and we may admit the singular beauty of his character and much of his moral and religious teaching, though we feel it to be unsound philosophically, and a morbid development in practice.

86. The impulse given by Law spent itself in the dreamland of mysti-

cism; a very different result followed the teaching of his admirer, and sometime disciple, John Wesley. Any adequate accounts of Wesley would have to include an estimate of his amazing activity as a leader of a great religious organisation. He founded a body which eighty years after his death could boast of twelve million adherents;[35] and its reaction upon other bodies was perhaps as important as its direct influence. Wesley's was a singular blending of strength and weakness. His strength lies almost entirely in the sphere of practice. He shows remarkable literary power; but we feel that his writings are means to a direct practical end, rather than valuable in themselves, either in form or substance. It would be difficult to find any letters more direct, forcible, and pithy in expression. He goes straight to the mark without one superfluous flourish. He writes as a man confined within the narrowest limits of time and space, whose thoughts are so well in hand that he can say everything needful within those limits. The compression gives emphasis and never causes confusion. The letters, in other words, are the work of one who for more than half a century was accustomed to turn to account every minute of his eighteen working hours. 'In person,' we are told, 'Wesley was rather below the middle size, but beautifully proportioned, without an ounce of superfluous flesh, yet muscular and strong, with a forehead clear and smooth, a bright penetrating eye, and a lovely face, which retained the freshness of its complexion to the last period of his life'[36]—in short, a human gamecock. His nervous energy was tremendous; he was never in low spirits for a quarter of an hour;[37] his talents for business and for spiritual influence are stamped upon his writings, and command equally our sympathy and our wonder. No such leader of men appeared in that century; and in a lower sphere he might have been a first-rate statesman or a general. As the guide of a religious movement—the highest duty which can fall to a human being —he was, as we shall see, deficient in the speculative insight which is so rarely combined with unusual practical energy; but for the immediate purpose of stirring the stagnating currents of religious emotion, no man could have been more admirably endowed. Few men have left more vivid portraits of their own personality than that which is embodied in Wesley's Journals. The detailed account of his labours surpasses in interest even the charming biography of Southey.

87. As a mere record of the quantity of work that can be got out of a single human being, endowed with untiring energy, and absolutely

[35]Tyerman's 'Life of Wesley,' i. 11.
[36]Ib. iii. 656.
[37]Wesley's Works, ix. 422.

devoid of at least the lower forms of selfish indulgence, it is encouraging to the strong and calculated to throw the weak into despair. For more than fifty years Wesley was the autocratic chief of his society, and not content with administration from a distance, personally inspected, at frequent intervals, every part of the machinery which he had organised. He travelled on his ceaseless round of duty some 4,500 miles annually; he preached two or more sermons a day; and it is calculated that in fifty-two years he travelled 225,000 miles, and preached over 40,000 sermons. The sermons were occasionally delivered to audiences of 20,000 persons,[38] and at the age of eighty-six (August 23, 1789) he records an address delivered to a congregation of 25,000.[39] Though he doubts whether all could hear, the feat, considered as a mere exhibition of physical energy, is something stupendous. He rose every morning at four, allowing himself only six hours of sleep, though we are told that he possessed the faculty, common to nearly all great workers, of falling asleep at a moment's notice.[40] He often rode seventy miles a day, and generally read as he rode, avoiding stumbling, as he tells us, by riding with a slack rein.[14] On his 85th birthday he ascribes his health to his constant exercise and change of air, to his powers of sleeping, to early rising, and regular preaching during sixty years, at 5 A.M., and to his having had little pain, sorrow, or anxious care during his life.[42] Any one who adopts the same methods should count upon a powerful constitution. The care of the churches, or the abuse of antagonists, never caused Wesley to fret. He was the most elastic, wiry, and invulnerable of men. This amazing soundness of physical health explains the character of his religion. He was too indomitably cheerful to dwell by preference on those gloomy imaginings which have haunted many of the greatest leaders of men. Calvinism revolted him. Mysticism seemed to him to be simply folly. His feet were on the solid earth; and he preferred the plain light of day to the glooms and the glories loved by more imaginative natures. His writings never have the questionable charm of a morbid sensibility. He is as thoroughly a moralist as any of his contemporaries. His aim is to stamp out vice; to suppress drinking and debauchery, and to show men the plain path to heaven, and force them into it by intelligible threats and promises. He differs, of course, from the ordinary moralists in the strong conviction that a blank collection of good precepts will never change men's lives without an appeal to their feelings and their imaginations; but the ultimate end of his labours

[38]Wesley, iv. 288, 293.

[39]Ib. vi. 210.   [41]Ib. iv. 436.

[40]Ib. vi. 270.   [42]Ib. vi. 163.

is to save his countrymen, to use his own dialect, from the clutches of the Devil, and, in any case, from the tyranny of vice and selfishness.

88. Wesley's strength and weakness are equally characteristic. His faith was on a level with the ordinary English mind; he shares the popular superstitions and the ordinary theological conceptions. He believes in the supernatural as frankly as Luther; though the Devil in the eighteenth century had become, even amongst the vulgar, a rather more shadowy being than he had been in an earlier generation. At every step we meet with some direct miraculous interference. If it rains during a sermon or blows during a sea voyage, Wesley prays, and his prayers are answered. If his horse runs away, the Devil has caused the mishap; when the horse stops, God has interposed. He collects stories of ghosts and visions and witches with a constant interest and perfect credulity. 'I cannot give up to all the deists in Great Britain the existence of witchcraft till I give up the credit of all history, sacred and profane.'[43] He holds that not only the Lisbon earthquake, but even a certain landslip at Whiston cliffs, in Yorkshire, which seems to have done no particular harm to anybody, was distinctly miraculous.[44] The Devil condescends at times to the smallest practical jokes. On one occasion he hoaxed Wesley and his brother by forcing them to laugh hysterically when they wanted to sing psalms.[45] The stories are for the most part of that provokingly prosaic turn which is characteristic of their origin amongst commonplace people. They do not recall the poetical, if hideous, superstitions of an age which has still a genuine mythology; but should rather be classed with De Foe's anecdotes in the 'History of the Devil' and the ghost of Mrs. Veal. Wesley's common sense, like Johnson's, breaks out unexpectedly against the strange stories of other people. He ranks the voyages of Captain Cook with those of Robinson Crusoe, because he will not believe that the natives of two islands, at a distance of 1,100 miles in latitude, can understand each other's language.[46] In the common phrase, he ridicules the credulity of sceptics—a phrase which simply means that, as his canons of proof are different from those of Hume and Voltaire, he sometimes rejects what they accept, as well as frequently differing in the opposite direction.

89. Thus we already find in Wesley that aversion to scientific reasoning which has become characteristic of orthodox theologians. He makes in one place the remarkable statement that he is convinced, 'from many experiments,' that he could not 'study to any degree of perfection either mathematics, arithmetic, or algebra, without being a deist, if not an

[43]Wesley, v. 100.   [45]Ib. ii. 33.
[44]Ib. xi. 397, &c.   [46]Ib. v. 110.

atheist.'[47] Others, he adds, may study those subjects all their lives without any inconvenience. His ignorance, of course, does not prevent him from forming some very decided opinions as to the value of scientific researches. He disbelieves altogether in the Newtonian astronomy. He doubts whether any man knows the distance of the sun or moon.[48] He thinks that Jones (of Nayland) has totally overthrown the Newtonian principles, though he may not have established the Hutchesonian;[49] and that Dr. Rogers has proved the whole framework of modern astronomy to be quite uncertain, if not self-contradictory. The scepticism of believers is at least as curious as the credulity of sceptics. A man who thus stands outside the whole sphere of scientific enquiry could of course have little interest in the speculative philosophy with which it was associated. He occasionally expresses a hearty contempt for the deists of the time, and for the moral philosophers of the Hutcheson school, whose optimistic complacency was abhorrent to all his views of human nature, and the system of divine government.[50] For the most part, he is content to leave the deistical doctrine to decay by its inherent weakness. Once or twice, however, he directly confronts the sceptic. In 1749, for example, he spent nearly three weeks in the 'unpleasing employment'[51] of answering Middleton's 'Free Enquiry.' The argument shows plainly enough that Wesley is trying to solve a problem requiring long and difficult historical investigations, by help of the data supplied by his antagonist. He can merely cavil at particular passages, without setting forth an independent theory of his own. The two, moreover, are not on the same plane of argument. The dilemma which Middleton put to his antagonist is meaningless for Wesley. You acknowledge, says Middleton in substance, that miracles have ceased; if so, why do you hold that they were ever wrought? To a man who believes that his prayers are daily answered by direct interposition, that the Devil is as busy as the constable, that modern diseases, like the old, were caused by devils, and that most lunatics are demoniacs,[52] the question has no significance. The position, which to Middleton seemed to be a *reductio ad absurdum*, was with Wesley a simple statement of everyday experience. As against Warburton or Sherlock, the argument was unanswerable. As against Wesley, it was so much empty parade.

90. I have already noticed Warburton's assault upon Wesley. As the typical enthusiast of the day, Wesley was equally offensive to the good and the bad instincts of his contemporaries, to their strong common

---

[47]Wesley, iii. 384.   [50]See *e.g.* Wesley, vii. 249, x. 14, 331.
[48]Ib. iv. 228.   [51]Tyerman, ii. 34.
[49]Ib. iv. 261.   [52]Ib. ix. 358.

sense and their easy-going indifference. Sermons and farces, grave appeals from the respectable classes, and coarse taunts from the debased
and the worldly-minded, showered upon the rising sect along with the
more tangible missiles of popular wrath. We need not ask what judgment was passed upon Christian in Vanity Fair. Nor is it necessary to
dwell at length upon the more respectable denunciations. The most
conspicuous assault was Bishop Lavington's 'Enthusiasm of Papists and
Methodists Compared.' It is an elaboration of a comparison suggested
by Warburton between Wesley and Loyola. Loyola, says Warburton,
was the most remarkable among 'the successful impostors which have
set out in all the blaze of fanaticism' and 'completed their schemes
amidst the cool depths and stillness of politics.'[53] Lavington drew out at
considerable length the parallel between the superstitious beliefs and
practices of the Wesleyans and those embodied in the lives of Catholic
saints. To the historical enquirer the resemblance is undoubtedly curious, and analogous phenomena might be discovered far beyond the
limits of Chistianity. A controversialist less short sighted than Warburton or Lavington would certainly not have inferred that the force
thus manifested was one to be despised and rejected by the official
guardians of a belief in supernaturalism. The Lavingtons of the time
were content, however indignant at the disturber of their calm, to call
Wesley knave, hypocrite, enthusiast, or papist, without being led to any
philosophical estimate of the disagreeable phenomenon. They accepted
the position, so naïvely interpreted by Warburton, and so skilfully
undermined by Middleton. They held that a church might safely rest its
claim to authority upon past miracles, and at the same time deny the
reality of modern interpositions of Providence. They combined, that is,
Hume's view of the eighteenth century with Wesley's view of the first.
They had thus put the religious impulse into a strait waistcoat, and
imagined that the force thus doomed to inaction could retain sufficient
power to be useful without being troublesome.

91. The conclusion of Wesley's answer to Middleton gives the key to
his position. The traditional evidence of Christianity might be destroyed
without injuring the faith. The believer would still be able to say to
those who were striking at it, 'Beat on the sack of Anaxagoras. But you
can no more hurt *my* evidence of Christianity, than the tyrant could
hurt the spirit of that wise man.'[54] The ultimate and incontrovertible
evidence is the evidence of the believer's heart. Christianity gives the
light for which we long; and the light is its own evidence. This is the

[53]Warburton's Works, viii. 382.   [54]Wesley, xiii, 256, 257.

sum of the believer's argument: 'One thing I know; I was blind, and now I see.'[54] This is the argument which may satisfy a woman or a child; not that historical argument which, according to worthy Lelands and Doddridges, might be made clear to a ploughboy. Here, in fact, we come once more to the sentiment which was the turning point in contemporary thought. Wesley, like Law, says seriously what Dodwell said ironically.[55] Christianity is not founded on argument, but upon sentiment interpreted as God's voice speaking to the soul. The phrase embodies the revolt of the emotional nature against an effete theological system. Men in whom the intellectual instincts were predominant became sceptical with Hume; men of warmer temperament, of greater imaginative power, and narrower logical faculty, might take shelter in Law's theosophical refuge; those in whom a strong moral sense, and a keen eye for the facts of life, were most strongly developed, would sympathise with Wesley.

92. The relation between Law and Wesley passed through several phases. Wesley never became a mystic, though much attracted by some of the mystical teaching. He not only wrote an angry letter to Law on breaking with him (in 1738); but eighteen years later (1756) he made a formal attack upon Law's mystical doctrines. In later years he softened towards his old master. His sermons frequently mention Law with the highest respect. In 1789 he speaks of the 'Serious Call' as a 'treatise which will hardly be excelled, if it be equalled, in the English tongue, either for beauty of expression or for justice and depth of thought.'[56] Elsewhere he speaks of Law's two practical treatises as 'sowing the seed' of Methodism, and first 'stemming the torrent' of infidelity and immorality, which had overspread the nation since the Restoration.[57] The force of Law's moral teaching was not obscured to him by his indifference to Law's theology.

93. Agreeing with Law's central method, and, like him, appealing to the heart from the intellect, Wesley's divergence was determined by the difference in character of the philosophical recluse and the active reformer. Law was more impressed by the inadequacy of the ordinary creed to satisfy the intellect or stimulate the emotions; Wesley by its impotence in the warfare with vice and corruption. Law retired from the world; Wesley sought to subdue the world. Law felt that a new philosophy was required to meet the searching scepticism of the day; Wesley was indifferent to all philosophical difficulties, and, instead of

[54]Wesley, xiii. 256, 257.
[55]See Wesley's reference to Dodwell's tract in the 'Earnest Appeal,' xii. 14.
[56]Wesley, x. 429.   [57]Ib. ix. 298.

endeavouring to cut away the logical standing-ground of scepticism, sought to overpower it by infusing a stronger zeal into the decaying organisation of the Church. So far as Wesley dealt at all in speculation, it was because certain difficulties were forced upon him by the mode in which his followers interpreted speculation into practice. To Wesley, as to Law, the resuscitation of religious emotions presented itself as a super-natural interference, or, as they would have said, as the outpouring of a divine influence into the human heart. Law, in his study, could aban-don himself to the current of his emotions, and set himself to frame a higher theology, free from the crude anthropomorphism of the ortho-dox creed. He could evade the cavils of the deist by adopting a more pantheistic conception of the Deity. Wesley had to meet very different difficulties. Law's pure and unselfish nature produced nothing but ele-vating visions under the raptures of religious excitement. But very different results followed when a similar stimulant was administered to thousands of ignorant and brutal human beings of the ordinary mould. The Warburtons and the Lavingtons inferred from the questionable phenomena which followed that the whole impulse was merely 'enthu-siastic,' or, in other words, the results of a debasing superstition. Wesley never doubted for a moment the reality of the influence, and could reply, with great cogency, that the belief in that reality was of the essence of Christianity. But he was sorely troubled by some of the mani-festations, which bore too strongly the marks of another than a celestial origin.

94. His early preaching produced many of those curious phenomena characteristic of great religious excitement. Men and women howled, foamed at the mouth, and went through dreadful convulsions, fre-quently lasting many hours, till the frame became exhausted, or the devil was cast out. Wesley argues that these symptoms were not ficti-tious, and infers that they must have been supernatural. As the first impulse died away, and sufficient proof appeared that a convulsive fit did not necessarily imply a permanent moral change, Wesley had an obvious explanation. The work, he thinks, was first divine; afterwards 'nature mixed with grace;' and, finally, 'Satan likewise mimicked this work of God, in order to discredit the whole work; and yet, it is not wise to give up this part any more than to give up the whole. At first it was doubtless wholly from God; it is partly so at this day (1759); and he will enable us to discern how far, in every case, the work is pure, and where it mixes or degenerates.'[58] A singular co-operation between

[58]Wesley, iii. 414.

God and the Devil! To keep these manifestations and other strange
aberrations of an ordinary intellect, when seized with what it takes to
be a divine frenzy, within tolerable bounds, was naturally the most
pressing of tasks for Wesley. It was necessary to provide a definite
framework of dogma to restrain the incoherent utterances of divergent
inspirations; a philosophy which might account for the varying impulses, without upsetting the validity of the general principle; and a
rigorous system of discipline to maintain decency and morality. The
last was supplied by the Methodist organisation, guided and impelled by
his own ceaseless energy. The dogma came from the Protestant tradition, or, as Wesley would have said, from the Bible. The text of the
Scriptures, interpreted, of course, with infantile faith in its literal inspiration, supplied a sufficient test for the utterances of the Spirit. Wesley
was content to assume, without in the least troubling himself with
speculative difficulties, that God had directly inspired the Scriptures,
and spoke directly to the individual, and that the two utterances must
be in perfect harmony.

95. One result is, that a large part of Wesley's writings deal with
what may be called the physiology of conversion. He inevitably takes
the keenest interest in finding the true explanation of the strange phenomena which he at once excited and controlled. His scientific apparatus
is simply the Bible, interpreted by his own common sense. What is the
meaning of conversion? What is a genuine and what a false conversion?
What change is wrought in the sinner's soul? How are his relations to
his Creator affected? What is the precise legal significance of justification, sanctification, and perfection? In what sense does the believer
become sinless? Is a relapse possible, or a recovery from a relapse?
These and other questions are canvassed with unceasing interest, as,
indeed, their solution vitally affected the welfare of the society. The discussions are not a mere scholastic logomachy, but are meant to decide
facts of immediate practical importance. The theology, however, must
necessarily be of the crude and rigid variety intelligible to the ordinary
intellect of the time; for men once lost in the mazes of mysticism would
fall into hopeless confusion. Wesley fully accepts the anthropomorphic
conceptions of God, and the 'debtor and creditor' scheme which revolted
Law's finer intellect; but he differs from Warburton and his like in so
far as God is regarded as an active administrator, not as a constitutional
sovereign who has retired from all immediate interference with the
affairs of his kingdom.

96. The 'Appeals to Men of Reason and Religion' (1743-5) and the
tract on 'Original Sin' (1757) are, perhaps, the writings most character-

istic of his intellectual position. The last of these books is in answer to
the Unitarian, Taylor, who is near enough to the deists to adopt their
protest against the theory of human corruption, and sufficiently a Christian to support his doctrine by the Bible, and therefore to come within
reach of Wesley. The greater part of Wesley's treatise is therefore occupied with a wearisome wrangle over texts, with little reference to the
deeper philosophical ground. The ever-recurring difficulty, indeed,
presses upon him; and he evades it as best he may. How are we to
reconcile the two fundamental articles of theology—the goodness of an
omnipotent Creator, and the corruption and misery of the creature?
Taylor had put his argument in a nutshell. 'If we come into the world
with' sinful propensities, he had said, 'they are natural; but if natural,
necessary; and if necessary, no sin.' From the goodness of God, then,
we must infer the goodness of man. To admit this consequence would
be to abandon Wesley's deepest convictions. Man is naturally wicked.
Must we, then, infer the injustice of a God who makes men sinful and
then damns them for sinning? Wesley shudders at the blasphemy. He
denounces, again and again, in various tracts, the hideous doctrine of
reprobation. He will not believe that God has foredoomed nineteen out
of twenty of his creatures to eternal torture. The escape, of course, from
the dilemma is made by the doctrine of free-will. The doctrine that
God has made twenty creatures with the certainty that nineteen will be
damned, and has left the selection to chance, is capable of being presented in such a way as to avoid the shock to the imagination. Upon
this subject, however, Wesley, though he wrote several tracts, did not
succeed in saying anything worth notice; for it belongs to a sphere of
thought in which he becomes hopelessly incompetent. He is content
with the ordinary reasonings; and, in fact, his dislike to Calvinism was
probably more of the practical than of the speculative kind. He is an
Arminian that he may preach repentance and avoid the popular fatalism
of antinomian enthusiasts. It is the instinct of the ruler of men, not of
the philosopher, which determines his creed.

97. To adjust the relations of speculative systems, to discover the
underlying truths of which they give a distorted view, and to detect the
fallacies by which they are vitiated, was not Wesley's peculiar province.
But God is good: men are bad; these propositions express his deepest
convictions—reconcile them who may—and he can enforce them with
the eloquence of perfect sincerity.

The treatise, for example, on 'Original Sin' opens with a vigorous
survey of man in all ages and countries. The colours are so dark that
the natural conclusion is purely sceptical. Can this world, we naturally

say, be the work of a good God? and can even Christianity have done much good? The classical nations were cruel and lustful under the thinnest veil of civilisation; the Jewish history is a record of 'astonishing wickedness.'[59] For centuries the Romans were godless, full of the grossest thoughts, and void of natural affection. Cato starved his old servants; Pompey was a monster of selfish ambition; and Cæsar of remorseless cruelty. The heathen at this day are little better than the beasts. Wesley had seen the 'poor Indians' of Pope's poetical sentimentalism, and declared that they were without God, and, without exception, 'gluttons, drunkards, thieves, dissemblers, liars.'[60] Any man would leave his wife at pleasure, and she in revenge would cut his children's throats. The Chinese had this in their favour, that they lived 7,000 miles off; but what Wesley knew of them was the reverse of the ordinary deist picture. The Mahomedans were as bad, and the Romanists generally infidels, unchaste, murderers, and cruel persecutors. The Protestants were not much better, and justified the account of Gulliver in Brobdingnag. The king of that country remarked that our recent history was nothing but 'a heap of conspiracies, rebellions, murders, massacres; the very worst effects that avarice, faction, hypocrisy, perfidiousness, cruelty, rage, madness, hatred, envy, lust, malice, and ambition could produce.'[61] And the theologian endorses the satire of the misanthropist. Coming nearer to his own experience, he points out all the evils which then affected English society; and he speaks as one knowing the evils which he describes. So black, indeed, is his description, that we are a little surprised when he discovers afterwards that Christians are better than heathen. He will not say that no heathen will be saved; but he will say that he never yet knew a heathen 'who was not a slave to some gross vice or other.' Bad, therefore, as nominal Christians are, he cannot yet 'place them on a level with the heathen;' and, indeed, he has a good reason; for if he believed with his opponent that the heathen might possibly be less vicious than the Christians, he would 'bid adieu to Christianity and commence heathen without delay.'[62] A more minute and, perhaps, effective description of English life is given in the second part of the 'Further Appeal.' The general irreligion of the nation; the extraordinary variety and extent of false swearing made necessary by the laws; the smuggling, sabbath-breaking, indifference to religious discipline, and political corruption, which was winked at by the sworn

[59]Wesley, xiv. 11.   [60]Ib. xiv. 23.   [61]Ib. xiv. 32.

[62]Ib. xiv. 152. Yet in his Journals (iii. 143) he says that the Indians learnt gluttony and drunkenness from the Christians, and asks, 'Oh, who will convert the English into honest heathens?'

defenders of the laws; the incessant drunkenness, the careless luxury of the higher orders, the gambling and cheating in every trade, the injury done by cunning lawyers under the name of justice, the squandering of public charities, the general disregard of truth; the profligacy of the army, the servility and carelessness of the clergy, and the utter indifference to the duties of their high calling; the immorality prevalent amongst the Dissenters, in spite of their claims to a stricter observance of duty; the worldliness of the Quakers, in spite of their affected simplicity—all these are described in the language of keen indignation; though they lead to a triumphant estimate of the reformation that has been worked by the Methodists.

98. Later writers have been too apt to assume that such denunciations as these, in comparison with which Brown's 'Estimate' is mere sham rhetoric, indicate a state of society really more degraded than that which existed before or since. It is enough to reply that a writer of equal eloquence, at any period and in any country, would be able to draw as dismal a picture. Whether the Englishmen of those days were really better or worse than the Englishmen of the seventeenth or of the nineteenth century is a question not to be so speedily settled. But the exertions of Wesley, and their success, are of themselves a sufficient proof that a work was to be done of which neither the rationalist nor the orthodox were capable. The creed of the one party was too negative, that of the other too lifeless, to satisfy the minds of the people. And, therefore, in Wesley's mouth the old creed uttered itself after the old fashion.

99. Wesley's eloquence is in the direct style which clothes his thoughts with the plainest language. He speaks of what he has seen; he is never beating the air, or slaying the dead, or mechanically repeating thrice-told stories, like most of his contemporaries. His arguments, when most obsolete in their methods and assumptions, still represent real thought upon questions of the deepest interest to himself and his hearers. He is not above familiar and telling illustrations, though to us they sometimes imply a childish credulity. He is at his best when striking home at the daily weaknesses of his disciples. We can fancy the venerable old man, his mind enriched by the experience of half a century's active warfare against vice, stained by no selfishness, and liable to no worse accusation than that of a too great love of power, and believe that his plain nervous language must have carried conviction and challenged the highest respect. It is rather curious, indeed, to find him saying, in his seventy-eighth year, that he had never yet preached a sermon expressly upon the danger of riches, though he had now and then touched upon

the subject.[63] Indeed, most of his disciples of that time suffered from a danger of a different kind. Wesley, however, could say that he had preached by example, and boasted that he would leave nothing but his books behind him. No man, at any rate, in that age spoke his mind more freely and forcibly as to the worst evils of the time. He gave his own notions towards the end of his life of what sermons should be. 'I dare no more write in a fine style,' he says in 1788, 'than wear a fine coat.' A man with one foot in the grave must waste no time on ornament. 'But were it otherwise, had I time to spare, I should still write just as I do. I should purposely decline what many admire—a highly ornamented style. I cannot admire French oratory; I despise it from my heart. Let those that please be in raptures at the pretty, elegant sentences of Massillon or Bourdaloue. But give me the plain nervous style of Dr. South, Dr. Bates, and Mr. John Howe. And for elegance, show me any French writer who exceeds Dean Young or Mr. Seed. Let who will admire the French frippery; I am still for plain sound English.'[64]

100. Wesley is his own best critic. We admire his sense and his sincerity. We respect his dislike to 'French frippery' and to that 'luxurious' style of eloquence of which it was a characteristic to apply the word 'dear' to Christ.[65] Abstinence from such language, he said, might check that kind of devotion which found expression in 'loud shouting, horrid unnatural screaming, repeating the same words twenty or thirty times, jumping two or three feet high, and throwing about the arms or legs both of men and women, in a manner shocking not only to religion, but to common decency.'[66] But it would not check proper devotion to him who was at once Man and God. Wesley is entirely free from some of the extravagances of his followers, and deals little even in impassioned appeals to the terrors of hell. He remains on the plane of terse vigorous sense. But it is also true that his eloquence never soars above the ground; if there is no bombast, there is little more rhetoric than may be found in a vigorous leading article, and if he wins our respect, he does not excite our admiration, or add to the stores of English rhetorical prose. He reminds us as little of Burke or Jeremy Taylor as of Massillon and Bourdaloue. His English is allied to that of Swift or Arbuthnot; but, unluckily, his thoughts run so frequently in the grooves of obsolete theological speculation, that he has succeeded in producing no single book satisfactory in a literary sense. In his rhetoric the threads

---

[63]Wesley, x. 102, 115.
[64]Ib. ix. 110. Dean Young was father of Young the poet.
[65]Ib. x. 424.   [66]Ib. x. 426.

of sound sense are crossed by others doomed to speedy decay, and the whole fabric has fallen into confusion. He did not look for the praise of critics, and he has hardly won it.

101. Wesley's writings are thus illustrative of the fact too often neglected by philosophical speculators. It is not only possible, but it is the normal case, that two and more currents of thought should exist side by side in a country with very little mutual influence. In the social stratum from which Wesley drew his followers the old ideas still prevailed in a slightly modified state. The arguments of the sceptics and the deists had scarcely penetrated to that depth. They were like so much idle wind stirring only the surface. Wesley is as indifferent to the doubts expressed by Hume as if the two men had lived in different hemispheres or centuries. The only relation is indirect. The field was undoubtedly prepared for Wesley by the fact that prevailing rationalism had paralysed the hands of the official cultivators. Men like Clarke or Warburton could no longer preach with the energy and the faith which alone can stir a popular audience. They had but half beliefs, and doctrines which they had demonstrated till their truth became doubtful. The growth of Methodism must be explained, not as an offshoot from the speculation of the time, nor yet, as is more commonly done, as a reaction against it. The true explanation is to be found in the records of the social development of the time, and in the growth of a great population outside the rusty ecclesiastical machinery. The refuse thus cast aside took fire by spontaneous combustion. The great masses of the untaught and uncared for inherited a tradition of the old theology. As they multiplied and developed, the need of some mode of satisfying the religious instincts became more pressing; and as the pure sceptics had nothing to say, and the official clergy could only say something in which they did not believe, Wesley's resuscitation of the old creed gave just the necessary impulse. Its want of any direct connection with that speculative movement could not stifle it, but it condemned it to barrenness. The want of a sound foundation in philosophy prevented the growth of any elevated theology, and alienated all cultivated thinkers. One outward symptom of the deficiency is the absence of any literature possessing more than a purely historical interest. The High Church revival of the present century differs curiously from Wesley's in this respect. Though less important in its moral aspect, it has to the speculation of the time the relation, at least, of reaction or misunderstanding, and has therefore produced some valuable literature. Wesleyanism in the eighteenth century represents heat without light—a blind protest of the

masses, and a vague feeling after some satisfaction to the instinct which ends only in a recrudescence of obsolete ideas.

102. When we turn from Wesley to the remarkable group of men who were his followers or allies, we find little but a less forcible utterance of the same order of ideas. The Methodists who gradually left the Established Church, and the Evangelical school which remained within it, furnish much matter for the ecclesiastical historian, but very little for the historian of thought or literature. The lively fermentation of religious feeling was confined to the classes for whom abstract speculation had no meaning, and to whom any artistic symbolisation of thought was profoundly uninteresting, if not provocative of absolute disgust. What literature they produced is valuable, so far as it has any value, for its contents, but not for its form. The psychologist may study records of the remarkable phenomena due to the presence of a vehement excitement, and observe with interest how curiously they repeat the experience of many different ages and races. But the literary student finds it difficult to peruse with any serious interest the incessant and often incoherent repetition of the cant phrases which may once have provoked the inarticulate shrieks of a revivalist meeting. A confused hubbub of the technical terms used in the Arminian and Calvinist controversies, of scriptural texts torn recklessly from their natural connection, and of semi-mystical phrases, occasionally bordering upon the erotic, is all that meets the ear. Such language is significant only from the absence of significance. It may throw light upon the nature and origin of the patient's excitement, but it does not express any coherent or intelligent view of the problems which occupied the genuine intellectual forces of the period.

103. We turn, for example, with a certain expectation to the sermons of Whitefield, the greatest orator, if we may trust the evidence of unprejudiced witnesses, of the Wesleyan movement. Franklin's well-known description[67] brings the man before us. To extort the copper and the silver and the gold from the pockets of that shrewdest of freethinkers was to win the most tangible of oratorical triumphs. One of Whitefield's assistants, Cornelius Winter, tells us that Whitefield wept profusely during his sermons, that he stamped and was overcome by his feelings, and that the physical effort was frequently followed by a loss of blood.[68] But the printed sermons, which appear indeed to have been imperfectly

[67]Franklin's 'Memoirs,' i. 161 and 166.
[68]'Life of Cornelius Winter,' by Jay.

reported, will draw no tears from the most emotional nature. In fact, they are the most striking proof that can be given of the familiar fact that oratory depends for its instantaneous effect upon the dramatic, rather than upon the intellectual, power of the orator. Here and there, there are passages of which we can believe that their defects of thought and language would not necessarily destroy our pleasure in a voice and manner of extraordinary excellence. There are apostrophes to God or to the sinner or to the Devil, in which, if we attend only to the situation and abstract our minds resolutely from the actual words, we can believe that a great effect might be produced. But nothing except the unequivocal testimony of facts could convince us that the greatest oratorical capacity could inform those tattered shreds of sensational rhetoric which are strung together to form the bulk of Whitefield's published sermons. It is, we know, the strength of the arm, not of the weapon, which gives force to the arrows of eloquence; and when Whitefield smote men to the heart with such blunt and brittle weapons, the secret of his success must have lain as much in the hearers as in the orator.

104. The controversy which divided Whitefield from Wesley brought out whatever speculative ability was possessed by their followers. The question at issue between Calvinists and Arminians has occupied many of the greatest intellects to be found amongst Catholics and Protestants; and, indeed, it is plain that the ultimate issues involved lie at the very root of a philosophical interpretation of the world. Wesley, as I have said, expressed very forcibly the sentiments natural to the autocrat of a great spiritual organisation. Such a man felt keenly the dangers of the Antinomian caricature of Calvinism, and was not able to distinguish the philosophical core of the doctrine from the perversions to which it is liable. If Wesley's treatment is ineffectual, there is not much interest in the controversy, which, after his abandonment of an active share in it, was carried on chiefly by Fletcher of Madeley and Toplady. Fletcher, indeed, was a man of singular beauty of character. The simplicity, purity, and warmth of his nature are stamped upon his biography, and are traceable even—where such qualities are most rarely to be found— in his controversial writings. An occasional tendency to sentimentalism reminds us that Fletcher was a countryman of Rousseau; though, fortunately for him, his emotions found a safer channel for utterance, and he was free from that dark stain of mental disease which poisoned Rousseau's life. But Fletcher, on the other hand, belongs as distinctly to a mere side current as Rousseau to the main stream of European thought. The quiet vicarage of Madeley was, in fact, a hermitage far less accessible than the Island of St. Pierre to the great forces of social upheaval.

There Fletcher could live in a bygone period, studying the theological problems which had been threshed out by the middle of the previous century. Formerly at the centre, they had now been banished to the very outskirts of speculation. A philosophical speculation may first lose its interest either for the intellectual leaders of mankind, or for their followers. When it disappears from the great arena of serious controversy, where the keenest thinkers reason under the healthy stimulus of contact with living men, it may retire to the schools or take refuge in country parsonages. Some minds enjoy a discussion all the more because they have to argue with the dead, and others have not yet discovered that it has ceased to have real vitality. If the pedant is contemptible, we feel at worst pity for men like Fletcher, who are discussing, in all earnestness, matters which to them are still of vital import. In this excellent man's 'checks to Antinomianism' and 'Scripture scales'—a characteristic title for a process of carefully balancing long chains of rival texts —we find mere relics of what once was thought, but scorn is rebuked by his simplicity. The good man really supposes that the battle is still to be decided by the use of the old-fashioned bows and arrows. We pass by, and feel that there would be a kind of profanity in exposing his weakness.

105. Toplady, his chief antagonist, seems to have been a man of considerable native powers of intellect, guided by a temperament of excessive fervour. His language towards Wesley is abusive and indecorous. He is in too great a passion to argue effectively. His chief work is an historical attempt to vindicate the Church of England from the charge of Arminianism, and he is still an intellectual contemporary of Calvin or Zanchius, and the early Puritan writers whom he quotes in utter unconsciousness that they belong to an antediluvian epoch. His latest authority is Jonathan Edwards, whose writings represent the blending of the old Calvinism with more recent philosophical thought. Toplady, however, shows a greater logical insight than his other allies and antagonists, and remonstrates very justly with Priestley, who inherited the ordinary hatred of the rationalist school for Calvinism, whilst abandoning the rationalist dogma of free-will. Priestley previously denied that the Calvinist theory had any relation to the philosophical doctrine of causation. Toplady regards the philosophical doctrine as a perversion of Calvinism; but the mere perception that there is such a philosophical doctrine suffices to distinguish him from most of his fellows. Their arguments are almost entirely confined to a fanciful interpretation of Scripture texts, implying a serene indifference to the very existence of Hume, Gibbon, or Voltaire.

106. The Evangelical school, who sympathised more or less distinctly with Wesley, included many men entitled to our sincere respect. We can admire their energy, though we cannot read their books. Throughout England sturdy sensible men, of the narrowest possible intellectual horizon, but the most vivid conviction of the value of certain teachings, were stirring the masses by addresses suited to indolent imaginations. What, they seemed to have tacitly enquired, is the argument which will induce an ignorant miner or a small tradesman in a country town to give up drinking and cock-fighting? The obvious answer was: Tell him that he is going straight to hell-fire to be tortured for all eternity. Preach that consoling truth to him long enough, and vigorously enough, and in a large enough crowd of his fellows, and he may be thrown into a fit of excitement that may form a crisis in his life. Represent God to him by the image most familiar to his imagination, as a severe creditor who won't excuse a farthing of the debt, and Christ as the benefactor who has freely offered to clear the score. Do not rest Christianity upon argument, but tell him dogmatically that every word of the Bible was dictated by God Almighty; and add that every word is as plain as the A B C. The doctrine may not be very refined or philosophical, but it is sufficiently congenial to the vague beliefs implanted in his mind by tradition to give a leverage for your appeals. By such means it was possible to kindle once more the dying embers of the old faith, and it is curious to remark how distinctly this power was recognised as the test of the truth. When a man like Berridge could throw a congregation into fits, and bring on all the phenomena of epidemic excitement, he took it for a plain proof that God was with him. Clarke or Foster might have preached till doomsday about the inherent and immutable essences of things, the everlasting laws of morality, and the conclusion that whatever is, is right, without producing more than a temporary glow of complacency. The common sense of Sherlock might be taken as sound advice, but could never send a thrill through the imagination. The Evangelicals discovered that by bringing out once more the old pictures of heaven and hell, and substituting dogmatism for abstract argument, they could still move an audience to frenzy, and permanently raise the warmth of religious feeling.

107. Energy exerted on behalf of a sincere conviction is commendable; and the early Evangelicals were, in their fashion, men of surprising vigour. The number of sermons which they preached was appalling. The example of Wesley and Whitefield was followed by the numerous itinerant preachers, who, with much zeal and little learning, bore the fiery torch throughout the country. Grimshaw, in the wild district fa-

miliar to modern readers of Miss Brontë's novels, preached habitually thirty-six sermons a fortnight—twelve in one week, and twenty-four in the alternate week; and his prayers were effectual enough to stop the Haworth races by continuous rain.[69] The sermons were measured out with no grudging hand. Newton remonstrated sensibly with a friend who seems to have been in the habit of talking for two hours so as to be heard 'far beyond the church walls.' Overlong sermons, says Newton, make the congregation think of the pudding which is in danger of being overboiled; and he judiciously limits himself to a single hour.[70] He could not 'wind up his ends' satisfactorily in a shorter time. 'I sometimes preach half an hour,' said one worthy performer, 'before God comes; and when he is come I can do no less than preach half an hour of three-quarters of an hour afterwards.'[71] Our more squeamish appetites are apt to be revolted at the thought of the torrents of clumsy exhortation, devoid of all merit except that of sincerity and strength of feeling. Of intellectual interest there could be none. Berridge lays it down for 'certain truth' that the cultivation of 'human science' implied the neglect of the Bible. 'Immorality and infidelity spread their branches equally with human science;' and when 'human science' reaches its highest pitch, a nation is ready for perpetual bondage.[72] Newton is equally clear as to the bad effects of æsthetic culture. It stimulates our 'depraved nature.' A cultivated imagination means the possession of a 'large stock of other people's dreams and fables.' Taste means a disposition for being 'humoured, soothed, and flattered,' which involves a dislike to the most important truths, unless concealed under delicate verbiage. People of taste, in fact, did not care to hear the Gospel preached—at least by Methodist preachers—and of course their dislike showed the corruption of their nature.[73] When poor Cowper was seeking distraction from the tortures of a diseased mind in the translation of Homer, Newton looked on with doubtful approval, and preferred to encourage the poet in the composition of hymns which stimulated his terrible religious mania. 'I believe,' says Newton himself, 'my name is up about the country for preaching people mad,' and he adds that there are nearly a dozen people in the neighbourhood more or less 'disordered in their heads, and most of them, I believe, truly gracious people.' Though he is grieved by the thought, he thinks them 'less to be pitied than the mad people of the world who think themselves in their senses, and take

[69]'Grimshaw's Life,' by Newton, pp. 18, 121.

[70]Newton's Works, ii. 163.   [72]Berridge, p. 238.

[71]Toplady, p. 501.   [73]See Southey's 'Life of Cowper,' i. 270.

occasion to scoff at the Gospel, as if it was only fit to drive people out of their senses.'[74]

108. The 'world' has pretty well taken Newton and his friends at their word. Cynics have called them madmen, and philosophers have called them fools; men of wide sympathy, revolted by their narrow dogmatism, which could see no good in human nature, and no chance of salvation for other sects, have satirised them as unctuous hypocrites; the adherents of the dilettante forms of religious sentimentality who measure the value of a creed by the prettiness of its external trappings, have been disgusted with their absence of any æsthetic charm; the intellectual cowards, who seek for the best mode of blinding themselves to awkward conclusions, have discovered that the ancient Church can hoodwink its followers more effectually. On all sides, the sect which called itself Evangelical has been ridiculed and despised, and but grudging justice is done, even by later believers, to its influence in awaking slumbering religious feeling. In truth, the chief moral for our purposes is a very plain one. The history of the Evangelical revival illustrates the limits of religious movements which spring up in the absence of any vigorous rivals without a definite philosophical basis. They flourish for a time because they satisfy a real emotional craving; but they have within them the seeds of decay. A form of faith which has no charms for thinkers ends by repelling from itself even the thinkers who have grown up under its influence. In the second generation the abler disciples revolted against the strict dogmatism of their fathers, and sought for some more liberal form of creed, or some more potent intellectual narcotic. The belief generated in the lower or middle social strata was utterly uncongenial to the higher currents of thought, and, thus confined within narrow limits, ossified into a set of barren theories, never vivified by contact with genuine thought.

109. As a whole, the Protestant movement may thus be regarded as a blind protest against the efficacy for the daily wants of life of the old deistic Christianity. The fundamental doctrine preached by all its advocates is the corruption of human nature. 'The mind of man,' says the typical rationalist Foster, 'is by nature so strongly attached to virtue that it cannot become totally corrupted at once.'[75] Henry Venn, in the 'Complete Duty of Man,' a book intended to supersede the cold morality of the 'Whole Duty of Man,' and containing the most formal statement of the creed of his sect, lays down the opposite principle. 'There dwells,' he says, 'in the heart of every man, till changed by grace, an aversion to

---

[74]Newton, i. 517.   [75]Foster's 'Discourses,' i. 387.

the very author of his being.'[76] The religion of nature, considered by all the theologians of the preceding generation as the basis of, if not identical with, Christianity, was thus, with the new school, the very antithesis of true religion, and meant a hatred of God. All the Methodists and semi-Methodists, Wesley and Whitefield, and Fletcher and Berridge and Toplady, agree in laying down this doctrine as the very foundation of their creed. The correlative doctrine necessarily follows. If nature is corrupt, the divine element must be supernatural. The Evangelists, therefore, trace everywhere the workings of the two antagonist principles—grace and nature. The hand of God was to be seen everywhere. Venn used to take his children to the window during a thunderstorm, and tell them that the lightning was directed by God's will.[77] Newton perhaps, more than any of the others, appears to be impressed by a constant sense of a superintending providence in the most minute events of life—a state of mind perhaps fostered by his early adventures as a slave-trader. Wesley's writings, as we have seen, are full of a doctrine which frequently leads to an unlovely superstition; and sometimes, as in the writings of Berridge, to a grotesque familiarity of address to a Being so constantly and tangibly present. As clearly it implies a vivid sentiment, never to be despised for its ugly clothing, and, as the example of the older Puritans showed, sometimes terribly efficacious.

110. A strong conviction of the evil side of nature may reveal itself in many forms, and is expressed in connection with very different theories by such men as Pascal, Butler, Law, Mandeville, and Voltaire. It is as naturally connected with scepticism as with faith. The special form which it assumed in England is indicative of the peculiarities of the national character and social condition. Wesley and Fletcher denounce the social evils of the country, and agree in supporting the authority of the English Government against America and religion against sceptics. In France the same passionate feeling took the form of a revolutionary assault upon the whole established order in Church and State. The effect of the English Methodist movement in thus diverting a great volume of discontent into the religious, instead of the political, channel is of an importance not easy to calculate; and I have already made some remarks upon its causes. The most marked result of the English agitation in the political field was the abolition of slavery. It is a triumph of which the Evangelicals have good reason to boast; but, however admirable in itself, the chief effect of the measure upon England was the great moral precedent of an appeal to conscience in a political question. Divorced

[76]'Complete Duty of Man,' p. 46.   [77]Life, p. 36.

from politics on the one hand, the movement, as we have seen, was divorced from speculation on the other. The old Protestantism had been an intellectual as well as a moral movement. It vindicated freedom of thought, besides attacking the moral evils of ecclesiastical tyranny. The revivers of the old phase of thought could no longer frankly reconcile themselves to reason which destroyed their first principles, nor, whilst retaining the old hatred of priestcraft, frankly oppose themselves to it; and this was, undoubtedly, their fundamental weakness. The moral efficacy of the preaching was necessarily lowered. A belief in the necessity of a miraculous change as the foundation of the religious life of every individual, tended to become merely superstitious as the general atmosphere was unfavourable to an intelligent belief in the supernatural. To believe in the literal inspiration of the Bible could no longer be the basis of a vigorous creed, except in ignorant or narrow minds.

III. The new Puritanism, excluding all the most powerful intellectual elements, was therefore of necessity a faint reflection of the grander Puritanism of the seventeenth century. The morality founded upon it showed the old narrowness without the old intensity. The hatred of the world was too often interpreted into a hatred of all that makes the world beautiful, combined with a hearty appreciation of everything that adds to its material comfort. The tendency which has been the most conspicuous weakness of the creed was the reflection of the tendencies of the English middle classes. Their religious emotions were coloured by the general character of their lives. Protestantism, as it has been developed amongst industrial communities, bears traces of its origin; and though it has produced an heroic type of character, it has always been hostile to the æsthetic development of the race, and to the more delicate forms of religious doctrine. The more general causes of this tendency, so far as they are logically connected with the primary data of the creed, would require an investigation beyond my present purpose. It may be assumed briefly that the great moral doctrine of Protestantism, the responsibility of the individual to his own conscience, and its consequent depreciation of all external observances, is congenial to this form of compromise with the world. Since, on the Protestant theory, heaven is not to be won by external observances, but by an inward change of heart, there is no ground for that exaltation of the ascetic life which, in corrupt times, and by the help of the vast organisation of the priesthood, becomes a mere sanctification of idleness. The Protestant, even in the Divine presence, is taught to shudder at the frivolities of the world, and to despise the frivolities of the Church; but there is nothing in his religion which forbids the severest application to any occupation not in itself wicked. I need not, however, enquire how far in this case the creed is influenced chiefly by the moral or by the social conditions. Protestantism divorced from freedom of thought, and without any qualification for enslaving thought, became but a shrivelled and narrow representative of the grand creed of the Reformation.

112. Wesleyanism and Evangelicalism thus illustrate the twofold truth that powerful religious movements often originate in social strata lying far beyond the reach of philosophy, but are doomed to sterility if they cannot assimilate some philosophical element. Between Wesleyanism and the belief of the cultivated classes there could scarcely be said to exist even the relation of contradiction. Wesley could as little appeal to the reason of Hume's scholars as Hume could touch the hearts of Wesley's disciples. A reactionary movement may gain some strength from the theories to which it is opposed; for thought generally progresses by antagonism. But Evangelicalism did not profess to have any genuine theory to oppose to Hume. It simply set Hume aside as irrelevant. A movement the roots of which are to be sought in the emotional instead of the intellectual nature necessarily takes the form of a reaction. Since the emotions cannot by themselves discover new creeds, they must clothe even a demand for change in the language of older creeds. Thus Wesley fell back upon the early Protestants, as the early Protestants had fallen back upon primitive Christianity; as, in a different sphere, the English political Radicals began by appealing to Hampden and Sidney; and as the literary reformers fancied themselves to be reviving the age of Shakespeare and Milton. When the heart usurps the functions of the head, even a progressive development will appear to be retrograde. The same cause obscures the true nature of the movement which we have now to consider.

VII. The Literary Reaction.

113. The opening of new intellectual horizons, the discovery of new instruments in the struggle with nature, the failure of the old organisation to meet the wants of a rapidly growing society, the failure of the old scholasticism and Catholicism to satisfy the intellect or the imagination, had led to the great outbreak which we call the Reformation and the Renaissance. Another crisis due to similar causes was about to take place. The revolt against the old dogmatism had not been sufficiently thorough. There was still dead social and intellectual tissue which had to be expelled. Though the old theological dogmas had become mere mummies, dead relics of their former selves, the scepticism which

showed their inanity could not replace them by a new synthesis, or afford satisfaction to the ordinary intellect of mankind. On one side, therefore, we have a dogmatism growing ever more frigid and lifeless; and on the other, a crude empiricism which takes fundamental questions for granted, or guides itself by the first hasty dictates of superficial observation. Corresponding to this, we have, in the imaginative sphere, frigid allegories in place of vivid symbols; mere personified abstractions for the living beings of the old mythology; and a conscious obedience to mechanical formulæ in place of the old free play of the imagination; for authority we have hollow demonstrations, and incessant arguing in place of appeals to the emotions. Simultaneously we have a vigorous, but too often prosaic, realism. The ordinary facts of everyday life are seen forcibly, but they are stripped of romantic association or philosophical significance. We do not see contemporary events as part of a vast series carrying us back to the dim past and inscrutable future; nor as standing out against a background of mystery. The divorce of philosophy from reality has impoverished both. Religious symbols which excite no genuine emotion, and facts which are never seen as lighted up by religious meaning, can evidently suggest no great imaginative work. The English literature, indeed, of the eighteenth century reflects the many admirable qualities of its writers, though it reflects them in an obscure mirror. Human nature does not vary, as we are sometimes given to assume, by sudden starts from one generation to another. I do not doubt that Englishmen a hundred years ago had as much imaginative power, as much good feeling, and at least as much love of truth as their descendants of to-day. I am only endeavouring to explain the conditions which limited for a time their powers of utterance, and then led them to find new modes of expression for the most perennial of human feelings. This last process took various forms. The last half of the century was marked in literature by the slow development of three distinct processes of reaction. A few hints, necessarily of the briefest and most imperfect kind, may sufficiently indicate their relation to previous modes of thought, and the peculiar nature of the English development. The sentimentalists represent, we may say, the vague feeling of discontent with the existing order of thought and society; the romantic and the naturalistic school adopted different modes of satisfying the yearning thus excited.

114. Wesley amused himself in one of his peregrinations with Sterne's 'Sentimental Journey.' 'Sentimental!' he asks in his journal; 'what is that? It is not English. He might as well say "Continental." '[1] It would

[1] Journal, February 11, 1772.

be rather difficult to answer Wesley's question with precision, after all our experience of the thing signified. Sentimentalism seems to be a name for several allied phases of thought which graduate imperceptibly into each other. It is the name of a kind of mildew which spreads over the surface of literature at this period to indicate a sickly constitution. It is the name of the mood in which we make a luxury of grief, and regard sympathetic emotion as an end rather than a means—a mood rightly despised by men of masculine nature. It is, again, the name of the disposition to substitute feeling for logic, and therefore to avert our eyes from whenever facts suggest unpleasant contemplations. But it may also be used to mean the sympathy of the good Samaritan for the sick and wounded in the struggle whom the orthodox Pharisee passes by with his official *non possumus*. It sometimes implies the tendency to substitute a rose-coloured ideal for a faithful portraiture of life; and sometimes the power of detecting the real beauty which is concealed from vulgar observers by their dread of vulgarity.

115. It would be futile to attempt to consider this fluctuating mood as closely correlated to any definite logical process. We may say, in a general way, that the growth of sentimentalism was symptomatic of a social condition daily becoming more unhealthy. In France an intelligent noblesse, having no particular duties to discharge, was beginning to play at philanthropy. In England, though the dissociation of the upper classes from active life was not so wide, there was a daily increasing number of rich and idle persons, who found the cultivation of their finer feelings a very amusing luxury. The virtue called 'sensibility,' which became so popular towards the end of the century, which was petted by the namby-pamby and Rosa-Matilda schools, and which was gently satirised in Miss Austen's novels, is the more colourless form of the sentiment which has recently taken theological masks. The 'man of feeling' of those days would in these days be a ritualist or a neopagan; and 'the tear of sensibility,' which used to bedew the eye of the fine ladies of the time, would be offered before the altar which has succeeded in adorning itself with lighted candles. We may trace the growth of the sentiment far back in the century. Wesleyanism was, in one sense, a development of sentimentalism. Wesley and his followers thought the symbols of the official theism too vague and effete for practical use, and tried to restore the old vivid concrete mythology. The writings of Shaftesbury may exemplify the kind of empty declamation against which they revolted. When we read his Hymn to Nature, we see that the feelings excited by so vague a deity can only give birth to a vague pomposity. Nature does not really excite the keen emotions appropriate

to the old God, and we must not contemplate the new idol too closely. It must be draped in all the apparatus of old-fashioned classical magniloquence.

116. But, when Wesleyanism came to be adopted by the more refined classes, a kind of compromise had to be effected. The modern imagination cannot feed upon the supernatural alone. The scenery of the lake of fire and brimstone became tiresome in the long run to contemporaries of Hume, however little they might be conscious of his direct influence. And thus, the religious world, naturally affected by the taste of its secular rival, tried to transplant into its own literature some of the faded charms of the Shaftesbury school of eloquence. Hervey's 'Meditations' (1746–7), for example, was one of the most popular books of the century; and it bears to Shaftesbury the same kind of relation which Young bears to Pope. Hervey was an attached disciple of Wesley; and a man of some cultivation and great fluency of speech. He tried to eclipse the worldly writers in their own style of rhetoric. The worship of nature might be combined with the worship of Jehovah. He admires the 'stupendous orbs,' and the immortal harmonies, but he takes care to remember that we must die, and meditates, in most edifying terms, amongst the tombs. Such works can hardly be judged by the common literary canons. Writings which are meant to sanctify imaginative indulgences by wresting the ordinary language to purposes of religious edification are often, for obvious reasons, popular beyond their merits. Sacred poetry and religious novels belong to a world of their own. To the profane reader, however, the fusion of deistical sentiment and evangelical truth does not seem to have been thoroughly effected. There is the old falsetto note which affects us disagreeably in Shaftesbury's writings. Hervey, after all, lives in the eighteenth century, and though, as his 'Theron and Aspasia' proves, he could write with sufficient savour upon the true Evangelical dogmas, the imaginative symbolism of his creed is softened by the contemporary currents which blend with it.

117. Hervey's chief book, the 'Meditations,' was, according to Southey, not more laudable in its purpose than vicious in its style, and therefore one of the most popular ever written. Dipping into its pages at random, we find everywhere specimens of that queer eighteenth-century euphuism of which Shaftesbury set, perhaps, the earliest example, mixed with phrases which recall the unction of the popular Evangelical preacher. If Hervey wants to say that certain herbs are useful medicinally, he observes that they 'impart floridity to our circulating fluids, add a more vigorous tone to our active solids, and thereby repair the decay of our enfeebled constitutions.' 'Breathe soft, ye winds!' he exclaims; 'O spare

the tender fruitage, ye surly blasts! Let the pear-tree suckle her juicy progeny, till they drop into our hands and dissolve in our mouths! Let the plum hang unmolested upon her boughs till she fatten her delicious flesh, and cloud her polished skin with blue.'[2] It is easy to conceive how this false gallop of rhetoric shades off into unctuous addresses to Christ, and is heightened by descriptions of decaying bodies or of hell-fire. Hervey's magniloquence is precisely of that kind which disgusts a cultivated reader, and passes with the half-educated for true eloquence. Very similar bombast is now manufactured with equal volubility to attract the readers of cheap newspapers; nor is it necessary to give further examples of a kind of rhetoric with which we are only too familiar.

118. Its interest for us consists chiefly in the fact that Hervey represents the blending of two streams of sentiment; of the religious unction of Wesleyanism, which is more explicitly given in his 'Theron and Aspasia,' and that vaguer enthusiasm for nature represented soon afterwards by Ossian and by Rousseau. His books may be described as a transitional form between the nature-worship of the deists, which was felt to be wanting in fire, and the nature-worship of Wordsworth, which had not yet dawned upon the world; the whole being rendered palatable to the ordinary reader by the admixture of Evangelical theology. Another writer who represents a somewhat analogous attitude is Henry Brooke, whose 'Fool of Quality' (1760, &c.), admired by Wesley and republished in later years by Kingsley, is a bewildering mixture of religious mysticism with poetical sentimentalism. Brooke's intellectual genealogy seems to be traceable to Behmen on the one hand and to Rousseau on the other; whilst a curious strain of Irish eccentricity runs through the whole, tempered by touches of the grace and tenderness of his greater countryman Goldsmith. The book resembles in some respects the friend of our infancy, 'Sandford and Merton,' though in that excellent performance the Rousseau element is not tempered by any theological admixture. Such performances indicate a current of vague feeling in search of some mode of utterance less constrained than that sanctioned by the practice of the Pope school, but equally ready to flow along the channels marked by Wesley or by Rousseau.

119. Another form of sentimentalism may be derived from Richardson. Richardson, as Johnson said, taught the passions to move at the command of virtue. That means that he discovered how a sincere profession of the narrowest code of morality might excuse a systematic dallying with seductive images. Byron held—and Byron was a good, if

[2]'Reflections on a Flower-Garden.'

a partial judge—that there was more danger in such books as Rousseau's 'Nouvelle Héloïse' than in the open and scoffing vice of 'Don
Juan.' This remark is equally applicable to 'Clarissa Harlowe.' Indeed,
it is hardly a new discovery that the casuistical moralist passes easily into
the prurient analyser of moral hotbeds; or that Abelard may with the
best intentions give rather dangerous lessons to Héloïse. Richardson
is never immoral in intention, nor, as a rule, immoral in effect; but he
is frequently morbid, and morbid in a significant direction. In fact, the
Pamelas and Clarissas of the day were rather tired, we may guess, of
the prosaic labours to which they were condemned, and of the prosaic
morality preached to them. They had, as Richardson's word-portraits
show, strong passions; they were tired of the old romances, and were
taking to books instead of needlework. The Spectator and his followers
preached excellent morality to women, but women want something
more than excellent morality. The old confessor had been abolished,
but not replaced. Richardson himself, the spiritual adviser of a little
circle of feminine worshippers, understood their needs, and gave utterance to their vague wants. The skill with which he prolongs through
eight volumes his variations upon the one theme of a feminine martyrdom, exhausting every phrase in the pathetic vocabulary, and accumulating misery until our sympathy becomes so pungent that we know
not whether it be more delicious or painful, makes 'Clarissa Harlowe'
one of the marvels of literature. That his morality was mawkish and
narrow is proved by the jovial contempt which gave a rebuff to Pamela
in 'Joseph Andrews.' That his sentiment had the power of original
genius is proved by the relation of 'Clarissa Harlowe' to the 'Nouvelle
Héloïse.' Rousseau is the greatest of the sentimentalists, and Rousseau borrowed more than the form of his most passionate work from
Richardson. When we think of the patient interest with which our
ancestors dwelt upon the long-drawn agonies of Clarissa, the moralising
of Pamela, and the virtuous declamation of Sir Charles Grandison, we
can believe that a weight of emotion, without adequate vent, was accumulating behind the old dikes and barriers of moral convention. As
the Clarissas were allowed to devote less time to needlework, and were
able to take advantage of circulating libraries, they might easily develop
a taste for literary stimulants.

120. Sentimentalism, pure and simple, needing neither the prefix of a
text nor the appendage of a moral application, was represented by a
later writer. It came into the world when Sterne discovered the art of
tickling his contemporaries' fancies by his inimitable mixture of pathos,
humour, and sheer buffoonery. No man of equal literary eminence

excites less respect or even less genuine sympathy. He showed, as we cannot deny, a corrupt heart and a prurient imagination. He is a literary prostitute. He cultivates his fineness of feeling with a direct view to the market; and when we most admire his books, we most despise the man. He is the most conspicuous example that could be quoted in favour of the dangerous thesis that literary and moral excellence belong to different spheres. The phenomenon, however, is hardly rare in its kind. The propensities to an actual and an ideal gratification of the virtuous instinct do not always accompany each other. Nobody could be more virtuous in imagination than Sterne. Fictitious misery excited his liveliest sympathy, because it need never shock his taste. We can believe that he wept genuine tears when he described Uncle Toby's oath, and the death of Le Fevre. And we weep too, for the moment, till a sense of the profound unreality disenchants us. We feel the insincerity when most cleverly disguised, and are less affected even by the death of Le Fevre than by a single touch of Cowper's pathos. The tinsel cannot pass itself off for gold. We resent the imposition, and accuse Sterne of laughing in his sleeve. Of course, he replies, I am laughing in my sleeve: why not weep for the luxury of weeping; and restore our self-esteem by mocking our own weakness? And then, if my sentiment disgusts you, would you prefer a bit of sham buffoonery, or a savoury morsel of obscene suggestion? They are quite at your service. The skill with which the varying moods are blended is marvelous, and we admit Sterne to be the best of the buffoons, and the most pathetic of the shallow-hearted. He buys our wonder by a degradation which would be a dear price even for the highest admiration. But no cleverer man ever put on the cap and bells, or catered successfully to the emotional wants, good or bad, of his generation.

121. Sterne is the typical sentimentalist. His eccentricity was too marked to suggest direct rivalry by any but the most servile of imitators. The best writer of his school is supposed to be Mackenzie, the 'Man of Feeling;' but the 'Man of Feeling,' from which he took his title, has passed from amongst the living. It is almost as much duller than Sterne as it is more virtuous. The sickly tone of feeling is relieved by no humour, and but slightly relieved by rather feeble satire. We might trace the influence of sentimentalism in Goldsmith's exquisite 'Vicar'—a book which affected Goethe as 'Clarissa' affected Rousseau. But the purity and healthiness of Goldsmith's feeling, which gives to his work a superiority over Sterne, not only in morality, but in art, makes it a less fitting instance of sentimentalism in its full development.

122. To assign any precise philosophical meaning to sentimentalism would, as I have said, be an absurd attempt. It is much more a social than an intellectual phenomenon. Yet it indicates certain tendencies which are connected with the development of thought. The modern sentimentalism may, perhaps, be defined as the effeminate element of Christianity. Th true sentimentalist accepts all that appears to be grace- ful, tender, and pretty in the Gospels, and turns away from the sterner and more masculine teaching which enables a religion to rule the world, as well as to amuse our softer hours. The tendency of the earlier gener- ation had been to transform Christianity into a code of mathematically demonstrable propositions, or to lower it into a system of prudential morality. As the Wesleyans tried to restore a sterner teaching, the sentimentalists tried to find expression for the more graceful teaching incorporated in the old doctrine. To attempt to make a religion out of the most effeminate elements is necessarily futile. Such a doctrine easily resolved itself into some variety of the cant, so heartily and rightfully denounced by Johnson. But the tendency to accept this milk-and-water version of the old theories was an indication that something was want- ing in the doctrine as well as in the social organisation of the time. Whilst Wesley stirred the masses, fine ladies and gentlemen began to play at sympathy with the poor and oppressed.

123. Meanwhile, however, one characteristic of the English sentimen- talists must be noticed. Their doctrine remained in the utterly unpracti- cal stage. When Rousseau wept rather too freely over the sorrows of his heroine, he regarded her as a type of the women of his time; and therefore was consciously aiming at a social and moral revolution. Sterne was content to weep without the slightest indication of any de- sire for a change. He shows no sense whatever of evils affecting the general welfare. He is a pure artist, and inclined, if anything, to preach the doctrine that things are very well as they are. If he weeps over a prisoner, he has no desire to destroy the Bastille. It would be rather a pity if some prisoners were not in existence to justify a little weeping. Even Goldsmith, though he laments the corruption,

> Where wealth accumulates and men decay,

is, as least, a good conservative, who delights in a pretty idyl, but does not want to see the state of nature revived. Prisons ought to be re- formed, and the country clergy better paid; but he has no grudge against the aristocracy which sends him venison, and no desire to upset the Church. He only wishes the rich to be better landlords, and charity to flow more freely.

124. Another peculiarity, less obvious, may be remarked. A more modern sentimentalist would probably express his feelings by describing some past state of society. He would paint some ideal society in mediæval times, and revive the holy monk and the humble nun for our edification. The sentimentalists whom I have mentioned, Richardson, and Sterne, and Goldsmith, and their followers, are perfectly content with imaginary persons derived from their own experience. They lay a new stress upon the advantage of tender-heartedness and sympathy, but they do not require to embody their imaginings in symbols drawn from a distant past. They are, in the first place, tolerably content with the society in which they live, and, in the next place, the historical tendencies of the age have not yet conferred tangible reality upon distant epochs. A change, however, was approaching. The last half of the century was, as I have said, pre-eminently historical. As civilisation progresses, as records are better preserved, and a greater permanence in social organisation makes men more disposed to look beyond their immediate surroundings, a tendency to historical enquiry is naturally awakened. This cause alone, without the more philosophical considerations which might lead a Hume or a Gibbon to turn from abstract investigations to historical enquiries, may account for the growth of antiquarianism in the later years. Men like Malone and Steevens were beginning those painful researches which have accumulated a whole literature upon the scanty records of our early dramatists. Gray, the most learned of poets, had vaguely designed a history of English poetry, and the design was executed with great industry by Thomas Warton. His brother Joseph ventured to uphold the then paradoxical thesis that Spenser was as great a man as Pope. Everywhere a new interest was awakening in the minuter details of the past. The antiquaries of earlier periods may have accumulated greater stores of knowledge; but they did not apply the same systematic and microscopic industry to the investigation of minute points of manners, language, or individual history. Something of the scientific spirit seems to have infected the modern school of infinitesimal research.

125. One result is remarkable. The first consequence of the breach with authority was an unreasonable contempt for the past. The modern philosopher who could spin all knowledge out of his own brain, the sceptic who had exploded the ancient dogmas, or the freethinker of any shade who rejoiced in the destruction of ecclesiastical tyranny, gloried in his conscious superiority to his forefathers. Whatever was old was absurd, and 'Gothic,' an epithet applied to all mediæval art, philosophy, or social order, became a simple term of contempt. Though the senti-

ment may strike us as narrow-minded, it at least implied a distinct
recognition of a difference between past and present. In simpler times,
people imagined their forefathers to be made in their own likeness, and
naïvely transferred the customs of chivalry to the classical or Hebrew
histories. To realise the fact that the eighteenth century differed materially from the eighth was a necessary step towards the modern theory
of progressive development. The history of the race suggested so much
continuity as is implied in the conflict between reason and authority,
instead of being a random series of unconnected events, or of events
connected by some supernatural, and therefore inscrutable, agency. The
sense that the thoughts and manners of past ages differed materially
from those of the present day began by encouraging the belief that men
must have been fools in past ages; but it soon led to the reflection that
their history might be worth examining. What was the nature of the
difference, and what were its causes? An antiquary is naturally a conservative, and men soon began to love the times whose peculiarities they
were so laboriously studying. Men of imaginative minds promptly made
the discovery that a new source of pleasure might be derived from these
dry records.

126. Few cleverer men lived in that century than Horace Walpole,
and few shared more fully the spirit of the Voltairian scepticism. But
Walpole passed his life as a trifler instead of an active combatant. He
was far too well off to be anxious to upset institutions, however corrupt, which gave him such comfortable shelter. He was quite content
with the permission to laugh at them. Amongst his other amusements,
Walpole took to antiquarianism. Possibly he had caught the contagion
from Gray; and he kept up judicious relations with various antiquaries,
such as Cole and Virtue. It was part of the natural duty of a born
aristocrat to turn the labours of meaner men to account, and Walpole
carried the practice into literature. His anecdotes of painters and royal
authors show the skill with which he could extract amusement out of
the heavy materials collected by more industrious miners in forgotten
history. He hit upon a more fertile device in the 'Castle of Otranto.' His
aim was, as he tells us, to combine something of the interests of everyday life with the interest of historical association. The combination is
not very skilful, and the product is flimsy enough; but Walpole had
made a real discovery. The 'Castle of Otranto' was the parent of Mrs.
Radcliffe's romances, and they broke ground for Scott's creation of the
historical novel. Walpole's position is typical. The idle sceptic of the
eighteenth century, looking about for a new amusement, found it in the
products of industrious antiquarian labour, and dressed it up as a

charming new toy. His scheme has been carried out more elaborately by later enquirers, but he has the merit which belongs to the origination of a new intellectual fashion. The 'Castle of Otranto' is to the literary romanticism what Strawberry Hill was to the modern revival of Gothic architecture. The fundamental vice of insincerity has not been removed from later and more systematic resuscitations of the dead.

127. Other manifestations of the same tendency might be noticed. Chatterton—the marvellous youth—seems to me to be marvellous chiefly from his youth. There is little, if anything, of permanent value in his writings. In one way, however, he showed an acuteness which may, perhaps, be fairly called marvellous. He showed an instinctive knowledge—remarkable in one so young—of the kind of intellectual food for which a demand was springing up in the country. His forgeries illustrate, as they no doubt stimulated, the growing taste for ancient literature. But two other publications of the same period are more remarkable. Every later writer has seen in Percy's 'Reliques' an impulse of great importance; and an impulse, in some sense even more important, is due to Macpherson's 'Ossian.' Singularly unlike as they are in most respects, there is a relation between the two publications. The ugly side of the modern romanticism is its confusion between fictions and realities, and its futile attempt to revive old modes of thought and feeling amidst an environment fatal to their real vitality. Walpole's performance begins that business of buff-jerkins and mediæval costumery which offends us in the inferior parts of Scott's writings. Romanticism has, however, its better side in its tendency to produce a true historical sense; and Percy's Ballads were more suggestive of the genuine lesson to be learnt from history. The study might suggest the propriety of falling back upon natural simplicity, instead of attempting to revive the external trappings of extinct social forms. The interest produced by 'Chevy Chase' and 'Childe Morice' was the interest of finding that our ancestors had been genuine human beings, capable of exploring manly emotions in a straightforward way, instead of an interest in their modes of dressing and swearing.

128. Macpherson's poem is a more singular performance. Its extraordinary effect upon the minds of contemporaries has often been noticed. The fate of a poem which excited the enthusiasm of Goethe and Napoleon, and which nobody can read at the present day, certainly suggests some curious problems. Briefly, we may assume that its vague and gigantesque scenery, its pompous mouthing of sham heroics, its crude attempts to represent a social state when great men stalked through the world in haughty superiority to the narrow conventions of modern life,

were congenial to men growing weary of an effete formalism. Men had
been talking under their breath and in a mincing dialect so long that
they were easily gratified, and easily imposed upon, by an affectation of
vigorous and natural sentiment.

129. But what is 'natural'? The question leads us to the third phase
of the reaction. The 'return to nature' expresses a sentiment which
underlies to some extent both the sentimental and the romantic movements, and which was more distinctly embodied in writers of a higher
order. To return to nature is, in one sense, to find a new expression for
emotions which have been repressed by existing conventions; or, in another, to return to some simpler social order which had not yet suffered
from those conventions. The artificiality attributed to the eighteenth
century seems to mean that men were content to regulate their thoughts
and lives by rules not traceable to first principles, but dependent upon
a set of special and exceptional conditions; and, again, that in the
imaginative sphere the accepted symbols did not express the deepest and
most permanent emotions, but were an arbitrary compromise between
traditional assumptions and the new philosophical tenets. To get out of
the ruts, or cast off the obsolete shackles, two methods might be adopted.
The intellectual horizon might be widened by including a greater number of ages and countries; or men might try to fall back upon the
thoughts and emotions common to all times and races, and so cast off
the superficial incrustation. The first method, that of the romanticists,
aims at increasing our knowledge; the second, that of the naturalistic
school, at basing our philosophy on deeper principles.

130. Two great poets at the end of the century gave an English
version of the cry for a 'return to nature.' Burns and Cowper sounded
a new note in our poetry, which was echoed by various writers of
inferior power or influence. What was the significance of their appeal?
The word 'nature,' as I have often had occasion to remark, is singularly
ambiguous. The whole significance of the early controversies of the
century may be described by saying that they represent the struggle between the religion of nature and the traditional religion. The result in
England was a kind of compromise. The traditional creed won a doubtful victory by concessions which destroyed its own efficacy. The doctrine
which emerged was thus Deism, or a religion of nature disguised by
traditional phraseology. And yet the revolt against it took again the
form of an appeal to nature. Obviously nature was used in different and
almost opposite senses. Wordsworth seemed to himself to be the antithesis to Pope, and yet Pope, like Wordsworth, preaches in one sense a

worship of nature. I must endeavour, therefore, to define more precisely the difference of conception which led to so vast a discord in practice.

131. The great revolution which was approaching had its social, its æsthetic, its political, and its philosophical aspects. The social movement seems to exhibit most distinctly the efficient causes of the changes, and the meaning of the new war-cry is there the least ambiguous. Briefly, we may say that the social revolution was an attempt to cast off the ossified crust of effete social organs which had become incapable of discharging their functions. To return to nature was with Rousseau and his followers to get rid of kings, nobles, and priests, who could no longer rule or teach. By sweeping away the accumulated rubbish of obsolete institutions, whose authority rested upon blind instinct instead of reason, we should come upon a pure, simple, reasonable, or 'natural' state of society. The state was vaguely conceived as having possibly existed in some remote past; as being preserved in certain primitive and uncorrupted societies of Alpine peasants, or even savage tribes; or as being that purely ideal state which would be made actual if every political or social institution rested upon pure reason, instead of including an arbitrary traditional element. The old doctrine of the social contract fell in with this theory; the contract being regarded as the embodiment of pure reason. In this sense, the return to nature meant little more with Rousseau than the immediate application to human affairs of the abstract theories which Locke had managed to interpret into harmony with the British Constitution. The metaphysical doctrine touched with passion, and applied to actual affairs, was suddenly endowed with destructive power; but there was no direct speculative advance. The theory had descended from the lecture-room into the street, but was not modifid in substance. Rousseau's sentimentalism breathed new life into the dead bones; or his followers simply adopted the most convenient phraseology for sanctioning their destructive energies. The doctrine, imported into England by such men as Thomas Paine, excited the wrathful denunciation of Burke's philosophical imagination, but scarcely took root in an uncongenial soil.

132. The English analogue is rather to be sought in the utilitarianism of Bentham, which rejected the old metaphysical method as well as the old traditional doctrine. Englishmen of this school sympathised with the return to nature, so far as they agreed in rejecting the ancient authority; but they would supplant it, not by abstract reasoning, but by a direct appeal to experience. I have sufficiently shown why this appeal was necessarily crude and unsatisfactory. It amounted, for the present, to an

assertion that all philosophy was unsatisfactory, and that the only method of discovering political and moral truths was a rough summary of individual experience. It was, in short, an appeal to a number of isolated facts, without any due perception of the necessity of discovering the general laws by which the facts must be organised and bound together. Such a method, though invaluable as a first stage towards a true scientific conception of history, was less fruitful for the imagination than even the destructive theory of abstract rights. The attempt at scientific methods began by cutting up the world into independent atoms, and limiting the view to what was directly appreciable by the senses. It rejected, that is, precisely those aspects of the world and of man which it is the office of the poetical and religious imagination to embody in vivid symbolism. In this sense, the return to nature meant, or would have meant—for the phrase was hardly used by thinkers of this school—an abandonment of all the old authoritative teaching, and of all philosophy, old or new, and an attempt to make a fresh start to knowledge based upon individual experience of the most tangible facts.

133. The philosophical and imaginative aspect of the movement took a parallel course. In the sphere of the imagination, the old symbols of the 'classical' or metaphysical school had become hopelessly effete. The life had departed, and they had become conventional or consciously fictitious. The muse of which Pope and his followers talked was an intolerable bore. The various abstract beings made by the use of capital letters, who play so great a part in the poetry of Gray,[3] were phantoms incapable of exciting the imagination. To return to nature was, therefore, primarily to sweep aside a set of arbitrary rules and symbols which had ceased to have any meaning. The philosophical movement explains the significance of the process. The weakness of the old theories consisted essentially in this, that it involved a complete divorce between reality and philosophy. God and nature, and the other high-sounding phrases of the earlier writers, turned out to correspond to barren abstractions which could not be brought into contact with the world of reality. The actual world in which we live and move and have our being was regarded by the metaphysicians as somehow made up of illusory phenomena; and we must sweep them aside before we could attain to

[3]Thus, in the 'Ode to Adversity,' we have in about fifty lines the following personages:—Adversity, Virtue, Folly, Noise, Joy, Prosperity, Melancholy, Charity, Justice, Pity, Horror, Despair, Disease, and Poverty. Collins's 'Ode to the Passions' is a characteristic, though very fine, example of the same tendency. Coleridge's sentence, 'Inoculation, Heavenly maid!' shows the natural result.

permanent truth. Inevitably, therefore, the God—whether called Nature or Jehovah—whose existence and attributes were proved by mathematical demonstration, could not be made to interfere in human affairs, and remained obstinately alienated from human affections. To remedy this divorce, to bring fact and philosophy together, so that the highest truths might be embodied in laws of experience, and not dismissed to a distinct world of transcendental entities, was the problem which, for the most part unconsciously, occupied men's minds. The reaction—so far as I have to consider it—is the result of an indistinct feeling after a gratification of this need by the most sensitive intellects.

134. Three distinguished poets, Pope, Cowper, and Wordsworth, mark three terms in this process. All of them were directly didactic; and all of them have used language which might be called pantheistic. Pope says, for example—

> All are but parts of one stupendous whole,
> Whose body Nature is, and God the soul;

Cowper, that

> There lives and works
> A soul in all things, and that soul is God;

and Wordsworth, speaking of the living principle of all nature, says—

> From link to link
> It circulates, the soul of all the worlds.

What is the difference between these utterances, alike in language, though marked by a profound difference in sentiment? With Pope the God who is nature is primarily the metaphysical God. Whenever he tries distinctly to realise the Divine character, or to show how that character is revealed to us, he necessarily falls back upon the dry ratiocination—or should we say word-manufacture?—of the school of Leibnitz. We have the arguments about the scale of being, the necessity of free-will, and so on, with which those reasoners tried to bewilder opponents rather than to satisfy themselves, and to spread a thin veil of theological phraseology over radically different doctrines. Pope's God is the God of the old ontologists. Wordsworth, on the contrary, habitually and systematically bases his pantheism upon immediate intuition. He is simply embodying the vague emotions of awe, reverence, and love generated in his mind by the contemplation of the phenomena of the universe. He feels profoundly the incapacity of the old metaphysics to satisfy his imagination. They may prove a God; but not the God who appeals to his sympathies. His emotions find a theological utterance; but the theology must be based on the testimony of facts, not of abstract reasoning. He hates science, because it regards facts without the imaginative and emotional colouring; because it seems to desire to reduce the universe to a set of unconnected fragments; and, in breaking it up for examination, to lose the principle of unity and continuity. His pantheism, therefore, if it could be logically formulated, would imply what we may call the deification of natural laws. It would be the expression of reverential awe in which man regards the universe when conceived as an organic whole. Pope, on the other hand, has logically to regard the visible universe as a troublesome and illusory intruder, to be dismissed from our minds when we try to rise to the highest contemplative altitude. Thus, though there are many curious coincidences of language, the tendency of the earlier writer is to separate the highest thoughts of man from actual experience; of the other, to see the facts transfigured by his imagination.

135. Cowper occupies an intermediate position. Unsatisfied by the dominant theology of his times, he had taken refuge in the more vigorous creed of the early Evangelicals. The starting-point of Cowper's feelings was a profound sense of the corruption of the existing order of society. He quotes and approves Brown's 'Estimate,' one of the earliest indications, as we have seen, of the new current of opinion. His early poems are satires, adhering in form to the precedent of Pope, though wanting in the brilliancy attained by Pope alone. They differ, however, in this respect—that Pope's interest is fixed upon the individual character; and that he does not seriously contemplate the necessity of any change in the structure of society. He attacks faults prevalent in his day; but apparently holds that they can be sufficiently put down by satire or by the general good sense of mankind. Cowper, on the contrary, holds that the society is tainted by a deeply seated disease, and has a cure to set forth. So far he agrees with Rousseau; but the remedy is characteristically different. Rousseau says, in substance, Upset the world; Cowper says, Leave the world. Rousseau looks for regeneration by a return to nature and reason. Cowper expects a regeneration in the sense of those who opposed nature to supernatural grace. The difference is characteristic of the difference of the national modes of development. In France, as I have so often remarked, the issues were more distinct and thoroughgoing. To attack the political or the social order was to attack the Church and the orthodox faith. There could be no medium or compromise. In England, as the religious movement was to a great

extent independent of the political, it was possible to be a reformer in
one sense, whilst remaining a dogged conservative in the other sense.
Cowper was nominally a Whig; but his Whiggism sat very lightly upon
him. It meant nothing less than revolutionary sentiment. He saw in the
poor not the victims of an oppressive caste, but sufferers from their own
vices. He admires liberty; but he explains that the true liberty is not
liberty from slavery, but liberty from the tyranny of spiritual evil. He
escapes, in short, from a corrupt and cruel world by becoming a religious recluse. Brought up as a good Protestant, he has no taste for asceticism; but his ideal existence is one of quiet contemplation and unob-
trusive benevolence, outside the hurry and the jar of the great turmoil
of life.

136. With Cowper, then, the appeal to nature has a narrow though a
most sincere meaning. The sight of nature—that is, of the external
world of animal or material existence—is as the drop of cold water to a
soul in purgatory. He escapes to quiet fields and brooks from the torture
of his own excited imagination, and from the agonies inflicted upon a
morbidly sensitive character by the conflict with his coarser fellows. The
pantheistic phrase which escapes him is merely an expression of the
sentiment that the divine element, no longer to be found in the hearts
of men, manifests itself in the flowers of the field and the harmless
animal creation. The position is not strictly logical. To a strict theologian, the curse which has passed upon human nature must appear to
have been inflicted upon the surrounding world. Suffering exists wherever there is feeling; and that struggle for existence, from which Cowper
had rescued his pet hares, was not entirely due to the interference of
man. Cowper differs from Rousseau in that he regards the natural man
as corrupt, and proves his case very forcibly by realistic pictures of the
savage and the simple peasant. But he presists in regarding inanimate
nature and its irrational dependants as still under the light of the
Divine countenance. The dogma of corruption is so arbitrary in its essence as easily to admit of such modifications. Many Calvinists, Jonathan
Edwards for example, have tacitly imposed the same limits upon the
sphere of corruption. If, according to their logic, the only refuge from
misery should be in deliverance from the bondage of the material
world, they are willing so far to depart from logic as to preserve some
visible symbols of the divine order. Cowper, therefore, might be sanctioned by the teaching of his creed, though he was undoubtedly influenced by the teaching of Rousseau and the school of Rousseau. Their
love of nature at least was congenial to him. Scornfully rejecting their
theories of the dignity of human beings, he shares their delight in an

escape to the fields from the corrupt air of streets or drawing-rooms. Indeed, his delight is probably keener than theirs; for these remnants of Paradise, left in the midst of a corrupt world, are all the more refreshing when contrasted with the supernatural gloom which, in his imagination, lay all around. Cowper's diatribes against the growth of luxury have become obsolete; his religious meanings are interesting to those alone who share his creed; but his intense love of calm scenery fell in with a widely spread sentiment of his age, and has scattered through his pages vignettes of enduring beauty. The pathetic power in which he was unrivalled, and which gives to two or three of his poems a charm quite unique in its kind, seems to belong to no age.

137. Of Burns—a poet who has left behind him an impression of power quite astonishing when compared with the fragmentary character of his works—it is needless to say much. Here, too, it is curious to observe how the spirit of the age manifests itself in a region at first sight quite beyond the direct influence of the great intellectual currents. Burns is the spokesman of a social order which might not unfairly represent the interpretation of Rousseau's state of nature. The strong healthy race of the Scotch lowlands, unconsciously absorbing the influences of a free open-air life, and far apart from all sickly sentimentalism, had produced for ages a race of poets whose ballads reflect their vigorous character. In the age of Burns life had become peaceable, and not luxurious. The society in which he lived had acquired a certain degree of culture, but had not yet been broken up by the restless movements of modern development. Burns, therefore, was qualified to stand forth to the world ripening for revolution, and give in a few vigorous touches the presentment of the truly vigorous peasant life, not stained by idyllic sentimentalisms, and with strong manly blood coursing through every vein.

138. In one sense he was consciously a revolutionist. The vigour of the Scotch race had expressed itself in the national religion. The religion had become an effete sham. When Burns was writing his glorious lyrics, Blair was mouthing his sham rhetoric. In earlier times, the Scotch vigour was best represented by its spiritual guides. A hundred years before Burns might have been a Covenanter, and have met the shock of Claverhouse's troopers at Drumclog. But the old Covenanting spirit had become a thing of shreds and patches—an effete idol no longer capable of rallying true men to its side. And therefore Burns puts his whole heart into such tremendous satires as 'Holy Willie's Prayer.' The peasant expressed his hearty contempt for the hypocritical leaders who tried to traffic upon his lingering superstitions to gratify their own lust or avarice. Such poems were a blast of doom to the old order. It would

no longer satisfy the manliest instincts of its subjects, for its creeds could no longer inspire worthy thoughts in their spiritual guides. Burns had no more direct consciousness than his brethren of the force of the philosophical argument against the orthodox creed; but the foundations of the creed had been so far sapped by argument, and by its own incapacity to develop, that it could no longer restrain the vigorous passions of the noblest of the race.

139. I have thus imperfectly and briefly sketched the chief leaders of the reaction. It remains only to make one remark. The various writers whom I have mentioned co-operated in a common movement; but, for the most part, their co-operation was quite unconscious. Neither Sterne, nor Richardson, nor Walpole, nor Macpherson, nor Cowper, had the smallest intention of fostering revolutionary tendencies. The religious movement of Wesley was so removed from any political influence that Wesley himself, and many of his followers, were strongly conservative; and, indeed, the movement itself was, perhaps, a diversion in favour of the established order. It provided a different channel for dangerous elements. The English movement thus differs from the French, where the revolutionary and the conservative elements were gathered into two different camps, and every attack upon one part of the order reacted upon all others. It differs, again, from the German, where a new philosophical impulse impressed a certain general direction upon the various movements of liberation, and made men more conscious of the general solidarity. The cause is, perhaps, due to the difference of national character, or to the social and political differences which threw the German movement into the hands of the speculative classes, instead of stimulating a direct political action. However this may be, the process as exhibited in England illustrates one, and perhaps the normal, variety of speculative development. The philosophers did not lead, but followed. Their aggressive influence had, indeed, been considerable; but it acted indirectly. It is less accurate to say that the old creed was destroyed by an undergrowth of new ideas, than that the decay of the old creed left a variety of instincts unsatisfied, and therefore made room for the development of a number of new and, apparently, unconnected movements, which had only this in common, that they were all attempts to supply wants produced by a common cause. Perhaps, as a new philosophy arises, these blind impulses, whether superficially reactionary or progressive, may be co-ordinated and directed to a common end. But at the conclusion of the century we see rather an intellectual chaos, in which no definite movement has attained supremacy. The sentimentalism of Rousseau or Sterne was represented by the feeble imitations of

such writers as Mackenzie, the 'Man of Feeling,' or Mrs. Inchbald, the hero of whose 'Nature and Art,' for example, is a rehabilitation of the conventional savage of Rousseau, or of Voltaire's 'Ingénu;' and by that sickly school amongst whom Miss Seward was an accepted critic, whose greatest luminary was Hayley, and whose poetical impulse is represented by the Della Crusca verses, remembered only as provoking Gifford's 'Baviad and Mæviad'—itself the forgotten and expiring utterance of the old Popian satire. For romanticism we have Mrs. Radcliffe, who reproduced on a larger scale, and in a more serious spirit, the machinery of Walpole's 'Castle of Otranto.' In the coming generation, the impulses thus briefly noticed gave birth to the romanticism of Scott, the natureworship of Wordsworth, and the sentimentalism of Byron or Shelley. But those great men represent a far wider and deeper and more complex movement of thought, nor do the names by which we label them at all adequately represent their significance. I have reached the opening of a new period in the history of thought; and here I must pause, without even venturing to cast the most perfunctory glance upon later developments.

NOTE TO CHAPTER XII

The following are the chief works of the principal writers referred to in this chapter:—

ADDISON, JOSEPH (1672–1719), 'Tatler,' 'Spectator,' and 'Guardian,' 1709–14. 'Cato,' 1713.

AKENSIDE, MARK (1721–1770), 'Pleasures of the Imagination,' 1744.

ATTERBURY, FRANCIS (1662–1732), 'Sermons,' 1740.

BERRIDGE, JOHN (1716–1793), 'The Christian World Unmasked,' 1773.

BLAIR, HUGH (1718–1800), 'Sermons,' 1777–1801. London: 1834.

BLAIR, ROBERT (1699–1746), 'The Grave,' 1743.

BROOKE, HENRY (1703–1783), 'Universal Beauty,' 1735–6. 'Gustavus Vasa,' 1739. 'The Fool of Quality,' 1766, 1770, 1777. 'Juliet Grenville,' 1774.

BURNEY, FRANCES (1752–1840), 'Evelina,' 1778. 'Cecilia,' 1782.

BURNS, ROBERT (1759–1796), 'Poems,' 1786, &c.

CHATTERTON, THOMAS (1752–1770), 'Poems,' 1777.

COLLINS, WILLIAM (1720–1759), 'Odes,' 1747.

COWPER, WILLIAM (1731–1800), 'Poems,' 1782. 'The Task,' 1785. 'Homer,' 1791.

CRABBE, GEORGE (1754–1832), 'The Library,' 1781. 'The Village,' 1783. 'The Newspaper,' 1785.

DODDRIDGE, PHILIP (1702–1751), 'The Family Expositor,' 1738–56. 'Rise and Progress of Religion,' 1745.

DE FOE, DANIEL (1660?–1731), 'Robinson Crusoe,' 1719.

FIELDING, HENRY (1707–1754), 'Joseph Andrews,' 1742. 'Tom Jones,' 1749. 'Amelia,' 1751.

FOSTER, JAMES (1697–1753), 'Discourses,' 1749–52.

GOLDSMITH, OLIVER (1728–1774), 'The Traveller,' 1764. 'The Vicar of Wakefield,' 1766. 'The Good-natured Man,' 1768. 'The Deserted Village,' 1769. 'She Stoops to Conquer,' 1773.

GRAY, THOMAS (1716–1771), 'Odes' &c. 1742–1769.

HAYLEY, WILLIAM (1745–1820), 'Triumphs of Temper,' and various works, 1778–1811.

HERVEY, JAMES (1714–1758), 'Meditations,' 1746–7. 'Theron and Aspasia,' 1753–5.

HOME, JOHN (1722–1808), 'Douglas,' 1756.

INCHBALD, ELIZABETH (1753–1821), 'A Simple Story,' 1791. 'Nature and Art,' 1796.

JOHNSON, SAMUEL (1709–1784), 'London,' 1738. 'Vanity of Human Wishes,' 1749. 'Irene,' 1749. 'Rambler,' 1750–2. 'Idler,' 1758–60. 'Rasselas,' 1759.

LAVINGTON, GEORGE (1684–1762), 'Enthusiasm of Methodists and Papists Compared,' 1749.

MACPHERSON, JAMES (1736–1796), 'Ossian,' 1762.

MASON, WILLIAM (1724–1797), 'Elfrida,' 1752. 'Odes,' 1756. 'Caractacus,' 1759. 'The English Garden,' 1772–82.

POPE, ALEXANDER (1688–1744), 'Pastorals,' 1709. 'Essay on Criticism,' 1711. 'Rape of the Lock,' 1712–14. 'Iliad,' 1718–20. 'Dunciad' (fourth book in 1742), 1728. 'Moral Essays,' 'Imitations of Horace' &c. 1731–1738. 'Essay on Man,' 1732–4.

RADCLIFFE, ANNE (1764–1823), 'Castles of Athlin and Dunboyne,' 1789. 'Sicilian Romance,' 1790. 'Romance of the Forest,' 1791. 'Mysteries of Udolpho,' 1794. 'The Italian,' 1797.

RICHARDSON, SAMUEL (1689–1761), 'Pamela,' 1741–2. 'Clarissa Harlowe,' 1751. 'Sir Charles Grandison,' 1754.

SECKER, THOMAS (1693–1768), 'Sermons,' 1770–90.

SEED, JEREMIAH (1700–1747), 'Sermons,' 1743, &c.

SHENSTONE, WILLIAM (1714–1763), 'The Schoolmistress,' 1742.

SHERIDAN, RICHARD BRINSLEY BUTLER (1751–1816), 'The Rivals,' 1775. 'The Duenna,' 1760. 'The School for Scandal,' 1777. 'The Critic,' 1779.

SMALRIDGE, GEORGE (1663–1719), Sixty Sermons, 1726.

SMOLLETT, TOBIAS GEORGE (1721–1771), 'Roderick Random,' 1748. 'Peregrine Pickle,' 1751. 'Ferdinand Count Fathom,' 1753. 'Sir Lancelot Greaves,' 1762. 'Adventures of an Atom,' 1769. 'Humphrey Clinker,' 1771.

STEELE, RICHARD (1672–1729), 'The Christian Hero,' 1701. 'The Funeral,' 1702. 'The Tender Husband,' 1702. 'Tatler,' 'Spectator,' and 'Guardian,' 1709–13. 'The Conscious Lovers,' 1725.

SWIFT, JONATHAN (1667–1745), 'Tale of a Tub,' and 'Battle of the Books,' 1704. 'Gulliver's Travels,' 1726.

THOMSON, JAMES (1700–1748), 'The Seasons,' 1726–30. 'The Castle of Indolence,' 1748.

VENN, HENRY (1724–1797), 'Complete Duty of Man,' 1763.

WALPOLE, HORACE (1717–1797), 'Castle of Otranto,' 1765.

WARTON, JOSEPH (1722–1800), 'Essay on Pope,' 1756, 1782.

WARTON, THOMAS (1728–1790), 'History of English Poetry,' 1774–81. 'Poems,' 1777.

WATTS, ISAAC (1674–1748), 'Poems,' 1706–1720. Sermons &c. &c. 1721–3.

WESLEY, CHARLES (1707–1788), Hymns, 1746–1781.

WESLEY, JOHN (1703–1791), 'Earnest Appeals,' 1750–58. 'Journals' &c. &c. 1737–90. 'Principles and Duties of Christianity,' 1799. Works. London: 1809.

WILSON, THOMAS (1663–1755), 'On the Lord's Supper,' Charges &c. 1734. 'Sacra Privata,' 1800.

WHITEFIELD, GEORGE (1714–1770), 'Sermons,' &c.

YOUNG, EDWARD (1683–1765), 'The Revenge,' 1721. 'Satires,' 1725–7. 'Night Thoughts,' 1742–5.

SUGGESTIONS FOR FURTHER READING

On Stephen himself see F. W. Maitland, *The Life and Letters of Leslie Stephen* (1906); Noel Annan, *Leslie Stephen* (1952); and Virginia Woolf, *To the Lighthouse* (1927). For comment on these three, see the Preface to Vol. I of this edition of the *English Thought in the Eighteenth Century*, p. v. There is a good brief account by Stephen's successor as editor of the *Dictionary of National Biography*, Sidney Lee, Lee, in *Twentieth Century Supplement, 1901–1911*, of the *Dictionary*. Stephen appears, appropriately enough, in A. W. Benn, *History of English Rationalism in the Nineteenth Century* (1906), Vol. II, pp. 384 ff. Maitland in Appendix I of his *Life and Letters of Leslie Stephen*, pp. 497–99, gives a very full list of Stephen's works.

For the reader who wishes to go directly to some of the thinkers here studied, the following paperback editions are available (in hard covers, most of them are of course readily found in good libraries): Thomas Hobbes, *Selections* (Frederick J. E. Woodbridge, ed., Scribner's); Bernard Mandeville, *Fable of the Bees* (Capricorn); Hume, *David Hume's Political Essays* (Charles W. Hendel, ed., Liberal Arts); Locke, *Of Civil Government* (Gateway); Samuel Johnson, *Rasselas; Poems and Selected Prose* (Bertrand H. Bronson, ed., Holt, Rinehart & Winston), and Johnson and Boswell, *The Portable Johnson and Boswell* (Louis Kronenberger, ed., Viking); Edmund Burke, *The Philosophy of Edmund Burke* (Louis I. Bredvold and Ralph G. Ross, eds., Ann Arbor), and *Reflections on the Revolution in France* (Thomas H. D. Mahoney, ed., Liberal Arts); William Godwin, *Caleb Williams* (George Sherburn, ed., Holt, Rinehart & Winston); Thomas Paine, *Common Sense and Other Political Writings* (Nelson F. Adkins, ed., Liberal Arts); Edmund Burke and Thomas Paine, *Reflections on the Revolution in France and The Rights of Man* (Thomas H. D. Mahoney, ed., Dolphin); Adam Smith, *The Wealth of Nations; Representative Selections* (Bruce Mazlish, ed., Liberal Arts); Alexander Pope, *Selected Poetry and Prose* (William K. Wimsatt, Jr., ed., Holt, Rinehart & Winston).

On the general field of this volume, there is Leslie Stephen's own *English Literature and Society in the Eighteenth Century* (1904). Volume I of Stephen's *The English Utilitarians* (1900) deals much

more thoroughly with Bentham and the origins of English Utilitarianism than does the present book of which *The English Utilitarians* is in
many ways a continuation. Another Stephen wrote critically and most
interestingly on the political phase of English Utilitarian thought—
Leslie's brother, James Fitzjames Stephen, *Liberty, Equality, Fraternity*
(1873). On political thought, there is the admirable general survey,
G. H. Sabine, *History of Political Theory* (rev. ed., 1955), and H. J.
Laski's brief survey, *Political Thought in England from Locke to
Bentham* (1920), one of his best books. Laski's later *Rise of Modern
Liberalism* (1936) is more orthodoxly Marxist and controversial. F. C.
Green, *Minuet* (1935), is a suggestive essay on Anglo-French literary
relations. No student of the history of ideas can neglect A. O. Lovejoy,
The Great Chain of Being (1936). Much pertinent to the eighteenth
century is in the same author's *Essays in the History of Ideas* (1948).
M. H. Carré, *Phases of Thought in England* (1949), is a good general
survey. Of histories of special disciplines here pertinent there are many:
notably for economics, Joseph Schumpeter, *A History of Economic
Analysis* (1954); for formal philosophy, W. R. Sorley, *A History of
English Philosophy* (1920); for literature, Albert C. Baugh, editor, *A
Literary History of England* (1948)—the currently appearing *Oxford
History of English Literature* (1945-) will be the latest word in bibli-
ography of the subject.

Many of the bibliographical suggestions in Vol. I of this edition of
English Thought in the Eighteenth Century are of course valid for this
second volume.

C. B.

INDEX

[*The First Number refers to the Chapter, the Second to the Section*]

ADAMS, W., viii. 25, 26
Addison, J., ii. 5, 11; iii. 45, note, 78; vii. 5; viii. 8, 15, 93; xii. 22, 24, 30, 33, 42, 44, 58, 76
Ader, iv. 51
Agnosticism, iii. 22
Aikenhead, ii. 11
Akenside, M., vii. 2; ix. 24; xii. 34, 35, 40, 41
Allegory, iv. 20, 32–34, 39, 45–48, 51, 73; viii. 19
Analogy and metaphor, iii. 21, 23, 24
Anderson, James, xi. 40
Annet, P., ii. 11; iv. 60, 63, 65, 82; viii. 63
Annet, P., Replies to West and Lyttelton, iv. 63, 65
Anthropomorphism, iii. 61, 62, 86; vi. 32; vii. 15–17, 20–22; viii. 41, 60; ix. 28
Arbuthnot, J., x. 30; xii. 100
Arianism, iii. 26, 68; viii. 52, 60–62
Asceticism, viii. 15; ix. 39, 102, 109
Asgill, John, ii. 1
Association, theory of, i. 44; ix. 65, 69–72
Atheists and divines, iii. 22–24, 86, 87; v. 9; ix. 29
Atonement, doctrine of the, iii. 48, note; v. 23; viii. 94
Atterbury, Bishop, iv. 26; x. 27, 33; xii. 18, 19
Attributes, divine, demonstrated, iii. 27–30
Attributes, moral and natural, iii. 86
Austen, Miss. xii. 115

BACON, Lord, iii. 82; vi. 37
Badcock, Samuel, viii. 63
Balguy, John, ii. 11; iii. 37; ix. 11
Bangorian controversy, x. part iii.
Barrington, Lord, ii. 11
Barrow, Isaac, ii. 6; xii. 9
Bartholine, iv. 51
Basnage, ii. 2
Bate, Julius, viii. 18
Bates, Dr., xii. 99
Baxter, Andrew, i. 68; v. 6
Baxter, R., xii. 9
Bayle, ii. 9; iv. 20, 22; vi. 8; vii. 2, 25; ix. 2, 22, 24; xii. 2
Beattie, James, vi. 29, note; viii. 9–13, 63, 65, 66; xii. 34
Beattie's 'Essay on Truth,' viii. 9–13
Beaumarchais, x. 111
Beccaria, ix. 62, note
Bedford, Duke of, x. 76
Behmen, Jacob, xii. 81, 84, 118
Benson, George, iii. 81
Bentham, Jeremy, ix. 2, 62, note, 103, 113, 136–140; x. 66, 79, 126, 128, 152; xi. 6, 27; xii. 132
Bentley, R., ii. 11; iv. 22, 27, 54, 56, 66; note to ch. iv; vii. 12; xii. 18, 22, 28

Bentley's 'Phileleutherus Lipsiensis,' iv. 23–25
Berkeley, Bishop, i. 21, 30, 38–44, 46, 61, 62; ii. 11; iii. 22, 24, 82; iv. 8, 53; v. 1; vi. 9; viii. 9, 10, 11, 13; ix. 25, 35, 38, 43, 45, 91, 92, 122; xii. 51, 62
Berkeley's 'Dialogues,' i. 38–42
Berkeley's 'Minute Philosopher,' iii. 22, 24; ix. 43, 45
Berkeley's 'New Theory of Vision,' i. 40
Berkeley's 'Principles of Human Knowledge,' i. 38–42
Berkeley's 'Siris,' i. 42
Berridge, John, xii. 106, 107, 109
Bible, corruptions in text of, iv. 25, 29, 30
Blackburne, F., viii. 53–55
Blackmore, ii. 11; xii. 35
Blackstone, x. 79; xii. 16
Blair, Hugh, x. 89; xii. 20, 21
Blair, Robert, xii. 41
Blount, Charles, iv. 10, 20
Blount's 'Oracles of Reason,' iv. 10
Bolingbroke, Lord, ii. 1; iii. 42, 74, 82–88; vii. 2, 3, 8, 15; viii. 2, 32, 96; ix. 20, 29, 74, note; x. 2, 43–55, 67, 69, 72, 97, 146; xii. 25, 36, 40, 69
Bolingbroke's political writings, x. 46–55
Bolingbroke's theological writings, iii. 82–88
Boscovich, viii. 65
Bossuet, ii. 1–3, 9, 10; viii. 82
Boswell, J., vii. 5; x. 70
Bott, John, v. 2
Bourdaloue, xii. 99, 100
Bower, A., viii. 25
Brontë, Miss, xii. 107
Brooke, Henry, xii. 118
Brown, John, ix. 35, 43, 46; x. 67–70, 128; xii. 98
Brown's 'Essay on the Characteristics,' ix. 43, 46
Brown's 'Estimate,' x. 67–70
Browne, Peter, iii. 20–24, 86; vi. 9
Browne's Reply to Toland, iii. 20
Browne's 'Analogy' and 'Procedure,' iii. 20–24
Browne, Simon, iv. 46, note
Browne, Sir T., xii. 45
Bryant, Jacob, viii. 66
Buffon, viii. 40
Burke, Edmund, i. 58; ii. 11; viii. 2, 56, 96; ix. 3; x. 62, 63, 71, 73, 77, 78, 79, 91, 93, part ix. 126; xi. 29; xii. 100, 135–137, 139, 152
Burke's American writings, x. 111–115
Burke's constitutional writings, x. 106–110
Burke's revolutionary writings, x. 116–125
Burke's 'Vindication of Natural Society,' x. 97
Burnet, Thomas, ii. 8; iv. 10, 20; viii. 19
Burns, R., xii. 1, 130, 137, 138

393